Yale Studies in Hermeneutics

Yale Studies in Hermeneutics
Joel Weinsheimer, Editor

Editorial Advisory Board
Zygmunt Bauman
Robert Bernasconi
Gerald Bruns
Fred R. Dallmayr
Ronald Dworkin
Hans-Georg Gadamer
Clifford Geertz
Frank Kermode
Richard Rorty
Mark Taylor

Secularism and Revivalism in Turkey

A Hermeneutic Reconsideration

Andrew Davison

Yale University Press

New Haven & London

cau

Set in Garamond type by The Composing Room of Michigan, Inc.
Printed in the United States of America.

Library of Congress Cataloging-in-Publication Data

Davison, Andrew, 1962–
    Secularism and revivalism in Turkey : a hermeneutic
reconsideration / Andrew Davison.
        p.   cm. — (Yale studies in hermeneutics)
    Includes bibliographical references and index.
    ISBN 0-300-06936-7
    1. Secularism—Turkey—History—20th century.   2. Islam and state—Turkey—History—20th century.   3. Turkey—Religion—20th century.
    I. Title.   II. Series.
    BL2747.8.D28   1998
    322'.1'09561—dc21
                                                                    97-49379
                                                                    CIP

A catalogue record for this book is available from the British Library.

The paper in this book meets the guidelines for permanence and durability of the Committee on Production Guidelines for Book Longevity of the Council on Library Resources.

10   9   8   7   6   5   4   3   2   1

Contents

Preface

This study demonstrates the indispensability of a hermeneutic approach to political explanation of secularism and theopolitics in modernity. Any such effort must critically confront misapprehensions about hermeneutics, both in political science, where hermeneutics is frequently seen as lacking much to say positively about "explanation," and in broader theoretical circles, where hermeneutics is assumed to be relevant only in matters of "tradition," a term narrowly understood as an ideological traditionalist might understand it.

In response to these and many other nonhermeneutic tendencies in the discipline of political science, I suggest that hermeneutics offers a clear vision for explaining the political lives and institutions of others in a critical, comparative, and compelling historical manner. I also suggest that the central hermeneutic concern with tradition is wrongly equated with traditionalist imperatives. Despite the traditionalism of some hermeneutic inquirers, the tradition with which hermeneutics is concerned is not the "tradition" prong of the truly narrow, modernity/tradition dichotomy. Rather, it is the *traditions* that constitute political options in modernity, modern and secular as well as traditional and religious. These categories need to be opened up and refined. My argument is that a hermeneutic disposition toward political inquiry enables us to do just that.

Support for the writing of this book was provided by the department of political science of the University of Minnesota, two Fulbright dissertation research grants administered by the Commission for Educational Exchange Between the United States and Turkey, the department of political science and international relations of Boğaziçi University, and the department of political science at Vassar College. I am extremely grateful for the assistance of all of the kind people from these institutions who have helped me, in one way or another, to complete this work. An edited version of Chapter 3, "Secularization and Modernization in Turkey: The Ideas of Ziya Gökalp," has been published in *Economy and Society* (vol. 24, no. 2 [May 1995]: 189–224).

I am deeply grateful to many people for their invaluable encouragement and support; thank you, especially, to Terence Ball, Bruce Baum, Dana Chabot, Mary G. Dietz, Nejat Dinç, Raymond Duvall, Süreyya Ersoy, Stephen Gerenscer, David Ingersoll, Ersin Kalaycıoğlu, Kemal Kirişçi, John Losee, William Lynn, Mark Miller, Marian Palley, Taha Parla, Chris Roark, Michael Root, Yurdanur Salman, Martin Sampson, Paul Soper, Ronald Steiner, Judith Swatosh, Binnaz Toprak, Zafer Toprak, Nilgün Uygun, Joel Weinsheimer, Greg White, and Maxwell, Barbara, Mark, Douglas, Ellen, and Lisa Davison. I am also grateful to Douglas Faneuil, Timothy Bagshaw, Caleb Elfenbein, and M. Nicole Soriano for their assistance in preparing the final version of this manuscript, and to Cynthia Wells and Joyce Ippolito of Yale University Press for their generous efforts. James Farr and Richard Matthews deserve a special, heartfelt thanks for their thoughtful concern and advice over the past several years.

Introduction

As the second millennium draws to its close, in one way or another the
ground is shaking under *everyone's* feet. . . . We are not talking about
family debates between the ideologies of the nineteenth century West.
Our drama—whatever the parts we have in it—is today being played out
in a theater with which we are unfamiliar, on a stage we cannot
recognize, and amid the unpredicted and unexpected, and insufficiently
understood, changes of scenery.
—*E. J. Hobsbawm*

The human attempt to understand politics may make little cognitive
headway; but it is going to go on.
—*John Dunn*

The apparent resurgence and efficacy of religious thought and practices in contemporary politics continue to baffle those interested in
the politics of secularization. Even as political inquirers seek to incorporate the so-called religious variable into explanations of contemporary politics—on questions of reproductive rights or school curricula
in the United States, divorce in Ireland, the Rushdie decree, or

the religiously conceived social justice and democratizing movements through-out the world—many social scientists consider it odd that we are still question-ing the relation between religion and politics, an issue that many believed was settled long ago. Did not some of the most brilliant minds of the nineteenth and twentieth centuries tell us that, as the processes of modernity take hold, religion would either fade away or enter the private conscience as new public, ethical moralities superseded theocentric ways of being in the world?

The sense that religion has no place in contemporary politics is evident in common claims that people "retreat" or "take refuge" in religion to escape so-called rapid sociopolitical change. The implication of this language is that theopolitical actors and movements are at odds with historical necessity (almost pathologically so), and should not be as predominant as they are.

In this book, I explore the theoretical dynamics of what might be called interpretive perplexity. Interpretive perplexity occurs when what we believed to be transparent or clear turns out to be anything but. It turns out to be more perplexing than anyone had suspected. The apparent rise in the role of religion in modern politics counts as an instance of such interpretive perplexity. Reli-gion's role in the organization and constitution of public life has not diminished inexorably, as many believed it would. The once-clear process of secularization now looks more complex than previously thought. Tied as it is to real-world political questions of enormous import, our perplexity beckons us to reconsider both why we believed that clerical prime ministers, senators, and other political activists were unlikely to become strategic power actors in our age and how we might become less perplexed now that they are.[1]

The former question, about our belief that the significance of religion would in some sense recede leads us to reconsider our substantive understanding of the character and the flow of secularizing, modern history. The issue of how we might be less perplexed leads us not simply to amend our explanatory frame-works with a new religious variable but to ask how to better understand contemporary politics. When the clergy hold political power (directly, behind the palace screens, or on the television screens) at the end of the twentieth century, we must ask how well equipped we are to grasp the dynamics of modern politics, to identify relevant factors and tendencies, and to anticipate certain outcomes as more likely than others.

Many social scientists are grappling with these issues. My aim is to address both issues while underscoring the indispensability of a hermeneutic orienta-tion to political explanation. I explore why perplexity over theopolitics charac-terizes the discipline entrusted to clarify modern politics, and how political inquirers might better understand certain aspects of this perplexity while accepting that perplexity is necessary in human social and political life.

The task of hermeneutic political inquiry is to grasp the meanings that constitute the features of political life—that is, political action, relations, practices, and institutions. Constitutive in the hermeneutic sense means, as Charles Taylor has put it, to make these features of political life what they are, such that without the meanings, human beings whose political lives we are trying to explain would not be doing what they are doing.[2]

It follows that the practices of political inquiry, like all human practices, are constitute by meanings. Thus, to understand practices associated with interpreting and explaining politics we must understand the meanings that make the practices of political science what they are. I argue that the practice of political inquiry in the secularization problematic has been constituted by a shared meaning—of the inevitable secularizing character of modern political history. Therefore, my response to the first question about the secularizing historical expectations that underlie our perplexity is that such expectations constitute what Hans-Georg Gadamer calls the prejudices—or pre-judgments—of a tradition of social scientific inquiry founded, as Dorothy Ross has put it, on "high expectations for modernity." Among the most important of these expectations is that as societies become more complex through demographic, economic, and social changes, the religious and public spheres become increasingly differentiated. Matters of government would become limited to regulating developing markets or organizing the functional units of a given society. Intimated here is what many—Marx, J. S. Mill, and Henry Maine among the most prominent—have characterized as a passage from one state to another based on understanding history as a continuous process of transformation through which the new would supersede the old, the modern the traditional, the secular the religious. I suggest that this view has been embedded in the self-understandings of modern social scientists to an extent that when the theopolitical resurfaces on the terrain of the modern, we are perplexed. We say that perhaps this is just a temporary phenomenon, a refuge from the hazards of modern life.[3]

It is important to point out that not all who predicted secularization *advocated* it, and those who advocated the separation of realms were not necessarily antireligious. Many of those who supported secularization understood the differentiation between religion and politics, especially after Thomas Hobbes and John Locke, as potentially good for both the life of a state and of religion: when liberated from the hands of politicians, religion could enjoy its own vitality. Many participants in political struggles (as well as observers of those struggles) understood the secularizing thesis as a historical "deal" between politics and religion that would allow for each to be free of the untoward influences of the other. History, many agreed, was the unfolding of an essentially secularizing process. Broadly stated, my response to the first question is: our explanations of religion in politics have been constituted by *our* meanings and understandings—our theories and judgments—that the outcomes of modern political history should be singularly secular in entailing the separation, privatization, recession, or cessation of religious theory and practice.[4]

Hermeneutic inquiry equips us to understand possibilities within the secularization problematic of modern politics because hermeneutics says that inquiry should not begin *and* end with an explanation of events in terms of their meaning and significance for *us*. We inevitably begin with such meaning (e.g., "secularization is inevitable," "religion will be privatized"), but we must not *end* there, because the hermeneutic imperative is to reflect on and communicate with those whose lives we seek to make authoritative claims about. Thus Taylor, drawing on Gadamer, has described the central demand of hermeneutic inquiry as the need to confront our language of explanation with the self-understandings of those whose political lives we seek to explain. Doing so entails trying to grasp the meanings that constitute other people's lives through reflection and communication. We should bring those meanings into *our* language.[5]

Consequently, we should explain better the lives of others in terms of constitutive meanings as well as expand our understanding of comparative political possibilities. In our context of religion in politics, hermeneutics enables us to understand the role and depth of religion in politics—because we seek to account for the constitutive meanings in theopolitical action and practice rather than await their historical demise *and,* as a consequence, it affords a richer understanding of alternative, comparative possibilities within the endlessly contested politics of secularization. My response to the second issue concerning how we might become less perplexed about the contemporary relevance of the theopolitical thus stresses the need to adopt a hermeneutic posture toward political explanation.

In sum I posit three general claims with explicit reference to anglophone political science, articulating each claim within the conceptual frame of Gadamerian hermeneutics, with special attention and emphasis on Gadamer's insights regarding illuminating and hindering prejudices in all interpretation. The first is that prejudices about the secular character and direction of modern politics—specifically, anticipations for the privatization and institutional separation of religion from politics—have hindered the interpretation of both secular and theopolitical phenomena in modernity. The second is that these prejudices have been supported by noninterpretive methodological commitments that are characterized by a failure to account for the shared and contested concepts that constitute political life. Because "constitute" means to make something what it is, the failure to account for the constitutive languages of politics in a context is a failure to account for what makes politics in that context what it is. Following this, the third claim is that an interpretive approach to modernity enables us to explain secular and theopolitical phenomena and the alternative modernities that they express more persuasively than noninterpretive approaches. After explicating each claim, I illustrate the difference that hermeneutics makes in two specific fields of inquiry. Both are drawn from the study of modern Turkish politics, and both are complexly constituted by secular and theopolitical aspects of meaning. Hence they illustrate the major theoretical claims of this work as well as demonstrate the indispensability of an interpretive approach to secularism and theopolitics in modernity.[6]

I begin by outlining Gadamer's understanding of prejudice. In the first chapter I critically examine modernity and the substantive character of the particular "secular modern" prejudice that I seek to evaluate. Because, as Gadamer argues, prejudice always and necessarily guides interpretation—mostly in unconscious ways—political investigators of contemporary secularism or theopolitics ought to aim not to shed their prejudices; rather, they should reevaluate aspects of their prejudices that they see as hindering, and attempt to improve understanding by introducing new prejudices. Operating within the Gadamerian frame, I claim that we need to rethink our substantive expectations regarding the secular or nonsecular outcomes of modern political history. In so doing, we may reconstitute conceptual aspects of the language of study in which we interpret modern politics.

For Gadamer, the recognition of prejudice, the discrimination between prejudices that illuminate and those that hinder understanding, and the adoption of new prejudices all occur within understanding, not outside it. This has two important implications. The first is that we cannot step into a prejudice-free zone. We *can* foreground prejudices and we *can* examine them, but these are not objective maneuvers, outside of understanding and free from prejudgment. They are within the hermeneutic circle, not above or beyond it. Similarly, there is no prejudice-free discourse to enter to critically adjudicate which prejudices hinder understanding and which illuminate it. We make such determinations only when we give our prejudgments "full play" in the context of understanding. We become conscious of them when they are provoked *in our attempt to understand.* This is, in part, how understanding occurs. To strengthen my case for hermeneutic political inquiry, I shall demonstrate that the hermeneutic perspective on language enables us to reconstruct how, in discriminating between illuminating and hindering prejudices, we may think of one explanation as more compelling than others.[7]

The second implication relates directly to this work as a critical enterprise. Because prejudice underlies all interpretation, my account in the first chapter of a kind of "secular modern" prejudice is not to be considered objective. I have jettisoned a frame in which objectivity about these matters is even desirable. My account is fruitfully thought of as a contribution to and an interpretation within a dialogue about the character of secularism and of modernity, a dialogue that has been provoked by the revival of theopolitics in the late twentieth century. This dialogue is my context for understanding in which my prejudices, most outside of my purview, come into play. My claims have emerged as part of broad discussions in the social sciences that are concerned with two particular issues: first, the secular and nonsecular conceptual and practical possibilities of modern politics, and second, the methodological identity of the discipline entrusted to explain those politics. These discussions and the phenomena that gave rise to them shaped this work, and this work participates in these discussions as well. Any attempt to conceive of a problem for investigation in such terms as prejudice, discrimination, and judgment risks being read as an attempt to make an objective evaluation of the facts; it might be seen as striving to step outside of the hermeneutic circle to pronounce a definitive and conclusive judgment. This is a danger in any critical enterprise, but as Gadamer's hermeneutics impressively demonstrates, we make even our strongest judgments within conversations, not outside of them.

Problems arise only if the conversation goes unrecognized, if interpretation is viewed as a subject-object confrontation in which the participants fail to see that they are interlocutors. They might believe, for instance, that one is the interpreter and the other the interpreted, one is the questioner and listener and the other the speaker, or one is the expert and the other the nonexpert. Such differentials underlie one reason why (noninterpretive) political scientists so often fall short in attempts to explain the political lives of others. They fail to engage in open-ended conversations (or metaphorically similar modes of historical research) with those whom they claim to understand. I hope that this work will illustrate that to suspend the dialogue—to stop making judgments, correcting misimpressions, declaring validity, and so on—is to impede understanding; indeed, it is to risk never truly understanding anything of substance in human affairs.

The conceptual discussion in Chapter 1 is followed by an exposition of the objectives and assumptions of interpretive political inquiry. I draw on the writings of Charles Taylor, Alasdair MacIntyre, Quentin Skinner, and John Dunn to guide a detailed exposition of what an interpretive explanation looks like with regard to various dimensions of politics and how hermeneutics can contribute to broader critical, comparative interests in the study of political thought and practice in modernity. Despite being widely recognized as an alternative approach to the study of politics throughout political science, the interpretive approach is still widely misconceived. As a response to this situation and for the purposes of my argument, I articulate the interpretive approach to political explanation and defend what I call the interpretive unity of political inquiry. The central thesis of interpretive political science is that political acts, relations, practices, and institutions express shared and contested, subjective and intersubjective, concepts and understandings within the language of a political culture (itself multiply constituted). The interpretive unity of political explanation derives from the fact that both linguistic political phenomena (like speeches) and ostensibly non-linguistic political phenomena (like migration) are conceptually constituted and cannot be adequately explained without those concepts. But to accept this is to accept several important implications for explanation in political science. To date, most political scientists are willing to grant the central thesis without grasping its implications for their project as a whole. The context is ripe for a restatement of these implications and a demonstration of the indispensability of interpretive political science.

As a project in political explanation and as a conceptual frame for making sense of politics, hermeneutics offers much for enriching our understanding of political life and for understanding comparative possibilities in the relation between politics and religion, or conscience and tradition more broadly. The general point is that there is an intimate link between our substantive historical expectations and our methodological commitments. Proceeding from hermeneutic premises about the nature of interpretation and of politics, I argue that political inquirers ought to make a dual shift: first in their historical understanding, by reconsidering their substantive historical judgments about modern political history, and, second, in their orientation toward political explanation, by adopting an interpretive posture. Doing so, as I argue in Chapter 2, will ensure more compelling explanations because our study of political life will be more consistent with who we—both the interpreters and the interpreted—are as human beings.

In elucidating guidelines for hermeneutic inquiry, I do not mean to imply that hermeneutics is practiced only by those who follow those guidelines; nor that hermeneutics is a form of political inquiry bearing no resemblance to existing qualitative modes of political science research. Overlapping interpretive concerns clearly exist between hermeneutics and those modes of qualitative research that establish imperatives for political inquirers to take context and meaning seriously. Indeed, although I think it would clearly be wrong to equate hermeneutics with qualitative social research, hermeneutics contributes to such fields by providing a second-order understanding of modes of inquiry that take language and meaning seriously in political explanation. Hermeneutics does not simply offer guidelines; it helps to reconstruct what is done by inquirers who seek to account for meaning.

Nonetheless, as my explication of hermeneutics will suggest, I believe that the language and conceptual frame of hermeneutics deepens one's grasp of politics and of qualitative political explanation. I believe, for example, that while it is one thing to point out the existence of (or patterns of) certain meanings in a context of study, it is another to show how those meanings constitute specific institutional power dynamics. (I take such dynamics to be the central, shared analytical concern of hermeneutic and nonhermeneutic political inquirers alike.) Moreover, I illustrate how hermeneutic political explanation makes a difference in understanding the outcomes of modern politics. And I show that Gadamerian hermeneutics offers a more compelling account of the relation between the interpreter and the interpreted than do commonly practiced qualitative methodologies, which, as much as they may emphasize contextual sensitivity, tend to relate the issues associated with interpretive prejudgments to problems of values and biases. From a Gadamerian perspective, these terms, partly expressive of an aspiration to be free from bias, constrain a deeper engagement with the relation between the interpreter and the interpreted, and, ultimately, between explanation and history. Thus in addition to offering guidelines for inquiry, the language of the hermeneutic approach—possibly obscure and cumbersome at first sight—contributes to the broader analytic aspirations of political explanation. At the dawn of the behavioral era, students of government, politics, and law shifted their understandings of their fields of inquiry toward becoming political scientists in search of law-like relations of causality that would allow them to "predict outcomes objectively." Indeed, participants in the discipline reconstituted the understandings that made up the various practices, institutional structures, and power relations in the study of politics in terms of the concepts and meanings of science. Constituting the practices of political inquiry has not ceased, and it should not: it should not be beyond the scope of our collective imaginations to incorporate the terms of the hermeneutic thesis, especially if they provide insight on understanding politics. Thus, the emphasis I place on elucidating the rules of thumb of hermeneutic inquiry stems from the costs that I discern in the discipline from their absence in the self-understandings of political inquirers, especially in light of the contributions that hermeneutics can make to understanding historical possibility when there is abundant perplexity of the sustained efficacy of theopolitics.

This efficacy is starkly evident in Turkey where, at the time of this writing, the Islamist prime minister claims that he and his party, the *Refah Partisi* (Welfare/Prosperity Party), are the "best guarantors of the secular state." While the serious dilemmas that Turkey faces in the politics of secularization are not entirely unique, there are highly contextualized features that make the Turkish case compelling for political reflection on the question of secularization today. Taking place on the geographic edge of the Islamic world and Europe, between East and West, the dialogue over the meanings and ends of secularization and modernization since the founding of the laicist republic in the 1920s has had world historical significance both for Turks and for interpreters of Turkey. In Turkey, a modern elite seized the reins of power from an empire that was heavily invested in Islam and effected a separation between religion and politics, something said to be rather unique in an Islamic context that was later emulated by other modernizers and promoted as a model by outside, modernist observers. I will show that the Turkish case is tremendously important for theorizing secularism and for understanding the phenomenon of religious revivalism in Turkey and elsewhere. Beyond the specifics of Turkish political thought and practice, however, the practices of modern states associated with secular politics must be sites for hermeneutics and for theorization about the politics of secularization. Thus my study of selected aspects of Turkey's experience in the politics of secularization, in addition to its intrinsic hermeneutic importance, also illustrates the general claims of this book.[8]

I offer detailed accounts of the history of interpreting two central and related aspects of Turkish laicist political thought and practice within anglophone political science, and I argue that these interpretations express a shared commitment to the unduly narrow secular modern prejudices discussed in the first chapter. As such, from an interpretive point of view, they express more about the meaning and identity—both substantive-theoretical and methodological-cal—of the history of political science than they do about those contexts that they were intended to capture. If our explanations are to be complete, they should, from an interpretive perspective, offer fully compelling accounts of both horizons.[9]

The two aspects of modern Turkish politics that I will consider are: first, the political ideas of Ziya Gökalp (1876–1924), the Young Turk nationalist thinker who believed that Turkey's modern turn could be reconciled with its Islamic traditions; and second, the practices, relations, and institutions associated with the original conception of laicist politics in Turkey. I address these two dimensions of analysis (texts as well as institutions and practices) to illustrate the interpretive unity of political science, but mostly to explore the interpretive issues that I have raised in two contexts, which are complexly constituted by secular/modern and religious/traditional aspects of meaning. After providing a history of explanatory attempts in the literature of anglophone political science research that fall short in their objectives, I offer alternative interpretive explanations of these aspects of study in this field. Gökalp's contribution to the secularization problematic in contemporary Turkish history cannot be understated. One of his interpreters has referred to him as the "only systematic thinker Turkey has produced in the twentieth century."[10] His significance stems from his considerable struggling with the articulation of a theoretical foundation for secular modern politics as the multiethnic and multireligious Ottoman empire was replaced by a Turkish nationalist and largely Muslim nation-state. As such, a study of his ideas is a necessary part of a study of the practices, relationships, and institutions associated with secularism and modernity in Muslim contexts in general, and in Turkey in particular.

These practices, which have roots in Ottoman efforts at bureaucratic rationalization and reform in the nineteenth century, accelerated under the leadership of Mustafa Kemal (Atatürk) during the 1920s. Atatürk promoted a nationalist version of positivist-scientific values as part of the sociocultural policy of the ruling Republican People's Party. Consequently, the once-prominent Islamic component of Ottoman politics and society was marginalized as the central elite undertook what they, and most of their interpreters in social science, took to be the construction of a republican, nationalist, populist, and secular polity and state. (As I argue in Chapter 3, the original conception of the politics associated with secularism in Turkey is better captured with the concept of laicism than with the concept of secularism.) Multiparty democracy after the Second World War enabled aspects of Islamic discourse to reenter politics within the framework of the laicist state, as rival candidates campaigned to represent religiously oriented constituent interests. The Islamic content of Turkish politics was extended after 1980, when coup leaders codified religious education in a new constitution and governing party officials articulated a solidarist-populist "Turkish Islamic Synthesis" to ensure stability and to challenge the left. Since 1983, multiparty (and military) institutions have continued to structure politics so that laicist and theopolitical aspects of Turkish political culture can be jointly expressed. Reconciliation of modernism and Islam in Turkey, however, continues to generate intense public debate about the meanings and the practical ends of secularism and laicism, especially with the electoral and parliamentary successes of the anti-laicist, theopolitically oriented *Refah Partisi* in both municipal and national elections since 1994. Debates over the original conception of laicism as well as over the nature of the modern secular state in an Islamic context underlie unfolding dynamics in Turkey.

The significance of this dialogue extends well beyond Turkey's borders and is of interest in comparative political studies of southeastern Europe and the Middle East and in broader policy circles. For many years, Turkey has sought full integration with the European Community, whose members are cautious of Turkey's Muslim character. Yet it is this so-called cultural fact that has enabled the United States and Turkey to promote it as a "secular, democratic, and market-oriented model," a bulwark against "Islamic Fundamentalism" for the Muslim countries of the former Soviet Union. For similar reasons, political scientists and economists in North Africa and the Middle East believe that they have much to learn from Turkey's experience. An interpretive account of Turkey's secular model has relevance in these domains of intellectual and political interest.

Textual analyses mainly of political science research on Turkey through 1995 have informed my accounts. I say "mainly" because the disciplinary boundaries between history, political science, sociology, and the other human sciences are always shifting. The best researchers in these disciplines read across these boundaries. Many essays written strictly in the discipline of history, for example, are fundamental to political science research. I have certainly found this to be the case in the study of Turkey. Following the multidisciplinary intellectual lineage of political science texts, I have developed a rich appreciation for the meanings that "Turkey" has in political science. It has not, however, seriously altered my first two general claims regarding historical frames and methods in political science. In addition to this cross-disciplinary textual analysis, the accounts of Gökalp and Turkey's laicist politics are informed by research that was conducted in Turkey during 1993 and 1994.

I conclude by summarizing my arguments, explaining what this work contributes to political inquiry, and outlining areas of future research. I also make several suggestions about the intellectual historiography of political science and about the (interpretive) responsibilities of political scientists in modernity. In general, this multilayered project has relevance to many specific research programs of contemporary interest. It contributes to studies in political science history, to theoretical and historical inquiry into modern—particularly secular—politics and existing alternative modernities, to attempts to sustain a viable and independent mode of interpretive political explanation in political science, and to debates in comparative political studies about Turkey's secular model.

POLITICAL SCIENCE HISTORY

The relevance of disciplinary histories of political science has been stressed in recent American political science literature. John Dryzek and Stephen Leonard suggest that such histories are ineliminable features of political science. They encourage us to "parse disciplinary histories for positive and negative lessons" of both a methodological and a theoretical nature. James Farr adds a practical interest to these "internal" dimensions, suggesting that the public functions of political scientists as civic educators and policy advisers raise questions of both local and global responsibility for which historical awareness is essential. One important contribution of these historiographical projects lies, as John Gunnell and David Easton suggest, in establishing the important connections between "historical reflections . . . and the enhancement and assessment of social scientific practice."[11]

My specific historical aim is to explain the engagement of political science with a specific context of inquiry to demonstrate the indispensability of interpretive inquiry in political analysis. Separate from my three general claims, however, I believe that studies in the historical development of the field as a whole can be extended fruitfully by exploring the work of individual political scientists in specific explanatory contexts. Too often, the great essays in the discipline's history (for example, presidential addresses of the American Political Science Association, classic paradigm-setting articles, etc.) are given sole credit for expressing the identity of the discipline. I seek to extend thinking about the history of political science by engaging its practice in specific contexts.[12] An examination of political science's practical engagement with Turkish politics, for example, illuminates disciplinary affinities for one model of westernizing politics, perspectives on the organization of religious and state power, and judgments about the place of Islam in modernity.

Four general questions guide my interest in the history of political science. First, what meanings do specific contexts have for political scientists who explain politics in them? Are they models of market reform? Illustrations of stable, institutional development? Are they overlooked? Second, in what conceptual frames (historical narratives, theoretical statements, assumptions) are specific contexts of inquiry interpreted, and what is the meaning content both of these conceptual frames and of the interpretations? Third, what is the relation between these interpretations and our methodological assumptions about political explanation? Finally, what are the links between the meanings of a specific context in political science and the meanings of that context outside political science, where anglophone political science fulfills its practical responsibilities? That is, are there any links between the meaning of a specific area of inquiry in the context of political explanation and in public arenas such as policymaking and analysis?[13]

THE IDEA OF "PREJUDICE"

"The hermeneutically trained mind" will make conscious the prejudices governing our understanding, so that the text, as another's meaning, can be isolated and valued on its own. Foregrounding (*Abheben*) a prejudice clearly requires suspending its validity for us. For as long as our mind is influenced by a prejudice, we do not consider it a judgment. How then can we foreground it? It is impossible to make ourselves aware of a prejudice while it is constantly operating unnoticed, but only when it is, so to speak, provoked. The encounter with a traditionary text can provide this provocation. For what leads to understanding must be something that has already asserted itself in its own separate validity. Understanding begins, as we have already said above, when something addresses us. This is the first condition of hermeneutics. We now know what this requires, namely the fundamental suspension of our own prejudices. But all suspension of judgments and hence, a fortiori, of prejudices, has the logical structure of a *question*.[14]

The essence of the *question* is to open up possibilities and keep them open. If a prejudice becomes questionable in view of what another person or text says to us, this does not mean that it is simply set aside and the text or the other person accepted as valid in its place. Rather, historical objectivism shows its naiveté in accepting this disregarding of ourselves as what actually happens. In fact our own prejudice is properly brought into play by being put at risk. Only by being given full play is it able to experience the other's claim to truth and make it possible for him to have full play himself.[15]

Using the concept of prejudice to identify my interpretive concern signifies the relevance of Gadamer's hermeneutics to this work. It also entails an explicit rejection of the terminology, more common in the vernacular of social science, of bias and values. These terms usually find expression in a frame that characterizes the influence of preconceptions and prejudgments on interpretation as entirely negative. When scientists—natural or social—speak of biases and values, the implication is that it is desirable to be free from bias, or to be value-neutral, either in general or with respect to certain values, when engaged in methodologically rigorous scientific explanation. Undergirding these views is the belief that it is possible to exercise control over our pre-understanding so that we may be objective. In this view, the interpreter's historicity may be set aside; history belongs to the scientist who can bracket it and thus "know" history free from its influence.

By contrast, to Gadamer, the interpreter belongs to history and can never be free from it. As such, the prejudices that are shaped in that history, and that largely reside outside the subject's full control, are not properly understood as hindrances to understanding. They are instead the precondition for all understanding; they always and necessarily guide interpretations, for they "constitute . . . the legitimate guiding for genuine understanding."[16]

Prejudices underlie all understanding—illuminating, hiding, promoting, concealing, and so on. Moreover, the ways that they are at work are never fully knowable by us. The prejudices involved in understanding are manifestations of our own historicity, of our belonging to traditions that are larger than the individuals who give them meaning. The hermeneutic view is that, belonging to history, we cannot—and need not—set it aside. We do not stand outside of it, we participate in it. The concept of prejudice, therefore, implies the tradition and historical-embeddedness of the prejudgments that inform and are hence necessary to understanding.[17]

Gadamer views the claim that prejudice is an obstacle to understanding as a pernicious corruption in Enlightenment thought, ironically over the term "prejudice" itself. It perpetuates the false view that through method we can exercise control over history and the process of understanding it. "We can know better: this is the maxim with which the modern enlightenment approaches tradition and which ultimately leads it to undertake historical research. It takes tradition as an object of critique." By stressing the historicity of prejudgments, Gadamer seeks to shatter this illusion. He argues that our consciousness of history is the "consciousness that consciousness is affected by history." Every act of understanding is, therefore, an act within history, within a tradition, and within the hermeneutic situation that aims at what Gadamer calls a fusion of horizons. Understanding involves grasping the relations and tensions between horizons that, in the process, maintain their difference as both are altered in the fusion.[18]

> Every encounter with tradition that takes place within historical consciousness involves the experience of a tension between the text and the present. The hermeneutic task consists in not covering up this tension by attempting a naive assimilation of the two but in consciously bringing it out. This is why it is part of the hermeneutic approach to project a historical horizon that is different from the horizon of the present. Historical consciousness is aware of its own otherness and hence foregrounds the horizon of the past from its own.[19]

This fusion of horizons lies behind Gadamer's claim that "real historical thinking must take account of its own historicity." Not to do so is to fall into the trap of objectivism, the belief that we can think historically without seeing our internal relation with history. For Gadamer, we cannot stand above history; consciousness is a historical effect and thus so too is our understanding of others. Thus Gadamer rejects the view that we can set ourselves aside, suspend all of our prejudgments, and proceed to understand.[20]

Because most prejudices remain outside our purview, we need to ask, how do some become conscious? According to Gadamer, prejudices are made conscious (foregrounded) when they are provoked in interpretation. Our "rais[ing] to a conscious level the prejudices which govern understanding," therefore, occurs within understanding. Moreover, only those prejudices that have been addressed by the text that we seek to understand are provoked; never all prejudices. There is no way to determine outside of interpretation what prejudices one must evaluate. When some are provoked, we become aware of the need to distinguish those that blind or hinder our understanding from those that illuminate it.[21]

Hindering prejudices are those that are a "cause of misunderstanding; and these it is certainly the duty of conscientious understanding to avoid." In conscientiously avoiding hindering prejudices, however, we are not stepping outside the hermeneutic situation. Similar to foregrounding, the separation between hindering and illuminating prejudices also occurs in the process of understanding. Understanding occurs in history, not above it. It is, therefore, both an opening up and a resituating in a historical frame whose contours we cannot fully describe.[22]

I seek to account for certain secular and modern prejudices in political science research that have been provoked by the resurgence of theopolitical phenomena at the end of the twentieth century. The conception of this project in these terms is possible because of a widely shared recognition that these prejudices have led to misunderstanding; as such, they have hindered attempts to understand the politics of others. I build from this recognition, not to jettison prejudice because that is not possible. I seek, rather, to reconsider those prejudices that we may now conscientiously reflect upon; political inquirers need to reconstitute those aspects of secular and modern prejudices of which we can be conscious in order to understand alternative, historically open secular and theopolitical possibilities in modernity. The task of interpreting alternative modernities remains crucial. We need to avoid the kind of misunderstandings that appear in studies governed by certain hindering prejudices without mistakenly thinking that we can step outside the history that shaped these understandings. Furthermore, we need to do this in a way that recognizes the openness of modern secular and theopolitical possibilities.

To improve our understanding, I argue, requires reevaluation of *both* our basic substantive understanding about modern political history and our methodological commitments. The problems that have been identified because they were provoked in recent history are founded as much on hindering methodological commitments as they are on hindering theoretical prejudices about the place of the theopolitical in modern politics. Thus we must consider both the methodological and the related theoretical bases of modern political inquiry. Commitments to non- or viciously anti-interpretive understandings of political inquiry must be reevaluated with our substantive historical expectations. The methodological commitments are not a prejudice to those whose faith in them is secure, but they are related to our continual failure to understand the political lives of others. In the context of inquiry that I discuss, the noninterpretive methodological commitments of political science continue effectively to sustain and support the problematic secular modern prejudices that I unpack in the first chapter. Thus, unless we conscientiously avoid certain substantive prejudices *and* make an interpretive turn, I fear that we will continue to misunderstand the complex dynamics within and between secular and theopolitical phenomena in modernity.

My evaluation of the problems we face thus places Gadamer's concept of prejudice at the center. Still, I must point out that my own interest in political explanation is different from Gadamer's interest in philosophical hermeneutics. While I believe that the foundational assumptions of my view of interpretive inquiry are wholly compatible with Gadamer's view of the basic nature of understanding, my own determination to improve understanding politics marks an immediate departure point. The reasons that I think my view of political explanation is compatible with Gadamer's hermeneutics are discussed in Chapter 2. What separates us, however, must be stated here.

In his foreword to the second edition of *Truth and Method*, Gadamer stresses his real concern: "My real concern was and is philosophic: not what we do and what we ought to do, but what happens to us over and above our wanting and doing." Gadamer's concern, in short, is what happens in all understanding.[23]

I am interested in what we do and what we ought to do in understanding politics, especially Turkish politics. To Gadamer, the "methods of the human sciences are not at issue here." To me, they are. To Gadamer, "it is enough to say we understand in a different way." To me, operating in the context of political explanation (where hermeneutics can be "deadly" as well as playful), we must say that an alternative understanding, while alternative, may be utterly uncompelling.[24]

Chapter 1 Interpreting Alternative Modernities

When one's feet are at Jerusalem, it is legitimate to emphasize that religious and literate societies are never wholly "traditional."
—J. G. A. Pocock

All philosophies of history proceed with the tale until they arrive at the happy ending to which our (modern) age is supposed to be destined. This is a highly unmodern idea. Among others, the novelty of our age consists of the openness of our horizon and the plurality of interpretations of both the present and the past. This openness allows for multiple projects. The multiplicity of projects is promising but at the same time threatening. The point is not that we are ignorant of the end of our story (a feature which we share with every human group and age), but that we are as yet ignorant as to whether our project will be viable in the long run. We have just begun to work in and on modernity.
—Agnes Heller

The resurgence of theopolitics at the end of the twentieth century has provoked widespread reconsideration of a shared belief in modern political studies, namely, that the outcomes of modern political history will be secular. The reconsideration, however, has elicited no consensus on how we might proceed or on how we should understand modernity. What does a recognition that we live in modernity require of us to understand the relation between religion and politics?

In this chapter, I argue that there are multiple possibilities for modernity and secularism, and that to understand these possibilities we must reflect on aspects of our interpretive prejudgments of which we have become aware. To this end, I delineate how theopolitical radicalism in modern politics has provoked certain hindering secular modern prejudices, and I identify problematic teleological, secular, and modern dimensions of these prejudices. I then consider how we might better judge modernity and its political possibilities, and conclude with several reasons for changing our expectations about modernity—especially regarding the relation between religion and politics—if we are to understand it.

THE PROBLEM WITH MODERN SOCIAL
SCIENTISTS ON MODERNITY

In the aftermath of the Iranian revolution, prominent western scholars of Iranian politics reflected that their pre-revolution accounts of Iranian politics exhibited a discernible tendency either to ignore or to downplay the political significance of those who became the victors in the revolution. Fred Halliday, for instance, reflected on the merits and shortcomings of his 1979 study *Iran: Dictatorship and Development,* noting that "there were several deficiencies in the book that subsequent events were to bring out." Among these, he ranked high his failure to appreciate the durability ("survival") and political potential ("significant oppositional role") of the "precapitalist sectors (for example, the bazaar merchants) and ideologies." Related to this deficiency was another: "In its discussion of the traditions and significance of political forces in Iran, the book placed too much emphasis on the secular opposition of the late 1940s and early 1950s, and underestimated the clerical forces of 1963. I knew of Khomeini from Iranian associates, but shared with many of them the view that he was a man of the past." Surprised by the endurance and political relevance of the precapitalist sectors, their ideologies, and their support for the political alternative represented by Ayatollah Ruhollah Musavi Khomeini, Halliday realized that he had interpreted all of these relative to the past, rather than the present.[1]

Halliday was not alone in reflecting on "relics" from the past in the politics of the present. James Bill, another renowned authority on Iranian politics, was influenced by a similar conception of the new power holders and of their

primary constituency. Bill argued that popular support for the Islamic opposition forces coalesced during the seventies when the "Iranian people took refuge
in religion and flocked to the mujtahids for social and political shelter." But,
Bill argued, the capacities necessary to attract support and to seize power are
different from those necessary to govern in the "modern world." Bill wrote that
for "Iran to come to terms with the modern world . . . the mullahs and
mujtahids will have to return to their accustomed roles as guides and guardians," where the "more flexible and better educated among them [such as the
moderate Islamic populists] will serve as the consciences of the new secular
leadership, whatever form that leadership may take." The leaders of the Kho-
meini-led "mullacracy," as he called them, "lacked the skills and experience to
operate effectively the modern economic, administrative, and technological
institutions that were in place." In addition, "by carrying all of their traditional
baggage of the past with them into the hallways of power within a social edifice
that must exist in the present and confront the future, the Shi'a political
extremists provided themselves with an impossible task."[2]

Bill expresses a view of the relation between the past and the present similar
to the one that governed Halliday's investigaton—authentic participation in
the politics of the present means "leaving one's traditional baggage in the past."
A crucial question arises: what is it that drives us to interpret religiously and
culturally different, yet politically efficacious, modes of expression and practice
as part of the past and not of the present?

Many contemporary thinkers concerned with the relation between religion
and politics in the modern world have noticed this habit of thought. Some
political scientists, for instance, have lamented that, as one scholar of Middle
East politics described it, "For too long biases, predispositions, and enthusiasms
have served instead of theory or even classification to guide research on the
politics of the Middle East."[3] Such comments suggest that predispositions only
interfere with understanding, and consequently we need to devise more sophisticated ways of restraining their influence. The amaranthine search for a general
theory or language of explanation is thus renewed.

Other commentators, including many outside of political science, have
engaged in extensive, critical considerations of these so-called biases to understand their character and the character of their influence in the context of
interpreting others. While these discussions are rarely framed in Gadamerian
terms, they can in part be conceived as such. More specifically, they are reflections on a particular form of secular modern prejudice that has been provoked
by theopolitical events in the late twentieth century. To understand the hinder-

ing nature of this prejudice, it is essential to reflect on various articulations of the problem as many now see it.[4]

These considerations take several different forms and address several different aspects of a relatively complex interpretive situation. Nonetheless, they may be organized along three general axes. The first concerns the role of teleological expectations in the explanation of traditional social phenomena. The second concerns the secular commitments of modern social science. The third concerns its stated modern or modernist elements. Much literature on each topic exists; an examination of representative criticisms of these dimensions illuminates important aspects of the conceptual frame in which modern politics is continually interpreted. This is not to imply, however, that these criticisms get to the heart of the puzzle presented here. While they help to explain some of the reasons why interpreters like Halliday and Bill assign less significance to theopolitical actors of the present by consigning them to the past, they do so at the risk of fixing the meanings of the important concepts of secular and modern in ways that are inconsistent with an explanatory disposition of an interpretive view of them.

Those commentators who draw attention to the untoward explanatory influence of "teleological temporalities," as the historical sociologist William Sewell calls them, criticize the tendency of modern social scientists to view history as the temporal unfolding of a law-like, inherent, inexorable logic of development. Sewell espies this tendency in what he calls the "common practice of labelling political or social movements as backward-looking or forward-looking." He writes, "The simple act of labelling movements in this way contains an implicit teleological explanation of their histories. Likewise, the term 'modern' often serves as a label for those processes or agents that are deemed by the analyst to be doing the work of the future in some present, while 'traditional' labels those equally current forces in the present that the analyst regards as doing the work of the past." Sewell contends that these teleological frames, and the habit of "labelling" that they condition, impede the sociologist's understanding of history.[5]

The belief that authentic politics in the modern present requires a secular supersession of "past" forms of theopolitical expression is also rooted in the history of anglophone political science. Its most systematic expression has been in the highly influential liberal and Marxist understandings of modernity and political development. According to these interpretations of political and historical change, certain phenomena—classified generally as traditional (and usually assumed to be historically inert)—pass through what Henry Maine in earlier days referred to as the "true lines" of historical "movement" and become modern. In that process, those things "of the past" either fade away or are relegated to private matters in the modern state. In turn, this state aims to promote and operate on variously conceived secular rationalities. Secular and modern futures have been explicitly juxtaposed to traditional and religious ones. In fact, with Sewell, it is possible to point to a lingering problem of teleology in political science as well, especially with regard to thinking about theopolitical phenomena.[6]

Theorists of comparative political inquiry, for example, suggest that religion, especially in non-Protestant forms, is dysfunctional for modernization. Lawrence Mayer underscores this point with reference to religions of the "non-western" world—noting that Buddhism and Islam especially, which "teach fatalistic views of the world" and "retain a far greater hold on the lives of the masses in the less developed nations"—"account for some of the slow rate of modernization" and failure to create "successful government in the modern world." His comments are not limited to the so-called developing context: "Since religious faith, almost in its essence, embodies final, absolute principles, the inability to create autonomous secular institutions would weaken the ability of that system to generate meaningful social change." The critique of teleology that I offer here suggests that it has become clear that religious institutions generate meaningful social change for those who participate in them. Nonetheless, for Mayer, modernization requires that religion—not only culturally different religions, but religion itself—assume its historically proper place. The non-westernness that Mayer refers to is essential only in the sense that non-western religions have not done what, in his account, religion in the West has done—namely, removed itself from public affairs and successfully entered the private realm. This is the proper historical place of religion in modern politics.[7]

Similarly, some of Samuel Huntington's reflections on development theory suggest that teleological assumptions may not always be couched explicitly in theopolitical terms. Huntington argues that culture differences may explain different patterns of economic and political development: "In contrast to the Western model [of sustained economic growth, equity, democracy, stability, and autonomy], another culture's image of the good society may be of a society that is simple, austere, hierarchical, authoritarian, disciplined, and martial. The image of the developed Western society . . . thus may not constitute a meaningful model or reference group for a modern Islamic, African, Confucian, or Hindu society." Huntington tries to accommodate the critique of teleology by suggesting that: "Maybe the time has come to stop trying to change these societies and to change the model, to develop models of a modern Islamic, Confucian, or Hindu society that would be more relevant to countries where those cultures prevail. . . . The need is to generalize from the East Asian experience and derive from that experience a developmental model of a society that is authoritarian, stable, economically dynamic, and equitable in its income distribution. The South American model might be one of class stratification, inequality, moderate growth, political conflict, economic penetration, and alternating democratic and authoritarian regimes." Huntington's concern for historical experience is to be welcomed, but what he actually does is not jettison teleology as much as substitute new culture-specific teleologies. The future development of different societies is not opened to various possibilities, contingent on external and internal factors (economic and political as well as cultural). A reified conception of "their own culture" defines this development. Huntington's suggestion to fashion new generalizable models of development for these broadly conceived non-western societies simply reproduces aspects of what was once tradition as telos.[8]

Beyond this interpretive move, Huntington's view of culture is determined by his understanding of especially non-western religions. Huntington uses the chart below to illustrate the variety of cultures (and hence, perhaps, the variety of development models) that exist in the world today:

Culture	Principal religion	Region/countries
Nordic	Protestantism	Northwest Europe, British settler countries
Latin	Catholicism	Southern Europe, Latin America
Arab	Islam	North Africa, Middle East
Slavic	Orthodox	Eastern Europe, Soviet Union
Indian	Hinduism	India
Sinic	Confucianism	China, Taiwan, Korea, Singapore, Vietnam
Japan	Confucianism, Buddhism/Shinto	Japan
Malay	Islam/Buddhism/Catholicism	Malaysia, Indonesia, Philippines
African	Christianity/Paganism	Africa south of the Sahara

Obviously, these categories neither exhaust all possibilities nor accommodate politically significant heterogeneity. There is, however, another, deeper problem.[9]

Recall that when Huntington characterizes different patterns of development he uses the concept of "culture," not "religion." Yet, referring to particular societies, he uses concepts that *by his own frame* are religious. For example, in stating the need for new, culture-specific models, he speaks of "Islamic, Confucian, or Hindu society." The table indicates that he must be speaking about (what he calls) Arab, Malay, Sinic, Japanese, and Indian cultures. But he does not once explicitly refer to either Arab or Indian culture, but rather the religious forms of Islamic or Hindu (both oversimplifications of all of the categories). These characterizations may be held by members of these societies. And, such conceptual parsimony avoids some repetition and specificity. Perhaps Huntington interchanges culture and religion in the interest of generality. Whatever the reason, by doing so in the context of identifying new culturally relative and teleologically different paths of development—what he has also discussed in civilizational terms—Huntington articulates Mayer's ideas only slightly differently: non-western religions are dysfunctional for economic growth, equity, stability, democracy, and autonomy. Religion is dysfunctional for sustained modernization, and the explanatory language of culture (or civilization), in this case, conceals that premise.[10]

I have discussed teleology at some length to illustrate its role in political studies of modernity. I do not intend to suggest that any religion or culture is easily made compatible with some models of democracy or other highly valued practices and institutions. That would simply reverse the error that I describe. My purpose is to identify the teleological assumptions that persist in comparative inquiry with explicit reference to the place of religion in modern politics. I will explain the complexity that is ignored in these situations, and why we cannot ignore it if we are to understand the politics of modernity. Huntington's attempt to bring culture (and, more generally, ascriptive criteria) back into comparative inquiry does not reach the heart of the theoretical or methodological problems that I investigate. The recognition that culture or religion should be considered a variable in our explanations does not lead us to rethink our expectations about the character of modernity or of the relations between religion and politics in the modern world.

To this end, recent critiques of the tendency to devalue theopolitics that focus less on teleology than on the so-called secular identity of political science are useful. Many commentators have argued that the failure to grasp the political significance of theopolitical phenomena in the present is a natural consequence of secular criteria of relevance in social science inquiry. These criteria, it is argued, incline inquirers to devalue the role of faith in history and politics and thus handicap political explanation in religious contexts.

Daya Krishna, for example, criticizes the "ontological sensualism" of the secular worldview that treats only what "is revealed and grasped and felt *by* the senses *through* the senses, and *for* the senses" as real and meaningful. In his view, as in that of Wilfred Cantwell Smith, secular social science exhibits a tendency to treat religion and the human curiosity about the transcendent as "eliminable in principle" from other human pursuits, or "as addenda that human beings have tacked on here and there," rather than as faith and traditions that remain effectual in all human projects—economics, philosophy, and politics included. It is not the world of faith that is "odd," as Smith says that secularists believe, but the secularist outlook. The corrective point, therefore, is not "that humanity is *homo religiosus;* it is just plain *homo sapiens.*" From this view, it is no surprise that secular social scientists ignore the religious dimensions of meaning in political thought and practice.[11]

Similarly, but with reference to political practice in the Muslim world, Dale Eickelman, James Piscatori, Michael Hudson, and John L. Esposito criticize the "secular bias of modernization theory" and the "secular presuppositions" of social and political science that fail to see dynamism within various Islamic religious traditions. In their view the problem is not solely ontological, as Krishna and Smith see it, but also a problem of theory and methodology. They suggest that the tendency to accept the mythology that Islam and political development are incompatible, for example, and to treat the "persistence or revival of religion in politics as regressive" or as "throwbacks or deviations" results directly from the intellectual traditions, disciplines, and methodologies of western social science that depend on the secular viewpoint of social and political development. Hudson succinctly states, "To put the matter crudely, by western standards political development is inversely related to religion in politics because secularism is a fundamental criterion of political development." Esposito echoes this view, arguing that secular presuppositions—such as "acceptance of the 'enlightened' notion of separation of church and state (or religion and politics)—constitute a "major obstacle to our understanding" of Islamic politics.[12]

For Hudson, secularism is also the handmaiden of the purported value-free project of the positivist, relativist, and empiricist tradition that relegates ethical issues "to a lower order of priority in favor of the search for trends and even laws of behavior." Secularism provides the view that politics and its study across contexts must transcend the variabilities associated with values. Thus, "secularism" is the pivotal support and constraint for researchers trying to explain, for example, unapologetically "ethical, normative" perspectives on political development found in contemporary Islamic political thought.[13]

There are more variations within these critiques of the secular identity of modern social science, but the result is clear. The "secular *Weltanschauung*" impedes understanding politics in the modern world. Almost by definition, according to these observers, secularism excludes either a "theocracy or even a polity in which religious identity or actors play a significant role." Where politics is concerned in these accounts, secularism treats religion as a phenomenon of the past, not of the present.[14]

Still, while the critique of a type of secular ontology found in the first perspective has the merit of a rich appreciation for the place of the nonsecular in life, it is not entirely clear that all forms of the secularism that Krishna and Smith criticize deny the significance of faith and tradition in all arenas of life. If we were to use Bill and Halliday as exemplars of the secularist approach, we might point out how both note a place for religion in social life. Bill, you may recall, suggests that religious leaders have a proper place as guides and guardians, and may even "serve as the consciences" of secular leaders. Similarly, Halliday notes that "all religions contain some ideas that favor progressive ideals." Such ideals have a place "in support of" political objectives. But, like Bill, he asseverates that "where religion has perhaps its greatest appeal is in the sphere of ethics and the major existential issues confronting each individual, not least death." Both agree that religion and politics must be separated. The problem of separating religion from life as addressed by Smith and Krishna is not entirely overcome in these statements, but it is also not clear that secularism or secular thought alone explains our puzzle. Why must religion be removed from politics? (This question is seemingly elementary to some but not others.) And, is there any relation between the answer to this question and the tendency to temporalize the difference between theopolitics and "secular and rational" politics (the terms used by Halliday and Bill)?[15] Hudson's critique addresses this more directly. Even if he readily accepts western social science's claim to value-free inquiry (as opposed to identifying its own normative force), his critique deepens our understanding of both the secular and the teleological dynamics at work when theopolitical phenomena of the present are consigned to the past.

According to the critical commentary reviewed thus far, the secularist expectations of certain types of western political thought in conjunction with a teleology that places ethical, normative issues either in the historical dustbin or in the private sphere has led political inquirers to overlook and diminish the relevance of religion in modern politics. By contrast, other scholars argue that it is the modernism of political inquiry—not its secularism—that conditions this perspective. The modern identity of the social sciences has been hotly debated in recent years. Similar to the critiques of secularism, the critiques of modernism are broad, but two aspects of the critiques speak directly to the dynamic at work when theopolitical phenomena of the present are read into the past.

The first critique is that modernism judges tradition to be part of the past whose basic function in the present is to serve, in Tilo Schabert's useful phrase, as an "object of critique to sharpen contemporary consciousness." Schabert argues that modernism exhibits an "aimless dynamism" in its relation to what it believes to be the past: it exalted human scientific inquiry over all traditional understandings of the world, thus constructing a "truth gap" between modernity and the past. This gap created two imperatives in modern thought:

> The most recent state of scientific development was also supposed to be always the highest, and consequently to legitimate the rejection of older findings of scientific endeavor as mere preliminaries. Consistently, the second imperative urged the maintenance of the epistemological difference between a present maximum degree of insight and earlier confusion of false opinions. A relapse into the seeming ignorance of earlier times could, however, at best be avoided by methodically barring any return to pre-modern stores of knowledge. . . . The imperative reading "Thou as a 'modern' shalt be superior to all that is past" (Condorcet), thus led to the ban on crossing the "barrier" between present and past. It excluded any attempt at recourse to premodern thinking *a priori*. The ignorance alleged to have prevailed in earlier times and now to be overcome must in no way be allowed to spread again.

In turn, these imperatives produced a distinctly modern standard: "any action is held to be justified if it replaces something 'older' by something newer." "'Older' doctrines, ideas, or theories do not count as models to be striven after. Instead, they are the object of criticism through which the contemporary consciousness sharpens itself." Modernism attempts to relate to any public assertion of the traditional as the intervention of an anachronistic predecessor. To Schabert, this is an "experiment that intrinsically cannot succeed." It posits the groundless view that the newer is always better and that nothing is better than whatever is newest. Anything of the past must remain there and be replaced by something else in the present that will be replaced in the future.[16]

An extension of this thesis is that modernism not only supersedes but also assaults the past. Invoking the "barbarous history of the twentieth century" as evidence for modernism's aimlessness, Jeffrey C. Isaac argues that modernity tramples excessively on meaningful traditions by considering the "mere illusions or impediments, anachronisms to be swept away before the altar of progress." Seeking a critical alternative to the modern, Isaac suggests a postmodern sensibility which, drawing on the "critical ideals and universalist principles of modernity," corrects for their excesses by treating religious identities as "guides to living in the world, *both publicly and privately*" (emphasis added).[17]

Significantly, in these critiques of modernism, it is not that the nonmodern is absent from the modern frame; it is that there is nothing for the nonmodern to do except to become modern, and to leave static traditional-religious identities in the past or in nonpublic spheres of life. From the perspective of criticisms such as those of Isaac and Schabert, therefore, it is fairly easy to understand how some modernists would interpret theopolitics in the present; they would, as perhaps Bill and Halliday have done, either ignore or neglect their relevance in the present, thinking of them instead as part of the past.

A second critique of modernism in political inquiry is that it is not simply that modernism fails to accommodate tradition, but that modernism distorts traditions such as religion to secure its hegemony over them. Susan Harding, for example, argues that the modern represents theopolitical others as of the past in part to secure its authority over them. She maintains that the conceptualization of the alternatives to modernism as vulgar and extreme dualities is an exercise of power in the discourse of modernism. The fundamentalist emerges as a "historical object, a cultural other, apart from, even antithetical to, 'modernity.'" Modernity is always the "positive term in an escalating string of oppositions between supernatural belief and unbelief, literal and critical, backward and progressive, bigoted and tolerant." Such representation enables modernism to secure its own historical legitimacy and its understanding of history as a neutral norm, superior to all others. Furthermore, usually appearing in an objectivist discourse of dispassionate, expert analysis, the representation effaces the exercise of power that is central to it. Representing the theopolitical in opposition to the modern is an exercise of power because it hides their internal relation. Fundamentalism, Harding avers, is an invention of modernist discourse. It is part of modernism's history. "Bible-belief is not an invention of modern discourses, but fundamentalism is. Fundamentalism is a part of modernism's history, not outside of it alien and anachronistic. It is not a dead or dying phenomenon, not an essentialized, oddly enduring, thing stuck in the past."[18]

Talal Asad considers a similar discursive phenomenon of modernist conceptions of the state. He suggests that the "historical narratives of modernity" that distort links between religion, public knowledge, moral identity, and political process are "central to the project of the modern nation-state." The widely shared modern belief, for example, that history will culminate in an emancipation from superstition accomplished by the structural "separation of religion from the state, and from science" (because "'religion' is everywhere and always the same") is a "simple story." This story, Asad argues, is necessary to the "strategic and administrative disciplines" of the modern state that assigns limits to religion (to secure itself against division and instability) and thus molds the structure of civil society and the citizen-identity of citizen-subjects according to that belief. The "scope, intensity and continuity [of this disciplining] exceed anything that religious reformers in premodern times could aspire to."[19]

Thus, from Harding's and Asad's points of view, consigning theopolitical phenomena of the present to the past represents an exercise of power, intrinsic to modernist discourse and effected by the modern state, in which modernist teleologies are secured by writing their competitors out of the legitimate history of politics in the modern world. Modernists represent theopolitical expression as universally outmoded to legitimize its marginalization or removal from public life in the present. Why do Halliday and Bill represent radical Islamism in Iran as of the past? Because in these accounts of modernism, the past is invented by modern discourse to conceal what it effectively produces: the modernist interest in controlling and subduing recalcitrant others. A power play exists in the concepts themselves, which the modernists—who believe either that discourse is power-free or simply use the story to conceal their designs—fail to detect. Consequently, modernism secures a belief that it is not we who need to change; they need to "get up to pace," to "go faster," to "get with it," to see the need to relegate to the private sphere, etc. To Harding, theopolitical expression is not an invention of modernist discourse, but the past is. The past is part of modernism's history, not external to it. This past (the theopolitical contestants of secular modernity) does not precede modern history, but participates with it in the present. Modern inquirers fail to see that this is directly related to the influence of modernism as a discourse of power.

It is not clear if either Halliday or Bill sees his conception of radical Islamist politics in Iran as a manifestation of modern discourses of power. Yet they both believe that history makes clear that religion is unsuited for modern governance, and both of their analyses legitimize the permanent removal of religion from politics with an exercise of power. Whether this is desirable politically here is a separate question. The important questions are, do the analyses of Halliday and Bill identify the concepts that they employ as central to the politics they favor? Are those concepts and analyses offered as an exercise of power, or are they assumed to be detached from politics, statements about others, not statements about their own historical interests and concerns? These important questions raised by the critiques of Harding and Asad cannot be answered adequately in passing. In subsequent chapters, I make some suggestions concerning the interpretive interests of interpreters of Turkey's political dynamics around the secular and nonsecular poles of political power.

From these perspectives on the influence of "secular" and "modern" dispositions of social science research on the place of religion in modern politics, one might conclude that the secular and modern identities of political inquiry have had an untoward influence on attempts to understand modern politics in general and the significance of theopolitics in particular. Secular and modern assumptions about the nature and character of public life, identity, history, and other features of the human landscape appear too singular, too limiting, in their characterization of the possible relations between religion and public life in modern politics. "Secularism" demotes religion from a prominent place in politics while "modernism" relegates all that is of the past to a similar status.

While these criticisms identify important shortcomings related to contemporary secular and modern understandings, the general indictment of secularism and modernity unnecessarily fixes these concepts as altogether problematic. The problems associated with this conceptual reification become apparent when both are viewed historically and in an interpretive frame. In this frame, both concepts express not just one problematic meaning, but many contested meanings. The need to elevate some of the meanings that have been trod over in warranted, but perhaps overly generalized, critiques is underscored insofar as the future of modernity remains a fundamental concern in the social sciences. Given the strong currents against the secular and modern identity of political inquiry, we need to rethink our expectations for modern political history, with specific attention to the meanings of secular and modern that inform our interpretive prejudgments.[20]

HISTORICIZING MODERN TEMPORAL CONSCIOUSNESS

I have proposed using the word "modernity" to define the consciousness rather than the condition of being "modern": as a concept, or what I believe is called a signifier, which people have used from time to time with a variety of effects. If it is a signifier, it is also an excluder; we call something (perhaps ourselves) modern in order to distance that of which we speak from some antecedent state of affairs. The antecedent is most unlikely to be of neutral effect in defining either what is to be called "modern" or the "modernity" attributed to it; and in understanding the uses of this whole family of words, it is usually important to understand what is being excluded from the "modern," to what past it is being relegated, and what structures of past and history are being imposed upon experience.[21]

In light of this need, I want to reconceive modernity, as distinct from being modern, based on two general claims:

1. Multiple modernities do exist (in past and present), are meaningful in the lives of many people who participate in the politics of modernity, and must be understood as such. We need to understand modernity differently and seek to understand others as they understand themselves rather than exclude them from modernity, even if they might appear to exclude themselves (philosophically and ideologically). Modern or not, political actors of radically alternative ideological orientations participate in and are shaped by the politics of modernity, and their significance in that context should not be devalued under any set of criteria.

2. Secularism, despite its recent bruises, remains a vital political project in the world (as religiously conceived politics do). This political project, however, is not amenable to generalization. Rather, it is variously constituted by attempts to define the relations between religious ideas (or matters of conscience and tradition more generally), institutions, practices, and politics. Moreover, the politics of modernity continue to center on these poles, and a judgment about the character of the history of modernity that enables us to reconceive secularism in political inquiry is fundamental to understanding our political world.

My interpretation focuses primarily on the meanings of modern and modernity. I will try to avoid giving modernity any explicit content except to say that modernists, postmodernists, premodernists, and traditionalists alike, all of various ideological orientations, participate in it. There is an important distinction between being modern and trying to grasp the dynamics and significance of modernity.

We are accustomed to thinking about modernity as those of the modern consciousness do—as an epoch that marks a transition between a broadly conceived premodern era and now. The nature of the transition varies depending on context: perhaps it is the use of technology derived from understandings gained in the advanced physical and natural sciences; perhaps it is urbanization that uproots previously stable and isolated communities and casts them into a new future; perhaps it is the acquisition of greater civil rights and liberties;

perhaps it is the change in authority relations that occurs when "legal-rational" relations replace patriarchal or patrimonial (Max Weber's ideal-types) ones. Whatever the root cause of the transition, we think of modern and consequently modernity as a period of distinction in history that marks the end of the old and the beginning of the new.

Not all participants in modernity think of modernity in these terms, however. This is also not consistent with how all modernists have historically understood themselves. These insights emerge if we think of both concepts as historically contested and variously constituted ones. "Modern" is contested because there exists no single definition of modern on which all those who have understood themselves as modern can agree. Importantly, the basis for the disagreement is not simply linguistic—it is political and historical. The contours of the epoch that modern picks out, as well as the relations with the nonmodern or premodern that it establishes, vary across contexts.[22]

The variability of the meaning of "modern" can be observed in the etymology of the word. "Modern" by definition connotes a division in time. Its root meaning is "just today" or "of today," marking a division of time from "of yesterday." The notion of an epochal shift is embedded in the meaning. What is not so clear is how the content of that shift must be understood. Does "of today" mean that what was "of yesterday" is no more (that is, does the shift entail a "negation or transcendence" of the old by the new)? Or, does "of yesterday" remain significant in "of today" (possibly a dialectical transcendence by incorporation, or a persistence)? Is the new forever new and the old forever old? Or, does the new only mark a moment in a process that will return to the old?[23]

There are historically modern consciousnesses that embrace several answers to these questions. Previous to the modern consciousness considered above, "modern" meant other things. As Jürgen Habermas has noted, until the Enlightenment "the term 'modern' appeared and reappeared exactly during those periods in Europe when the consciousness of a new epoch formed itself through a *renewed relationship* to the ancients—wherever, moreover, antiquity was considered a model *to be recovered* through some kind of imitation" (emphasis added). Both he and Schabert tell us that "modern," in this sense, was first used in the fifth century to distinguish the new German Christian present from the Roman past. Schabert suggests that Cassiodorus (485–580), the historian of Theodoric the Great, was the first to distinguish between *antiqui* and *moderni*. He saw the modern as a renewal of the ancient to clarify lines of "uninterrupted continuity." The modern was not a "break in the cultural traditions of antiq-uity," it was the "old reacquired and renewed."[24]

The modern idea of a secular past as a predecessor to a religious present (with its own eschatological view of time) no doubt strikes our modern ears as odd. But modern identities are and have been variously constituted and understood in our ancient past. We may even wonder, beyond Schabert and Habermas's observations, how time was considered by these old "moderns," in light of S. N. Eisenstadt's work on the pre-Axial civilizations of pre-antiquity. These pagan cultures, he suggests, did not divide time into past, present, and future as most do today. They saw it as cyclical, in which the "difference between the major dimensions—past, present, and future—were only mildly articulated." The Axial Age civilizations—Ancient Israel, Second Commonwealth Judaism, Christianity, Ancient Greece, Zoroastrian Iran, Early Imperial China, Hindu-ism and Buddhism, and Islam (the latter extended beyond the Axial Age)—saw a disjunction in time that the pre-Axials did not. This derived largely from the Axials' need to reconcile the time of the mundane world with the time of the transmundane or higher world. This project is still with us. Could it be that the concept of modern in the fifth century was not simply an attempt to establish a relation with the pagan past, but a critical challenge to the eschatologi-cal/progressive view of history posited by Christianity (following its great Axial predecessors)?[25]

These Christian views, argues Pocock, saw Jesus as the first modern, and thus had a different meaning for modern than Cassiodorus did. "[Jesus'] life was held to have marked the supersession, in sacred and therefore in secular history, of both 'antiquity' and the 'old dispensation': of Greco-Roman politics, letters, and philosophy; and of Jewish law, covenant, and sacrifice." Over time, this historical outlook gave birth to competing traditions in Christianity—first the *via antiqua* and later the *via moderna*. The former hoped to reconcile dispensa-tion with ancient philosophy (epitomized in the reflections of Thomas Aqui-nas) and the latter to preserve the original purity of grace by faith alone. The *via moderna* emerged with William of Ockham, in response to the pope's usurpa-tion of the Christian Church. These Christian moderns sought a return to the original sources of grace. This modern view also saw its relation to the past as one of renewal and recovery, rather than negation and transcendence.[26]

Joining the Christian moderns in this period were alternative understand-ings of modern in pagan discourse that also preserved this tie to the past. Cassiodorus's concept of modern did not die. Pocock sees it in Renaissance neopaganism, which "invented the medieval" and may have been the first to "perceive a connection between 'the triumph of barbarism' and 'religion'." The institutionalization of Christianity in the Greek and Latin ecumen was said to have resulted in barbarism. This new paganism invented the "medieval" to distinguish their project of imitating the ancients from Christian vias. According to Pocock, "Contemporaries might describe themselves as 'moderns' who had at last the opportunity to imitate, emulate or surpass the 'ancients,' or they might denounce as 'moderns' those who had preceded them or were still failing to do so; in either case, however, imitation was of a pre-dispensation, 'pagan' or 'secular' antiquity."[27]

Among the interesting implications of these historical insights is that differently oriented moderns coexisted in chronologically shared time (even if they did not see themselves as historically synchronous). This would not be the last time that this would occur. Pocock captures the significance of this moment from the perspective of those trying to grasp the meaning of modernity: "Two restorationist self-identified 'modern' impulses were at work. A 'return' might be undertaken in search of a classical rhetoric and philosophy which had arisen before and without dispensation, or in search of the sources of grace which had been established by the second dispensation and might be found in the mere act of a return to it. . . . The neo-pagan philosopher and the antinomian enthusiast, deeply antipathetic to one another, might find themselves travelling in the same company. The metahistorical frameworks before the minds of late Latin men were diverse and contradictory, and the meaning of 'modernity' highly problematical."[28] By 1800, the sixteenth-century extensions of these two modernities had developed into modernity.

The real break with time and with the old understanding of modern was inspired by developments in the natural sciences. Schabert charts this aspect of the modern consciousness from its inchoate form in Renaissance neopaganism, which aimed to surpass the ancients, to its maturity in the Enlightenment thought of the eighteenth century. Renaissance neopaganism generated a heightened tendency to see history as a progressive distancing from the past, originating when Renaissance thinkers suggested that the passage of time meant progress toward truth (*veritas filia temporis*). Impressed with demonstrable advancements in the sciences, they boldly asserted, "We can know more [than the 'ancients']." Francis Bacon put it this way: "We have reason to expect much greater things of our own age . . . than that of antiquity." Similarly, Jean Bodin believed that the ancient "inventors of the arts and sciences" deserved thanks for their efforts. But he made it clear that "they also left behind much that is incomplete, which we will finish and pass on to our descendants." He asserted that "looking at the matter carefully, no one can doubt that in a comparison between our inventions and discoveries and those of the ancients ours must clearly be given precedence. Thus, among all things Nature there is nothing more wonderful than the magnet and yet the ancients understood nothing of it and its use: they had to confine themselves to the Mediterranean basin, while our contemporaries every year sail around the globe and have settled a new world."[29]

At the end of the seventeenth century, the modern finally ceased to have anything to do with the ancient. Moderns began charting an independent course. It is significant that Hobbes and René Descartes wrote some of their books in their native tongues rather than in Latin. This demonstrated "that henceforth even the abstract meaning of learned minds could be expressed in the 'modern' languages, and the language of the 'ancients' consequently given up."[30]

Renaissance neopaganism matured in Enlightenment thought that extended these tendencies: man replaced God as the creator of existence; secular criteria replaced the moral discourse of Christianity; universal truths replaced myths; and instrumentalism vis-à-vis nature replaced design. The Enlightenment motto—through reason we (aware of our responsibility to others) can know and act to improve our world—gave birth to a new modern consciousness. In Schabert's view, there were alternatives: "To be sure, Bossuet and Vico were again to portray the process of history from the viewpoint of divine *providential.* But they were drowned out by those like Fontenelle or Voltaire who now interpreted history from the viewpoint of their belief in progress, so as to discover a *historie de l'historie* immanent in the world. From this epoch-making transition of European thought towards modernity there arose the modern form of consciousness."[31] This understanding of modernity reproduced the epochal distinction embedded in the concept of modern, but it did so while altering the temporal relation between the modern and the premodern. Time became an arrow, or even an upward spiral, and whole societies could be measured according to their place on the arrow. The criteria were relatively simple: those societies that were taking advantage of the sciences were modern and future-oriented, and those that were not were of the past, living a torpid life of ignorance. Peter Gay, who preceded Habermas in fending off the antimodernist, conservative critics of the Enlightenment, has interpreted the Enlightenment's modern disposition in the following way:

> In general, the Enlightenment thinkers held that knowledge is better than igno-
> rance—that if social problems are to be solved they can be solved only through
> action based on research and analysis rather than through prayer, renunciation, or
> the patient waiting for God—that reason is better than fanaticism—that reason
> must come to terms with sentiment and act in accord with it—that barriers to
> inquiry, whether barriers of religion, tradition, or philosophic dogma, are always
> pernicious since only rational inquiry can understand reality.[32]

This understanding of the temporal relation between the traditional past and
the Enlightenment present was not, as Schabert hints, uncontested within
Enlightenment thought. With an eye on the English and Scottish modernities,
Pocock cautions against constructing an explicit and necessary dichotomy
between reason and religion, or between belief and research. Again, the history
of modernity is more complex than many modernist categories allow. The
English and Scottish Enlightenment contained competing views of the relation
between religion and modern life.

Pocock notes that by 1700 the "wars of religion and the Puritan Revolution
had burned into elite consciousness the determination that 'enthusiasm' should
by any means necessary be contained within the secular disciplines of culture
and society." In this context the "new philosophy" of modern science arose. But
the elite that rallied around it was by no means entirely secular.

> We are accustomed to think of this [new philosophy] as a radical liberation of the
> powers of the mind to conquer nature and history; but it is equally valid to think of it
> as conservative, a successful reduction of metaphysics and enthusiasm within the
> bounds set by experimentalism and empiricism. Anglican, Armenian, and Lutheran
> clerics joined the academies and salons in welcoming Newtonian science as the
> demonstration that the Creator was not immanent in his creation (to hold that he
> was seemed the ultimate "enthusiasm"), but stood apart from it, ruling it by laws to
> which the human intellect might gain access by self-imposed limitations. . . . Much
> of the Enlightenment is conservative, a demonstration that reason enjoins author-
> ity. . . . Clerics were anxious to restore the Word to the Flesh as *philosophes* were to
> subject the sacred to the secular.

Thus, both nonsecular and secular participants shared these modern world
historical moments. ("Theological modernism" expresses the continuity of this
nonsecular modernism. The modern cannot be easily collapsed historically
with the secular.) They were not alone. Others—such as those whom we might
describe as traditionalists or as non- or premoderns—and whom we might
have considered enthusiasts at the time—coexisted and contested the political
configurations that were developing. In what we generally consider the birth of

modernity and modern politics, alternative, contemporaneous forms of life and politics coexisted, cooperated, and conflicted over the emerging bases of public life. The political significance of each alone cannot be understood outside of the context that they all shared. Even the two more modern secular and theological movements that have significantly defined modernity in our own time attached different meanings to these modern developments.[33]

For the nontheological modernists, the passage of time meant more types of control over nature (over things once believed that only gods could do). Such control had consequences both for the understanding and the structuring of public life. God, and indeed all value judgments, could be removed from public policy considerations. The public would become the exclusive domain of reason. For the sacred modernists, this conception of the public "was by no means at odds with [their] demands of a conservative religiosity." Indeed, religion became a personal matter, and a rightly conceived politics was consistent with this need. Politics, however, was not meaningful from this vantage point because it was "secular" as much as it was how it ought to be from within a "religious" frame (or in a frame of faith-in-history). Indeed the two were mutually reinforcing: the right religious upbringing could serve the citizen well. The individual "who specialized himself accepted his limitations and the authority of the creator over him, and did not believe [because he *believed*] that he was the vehicle of immanent spirit." One need not divorce God or faith-in-life from meaning in everyday political life in order to accept the necessity for a (so-called) modern politics, even one that separated matters of faith and matters of politics. The importance of God in life has been historically—in the West after Hobbes and Locke—the basis for such an acceptance.[34]

The historical lineage between neopagan, secular Scots and North American political science shows both the scope and the limits of our appreciation of the Enlightenment in modern political science. For the general health of the public, political scientists have aimed to discover and to identify generally applicable antidotes, as Adam Smith called them, to the "excesses" and delusions of "enthusiasts" of all kinds, including and especially theopolitical ones. Science—especially in its positivist and neopositivist forms—seems, and perhaps is, too good to be true: it "not only identifies itself as the opposition of ideology, it promises an end of ideology." Its claims on truth, and the divisions among humans and history implied by its newest revelations, continue their appeal in the modern political sciences. But science in this form has never revealed much about what human beings understand to be true (except perhaps that science has a special claim to truth). With scientific truth we have enabled ourselves both to remain unfamiliar with the particularities of human living (especially the concepts that give life—private and public—the meanings it has) and to justify that unfamiliarity as part of the modern project.[35]

From our historical vantage point, and from a hermeneutic frame, this appropriation of the Enlightenment is fraught with errors. Despite incremental advances, political scientists continue to believe that understanding can be free from prejudice; to consign nonsecular, alternative, and contemporaneous modes of public living to the past; and to reduce politics essentially to so-called secular matters (for example, interest aggregation, capital accumulation). Modernization theory—which arose in the 1950s, and is both preceded and succeeded by different understandings of modernity—was and remains the crudest (and most brilliant?) expression of each premise. Even if we recognized the contingency of our situation, we could rest knowing that all others would come to see things as we do. Describing the still-dominant pluralist frame, Leonard Binder has written: "Political freedom is defined as this capacity to change constantly, just as political development is defined as the willingness and enlightenment to want to change continuously. The reason why one should want to change continuously is that the world, nature, all of creation is changing continuously. Not to change continuously is to be submerged in ignorance . . . well-being can only be attained by changing. Alienation from the world can be overcome only by adapting to a constantly changing world."[36] The problem is that *not all of those who recognize change as reality, and hence participate in modernity, share the same understanding of "contingency."* Can self-consciously modern researchers reconsider their historical prejudgments in such a way as to see modernity as a much more hotly contested set of realities, consisting of different modernities as well as traditionally based, but dynamic, responses to ongoing changes in life?

REAPPRAISING MODERNITY

Thinking of modernity solely as a patterned transition from the old to the new obscures the contest over the constitution of public life that it marks. One need not impose a strict notion of transition to see that modernity is generally marked by complex alterations, some of which may include certain types of transitions, others of which may not.

Consider, for example, the variety of temporal relations that may exist between legal-rational and patrimonial authority relations. Weber intended these "ideal types" to capture heuristically the difference between hierarchical relations in modern, as opposed to traditional, contexts. He suggested, for example, that the spheres of competence between superiors and subordinates in modern authority relations are governed by impersonal, but intersubjectively knowable, rules; whereas in traditional authority relations, these spheres are ambiguous and shifting, subject to ad hoc definition by those in superior positions. Social scientists gain much interpretive purchase from both types in historical and political explanation.

Yet, given the stark contrasts between the types, the question arises concerning how to conceive of their temporal relation. For many years, we assumed that the traditional would fade away and be replaced by the modern. This is the core of the "transition-by-replacement" model of modernity. Change occurs in whole packages as homogenously conceived societies pass through heterogeneously conceived progressive stages of development. In political inquiry, many assumed that changing sociocultural dynamics would give rise to new modernizing classes that would serve as agents of progressive change (both bureaucratic and entrepreneurial/bourgeois). These classes would build modern nation-states that would partly be devoted to undermining, subverting, and replacing the structures on which old authority relations were built. Along the way, loyalties to the new nation-state would replace old loyalties and ascriptive character traits necessary to traditional structures. The individual, previously imprisoned by the customs of the traditional social world, would be freed to be a participant and citizen in the new modern state. Indeed, John Stuart Mill's "struggle between Liberty and Authority" would be played out as the advent of modern institutions and ideas altered traditional authority relations.[37]

This assumption was based on the thesis that traditional societies were incapable of accommodating rapid change brought about by the processes that we associate with modernization (or capital accumulation and class formation). This assumption has been debunked. To quote Pocock making a point that he does not believe has been sufficiently grasped, what had been considered tradition "contained within itself a dialectic far more complex than the word 'traditional' can convey." Indeed, consideration of the variety of structural and cultural dynamics embedded in Weber's traditional frame shows that any system that nearly approximates the patrimonial ideal type is quite capable of great dynamism (depending on technologies, perhaps, to defend itself). Neopatrimonialism can replace patrimonialism, without any thoroughgoing change in authority relations or expectations. Conversely, legal-rational bureaucracies can encompass patrimonial relations without any thoroughgoing transformation to purposive-rational behavior. In addition, the idea that modern societies are or would be fully dynamic has suffered criticisms. Readers of Weber are familiar with his thesis that a society constituted structurally and culturally by legal-rational assumptions faces the danger of becoming an "iron-cage," wherein freedom from arbitrary rule of the traditional type is replaced by the tyranny of rules themselves (no particular person is in charge, but no one is free either; postmodernism is one expression of this in modern life).[38]

That both systems can accommodate change is important for my purposes. Change does not bring about the replacement of the old with the new but rather a complexly constituted array of specifically articulated formations, all experiencing change. Perhaps more is preserved than is altered (Gadamer). One general label does not capture the complex dynamics at work as various modern understandings and structures intersect with, interpret, or approach various traditional ones, or as traditional understandings and structures incorporate, interpret, or respond to modern ones, vice versa and so forth. This dynamic, of course, now includes postmodern ones as well. Whatever the context-specific dynamic, it is clear that there is no quick replacement. Indeed, even Weber described transitions in forms of domination as vague and changing. This is partly because traditional structures accommodate change and partly because their constitutive understandings do not fade into history, instead remaining efficacious in their new and changing forms.[39]

Modernity is thus not a replacement of the old by the new. It is this process of evolving newer relations (some of which include new "fixed" ones), a process whose specific attributes cannot be adequately described a priori or in general. Its processes can be understood only in context, given the variety of articulated historical factors that shape it. Modernity thus understood does not effect the climax of any grand narrative; it marks the contest among them in which all of the participants recognize the existence of the contest. They do so in part because one cannot assume (if one ever could) that things will remain the same. In addition, they do so variously: believing or nonbelieving in God, defining and contesting time, history, power, present, past, future, innovations, progress, memory, rationality, institutions, ideologies, authentic politics, science, and relationships to each other and to the cosmos (among other things). They participate with a shared recognition of the reality of change and the need to respond to it. Niccolò Machiavelli may have been the first thinker of modern politics: he realized that the constitution of public life was part human and part *fortuna,* and that the players in the contest over the character of public life could be believers in God or in the Greek virtues as much as they may be believers in liberty or in greed. They could act within the frameworks of the present or the past.[40]

Participants in modernity, moreover, understand this dynamic. Their recognition is expressed in the various criteria (or "essential differences") that they themselves impose on the epochal transition that modernity marks:[41] lower/higher, irrational/rational, ignorant/knowledgeable, primitive/civilized, fallen/saved, benighted/enlightened, reactionary/progressive, closed/open, imprisoned/free, superstitious/clearheaded, etc. (As it turns out, it may be the contest over real power relations rather than any ideological or theoretical commitments held by the participants that best explains the tendency to consign alternative, contemporaneous political phenomena, theo- or not, to the past.) If we think of modernity only in such dichotomies, we may neglect the significance of one because of our interest in the other. These evaluative criteria may become criteria of analytical relevance. This is why Fred Halliday and James Bill consider theopolitical phenomena of the present to be traditional baggage of the past. They impose a set of temporally dichotomous historical criteria on chronologically similar phenomena so as to read them as historically non-synchronous. This evaluation is partly determined by the meaning of modern as an epochal term.

Furthermore, in Gadamerian terms, this evaluation constitutes their prejudgment or prejudice. Halliday's later recognition that his analysis exhibited shortcomings that were guided by this prejudice illustrates the nature of interpretation. The prejudice constituted and guided his interpretation in ways that Halliday was unaware of when he offered his account of Iranian politics. But this prejudice was foregrounded by events in Iran, namely the victory of an Islamist group during the revolution. The content of this prejudice—a specific kind of secular modern prejudice—has been theoretically scrutinized from many vantage points. All of these perspectives—guided by prejudice as well—contribute to a process in which we are able to rethink our approach to the study of secular and theopolitical phenomena. If Gadamer is correct, we cannot and should not aim to rethink all of our prejudices, since most are beyond our immediate purview. But we can reconsider those that have been provoked. Moreover, we must do so, otherwise the recognition of prejudice is fruitless from the perspective of grasping constitutive meanings and of coming to a new understanding of the conceptual lives of others. We should converse with those we study. Unless we allow ourselves to change our understandings in that conversation, we have not expanded our possibilities for understanding; we have not, as Gadamer stresses, understood at all, as I discuss in the next chapter.

My point is simple. The exclusion that is made possible by the type of secular modern prejudice exhibited by Halliday's earlier work need not be repeated, whether our concern is another fundamentalist revolution *or* a new articulation of secularism. We will, of course, always exclude. If we exclude is not the question. The question is whether or not we can change specific dimensions of our posture toward explaining political possibilities in modernity, because changing is fundamental to understanding. We must rethink our judgments about modern political possibilities to account for the multiple modern political actualities.

The point is not simply that tradition is an insufficient characterization of the past, which now must be reacquired (perhaps as a cultural—traditional—variable), to fully explain the challenges of modern politics. Nor is it that modernists are wrong to see the protection of the individual from higher arbitrary authority as a step toward an open society and more legitimate power arrangements. (To be modern is to herald a new era in which old ways will be discarded as we fight for new.) The Iranian revolution illuminated the difference between changing one's thinking about the concept of tradition and changing one's expectations concerning the path of political history. We might reconceive tradition to have a relevance that we never believed it would. We might, that is, extend the scope of our variables. But can we make room for tradition in our understandings of modern history? There is an important difference between seeing religious traditionalism (apparently on the rise throughout the world) as a meaningful response to change, and seeing it as a refuge (Bill) from rapid sociopolitical change. In both cases, tradition may be recognized as an enduring feature of the political landscape. But the latter expresses an assumption that traditionally meaningful responses are inappropriate. It is the difference between seeing traditions persist almost out of place in the modern world and seeing them exist as alternative, contemporaneous forms of life in the modern world.[42]

Therefore, various modernist and nonmodernist expectations must be seen within a picture of modernity that does not obliterate, and indeed accounts for, the contestation that is essential to it. Thinking of modernity's past or future as a transition-by-replacement prevents us from seeing that it marks a moment of contestation. Yes, things have changed, and indeed, they might change more according to one's highest expectations. But the change that has occurred is one that has occurred in the habitually established system of the old, which is never fixed. It is wrong *to expect* transition, both the ongoing unilinear, evolutionary transition that has come to indicate the modern model (to both its proponents and critics), and even smaller scale transitions. It is more fruitful to see alteration and contestation. For example, the public liberties of women have largely been won in fights with patriarchy, and yet patriarchy (in various forms) continues to constitute nearly all relations between men and women. Fighting for the liberties of women is not over, and may never be over. The modernity that marks a moment in the universal transformation from one society to another is not a mere transition. There are few grounds to believe that such a transition is necessary. Modernity marks an awareness that transition and alteration are possible—and this is an awareness that all of the contestants over the constitution of public life share, and to which they direct their attention. (Within this awareness, we must also anticipate new forms of "fixed relations.") The imposition of a grand narrative of transition-by-replacement on what are only small and incremental changes away from, and even perhaps in the context of, arbitrary rule clouds what is occurring. Similarly, to view our conception of tradition as the only problem with the modernization schema is to miss how the entire set of historical expectations, in which the traditional is temporally juxtaposed with the modern, is an inadequate conscious prejudgment about the character of modern political history.

Thus, merely because participants in modernity do not think that they share a history (or occupy the same temporal world) does not mean that we should think so as well when we try to understand the politics of modernity. To do so is not only to risk closing history or ending modernity. It is also to succumb selectively and uncritically to the comprehensive validity of the participant's belief. To succumb to this is to close inquiry, and not anticipate that we will find not only what we are looking for but also other conceptual and institutional possibilities, subtle and nuanced in particular ways, whose significance we can begin to understand only if we are ready to see them. We have for too long participated in the modern tradition of relegating to the past or to irrelevance those things that we do not agree with or do not find relevant in our projects of the present. We have thus overlooked how significant they are or may be in the politics of a shared present. Can we conceive of the temporal history of modernity in a way as to not relegate theopolitical (and/or secular politics) to the past?

CHANGING EXPECTATIONS

The need to rethink the concepts that constitute our understanding of modernity is based on several considerations. I will discuss four of them in this conclusion.

The first is that there has been a general, and increasingly shared, recognition that modernity is not reducible to one criterion or pattern. This is not to suggest that there are *no* intelligible patterns or what Charles Tilly calls chronologies of salience in modernity. It is, however, to reaffirm the need to see modernity as made up of various possibilities. Tilly argues that change must be seen "not [as] a general process but a catchall name for very different processes varying greatly in their connections with one another." Similarly, Eisenstadt stresses the varied symbolic and institutional constellations of modernity, of different modern civilizations, of "different modes of incorporation and reinterpretation of the premises of modernity; of different symbolic reactions to it; as well as the development of various modern institutional patterns and dynamics." The unidimensional exclusivity of our collective judgments about modernity, supported by inadequate historical expectations, must now be reexamined.[43]

As an instructive example, Tilly considers the expectation, derived from social evolutionary thought and shared by historical and political inquirers, that one inevitable outcome of modern history would be the progressive differentiation of social processes and structures. Tilly agrees that differentiation is "one important process of change, [but] many of the fundamental changes in our era actually entail *de*differentiation, and to some of them the question of differentiation is secondary or even irrelevant." As evidence, he cites processes such as linguistic standardization, mass consumption, and religious diffusion. Differentiation as one outcome of political history is one of many possible outcomes of modern history. It is a process applicable to some specific contexts, but in no sense generally applicable. As an alternative, Tilly suggests the broadly conceived notion of abstract specified processes as outcomes of political history. This conception opens up our expectations to see various processes—some of which entail differentiation, others standardization, and others even different formulations—as emergent modern ones.[44]

This leads to a second reason for reappraising our understanding of modernity. If we do not alter our views, we will continue to fail to see and to grasp the significance and influence(s) of religiously conceived participations in modern politics, what I have been calling theopolitical ones. From the criticisms reviewed above, one may conclude that our collective judgments about religion in modern politics must be reexamined. Still, many in political science—which is deeply influenced by the secular modernist ideal criticized in these pages—are reluctant to abandon what they describe as solely secular bases for legitimate modern politics (though "secular" is understood in many ways). To ignore the sometimes intimate relation between faith and public life, however, is to ignore the evolving meanings of politics both in the East and in the West. Eliot Deutsch has charted the connection between religion and other identities that cannot be defined within the framework of ideas normally associated with modernity. Deutsch argues that the serious questioning of this framework in the East and the West does not mean that modernity is over; nonetheless, the "emphasis is clearly on getting behind . . . the 'single vision' of Western views of modernity." Current history, argues Deutsch, illustrates that all societies have much to contribute to the "meaning of modernity in the West."[45]

Going further, as Richard Rorty does, the West (and hence the meanings of modernity in it) is not a "finished off object." Rorty espies a lingering, "distressing tendency to essentialism" in "our recent willingness to talk about 'the West' not as an ongoing, suspenseful adventure in which we are participating but rather a structure which we can step back from, inspect at a distance." The West has "not exhausted its possibilities"—secular and theopolitical—either. More concretely, the meaning of the relations between religion and politics is constantly evolving here as well as in other places in the world. In Poland, for example, the prominent opponent of the Communist regimes, Adam Michnik, criticizes a "reflexive anti-clericalism that has been the hallmark of the Left in Europe ever since Voltaire." Martin Jay, thinking about Lyotard and postmodernism, has observed that "in the disappointing aftermath of the 1968 events, . . . one of the most arresting developments in France was in fact a new appreciation for the legacy of Judaism." In North America no day goes by without understanding how central questions of religion and faith are to modern governance. These questions involve not only radical theopolitical activism, but also implicate a variety of differently nuanced, religiously conceived public articulations, ranging from social justice sojourners to persons engaged in "shamanism, magic and longing for miracles."[46]

The relevance of religion is certainly underscored in places where the principal religion is Islam. In the lives of people in the "Dar al-Islam" (the "abode" of Islam), faith-in-history has real public significance. The growing body of literature emerging from political research in these contexts stresses the need to get beyond the old secular and modern habits of consigning all articulations of Islam to the past. This literature extends far beyond Maxime Rodinson's case that Islam, once perceived to be compatible only with precapitalist (premodern) economic systems, is compatible with capitalism. Today, Sunni radicals are being compared to Protestant radicals, and Shiite ulema to Calvinist preachers. The research of Saad Eddin Ibrahim is frequently cited to show that many Islamist activists include science and engineering students, as well as members of the urban poor or traditional economic sectors. This is significant because it contrasts with the historical expectations of social scientists who believed that the scientifically educated young would constitute a new middle class that would usher in a secular modern future. Increasingly, those in this class see their role in science, commerce, or politics through a faith-in-history lens.[47]

The need for a view of modernity that admits a place for Islamically generated articulations in modern politics is more than just a need to reformulate new theories of the middle class, however. We can no longer afford to reduce Islam to a system that has one proper historical place. Some Muslims living in or experiencing life in contemporary Islamic contexts will not conform to our expectations. Hisham Sharabi has described the fundamentalist insistence on "independent interpretation and scholarship that is not Western derivative." There is an important convergence between this insistence and assertions in the West seeking to get beyond one fold for modernity, as seen in Rorty's comment that the West must necessarily remain open to what are presently unknowable self-definitions. Assertions such as that of Abdelwahab El-Affendi on the "vitality and dynamism of Islam" and Rorty's idea of the West as an unfinished complex of attitudes are both chronologically and historically synchronous. They are responses of various historical forces to ongoing, changing contexts in the politics of modernity. As such, they represent the fully contested character of modernity.[48]

To clarify, my argument is not intended to open our understanding so wide that we see every religious revivalist leader as modern. Such a general cast blurs relevant substantive and philosophical distinctions among the active participants in the contest over modernity. It is an argument, however, for us to open up so that we see revivalists as participants in the contest of modernity, and not simply as relics from the past. To understand modern politics (to borrow from one of Quentin Skinner's examples), we cannot "exclude in advance the possibility that those who believed in witches may have done so as a result of following out some . . . recognizable chain of reasoning" that is in need of understanding. To exclude in advance is to block the path of inquiry.[49]

We will best avoid blocking inquiry by altering our expectations about modernity—opening them up to things previously considered irrelevant— and then trying to grasp how others define themselves in light of this alteration. (The next chapter on interpretive inquiry deals with the latter.) Again, even as we see and interpret, we will always miss and exclude; prejudices are always at work.

As discussed in the next chapter, however, we must adopt a posture toward those we study that enables us to see, as best as possible, the varieties of modernities as well as the varieties of assertions made about the relation between religion and politics in alternative, contemporaneous, modern contexts.

In this regard, the third reason for reappraisal arises: just as we need to create a space for theopolitical formulations in modern politics, we need to reevaluate our expectations about what is secular. The path of modernity has been circumscribed by a narrow understanding of the relation between religion (or, more generally, matters of conscience) and politics. Some call this secularism and the secular standard. As I argue, the criticism is warranted in some articulations of secularism, but we are not at a standstill here any more than we are regarding articulations of modernity. What is secular, what may be meant by secularism and its different modes in modernity, and, consequently, in the practices, relations, and institutions associated with secularism are historically contested and various.

Like modernity, secularism as an idea and secular institutional relations as practices make no sense apart from the understandings that people have of them, and many who participate in the politics of modernity do hold various secular understandings. As such, secularism is a constantly evolving and reinterpreted tradition in modern politics, as religiously conceived participations are. In the same way that the tradition/modern dichotomy has been too narrow to capture the plurality of traditions and modernities, so too the religion/secular dichotomy is too narrow to understand the religions and secularisms. In opening up our historical anticipations, we need not jettison either religion or secularism. We must consider existing, past, and future formulations by political actors grappling with reconciling faith *and conscience* (religious or otherwise)-in-history with the politics of the modern state, economy, and so forth. Indeed, given the publicly expressed varieties of authoritative religious theory and practice, to lose sense of viable, contextually specific, secular political possibilities would be costly. We need to be open to seeing and to understanding these formulations.

A fundamental belief underlying this work is that a concept of secularism is crucial to a fruitful conception of politics in our time. If it is part of our modern situation to see the contestation/conflict/cooperation that marks modernity, we must see the nonreligious and vital secularist traditions as participants as well. If we are to confront the increasingly awesome questions about the place of religion in modern states, the size and content of this sphere in different contexts must become a concern for comparative inquiry.

An example of secularism's vitality may be found in the work of the same scholar who illustrates the powerful significance of theopolitics in the Middle East. Ibrahim has observed small but significant challenges to Islamic politics in Middle East contexts. His observation appears in a discussion about how Islamists continually develop the "arts of mobilization and articulation" in competitive electoral politics. Ibrahim notes that some of these lessons have come from defeat as well as success:

> [The Islamists] have also learned the imperatives of appealing to circles wider than their own if they are to win elections. Egypt's Muslim Brothers learned that lesson when they lost a reelection contest *in the pharmacists association in 1992, gracefully conceding their first defeat in ten years* [emphasis added]. The case of the pharmacists has shown that the march of Islamists is reversible, not only in professional associations but also in political contexts at large. In Irbid, Jordan, such a reversal took place two years after Islamists swept elections in 1990. Even the dazzling victory of Algeria's FIS [Islamic Salvation Front] concealed the fact that FIS lost 1 million votes between the municipal elections of 1990 and the parliamentary elections of December 1991.[50]

It is not clear to me if these developments mark a historical reversal, as Ibrahim's remarks imply. And, despite the professional contexts for these challenges, the identity of the opposition is also not clear. There are differently oriented secularizing movements in these contexts: new professional secularizing movements as well as new movements of secular cultural criticism seeking to "go beyond mainstream Western scholarship . . . to establish its own independent perspective." In any event, the evidence suggests that something more complex than a simple theopolitical assertion may be occurring. We must be open to listening to one another in this context, and to considering alternative, contemporaneous, secular ways of relating religious belief and practice (and matters of conscience and culture) to matters of politics.[51]

By understanding these new formulations and the multihistorical lineages on which they are based, political inquiry, especially inquiry in political theory and comparative politics, can make distinct contributions to thinking about modern politics. If, however, we continue to rely on only those prejudices that we recognize as hindering—or if we try to bracket prejudices in search of a neutral vantage point—we will be left with only prejudice in the narrowest sense imaginable. We will fail to confront the important dimensions of the crucial contests in modern political life. We will also fail to appreciate what Hannah Arendt once called the dimensions of depth of human existence in their historically evolving forms.[52]

Herein lies the fourth reason for reappraisal: we need to think of our histori-cal moment—shared with alternative, contemporaneous modes and formula-tions—in a way as to appreciate the depth of human experience in modern politics. This depth takes various forms, some of which we may wish to actively oppose. But we must try to grasp this depth to succeed in our project of political explanation. My general thesis is that what we may now see as hindering prejudgments supported by anti-interpretive methodological tendencies have consistently kept us from understanding this depth.

To sum up the need for reappraisal: modernity does not entail the victory of one form of living or politics over others. It consists of multidimensional responses from many participants whose understandings and relations are contested and sometimes conflictual, sometimes compatible, sometimes transi-tional, but always potentially subject to alteration. This understanding of modernity should be the basis of a new prejudgment, albeit a conscious one, about the possibilities and directions of modern politics. When we venture into the study of and accept responsibility for explaining the politics of others, we must be open to the unexpected. We must be prepared to write others into, rather than read them out of, the history of modernity. We cannot escape from the real, present possibility that the outcomes of political, social, economic, and cultural change are varied and, to borrow a term from O'Donnell and Schmit-ter, indeterminate.[53]

Changing expectations is no small task. The modern social sciences were founded with high expectations for modernity, and we must recognize these expectations to understand our situation.[54] This project entails reconceiving secularism and modernity as contested and historically variable concepts. This approach, accompanied by the interpretive methodological shift described in the next chapter, will help us to see the history of modern politics differently as well as to appreciate more deeply the role of hermeneutic political inquiry in it. In emphasizing the need for a hermeneutic approach to understanding, Charles Taylor compares what he calls a purely acultural theory with a cultural theory of modernity. A cultural theory, unlike an acultural one, accounts for others' "understandings of person, nature, society, and the good."[55] An acultural theory assumes that understanding modernity does not require such knowl-edge. Modernity, an acultural theorist might suggest, can be understood as the sum of several large-scale, quantifiable processes such as industrialization, ur-banization, literacy, and so forth. Taylor's description of the difference between the two is an appropriate introduction to the next chapter in which I draw on many of Taylor's methodological reflections:

A purely acultural theory distorts and impoverishes our understanding of ourselves, both through misclassification . . . and through too narrow a focus. But its effects on our understanding of other cultures is even more devastating. The belief that modernity comes from one single universally applicable operation imposes a falsely uniform pattern on the multiple encounters of non-western cultures with the exigencies of science, technology, and industrialization. As long as we are bemused by the Enlightenment package, we will believe that they all *have* to undergo a certain range of cultural changes, drawn from our experience, e.g., "secularization" or the growth of atomistic forms of self-identification. As long as we leave our own notions of identity unexamined, we will fail to see how theirs differ and how this difference crucially conditions the way in which they integrate the universal features of "modernity."

In short, exclusive reliance on an acultural theory unfits us for what is perhaps the most important task of social sciences in our day: Understanding the full gamut of alternative modernities that are in the making in different parts of the world. It locks us into an ethnocentric prison, condemned to project our own forms on everyone else, blissfully unaware of what we are doing.[56]

Acultural theory, despite its ostensible objectivity, turns out, from the perspectives of those it seeks to understand, to be a "rival orientation," unconscious of its own partisanship. We can no longer afford to exclude the past from the present, as we can no longer afford to reduce the "other" to the "same." We must see political and historical relations where we have usually imposed negation and transcendence.[57]

In the subsequent chapters, I attempt to contribute to the understanding of alternative modernities of today by explaining aspects of modernizing and secularizing thought and practice in the early Turkish Republic. I examine the influence of the particular secular modern prejudgments discussed in this chapter on the understanding of aspects of twentieth-century Turkish political history and reinterpret particular phenomena in light of the reappraisal of the substantive character of modernity I have argued for here. It is time to open up our understandings of the conceptual and practical possibilities of what we have understood to be the secular politics in modernity by critically examining and explaining their constitutive character from a self-consciously interpretive perspective.

Chapter 2 The Interpretive Commitment in Political Science

The *expert,* that figure who so often justifies financial subsidizing of the social sciences by public and private corporations, turns out to be a mythological beast. Like the unicorn, a social existence and social importance is conferred upon him as long as people believe in him. The expert's claim always takes this form: his taxonomic ordering represents the determinativeness of a future not available to ordinary agents. He thus legitimates the treatment of the surface phenomena of social life in one way rather than another by invoking the notion of deeper structures. . . . As the prophet and the priest would on occasion invoke their alleged deep understandings against the social order, so the expert and radical critic can appear in a similar role.
—*Alasdair MacIntyre*

It is the mark of the trained mind never to expect more precision in the treatment of any subject than the nature of that subject permits.
—*Aristotle*

Because Gadamer's hermeneutics "explores how understanding occurs at all—not how it should be regulated in order to function more rigorously or effectively," it would be unwise to consider his insights as rigid methodological guides for human inquiry. Indeed, one of Gadamer's principal contributions to discussions in the philosophy of political inquiry is that understanding is not and cannot be wholly governed by method.[1] Although this view is not stated forcefully in the writings of theorists of interpretive political inquiry whose ideas I explore here, I see it as an essential part of the interpretive commitment in political science to resist "counterposing one highly sound method to a putatively unsound one." In interpretive inquiry, good judgment, good sense, and a "certain measure of insight" are indispensable, and these "cannot be communicated by the gathering of brute data, or initiation in modes of formal reasoning, or some combination of these."[2]

Nevertheless, most interpretive political theorists—well aware that their interpretations are interpretations—do wish to sustain notions of adequate and inadequate, correct and mistaken, and true and false. In doing so, they agree with John Dunn, who avers that "just because there cannot be a guaranteed method of discovering what is true about some matter does not imply that nothing *is* true about that matter." We need to understand truth, therefore, in the context of interpretive claims on political explanation. Sometimes, for example, stating what is true about some matter amounts to countering what has been "falsely" said about it. Thus, it makes sense—especially when striving to understand the variety of phenomena subsumed under the name of politics—to "attempt to judge methodologically" how it is sound to say something true of others. I do this by articulating the framework of assumptions about political life and explanation that inform interpretive political inquiry. From these assumptions we may derive certain rules of thumb to guide political explanation.[3] These rules of thumb will neither produce objective truth nor enable us to distinguish conclusively between true and false. They will, however, enable us to distinguish between interpretive and noninterpretive explanations. As my analysis shows, I believe that an interpretive explanation is always closer to the truth than a noninterpretive explanation in the context of understanding political life. As Dunn has said, "There cannot be *rules* of sociological or historical method; but there can be and are many bad historians and sociologists."[4]

My exposition of interpretive political inquiry begins with a discussion of the background for contemporary articulations of the interpretive approach in political science. The conceptual frame of interpretive inquiry—despite many misunderstandings and misrepresentations of it—is fundamental to the idea of political science. I offer suggestions about why the significance of interpretive inquiry continues to be overlooked. The absence of an adequate understanding of interpretive inquiry is linked with our failure to understand political life. It also has implications for our conception of the critical responsibilities of political science. By clarifying the assumptions of the interpretive approach—its view of human beings, language, politics, and criticism—I clarify what political scientists can gain by making an interpretive turn. A commitment to interpretive inquiry is a commitment to viewing political actions, practices, relations, and institutions as fundamentally related in an interpretively defined way. In addition, interpretive inquiry supports an understanding of history in general and of modern political history in particular as comprised of various possibilities. In this way it is suited to explaining modern politics.

THE INTELLECTUAL CONTEXT

Interpretive political inquiry is part of the larger tradition of hermeneutics. *Hermeneutics* (from the Greek *hermeneutikós*) is the study of interpretation, particularly interpretation of classical texts and scripture. Although the idea is much older than the word, the field was developed to determine the truth and authority of contradictory versions of religious texts. The concept invokes the Greek mythological figure Hermes, whose task was to interpret the messages of the other gods for mortals. Hermes needed to be conversant in the idioms of both parties: "He had to understand and to interpret for himself what the gods wanted to convey before he could proceed to translate, articulate, and explicate their intention to the mortals." Hermes' task has been embraced in modified form throughout the social sciences, following an awakened interest in understanding and meaning as part of the linguistic turn of the post-positivist era. Consequently, recent interest in hermeneutics spans many areas of inquiry, including anthropology, law, literary theory, psychology, geography, and political science.[5]

Hermeneutics in the social sciences is part of a larger tradition of inquiry that has sought to distinguish the study of human history and culture from the study of nonhuman nature. This distinction has been asseverated against a dominant mode of thinking throughout the sciences that aims to subsume the study of human behavior under the study of all nature. The variety of approaches in both the natural and human sciences make this distinction imprecise today. When it was first offered, however, the arguably hegemonic model in the study of nonhuman nature was methodological naturalism (or positivism) derived from Comtean sociology. This model had a growing appeal among social scientists who hoped, in the study of society (especially in sociology and political science), to emulate the methodological and nomological achievements of the natural sciences. As I discuss in detail, methodological naturalism is not dead in the social sciences. While the overall appeal of the model may have lessened, many of its core assumptions—despite being debunked by decades of philosophical argumentation—remain at work in research (mostly as a result of a persistent antagonism between philosophy and practice, theory and research requirements in political science). Thus the critique of the methodological naturalists' attempt to subsume the explanation of human behavior under their model of explanation remains significant.[6]

According to this model, social scientists attempt to understand the universal, invariable relations of dependence between (manipulable) conditions of behavior and their consequences. In practice, scientists employ various techniques of observation and measurement to *discover* and to *specify*, in general terms, the initial and boundary conditions under which events of various sorts occur. Knowledge of these conditions and the patterns of interaction that result from altering them constitutes the explanation of an event. Additionally, the formalization of this knowledge as an argument of deductive logic enables the prediction of similar events. A statement of the event's occurrence is deduced from general statements that specify (a) the existing understanding of the relation between the conditions under the event (theories, laws, or "covering laws") and (b) the conditions under which the event takes place. Science, by articulating both the necessary and the contingent relations that exist among a wide array of measurable variables under a variety of conditions, aims for an ever-increasing, objective body of knowledge to enable effective, predictable human intervention (action) in the world. The potential for such intervention and the power over the determinants of public life that it entails, not to mention the promise of "unifying" the sciences, are aspects of methodological naturalism that have appealed to generations of social scientists.[7]

In rejecting the applicability of these methods to the study of human behavior, theorists of the human sciences have argued that the human capacity to give meaning to action makes it impossible to understand, much less explain, human behavior simply by "observing" what human beings are doing. Moreover, the deductive-nomological view of the natural sciences in the interpretive view simply generalizes our puzzlement. The question remains: "Why did these human beings act the way they did?" There are many different answers to this question from those who reject methodological naturalism. The hermeneutic response begins, as did Weber, by stressing the need to understand the meaning of action, not simply its conditions, causes, and consequences. From this point on, hermeneutics offers no generalizable perspective on the context, nature, or goals of understanding. Each has many different hermeneutic understandings. Joel Weinsheimer describes the field of hermeneutics as "rife with struggle between opposed positions, each claiming to subvert or supersede the others." As a result of such contestation, to speak of interpretation is to invite attention to many articulations. The category of interpretive analysis is broad, and, indeed, hotly contested.[8]

This is true in political science as much as anywhere else. In political science, however, the category of interpretive analysis is broad not only in the sense that it is developing into several different articulations. Its broadness is evident in the misrepresentations and distortions of it by political scientists who for many years have missed the point of interpretive inquiry. Many political scientists continue to misrepresent the type of qualitative political inquiry that interpretive inquiry offers. It is said, for example, that interpretive research entails studying others from their point of view alone, or that interpretive inquiry offers only understanding, as opposed to explanation. There are a variety of institutional and conceptual reasons for these understandings. Almost thirty years after the initial interpretive intervention into the discipline there remains a need to reassert it and to restate its indispensability for political explanation. Therefore, that there is no one interpretive political inquiry is less important as a point of departure for this book than that what constitutes interpretive inquiry in its most sophisticated manifestations is poorly understood throughout the discipline. Thus, while I address some of the differences of opinion in interpretive inquiry, I focus on developing a coherent account of what I think holds it (or should hold it) together against the dominant anti-interpretive tendency to distort and reject it.

In interpretive political inquiry, the central hermeneutic point concerning the relation between meaning and political explanation is stated in a distinctly humanist manner: the capacity of human beings to give meaning to their actions, relations, practices, and institutions, and to communicate this meaning through reflection and communication in speech—in short, the human capacity for language in this sense—makes understanding human experience different from understanding nonhuman nature. The roots of this view reach back, as the tradition of hermeneutics, to the classical world of ancient Greece. In its contemporary forms, many point to the enduring influence of Ludwig Wittgenstein's notions of "language-games," "modes of life," and conceptual "family likeness (or resemblance)."[9]

In post-Wittgenstinian political science, several prominent inquirers with a shared concern for a range of explanation in political science (texts, elections, revolutions) have delineated the principles of interpretive inquiry. If only because these inquirers focus on issues raised specifically in political explanation, political scientists should give the works of John Dunn, Alasdair MacIntyre, Quentin Skinner, and Charles Taylor as much attention as they do Weber and Peter Winch.[10] To do so might begin to close the gap between the interpretive approach to political inquiry and perceptions of it in political science. While the ideas of Dunn, MacIntyre, Skinner, and Taylor differ in interesting ways, my claim is that their assumptions about a self-consciously interpretive approach are nearly the same. Their shared concern is how political inquirers may best understand and claim to explain the political lives of others.

Despite this concern, however, both their writings and the significance of their approach have eluded the sustained attention of many political scientists. There are many reasons for this situation, four of which set the context for my account of their contributions to hermeneutics in political science. The first reason relates to the organizational structure of political science in the United States. The discipline is organized into subdisciplines (American politics, comparative politics, political theory, international relations, public policy and administration, methodology); Dunn, MacIntyre, Skinner, and Taylor are usually placed in the theorist wing, where questions of interpretation have been routinely relegated. This institutional situation implies that the significance of their views is confined to political theory. These perceptions are unfortunate, because these thinkers have made their contributions regarding political interpretation as contributions to the discipline as a whole. Still, while their names are well known, their ideas are frequently excluded from the discipline's broader self-conception. As a result their reflections on the philosophy of political inquiry are checked at the sometimes strictly defined—almost statelike—borders between the subfields of political science. These borders are as rigid in the self-conceptions of many students and practitioners as they are in course catalogues. And, despite efforts by many to shatter the assumptions that they are founded on, they maintain their influence on our view of both the field and the study of politics. Interpretive theory seeks to end the "protectionist policy of intellectual isolationism" in political science by stressing the fundamental interpretive dimension common to all of its subdisciplines, or what I call the interpretive unity of the practice of political inquiry.[11]

A second, related reason for this exclusion is that the work of Dunn and the others is seen as relevant only to the history of the discipline rather than to ongoing dilemmas in political research. Interpretive theorists are seen as having once successfully debunked certain assumptions of positivist political science but not as having much else of substance to contribute to political explanation. Taylor's critique of value-free inquiry is a good example. In several widely read essays, Taylor criticized the objectivist pretensions of political science. But, his debates are seen by many as debates of the past. The proper place for Taylor's study on value-freedom and other similar works is in the archives of political science.[12]

This view, like the first, is unfortunate. These papers, as well as subsequent elaborations on the interpretive approach, remain relevant contributions to political explanation. To view the debates as relevant only to the history of the discipline is to assume that these debates were solely about positivism and its prospects when they were about understanding political life in general. Interpretive theorists were not simply playing the role of estranged gadflies, as John Gunnell has implied. As early as the late 1960s, theorists of interpretive inquiry articulated an alternative thesis for understanding politics generally, not simply one on the shortcomings of positivist or empiricist approaches.[13]

Moreover, to view the debates between the defenders of political science and the defenders of interpretive inquiry as belonging to the past is to underestimate the persistence of different forms of problematic methodological understandings and assumptions once associated solely with positivism, such as the value-free claims. I discuss this tendency to relegate present issues of significance to the past in the previous chapter. Nonetheless, this problem is not limited to our vision of secular and modern political possibilities. Positivist assumptions have not died in political science as much as they have dispersed into all research designs, wherein, as Dunn has stated, "rather substantial disagreements as to just how human values are to be appraised and taken into account" remain. This is a third reason that the significance of interpretive inquiry is overlooked. Methodological naturalism, especially in its "neo" forms, remains efficacious in political science. Its continuing influence is not an explicit focus of this chapter, but I will address it indirectly. The core theses of the interpretive approach are incompatible with neonaturalist and neopositivist approaches to political inquiry. My discussion of interpretive inquiry assumes that the assumptions of positivism are dead in political science in name only.[14]

Related to this is a fourth reason why the significance of the interpretive view continues to be missed. Captivated by increasingly sophisticated quantitative and computer modeling techniques, many practitioners of political science demand that political explanation should provide a measurable kind of certainty that is unavailable from the hermeneutic approach to meaning. Quantitative and qualitative inquirers alike frequently equate explanation with method-driven ways to produce definitive analytical certainty (including about margins of error). Interpretive inquiry is thus seen as insufficiently scientific or rigorous, because it will not satisfy this demand. The expectation that any approach to political inquiry should yield regulated certainty has led many to mischaracterize the interpretive commitment as a set of methods (that is, to think problematically about what interpretation involves, or to ignore the significance of interpretive inquiry when no such set of methods seems available). Unfortunately, more than a few texts dealing with the scope and methods of political science place the interpretive "method" next to other methods of political research.[15]

The upshot of these factors is that, although methodological discussions are, as David Easton said, still evolving, the situation does not radiate optimism for interpretive inquirers hoping to invigorate political science with a new interpretive consciousness.[16] The work of interpretive theorists is often not read with an interest that defines or understands its proper relevance. Hoping, for example, to transcend causal assumptions about the relation between language and political action, interpretive theorists usually find that these assumptions are powerfully held and transmitted from one generation to the next in the discipline. Practitioners of political science respond not always by accepting what I will refer to as the constitutive thesis, but rather by distorting it. My delineation of the rules of thumb of the interpretive commitment takes this and similar responses into account.

LANGUAGE AS EXPRESSIVE AND MEANING AS INTERSUBJECTIVE

The cornerstone of the interpretive commitment in political inquiry is that the relation between linguistic and nonlinguistic aspects of political life is constitutive. To say that "language is constitutive of reality" is to say that language, as Taylor said, "is essential to its being the kind of reality it is." I employ a broad concept of language here that is "not amenable to straightforward definitional settlement." Language encompasses a wide range of subjectively and intersubjectively held concepts, symbols, and beliefs that make up the communicative apparatus for human relations. From the perspective of interpretive inquiry, these concepts are accessible and hence graspable through reflection and communication (or metaphorically similar modes of historical research) between the interpreter and the subject of interpretation.[17]

To understand this frame, it is necessary to locate the interpretive view of the constitutive relation between language and reality in an account of language and meaning. Few political scientists are accustomed to thinking about "accounts of language" (also called theories of linguistic meaning). While political inquirers often think about the tactical purposes for which certain things are said (and others not) and about different meanings that concepts have, rarely do we think about our view of those concepts and of language, including the language of explanation. Different accounts of language see the significance of language—its composition and its relational place in the context of life—differently.

At the heart of the interpretive commitment to political explanation lies what I refer to, following Taylor, as the expressivist account of language and the constitutive relation between language and politics. This account can be understood in contrast to the dominant account in the social sciences, the designative account of language. The designative account of language states that the relation between language and life is disjunctive. Understood disjunctively, the two can be separated; understood constitutively, they cannot.

According to the designative account, the meaning of words or signs is what they designate; hence, to explain their meaning one must identify how words or signs designate, depict, or represent nonlinguistic or other linguistic phenomena. Taylor argues that the history of the designative account illuminates how the designative, depictive, and representative functions of language are fundamental to it. Originally part of the seventeenth-century medieval nominalist repudiation of the existence of abstract universal (theocentric or platonic) meanings, this account sought meaning in a this-worldly frame. Words, it was understood, gain meaning when correlated with this-worldly states of affairs, not outside of them. It follows that the world can be studied from an objective, nonmetaphysical position through language. Language is understood as a "set of designators, words we use to talk about things," the world is external to the language that describes it, ideas are "little [verifiable] units of representation," thought is "how these ideas are put together," understanding is "breaking the ideas down and then putting them back together," thinking is "assembling clear and distinct ideas," and knowledge is an objective appeal to the designators.[18]

By contrast, the expressive theory of meaning, while not in conflict with the idea that the meaning of language lies partly in its designative use, nevertheless sees the designative theory as a postponement of the study of language. By posing such questions as what are the things that language designates and, how can that designation be clearer and more precise? the designative account creates an interest in the uses of language, but it does not explain what language *is* for human beings—what its status is in their lives. To know that I use this word in this way and that one in another, or that I attach this set of meanings to that experience and that to another, is to know that we find language sometimes instrumentally or descriptively useful. But what is it about language that makes this possible? In its challenge to metaphysical approaches to meaning, the designative theory illuminates one function of language, but it occludes engagement with the nature of language, and because of this, with the nature of the relation between language and the world.

In the expressive view, words do not only designate or represent. Words express. They do not only depict the matters of our lives, they disclose life. Language does not only designate "externals." It makes life possible, where the life that is made possible is not only that of a self that uses language or expresses itself. It is the life of an intersubjective, language-speaking community.

Unpacking this view, Taylor draws on Gottlob Frege, J. G. von Herder, Wilhelm von Humboldt, and Martin Heidegger to identify three functions, beyond the designative, "for which language seems indispensable." The first is the formulative function. Language enables us to "formulate things . . . to bring to explicit awareness what we formerly had only an implicit sense of." In this way, language is not reducible to a set of words that designate. Language is realized in reflection (as distinct from verbalization). It is a vehicle for reflecting on our beliefs and feelings. Second is the "founding" function. Through speech, language enables us to "put things in public space," to "place certain matters before us." In so doing, it founds public space in a way that "bring[s] us together *qua* participants in a common act of focusing." Finally, language fulfills a characteristically normative function. It "provides the medium through which some of our most important concerns, characteristically human concerns, can impinge on us at all." Without it, we would lack the medium to "be sensitive to standards as standards," or to make fundamentally human discriminations or "distinctions of worth" (for example, between right and wrong, good and bad, etc.).[19]

All three functions "involve different ways of disclosing, of making things plain." Together they identify the *expressive* nature of language, its character of making life plain. Language expresses or discloses (*Erschlossenheit*), it reveals and realizes. In reflection, it "bring[s] to light" (*Lichtung*); in articulation, it manifests, making "visible, something out there between us" (*entre nous*). In this sense, expression, not designation, is fundamental.[20]

Expression here implies that language is not set apart from the life that it expresses. This is central to the constitutive thesis: meanings and understandings that constitute the actions, relations, practices, and institutions of life are expressed in and through language. "Constitute" here means to make these aspects of political life what they are. Interpretive political inquiry seeks to grasp these meanings as well as dimensions of their significance. From this perspective, interpretive inquiry stipulates that the task of political explanation is not fulfilled unless it accounts for the meanings and understandings that constitute political life as they are expressed in the concepts and language of that life. This is the first rule of thumb of the approach. Because language expresses meaning and meanings constitute life, life cannot be adequately understood apart from the meanings that constitute it. The "delineation of a society's concepts becomes a, if not perhaps the, crucial step in the delineation of its life." This is the benefit of the expressivist account of language. In the designative account, language (and hence the meanings it expresses) is said to be separate from life. The expressive-constitutive account rejects this thesis as an inadequate representation of language. Meaning constitutes life. To separate language and life is to separate life from what makes it what it is.[21]

Contemporary interpretive inquiry offers an important extension beyond earlier versions of the expressive account that raises important questions concerning the conception of meaning in political science explanation. The eighteenth-century version of the expressive account shared with the designative account an interest in transposing meaning to the human self, thus stripping meaning of its metaphysical and/or divine origins. "Expression was self-expression. What comes to full expression are my desires, my aspirations, my moral sentiments. What comes to light in the full development of my expressive power is precisely that what was striving for expression all along was the self." This statement expresses the idea of *subjective* meaning, one understanding of meaning that has become a central feature especially of contemporary Weberian approaches to interpretive inquiry. The premise is that it is impossible to explain anything about human beings without an account of the meanings that individual agents give to their actions, the meanings constitutive of those actions. Such meanings are private from an individual viewpoint, but accessible through reflection and communication (or other forms of metaphorically similar modes of historical research) in which the interpretive inquirer grasps the aspects of meaning that make the individual actions what they are.[22]

The emphasis on the self that is in command of meaning is contested by interpretive political theorists who seek to stress, following Wittgenstein as well as Weber, both the subjective and the *inter*subjective nature of meaning. A Wittgenstinian might allow that meaning is subjective, but it is not mainly subjective, for meaning is expressed in concepts that are shared among participants in a language-using community. Viewed as such, meaning is intersubjective, and accounting for shared concepts enables us to account for the constitutive meanings of human relations, practices, and institutions as well as individual actions. Thus, interpretive inquirers must account not only for subjective meanings, but they must also account for the intersubjective matrices of meaning that constitute political relations, practices, institutions, policies, and other forms of collective human endeavor. Since language, as Taylor argues, "originally comes to us from others, from a community," it is "not unambiguously clear that [all expression] ought to be considered as self-expression/realization." There are meanings, shared and contested, among participants in collective political endeavors such that without those meanings the endeavors would not be what they are. Thus interpretive inquirers must account for intersubjective meanings that are not solely the possession of the self. What the self manifests in expression is not simply a self, but what Terence Ball, James Farr, and Russell Hanson describe as the preconstituted linguistic world of which the self is a part. Language is "always more than we encompass." "We express ourselves, and a larger reality of which we are a part." A "speech community," not simply speakers, "is always a subject of speech."[23]

All of the interpretive theorists that I review here accept this, seeking to open meaning to its intersubjective dimensions without obliterating a notion of the human agent that participates in those dimensions. While the self does not exclusively control meaning, it does manifest, express, and participate in creating, even reconstituting, meaning. The self's capacity for interpretation, for reflective awareness, always exists in a linguistic web (Herder). The self does not dominate this web and the web does not dominate the self. As Taylor conceptualizes it, self-interpretations, as expressions of the uniqueness of an individual's experience, are always "drawn from the interchange which the community carries on." In this way, the language community is "constitutive of the individual." At the same time, as "self-interpreting animals" who formulate understandings through reflection, and who found common places with others in communication, we constantly reshape the communities in which we exist. To be self-interpreting, to have an identity as a self, is part of what it means to be human.[24]

The interactivity between the web and the self that is always subject to change has two important consequences for understanding meaning. The first is that the "human being alone is an impossibility, not just *de facto*, but as it were *de jure*. Outside of the continuing conversation of a community (or tradition), which provides the language by which we draw our background distinctions, human agency [as reflective, self-interpreting, language-using beings] would not be just impossible, but inconceivable. As organisms we are separable from society . . . but as humans this separation is unthinkable." Understanding expressions of meaning, therefore, requires understanding self-interpreting agents as participants in broader, intersubjectively constituted and fundamentally dialogical processes of social life.[25]

The second consequence as described by Taylor is: "Reshaping [the web] without dominating it, or being able to oversee it, means that we never fully know what we are doing to it; we develop language without knowing fully what we are making it into." This is important enough to be reformulated as a second rule of thumb for interpretive inquiry: meaning is intersubjective, and the web of intersubjective meanings and their significance always exist in part beyond the grasp of the self that expresses and gives shape to them. This point strongly implies that an interpretive inquirer should never expect to provide a comprehensive account of meaning in any interpretive political explanation.[26]

That many dimensions of meaning exist beyond the immediate grasp of any given self in any given speech community, wherein meanings are shared and contested and thus constantly altering, makes the definitive account of meaning an elusive goal. The status of the interpretive inquirer is implicated here, for inquirers too are "selves" within this frame. Interpretive explanation is perpetually unfinished. As essential as it is to account for constitutive meanings in any political explanation, we can never expect either the individuals who express meanings, or ourselves trying to grasp meanings, to provide a single, definitive account of them. The web is bigger than any self that attempts to account for it. It is important to stress, however, that this perspective on interpretation is not a shortcoming of political explanation. Rather, it is a statement about the form and limits of explanation. A definitive interpretation of constitutive meanings—and by consequence of the politics constituted by those meanings—is not available to us. Because meaning is both subjective and intersubjective, and not simply subjective, interpretation is always open ended.

Where meaning may be construed in both subjective and intersubjective terms, interpretive inquiry may take many different forms. The different forms stem from differing judgments regarding the nature of and relation between the subjective and intersubjective dimensions of meaning. Does a meaning belong to one more than the other? If so, how ought the relation between subjective and intersubjective meaning be conceptualized? The theorists whose work I draw on, while differing in emphasis, agree that one should consider both forms of meaning in any analysis of social life. As such their work is, at least in part, agent-centric in that meaning is significantly subjective, and that accounting for subjective meaning that constitutes political life is indispensable to any explanation of political life.

Their agreement on intersubjective meaning poses a critical challenge to dominant epistemologically individualist research programs in political science that are based on gauging individual preferences. These programs assume that "all knowledge may be reconstructed from impressions imprinted on the individual subject." Subscribers to this thesis raise several criticisms of intersubjective meanings that interpretive inquirers should take seriously, especially because they raise valid ethical and sincere methodological concerns. Noninterpretive theorists argue, for instance, that positing the existence of intersubjective meaning implies the absence of subjective meanings; is equivalent to presuming a consensus of meaning; and legitimates "going beyond" self-understandings, a move that lacks any valid justification and raises many practical dangers.[27]

As we have seen for various accounts of language, the view that meanings are anthropocentric rather than theocentric opens up several possible understandings of meaning. Within these possibilities, the interpretive approach attempts to establish philosophically valid reasons for thinking that meaning is expressed by agents who formulate it through reflective awareness but is developed in the "social matrix in which individuals find themselves and act." This social matrix is constituted by intersubjective as well as subjective meanings, and the line between the two is always shifting. It is shifting, not nonexistent. There is no reason to think of meaning as wholly subjective. It neither resides entirely in the minds of individuals nor entirely outside of them. The interpretive approach does not annihilate subjective meanings as much as enrich our understanding of their subjectivity.[28]

From this, however, one should not conclude that meaning is assumed a priori to be consensual or that the aim of intepretive inquiry is to identify consensus. Judith N. Shklar suggested this implication when she criticized the interpretive attempt to get "subjects of investigation . . . to recognize their hidden unities of belief." To think that interpretive inquiry aims to identify such unities is to miss the point of its account of meaning. Interpretive inquiry, as I demonstrate in subsequent chapters, is concerned to illuminate intersubjective spaces of contestation as well as of commonality. Indeed, identifying contestation is fundamental to an interpretive political explanation. Moreover, the interpretive interest in commonality is not reducible to an interest in consensus or unities of belief. "Commonality" is not synonymous with either. Taylor uses "freedom" in the United States to illustrate this. In part, what makes freedom a common meaning is that it is differently articulated by different groups. The objection mistakes the claim about the nature of meaning and its intersubjective and subjective dimensions for a claim about a new class of meanings. In an interpretive frame it is as ludicrous to presume that all meaning is consensual as it is to presume that all meaning resides in the individual.[29]

Of course, by saying this, the interpretive inquirer may be committing one of the worst fallacies in contemporary political science research: going beyond individual preferences or understandings in the process of explanation. This objection may have some merit. An interpretive commitment to intersubjective meanings expresses an interest in identifying aspects of meaning that exist beyond self-understandings.

The view that "going beyond" understandings is a problem with *any* explanation is premised on a view that understandings should be reported exclusively in the frame of meaning of the subjects that we study. The qualitative researcher, it is said, "suspends, or sets aside, his or her own beliefs, perspectives, and predispositions." This is a version of the claim that to understand any "other" (culture, time, etc.) one needs to adopt the viewpoint of that other. Going beyond what subjects understand about their lives, in this view, contaminates explanation by introducing the bias of the researcher.[30]

This view misconstrues the hermeneutic situation as understood in Gadamerian hermeneutics. As discussed above, all interpretation involves already "being beyond" the understandings of those we study; we never read the world from a clean slate. We are always "beyond" those we study insofar as our accounts and explanations are shaped by our subjective and intersubjective prejudgments, foremeanings, and expectations—many residing outside our consciousness. These elements of our preunderstanding, as Taylor calls it, are "what we have to draw on to make other people intelligible." Anything I say about your life is also about my life. The interpretive hope is that what I say will be something that we both agree is true about your life when it is expressed and explained by me. We should not fool ourselves into thinking that at some point we fully capture another's conceptual world and at a different point we are "going beyond" it, though this does not necessarily mean that we will fail to capture theirs.[31]

The view that one should avoid going beyond understandings by "getting entirely inside the other's head" to understand others is intrinsically related to the positivist view that one needs a neutral language for explanation, even though the two views are usually held up as opposites. The latter is based on the claim that common sense or ordinary language is less systematic, too variable, and radically incomplete for cross-cultural generalization (in the search for theories and laws). Robert Holt and John Richardson argued that comparative explanation could and should avoid ethnocentrism by employing "non-culture bound concepts." In a similar vein, Richard Rose recently defended the use of generic political concepts in comparative analysis "to relate knowledge across national boundaries." The search for this neutral language (one not bound by culture) is related to going indigenous (to lose one's own language and adopt another) in that both assume that it is possible and desirable for the inquirer to bracket himself or herself to understand others. The unbracketable character of prejudgment, however, suggests that neither accepting the native's viewpoint as the language of explanation nor getting outside of culture is possible. The interpretive approach recognizes that a language and conceptual world that are the interpreter's and not the agent's are always part of interpretation. This point underscores one dimension of the significance of "prejudgment" in hermeneutics. Given that an interpretive disposition toward explanation aims to grasp constitutive meanings, and that an objective point of view is beyond our reach, we must reconsider the explanatory ends of interpretive inquiry. How are we to understand the aim of explanation, the language of explanation, and, perhaps most significantly, the relation between the language of explanation and the languages for which we seek to account?[32]

Rather than thinking of interpretive explanation as staying with or going beyond self-understandings, it is appropriate from a Gadamerian perspective to think of it as eliciting multiple meanings, in which these meanings result in what Gadamer has called a fusion of horizons. This fusion can be achieved only in conversation—or in metaphorically similar modes of historical research, what William Outhwaite calls a "virtual dialogue"—with those we seek to understand. Understanding others always involves understanding more fully by broadening our conceptual horizons relative to those of others. This occurs through insight and comparison expressed in a common language between interlocutors.[33]

Understanding thus requires bringing the constitutive concepts of others into our language without distortion, in all the natural parameters of understanding discussed thus far. In that process, our initial understanding is expanded (altered) in reflection and communication with those whose constitutive languages we seek to grasp. By expanding our language and incorporating other languages we cease to understand solely through our prejudgments. The language of explanation that expresses our new understanding is what Taylor calls a language of perspicuous contrast. As the language of interpretive explanation, it is neither exclusively our language nor the language of those whose lives we are studying. It is a language in which meanings in both languages can be comparatively and perspicuously articulated.[34]

Taylor's choice of the concept of perspicuous is instructive, for the term is derived from the Latin word *perspicere,* meaning to look or to see through. Interpretive inquiry offers an alternative understanding of observation (alternative to the norms of positivist/empiricist social science) in which the imperative of inquiry is to render clear by observing the constitutive concepts of political life. Conversation here is the context for knowing. Zygmunt Bauman aptly calls it an "endless process of re-evaluation and recapitulation," and Clifford Geertz a "hopping back and forth." The image conveys how dialogue enables us to arrive at a common language that brings the constitutive concepts of others' lives to ours so that we may express their meanings in a language that "makes them accessible for us."[35] Taylor describes Gadamer's fusion of horizons: "We have to learn to move in a broader horizon, within which what we have formerly taken for granted as the background valuation can be situated as one possibility alongside the different background of the formerly unfamiliar culture."[36] To do this without distortion, while recognizing also the necessary open-endedness of the project, is to be able to explain something that is true of others. It is to offer a compelling interpretive account. This language of perspicuous contrast "formulates both their way of life and ours as alternative possibilities in relation to some human constants at work in both." This language, then, is necessary for explaining—in the hermeneutic sense—alternative modernities, as I pose in the first chapter. The language of perspicuous contrast "allows for the fact that their range of activities may be crucially different from ours, [and] that they may have activities which have no correspondent in ours, which in fact they turn out to do."[37]

Interpretive theorists have discussed problems related to translating another's language as a way of illustrating what is meant by recognizing and identifying crucial contrasts. "There will often be no prospect of translating terms in an alien language by means of anything approaching counterpoints in our own," observes Quentin Skinner. "But," he argues, "this does not prevent us from learning alien terms, and in consequence finding out what discriminations they are used to make." Or, in general, "that we can understand completely what is being said in some language other than our own never entails that we can translate what we understand." Grasping discrimination points is part of the interpretive process of identifying constitutive meanings and understandings that we hope to account for.[38]

Furthermore, that grasping the meaning of constitutive concepts is more like grasping points of discrimination than like translating them reminds us of the crucial difference between understanding "concepts" and "words." Interpretive inquiry aims to grasp the meanings that concepts express, not simply when and how words are used. The difference is crucial. A concept can exist without a word or phrase to express it. Skinner observes, for example, that one could never have concluded that John Milton understood " 'things unattempted yet in prose,' . . . by examining Milton's use of the word *originality*. For while the concept is clearly central to his thought [even if his topic is not], the word did not enter the language until a century or more after his death." Skinner formulates what for us can be another rule of thumb: "The possession of a concept will at least *standardly* be signaled by the employment of a corresponding term. As long as we bear in mind that standardly means neither necessarily nor sufficiently, I think we may legitimately proceed."[39]

That we can't "go native" or create a general language of explanation need not, therefore, leave us in utter despair. Both directions seek to escape human constants at work in all interpretation. In the interpretive view, explanation always expresses the prejudices and preunderstandings of the inquirer. It is ethnocentric only "if we stick with" our "provisional identifications." The point of interpretation is to place our language out in front, opening it up to a dialogue with those we seek to understand. In that process, understanding occurs when our conceptual frame is expanded. This may require critical dialogue in which we lay bare our prejudgments to others, thus eliciting their strongest, most powerfully constitutive understandings. Any criticism that keeps the conversation going is entirely apt, even necessary, for fuller understanding to emerge. To withhold oneself (or to operate under the false assumption that it is possible to remove oneself) is to fail to make understanding possible. To repeat Gadamer's maxim, "We understand differently, if we understand at all." Many in political science would like to interpret this as "We understand differently than you do." This would insulate our language, but it is difficult to see how we could claim to understand the political lives of others. *To understand others, it is we who must understand differently.* The so-called neutral ("acultural") language of explanation in political science often expresses more about the understandings of political scientists than about those whose lives they claim to explain. To reiterate the first rule of thumb: no truly comparative explanation can be adequate unless it attempts to bring the constitutive languages of others to our own language while making intelligible contrasts between our frames. It is therefore absurd to suggest that either total immersion or neutrality is possible, or even desirable. Engaging in interpretation through a language of perspicuous contrast involves arriving at new understandings and new prejudices, where both are not always neatly separable.[40]

Thus another rule of thumb emerges: while trying to grasp the meanings that constitute political actions, practices, relations, and institutions, seek to identify perspicuous contrasts between meanings in the language of those you study and meanings in your language. Moreover, find a common language in which those contrasts can be stated perspicuously without distorting the meanings. "The aim is fusion of horizons, not escaping horizons."[41]

From the foregoing discussion we can see how the interpretive/constitutive perspective borrows heavily from the expressive view of the relation between language and life. It takes issue with subjectivist understandings of meaning, favoring a fruitful understanding of meaning as intersubjective. Interpretive inquiry is not simply a matter of listening to others talk or of reading their texts. What we assume about meaning when we listen or read can make a great difference in what we understand. The implication is that interpretive inquiry does not consist solely in archival research, discussion, or qualitative interviewing. If interpretation is divorced from the expressive account of language (or theory of meaning), the thinking that is necessary in interpretive inquiry is overlooked, and the point is distorted. If the expressive/constitutive view is correct, then understanding political actions, relations, practices, and institutions must begin by attempting to grasp the meanings, expressed in language, that constitute them. And doing this requires that we converse (though not necessarily agree) with those we seek to understand.

The constitutive thesis in political explanation—the problem of action: In this interpretive frame, we are beyond the idea that an adequate account of political action can be articulated only through observation of overt behavior. As MacIntyre neatly states, "The same overt behavior may fall under a whole range of descriptions that are inaccessible to any one who derives his or her knowledge from the observation of overt behavior." Thus, understanding what someone is doing requires understanding what that person understands he or she is doing. When you find me working with the soil, I could be digging the garden, taking healthful exercise, pleasing my significant other, making sure that we have vegetables this summer, and so on. While I may be doing all of these, each understanding may not be equally significant to me. You must attempt to grasp the significance that the action has for me (even it is distasteful to you) to understand my action. You must try to understand the language and concepts of my life. Moreover, none of the discriminating concepts in the above descriptions are simply "mine"; "significant other," for example, marks a type of practice that is constituted by shared meanings in a given speech community. Still, no meaning can be assumed; the central concepts and the practices that they constitute have various meanings and are contested by its participants. Thus, understanding my action requires thinking of me as a participant in a broader linguistic community, with distinctive, shared, and contested parlances, grammars, etc. Would I be digging if it were not my responsibility to do so (hence I may value "being responsible"), if the government had not legislated against meat-eating (hence I may be "obedient to the law")? Would I be doing so even if I did not know that it was good exercise (good exercise may be an "excuse;" I believe that eating meat is a "sin")? The action cannot be understood adequately from an interpretive view without understanding how my understandings—subjective and intersubjective—constitute the action. My beliefs are not antecedent causes, "distinct and separately identifiable social phenomena" (as an interpretation adopting the designative account of language may have it). My actions are "uninterpretable and unidentifiable apart from" my beliefs, expressed in my own concepts, but not solely mine, because they identify my relation to a broader linguistic community. These actions have meaning because of the beliefs that I have of them.[42]

What is true of bending down and digging is true for voting, exploiting, canvassing, disrupting, and assassinating. MacIntyre perspicaciously identifies the depth of the relation between subjective and intersubjective meaning in his exposition of the interpretive idea of a "dramatic narrative":

> The action of assassinating a tyrant [presupposes a whole] web of political beliefs. For the agent and others to see his actions in the same light, a certain community of shared beliefs is a prerequisite. But social community can coexist with a great deal of divergence of belief. That it does so is one reason why it is indeed a task to make what others are doing intelligible to ourselves. Consequently . . . our beliefs about, and our beliefs which bear upon, our actions always have as part of their content explicit or implicit reference to what others believe about our actions, and *a fortiori* to what others believe about our beliefs. Nor are matters as simple as this. Our actions express our beliefs, including our beliefs about what others believe about our actions and

beliefs, but their beliefs are similarly informed by beliefs about what we believe their beliefs to be, including their beliefs about our beliefs.

"The" action, about which so many theorists write, cannot therefore be identified independently of the beliefs of the agent and of the others with whom he interacts, and, of course, of their actions as well. One crucial way in which this has to be understood is in terms of the dramatic narrative forms into which we and others continually reorder our lives. These forms make our actions intelligible not only in relation to what has gone before, but also to future possibilities. It is of prime importance here to note that any action may be a response not just to the immediate past but to any point in the recollected past, and that it may be, at one and the same time, a response to a number of past episodes and present situations. Moreover, any given action or string of actions may be situated in a number of historical sequences from the recollected past of the agent, so that different features of that action may be responses or sequels to quite different pasts.

The production of the dramatic and narrative forms through which we make our actions intelligible to ourselves as well as to others is of course a cooperative affair.[43]

Thus, an interpretive account of an assassination must try to grasp both the "coherence between the actions of the agent and the meaning of the situation" for the agent—the subjective dimension—and the relation between that coherence and statement of meaning, and the intersubjective meaning context. We must seek to identity the assassin's purposes as they are informed by the intersubjective meaning context.[44]

Identifying coherence may be stated as a rule of thumb. Importantly, coherence does not imply consistency. As Taylor notes, the "meaning may be full of contradiction and confusion." An interpretively adequate explanation must attempt to make sense of this contradiction (not try to correct for it). The purpose of inquiry is to try to make clear both the "agent's criterion" and why the agent "made use of this criterion rather than another," however confused either appears from the perspective of the inquirer. This purpose lies behind Skinner's "golden rule": "However bizarre the beliefs we are studying may seem to be, we must try to make the agents who accepted them appear (in Martin Hollis's phrase) to be as rational as possible." By "rational" Skinner means situationally rational: beliefs are those "suitable for them to hold true in the circumstances in which they find themselves."[45]

Skinner distinctly contributed to interpretive inquiry in his approach to understanding a class of action, namely "speech acts." In a series of articles over twenty-five years, Skinner has articulated, defended, and clarified his views on understanding texts as speech acts. No introduction to interpretive inquiry can ignore this contribution, even if Skinner himself does not consider it, as he has said, "anything particularly novel." His views reflect the contextualist or Cambridge school of political inquiry, profoundly influenced by the ideas of, among others, R. G. Collingwood, J. L. Austin, H. P. Grice, J. G. A. Pocock, Peter Laslett, and especially John Dunn. Collingwood's view of the history of political thought and Austin's notion of illocutionary acts were especially significant in both Skinner's and Dunn's articulations of the interpretive view.[46]

Collingwood suggested that the "history of political thought is not the history of different answers to the same questions, but the history of a problem more or less consistently changing, whose solution was changing with it." Both Skinner and Dunn sought to draw out this view as a response to a shared "dissatisfaction with the range of genres prevalent in the mid 1960s in the historical study of human thinking." In their view, these genres misunderstood thinking in two fundamental ways. First, thought was divorced from action; theorizing was not seen as "effortful activity" in need of interpretive explanation. Second and consequently, thought was divorced from the subjective and intersubjective contexts in which it occurred. Skinner and Dunn sought, therefore, to delineate an interpretive approach to understanding political thought.[47]

To explicate the first point referring to the interpretation of the history of political thought, Skinner turned to J. L. Austin's discussion of linguistic acts and H. P. Grice's discussion of meaning and intention. Austin argued in *How To Do Things With Words* (1955) that "any agent, in issuing any serious utterance, will be doing something as well as saying something, and will be doing something *in* saying what he says, not merely as a consequence of what is said." This is to say that in issuing a serious utterance, one is acting (doing) as well as saying. All serious speech acts have this illocutionary or performative "force" as a quality of them; these acts are active (like performance), and "deliberate and voluntary" (and thus meaningful) in this sense. Skinner discusses these aspects of speech as a "way of describing, and thereby calling to our attention, a dimension and hence a resource of language that every speaker and writer exploits all the time, and which we need to identify whenever we wish to understand any serious utterance."[48]

Austin believed that it was possible to understand what the agent was doing in saying something by gaining "uptake" of the illocutionary force. Was she commanding, promising, deliberating, manipulating, sending encoded messages? Skinner redescribes Austin's point by suggesting that understanding the illocutionary force is equivalent to understanding intentionality. For Skinner, to understand a speech act means to grasp the author's intentions that constitute the act and make the utterance what it is. Dunn put it slightly different: to gain uptake is to grasp the original point of the intellectual enterprise. In distinguishing what a text means from what its author meant, Skinner identifies his interest in grasping the latter, those intentions that "are a feature of the work itself," intended meanings that are *in* the text as a result of the author's illocutionary force.[49]

> Any text must include an intended meaning; and the recovery of that meaning certainly constitutes a precondition of understanding what its author may have meant. But any text of complexity will always contain far more meaning . . . than even the most vigilant and imaginative author could possibly have intended to put into it. So I am far from supposing that the meanings of texts are to be identified with the intentions of their authors; what must be identified with such intentions is only what their author meant by them.[50]

While there is much controversy about the extent to which Cambridge historians think that they can grasp intent, their general account of inquiry fits well in the hermeneutic enterprise of interpretive political inquiry. Skinner's argument forces us to grapple with identifying the meanings of actions for those who perform those actions. To fail to grapple with these meanings is to risk misinterpreting the actions, perhaps to understand them with our meanings only (Dunn). It is to "assume what has to be established." As in studying other individual actions, we should seek coherence between the action and the meaning of the situation for the speaker.[51]

To this end, Skinner and Dunn have identified three crucial aspects of what Austin described as the context (or "occasion of an utterance") that must be accounted for to grasp illocutionary force. One is the intersubjective context, variously referred to as the linguistic, ideological, rational, argumentative, discursive, rhetorical, or intellectual context. This aspect of context is comprised of prevailing assumptions, vocabulary, conventions, debate styles, conceptual discriminations, and so on—those features of the intersubjective meaning context that help to make the "best sense" of speech actions. The second aspect is the "general social and intellectual matrix" in which speech actors participate and issue utterances. The matrix of social and political circumstances—or the interpretations of those circumstances by participants in them—"set the problems" for speech action and must be accounted for to make sense of that action. Finally, the third aspect is the speaker's personal biography, his or her "life." Providing an account of the author's personal history relevant to making sense of his or her meaning is essential to exploring the subjective dimensions of meaning and trying to account for their relation to, and within, the intersubjective context.[52]

Again, accounting for context in these senses must be understood in the set of possibilities and constraints in which any interpretive explanation is offered. To forget these conditions for all interpretation is to exit the frame of interpretive inquiry. Skinner's acceptance of the scope and limits of the conversational mode of inquiry has been much debated. In my opinion, Skinner's approach falls well within the project of articulating languages of perspicuous contrast. He accepts the reality of prejudice in all interpretation, rejects epistemological individualism, and believes that interpretation never stops. Furthermore, what he says about "doing" interpretation he says by offering "precepts," not methods, for "how best to proceed; they are not claims about how to guarantee success." He stresses, for instance, that he has not intended to offer a "method for doing the history of ideas." Rather, he aimed to "articulate some general arguments about the process of interpretation itself, and to draw from them a series of what I take to be its methodological implications."[53]

> The outcome of the hermeneutic circle can never be anything approaching the attainment of a final, self-evident and indubitable set of truths about the utterance concerned. It scarcely follows from this, however, that we can never hope to construct and corroborate plausible hypotheses about the intentions with which a given utterance may have been issued. We can frequently do so in just the manner I have tried to set out. We can focus on the intersubjective meanings of illocutionary acts, and then seek further corroboration for such ascriptions of intentionality by inquiring into the motives and beliefs of the agent in question and in general the context of the utterance itself.[54]

In addition to these suggestions on context, Skinner also makes specific suggestions regarding how utterances, especially unfamiliar ones, should be received by the social inquirer. These suggestions, too, can be considered rules of thumb for producing an interpretive explanation. Two are particularly important for our purposes. Both are derived from his abovementioned "golden rule." The first is what Skinner considers the "*sine qua non* of the whole enterprise." This is that the interpreter should "treat utterances as straightforward expressions of belief." We need to assume a "convention of truthfulness": agents are being truthful about what they believe. This is the only way to begin an inquiry into meaning and intent. The second is closely related to this. However unusual they seem, utterances must be taken at face value. We must assume that "this is exactly what they believe." This avoids a number of errors that frequently accompany interpretation from cultural or temporal distance. We might, for example, be uncomfortable with the beliefs of those whom we study, and hence refuse to believe that what is uttered is what is meant. We might, in such a case, abandon the focus and the concern for meaning and seek some structural explanation for their beliefs, thus impeding understanding from an interpretive perspective.[55]

The constitutive thesis in political explanation—the problems of practices, relations, institutions: How do we account for practices and relations such as those associated with representation, interest articulation, revolution, administration, coups d'etát, or deliberation? What is true of an account of individual action is also true of an account of political practices, relations, and institutions: "The kind of footings we can be on with each other," writes Taylor, are "constituted in and shaped by language." Practices and relations cannot be adequately identified apart from the matrices of meanings and understandings—contested as well as shared—that constitute them. As such, an interpretive explanation must account for those meanings and understandings: "It is not just that people in our society all or mostly have a given set of ideas in their heads and subscribe to a given set of goals. The meanings and the norms implicit in those practices are not just in the minds of actors but are out there in the practices themselves, practices which cannot be conceived as a set of individual actions, what are essentially modes of social relation, of mutual relations."[56]

If, for instance, one is "living with one's significant other," does this mean that one is married, or participating in the social, and legally sanctioned, practice of marriage? From an interpretive perspective an adequate understanding, and hence explanation, of the living situation requires accounting for the matrix of meanings and understandings of those living in it. This is not to say that other interpretations are unavailable. Rather it is to involve us in conversation with those about whose lives we make authoritative claims. The practice of living together differs from other living situations, including marriage, even though they may look like the same behavior. Of course, there is wide variation. Two couples may be married and have vastly different understandings of marriage because it is a shared and contested concept. From an interpretive perspective, we raise the question of whether differently understood relations and institutions are the "same" institutions or whether they are meaningfully distinct. Any political science survey research that presumes to tell us something about married couple attitudes thus is indecisive from an interpretive perspective. Should we use the state's definition of marriage or the widely shared and contested definitions? Who is in, who is out, and how are we to formulate generalizations about married couple attitudes when the practices that are associated with marriage are highly contested? How would we do a national study, especially given wide cultural variations on understandings of marriage? If persons have different understandings of the practices in which they participate, those practices are not necessarily the same.

How then are we to understand policymaking practices? Should we construct abstract ideal type models and seek their explanatory power in alternative contexts, or does this procedure, conducted in a noninterpretive manner, risk missing the practice entirely? By saying that practices and relations are constituted by the understandings that people have of them, I am saying that those practices and relations are not possible without those understandings. Any adequate explanation of those practices must account for the meanings and understandings that constitute them. Grasping these understandings requires grasping them as they are realized (through conscious reflection and communication in speech) in the concepts and language of those whose lives we claim to explain.

Representation and policymaking take place in committees, parliaments, the national security council, convention halls; coups d'etát emerge from networks in army units or between such units and members of a cabinet; economic policy develops in and through money, the Federal Reserve, international loaning institutions; protests occur in the organizational structures of social movements. These institutions and structures of power, as with the practices and relations within and across them, cannot be adequately explained apart from the understandings of those who participate, often differently and differentially, in them. The meanings and beliefs expressed and expressible in language constitute these institutions so that the institutions cannot exist as they are without them. "A given piece of paper or metal," MacIntyre writes, "has the value it has not only because it has been issued by a duly constituted authority, but because it is accepted as having that value by the members of a particular currency-using population. When this condition is not generally satisfied, as in Germany and Austria in 1923, the currency ceases to have value, and this ceases to be currency." The same is true of an army, a parliament, a city council, or a social movement, and the positions that persons hold within them. The meanings and understandings constitutive of these institutions and institutional positions make them what they are, and for a political scientist to make claims about them apart from what they are seems to fail grossly in his or her task. "It is impossible to identify an institution except in terms of the beliefs of those engaged in its practices."[57]

We may formulate a rule of thumb for understanding political practices, relations, and institutions. Drawing explicitly from Wittgenstein, Taylor suggests that an "essential condition of anything we would count as grasping some social practice" is to "understand *what it would be like to be a participant* [emphasis added]." From an interpretive perspective, understanding practices, relations, and institutions requires "some degree of participant's know how, some ability to 'call' the right response" *in* the practical, relational, and institutional contexts in which the participant lives. We can do this by grasping the concepts that constitute these practices, the points of discrimination that they express, and their significance both in the subjective understandings that we have access to and the intersubjective context that they illuminate. For institutions, we must account for interpretations of institutional rules (not just the rules themselves) as well as norms, expectations, and aspirations that participants hold within those institutions. "You have to grasp what would be the appropriate thing for a participant to do in certain situations" to claim to understand these situations. To do this, we must focus on language, and if those that we seek to understand are still alive, we must communicate with them.[58]

At this juncture, a frequent objection to interpretive inquiry must be addressed. This objection focuses on the apparent lack of concern in the interpretive frame for nonlinguistic aspects of political reality that impinge significantly on political life and hence should appear in a political explanation. What about, for instance, the relations between action and social status, power, or class position? What about historical context? How are we to claim that we understand anything about the International Monetary Fund, for instance, unless we account for the international political economic context in which it operates and on which it sustains itself? Or, alternatively, how does interpretive inquiry help us to account for protests against government price hikes on basic necessities (for example, so-called food riots)?

The interpretive explanation does not deny that relations of power, privilege, property, style, and so on shape actions, practices, relations, and institutions. What it maintains is that these relations cannot be adequately identified without accounting for the understandings of their participants. To participate does not necessarily connote "equally" or "willfully"; nonetheless, these relations are what they are because they are constituted by a shared and contested, subjective and intersubjective vocabulary that interpretive inquiry aims to account for. The objection presumes what is in the interpretive view an artificial distinction between a social reality and the language of description of that social reality. It presupposes a designative view of language, wherein language depicts or represents, and meanings are understood to be, from the perspective of explanation, something extra, attached to objects rather than constitutive of them. Against this, the interpretive view suggests that language expresses or discloses. As Taylor has said, "Language marks the distinction among different social acts, relations, and structures"; the "point is that relations of power, and property themselves are not possible without language; they are essentially realized in language. Language is essential because these footings represent in fact different shapes of the public space established between people; and these spaces are maintained by language." Therefore, the constitutive social languages must be analyzed, and the most effective, efficacious, or centrally constitutive concepts—"powerful" in this sense—identified. Relevant contextual history must be interpretively described; this is true of the political economic context for the IMF as well as for food riots. It is essential to study the power relations of class or oppositional politics interpretively. We cannot understand why certain people join together for certain purposes without understanding the meanings constitutive of that joining. The aim is to deepen our grasp of these meanings, not to ignore or to neglect them.[59]

To summarize, what should an interpretive account accomplish in the study of political actions, practices, relations, and institutions? In the framework of the fusion of horizons, we should seek coherence between an individual action and the meanings of the situation for the agent. This requires us to understand the rationality of the situation for the agent. In understanding speech acts, accounting for the illocutionary force is indispensable. To understand practices, relations, and institutions, we must consider what it would be like to participate in them. We must seek to identify the meanings and understandings that constitute those dimensions of politics and their significance in those dimensions. They are guides for the explanation of political life. We must learn the concepts that are embedded in the meanings and understandings of those whom we seek to understand and whose political lives we claim to explain. We must engage in mutual self-clarifying exchange with those we study. There must be communication (or metaphorically similar historical approaches) with those we purport to understand.[60]

From an interpretive view of political life, there is a fundamental relation among the study of actions, practices, relations, and institutions. Each dimension is linguistically constituted, and interpretive inquiry attempts to bring these languages out.

HOW THIS TASK RELATES TO EXPLANATION
AND CRITICISM

Interpretive inquiry is frequently understood in political science to be more concerned with understanding than with explanation. It is also, as a consequence, understood to provide no basis for a critical social theory. In this section I provide an interpretive view of explanation and criticism. Unless these two aspects of the interpretive project are understood, the indispensability of hermeneutic political explanation to comparative political inquiry cannot be fully appreciated.

The objective of interpretive political inquiry is to achieve explanation as well as understanding. But by explanation I do not mean the methodological naturalist model (explanation and prediction on the covering-law model). Moreover, I believe that to interpret means more than to translate and to understand. It means to provide an account that speaks to our explanatory curiosities by answering such questions as, why this act and not another? What was the nature of this relation (between actor and action, institutions and practices, etc.)? What other narratives attempt to explain these relations? Are there continuities, changes? Are there relevant anomalies, aspects of political reality that challenge our account?

Positivist ideology has so captured the language and imagination of political scientists that explanation is often reserved only for those who seek generalization and prediction. There is no reason to think of this as a necessary or historically conclusive claim on explanation. To those who question interpretation as explanation, the question should be reversed: how can questions such as, why this act? why then? and so on be answered without accounting for constitutive meanings? What interpretive inquiry says is that no explanation is empirically adequate without accounting for the meanings and understandings of those we study.

Nonetheless, as many have argued, adopting an interpretive mode of explanation requires reconsidering what political inquirers should expect as an outcome of their explanatory efforts. First and foremost, the type of prediction that scientific social scientists strive for is impossible or fortuitous in interpretive inquiry. Not only does the thesis concerning intersubjective meaning require that our accounts remain open ended, the thesis concerning humans as self-interpreting creatures tells us that humans continually formulate and reflect on their lives (though not necessarily always) in their engagements in changing linguistic and conceptual, and hence practical, contexts. Through reflection they become aware of things that may have previously been to them only implicit or inchoate. Perhaps they reconsider a nagging problem and come up with a new way of thinking about—or conceptualizing—a set of power relations in light of some new experience. This may happen in common acts of focusing such as conversing, listening, training, campaigning, producing, or conflicting; or it may happen on a walk in the woods, or while cooking a meal. Reflection brings about both vision and change in who we are. It is not simply that human beings see things previously unseen; it is also that human beings are capable of seeing their lives differently, thus changing the understandings that constitute life.[61]

This is the crucial point: human beings are self-interpreting creatures whose interpretations change dynamically over time. The practical evidence is that institutions, practices, and relations change as understandings do. From an analytical perspective this insight instructs us not simply that our interpretations are endless, but that the "very terms in which the future will have to be characterized . . . are not available to us at present." As self-interpreting beings, our formulations that constitute our present lives—always partial "readings" within a constellation of meanings—are fundamentally unpredictable. They cannot be adequately posited in advance. "To have predicted the wheel," writes MacIntyre, "it would have been necessary to characterize the wheel; but to have been able to characterize it would have been to have invented it already. Where basic conceptual innovation is involved, we cannot predict, because to predict we would have to apply the new concepts that have yet to be articulated." Thus, given the constitutive view of political reality, we cannot predict political life with the certainty that naturalisms and neopositivisms—explicitly teleological or not—seek. "To any stock of maxims derived from empirically founded generalizations the student of politics must always add one more: 'And do not be surprised if in the event things turn out to be otherwise.'" Human history is non-nomological in all of its dimensions, past, present, and future.[62]

Interpretive inquiry does not, however, rule out a certain type of prediction, or, better, prediction understood interpretively. The Wittgensteinian notion that we aim to explain what it would be like to participate in relations in order to understand them makes it possible that we may, as political inquirers interested in understanding future possibilities, anticipate certain moves (actions, relations, practices, policies, etc.) in relational contexts that we have explained. An account of the rules and languages constitutive of these relations enables interpreters to anticipate a range of possible behaviors. But this must always be qualified by the ultimate unpredictability of interpretive explanation that is based on the reality of conceptual innovation and alteration of conceptual consciousness discussed above.

As a second consequence of the open-endedness of interpretation, no interpretive account is necessarily more objective than others. Alternative accounts are better understood as rival interpretations in the hermeneutic circle, interpretations that we consider *within the interpretive frame* as correct or incorrect, compelling or less compelling, right or wrong, and even true or false as we continually engage in the field of those we study. As Taylor notes, "The demand has been for a kind of certainty which can only be attained by breaking beyond the circle."[63]

Not all political scientists, however, accept this view of alternative accounts, especially those seeking generalized explanation. John Ferejohn, for instance, has criticized the interpretive "method" for not providing a "criterion within the approach to decide between" rival interpretations. He writes, "Taylor calls this the 'hermeneutic circle'; I call it incompleteness." Ferejohn, however, confuses the claim that there are only rival interpretations with the claim that there is no way to adjudicate between them. Interpretive inquiry is committed to the first but not to the second. That there are no specifiable rules for adjudication does not mean that there is no way to adjudicate. This is where the rules of thumb that are posited here may clarify the objectives of interpretive inquiry. Contrary to Ferejohn's claim, there are certain standards for a "better" interpretive explanation. Inquiry that strays from the rules of thumb derived from the constitutive thesis that I have outlined here is bound to generate less compelling and less adequate explanations than inquiry that is centered in them. The practice of political inquiry must aim to articulate languages of perspicuous contrast that make intelligible the shared and contested, subjective and intersubjective meanings and understandings that constitute political life. This entails grasping the expressed languages of political life such as constitutive criteria for individual action and relational understandings of participant know-how in collective political endeavors.[64]

Beyond constituting the practices of explanation according to these guidelines, we must, however, also accept a certain "incompleteness" as a necessary feature of interpretation. An interpretive claim against a rival might be something like the following: "I understand your argument, but I will try to show you something that you have not seen yet." The claim is based on the premise that self-interpreting beings—interpretive theorists as well as the subjects of their interpretive accounts—alter their interpretations because they belong to language communities in which particular, shared meanings and understandings are subject to reconsideration and alteration ("innovation").

> If an interlocutor does not understand this kind of reading, or will not accept it as valid, there is nowhere else the argument can go. Ultimately, a good explanation is one which makes sense of the behavior; but then to appreciate a good explanation, one has to agree on what makes good sense; what makes good sense is a function of one's readings; and these in turn are based on the kind of sense one understands.[65]

In adjudicating rival interpretations, therefore, we are forced to return constantly to the languages of understanding—both the self-interpretations of those whom we seek to understand and to our own previous formulations. We do this inexorably. "We can never expect our debates about interpretation to have a stop." This is why it is crucial to be committed to interpretive inquiry to grapple with *our* understanding politics in modernity. Noninterpretive methods, usually supporting hindering prejudices like the narrow secular modern ones that I detail in the previous chapter, have for too long occluded our explanation of the contested, alternative, contemporaneous actions, relations, practices, and institutions in modern politics and in the theoretical preunderstandings of social inquiry.[66]

In the interpretive frame, therefore, the question of whether interpretive inquiry is critical is improperly posed. The question is not, should we or can we criticize? The question should be, when is interpretive inquiry not critical? The engagement with the study of politics that is offered by interpretive inquiry is inherently critical, but its understanding of criticism does not satisfy the demand frequently made in social sciences that we criticize those whom we claim to understand without adequately accounting for their understandings and the intersubjective contexts in which they must be situated. Nevertheless, it would be a gross oversimplification of interpretive inquiry to suggest that all interpretive theorists are united on this question. There are two related kinds of criticism that interpretive inquiry enables.

The first type of criticism comes closest to the demand for "criticism of others" in the social sciences without leaving the interpretive frame. This is the view that an interpretive posture toward political explanation makes room for correcting, supplementing, or even repudiating subjective understandings, both the interpreter's and the interpreted's, although the focus of this first type of criticism is on the latter. This is a complex claim and it must be viewed in the context of the general interpretive thesis that I have delineated; that is, it is based in a fusion of horizons in which one comes to grasp the constitutive subjective and intersubjective dimensions of meaning by agents who express them, although not always fully. Criticism of this first kind aims at keeping the conversation going by inquiring whether any agent will accept as true an alternative reading of his or her "meaning context," subjective or intersubjective. Thus, criticism as correcting, supplementing, or repudiating claims must be part of coming to a deeper understanding of the constitutive meanings for which we seek to account. The standard for such critique is that it be articulated to show how it makes sense "within an agent's own mapping of his 'problem situation' or 'set of problem situations' (action context)." "Criticism" of these types must be articulated during mutually self-clarifying exchange seeking to elicit, paraphrasing Dunn, the best expression and the best account of the best description. Dunn comments on the latter:

> Any supplementation, for instance, must remove anomaly within, or add information to, the best description which he himself is able to offer; and it is because they must do so that it is tempting (though plainly wrong) to insist that they must provide characterizations which an agent could or even would in practice accept. When we have the best description which he is able to offer, we may well be able to illuminate him to himself, perhaps even to show him that some of his initial statements are the reverse of the truth; and our potential ability to do so will not be impugned should he not in fact wish for further illumination, wish to understand himself any better. What we cannot do is to claim to *know* without access to the best descriptions which he is able to offer.[67]

This is the central point that differentiates criticism that is correcting, supplementing, or repudiating in an interpretive frame from criticism within an anti-interpretive one. Taylor is useful to quote as well:

> Social theory . . . is very much in the business of correcting common sense understanding. It is of very little use unless it goes beyond, unless it frequently challenges and negates what we think we are doing, saying, feeling, aiming at. But its criterion of success is that it makes us as agents more comprehensible, that it makes sense of what we feel, do, aim at. And this it cannot do without getting clear on what we think about our action and feeling. That is, after all, what offers the puzzle theory tries to resolve. And so there is no way of showing that some theory has actually explained *us* and *our* action until it can be shown to make sense of what we did under *our* description (where this emphatically does *not* mean, let me repeat, showing how what we did made sense). For otherwise, we may have an interesting, speculative

rational reconstruction . . . but no way of showing that it actually *explains* any-thing.[68]

The demand for locating criticism in the web of the subject's intersubjective context establishes a high standard for interpretive political inquiry. Moreover, it identifies interpretive inquiry as a critical examination of politics; interpretation is not simply "understanding" or "interviewing." "The arrogance of ideological explanation of the thought of others lies in the claim to understand another's thinking more deeply than he does himself without being in a position to provide true descriptions of almost any of it. It is a routinized claim to authority where routinized claims must be false, where all authority must be earned in detail and where the mode of its earning is by explaining persons (and their situations), more lucidly to themselves. . . . If we claim to *know* about others, we must try as best we can to give them what is their due, their right."[69]

The possibility always exists that our attempts to criticize others may lead to sharp repudiation from our interlocutors. In actual conversation, as opposed to metaphorical historical dialogues, they may end the conversation. Such an occurrence need not hinder understanding. It may provide great insight, wherein we discover the understandings that set us apart conceptually (and thus perhaps ethically and politically as well). We should attend carefully to such moments and account for conceptual expressions indicative of strong disagreement in our common languages of perspicuous contrast. Nothing that is said about achieving a common language for explanation implies achieving agreement on all matters. It implies achieving agreement on understanding constitutive meanings. But there are no rules here, for the closure of communication may signal our need to return to the conversation, to converse differently, to understand better.

In addition to challenging subjective understandings of others, interpretive inquiry provides a frame for challenging ourselves.[70] This is the second kind of criticism enabled by interpretive inquiry. An interpretative understanding of politics opens us up to "making and remaking the forms and limits" (Taylor) of our own understanding. In dialogue with those whose lives are presumably different than our own, alternative possibilities—past, present, and future—come into view. As Peter Winch understood, interpretation makes possible "learning different possibilities of making sense of human life, different ideas about the possible importance that the carrying out of certain activities may take on for a [person], trying to contemplate the meaning of life as a whole." Thus, mapping moral and political possibilities (Ball, Farr, Hanson), perhaps even taking them seriously, is what interpretive inquiry provides us: "Our encounter with alien traditions, may and indeed ought to, compel us to reflect critically on our own intellectual and cultural situation" (Gerald Bruns). Because our language of explanation is always a language of perspicuous contrast, we, and not simply others, are challenged to think differently about life in general, and about the meanings of our own lives in particular. (Is this not the essence of the critical impulse?) Interpretive inquiry "is inseparable from an examination of the options between which [we] must choose."[71]

Therefore, the process of interpretation that is offered here, in addition to being intrinsically critical in several senses, is also necessarily comparative. It enables comparisons among alternative actions, relations, practices, and institutions by mapping out the matrices of meaning that constitute them in various contexts. For this reason also we must engage the comparative study of alternative modernities interpretively. The alternative is to avoid a critical confrontation with our own judgments in history and to fail to account for those of others. It is to fail to see alternative options. Anti-interpretive methods have for too long occluded critical engagement with our own perspectives as well as the perspectives of others in modern politics.

Finally, interpretive inquiry's claim to illuminate possibilities that are fundamentally unpredictable has an important consequence for interpretive political inquiry: all inquiry is inescapably historical. We are always considering historically different options. This view underlies the various interpretive pursuits in political science that append history to their label: the history of political consciousness, conceptual history, and comparative histories. The domains of inquiry include revolutions in Africa as well as the speech acts of William of Ockham and Locke. It is thus unfortunate that "history" in political science is sometimes considered to lack relevance to political explanation. The study of political languages is intimately related to the study of history because it is dedicated to examining judgments of possibility in human affairs. As such, history "becomes essential, not incidental to the study of politics."[72]

I agree with Skinner's response to criticisms that his mode of inquiry is "purely historical" and "without modern relevance," driven by nothing more than the "dustiest antiquarian interest." He suggests that it is "needlessly blinkered to suppose that intellectual history [or comparative histories] can only be 'relevant' if it enables us to reflect our current beliefs and assumptions back on us," a version of what Gunn refers to as the "whiggish insensitivity to the past." This is a shared view among those who take interpretive inquiry seriously. We may find, for instance, as a result of engaging in such studies, that some of what we currently believe about, say, our moral and political arrangements is actually false. We are prone, for example, to think that the concept of individual responsibility is indispensable to any satisfactory moral code. But Adkin's analysis of ancient Greek values casts considerable doubt on that article for faith. We are prone to think that there can be no concept of state in the absence of centralized systems of power. But Geertz's study of classical Bali shows how the one is perfectly possible in the absence of the other.[73]

So the question of critique is returned to the objectors: Is a "stepping back from our own prevailing assumptions and structures of thought and . . . situating ourselves in relation to others and very different forms of life" (for the interpreters as well as the interpreted) irrelevant? Is it *un*critical? I think not. Political inquiry conceived of as situating ourselves in relation to historical possibility equips us "with a new means of looking critically at our own beliefs *in light of* the enlarged sense of possibility we acquire." It enables us to engage critically with the world of politics, and possibly to alter it, with new meanings for our political actions, practices, relations, and institutions. From one point of view, by explaining the constitutive nature of meaning, interpretive inquiry shows how a change in constitutive meanings enables a change in the practical institutional relations in the world. By offering interpretive explanations and accounts of available options, does not hermeneutic inquiry lay the basis for making world historical change possible? On what basis do we as human beings act? *What is* the relation between understanding and action? To quote Taylor, in interpretive inquiry "there can be a valid response to 'I don't understand' which takes the form, not only 'develop your intuitions,' but more radically 'change yourself.'"[74]

If our purpose in political science is to understand and to explain, then we must view the understanding of actions, practices, relations, and institutions—separated by artificial boundaries in modern political science—as fundamentally related. There is a unity in political science across these dimensions of analysis that continues to go unnoticed and insufficiently appreciated in the discipline. Understanding is conceptual, comparative, historical, and open. Grasping the expressed concepts and grammars of those we study means our understanding their political lives as they do. Comparison, intertwined within critical interpretation, opens up their possibilities in a historical relation to ours. The disciplinary boundaries—that uphold the distinctions between conceptual analysis, historical analysis, and comparative analysis which perforce divert us from a hermeneutic disposition toward political explanation—must be broken down.[75]

WHY TURKEY AS A FIELD OF STUDY

My thesis is that secular and modern prejudices, sustained and supported by noninterpretive methodological commitments, have governed the study of modern politics, especially in culturally different contexts. Turkey is one of those contexts. Moreover, the declared commitment of its founding political elites to supplant the "old ways of life," based in what they referred to as superstition and ignorance, with "new" ones, based in science and reason, has made Turkey a site of great interest for modern political scientists. It has been said that the western modernization and nation-building literature of the 1950s and 1960s "could, in spirit, have been written by Atatürk." In a speech in August 1925 promoting his sartorial reform policies, Atatürk is said to have declared the following:[76]

> The aim of the revolutions which we have been and are now accomplishing is to bring the people of the Turkish Republic into a state of society entirely modern and completely civilized in spirit and form. This is the central pillar of our Revolution, and it is necessary utterly to defeat those mentalities incapable of accepting this truth. Hitherto there have been many of this mentality, rusting and deadening the mind of the nation. In any case, the superstitions dwelling in people's minds will be completely driven out, for as long as they are not expelled, it will not be possible to bring the light of truth into men's minds.[77]

The Kemalist reforms thus ushered in a future that he and his colleagues hoped would free the people of Turkey from, as Şerif Mardin has put it, "what [Atatürk] may have agreed to call the 'idiocy of traditional, community-oriented life.'" He "was very much of the opinion that baggy pants and the fez were part of a 'carnival.'"[78]

Thus, as the modern political scientists believed that religion should defer to secular identities in modern politics, Atatürk and those who seized power believed that it was necessary to bring Turkey out of its premodern "religiously anchored" present and elevate it to a new future. In believing this, Atatürk and his colleagues were neither alone nor unchallenged. They were participating in one tradition of Turkish national thought that understood Turkey's chances for an independent, respected, and prosperous future as dependent on this radical transformation of Turkish national identity. The ideologist of Turkish nationalism, Ziya Gökalp, summed up this view when he declared favorably that a "modern nation is a creature which thinks in terms of the positive sciences." Turkey, it was believed, needed to come of age.[79]

To interpreters of the possibilities for secularism in the modern world,

Turkey is a site of world historical significance. "I think of Turkey," wrote the sociologist Donald E. Webster, "as a country which is coming of age." In political science, Daniel Lerner's thesis on the "passing of traditional society" took Turkey as its paradigm case. Lerner and Richard Robinson expressed the widely shared view that Kemalist policy signaled the epitome of pragmatic modernization politics: "Each policy and program was evaluated by what the ruling elite conceived to be the public welfare, not according to some *a priori* religious doctrine or political ideology." To these interpreters, it was unbiased science in practice superseding the theological stage of history (Auguste Comte, among others).[80]

My central claim with regard to Turkey is that while the building of a secular modern future may have been a goal of Turkish national politics, the constitutive meanings and ends of this project within Turkish political discourse have been inadequately attended to by anglophone political scientists whose interest in Turkey has been defined by narrowing secular and modern prejudgments and whose methods have been noninterpretive. In consequence, the original character of Turkey's secular state has not yet been adequately explained, and thus we have yet to grasp the understandings that constitute our perplexity about the rise of theopolitics in that context. There are, of course, always exceptions and qualifications to any such claim. But, as I argue, the broad general claim is defensible: governed by narrow secular modern prejudices (such as the inevitability of the privatization or the structural separation of religion), sustained and supported by noninterpretive methodological commitments, interpreters of Turkey have offered great insight on numerous power dynamics that are associated with the politics of secularization, but have failed to offer fully compelling accounts of Turkey's secular identity from an interpretive perspective.

My project vis-à-vis Turkey begins with a growing awareness in Turkish studies that significant aspects of Turkish political history remain open to interpretation. Inside Turkish academia, new understandings are emerging concerning many historical issues related to the Republic. Led by the new Turkish historians, research has begun to challenge accepted Kemalist views of Ottoman and Turkish history. Non-Turkish historians have also contributed to these debates. Even in political science, there is agreement that interpreting Turkish political history remains open. As George Harris has stated, "studies of Turkey have not progressed to the point where a 'standard' view of the country and its prospects has emerged. Thus far, attempts to present Turkish reality as a coherent whole have been rapidly outdated; the polemical literature of recent years remains less than satisfying as well. Indeed, all too many major questions of historical controversy still have not been convincingly resolved."[81]

I differ from Harris (and most mainstream political science views of history) in thinking that these controversies will ever be resolved—interpretation is necessarily open. But I do agree that the project must continue. The existence of an open interpretive field and the need to understand the alternative modernities of today—among other pressing and I dare say relevant matters that we must address in considering the possibilities for secularism—make Turkey a rich field of study for an interpretation of the complex issues that I have articulated thus far.

Chapter 3 Secularization and Modernization in Turkey: Interpreting the Ideas of Ziya Gökalp

The essence of life is creative evolution.

Human culture is nothing but a synthesis of national culture and international civilization.
—*Ziya Gökalp*

For the intellectual elite in the Young Turk movement, the last days of the Ottoman Empire were " 'a time of revolution' when old values were being pulled down and new ones were being invented." The promulgation of a distinct "Turkish" national identity by the Young Turks brought a "certain newness (*yenilik*)" to the "quality of a Turk (*Türklük*)." In this context of conceptual innovation and change, and beyond the immediate practical-political problem of how best to secure failing Ottoman political and economic structures, the foremost minds of the day tried to give substance to this newness. They asked what has turned out to be one of the most enduring questions in Turkey: who is a Turk and how ought this national identity be understood in relation to Islamic identity and modern scientific-rational identity?[1]

Nearly all analysts of the late Ottoman and early Turkish national period estimate that one thinker stands above all others in answering this question. This was Ziya Gökalp (1876–1924). Niyazi Berkes refers to Gökalp as the "most original and influential among Turkish writers of the twentieth century." Taha Parla writes, "It is no mean achievement to have laid the only plausible comprehensive cognitive map for Turkey's passage from a six-hundred year empire to a new nation-state." For Parla, Gökalp "stands out in Turkey as the one person who was able to go beyond narrow ideological blueprints to a systematic theoretical construction. With him, and in contrast to the Young Turks, loose ends come together; eclecticism is replaced by synthesis; the discrepancy between what is prescribed and what is practiced becomes smaller; imitative and idiosyncratic westernisms are supplanted by a critical appreciation of the West; radical chic is superseded by a sense of proportion and totality."[2]

The setting for Gökalp was characterized by the dissolution of the culturally, ethnically, and religiously heterogeneous Ottoman Empire and the rise of nationalism among both Muslim and non-Muslim populations under Ottoman suzerainty. Ottoman elites had tried through the nineteenth century to secure their state by adopting military, political, legal, and administrative techniques from states to their west. The famous Tanzimat—literally "reordering"—edicts (1839, 1856) concretized their interest in westernizing reforms, but also sparked a debate in the empire on the relation between new European ways and old, but changing, Ottoman-Islamic ones. The prominent "Young Ottoman" ideologue Namık Kemal, for example, argued for interpreting Islamic jurisprudential traditions to fit newer constitutional and parliamentary governing structures. His ideas contributed to the 1876 constitution and parliament that were prorogued only two years later by Sultan Abdülhamid II as the weakening of the Ottoman Empire accelerated. The sultan intensified so-called modernization reforms, but he did so in an Ottoman-Islamic, not a westernizing, conceptual frame.[3]

His virtual overthrow by the Committee of Union and Progress (in the "Young Turk revolution") led to the restoration of the constitution and parliament. The CUP encompassed varying ideological tendencies, but the presence of a Turkish nationalist group marked the end of the political hegemony of solely "Ottomanist" ideas. The nationalists, like their chief ideologue Ziya Gökalp, would confront similar problems of reconciling changes induced from the outside, but they would do so, especially after the losses of the Balkans in 1911–1913, with the goal of fashioning a distinctly Turkish national synthesis.

CUP rule ended with the Axis defeat in the First World War, and some CUP leaders, including Ziya Gökalp, were sentenced to a British jail in Malta. Still, the nationalist project gained steam after the victorious Allies attempted to implement their designs on Ottoman territory (Treaty of Sèvres, 1920). A national liberation movement culminated in 1923 with the declaration of a new Turkish Republic, in whose formation Ziya Gökalp's ideas played a significant, though still contested, role.

As an engaged public intellectual and ideologue, Gökalp participated in attempts to make sense of the transformations of the time and gave clarity to them. He did this conceptually in two related ways. The first was by investing the concepts of "nation" (*millet*), "religion" (*ümmet*), and "modernization" (*muasırlaşma*) with new meanings. The second was by offering, in a context of rapid political, economic, social, and ideological change, a new understanding of the relation of Turkish national culture, Islam, and modern civilization. In short, he believed that the necessity of grasping the crucial conceptual differ-ence between what he called their culture and what he called their civilization underlay the ability of the Turks to retain both their national culture and their Islamic religion while also absorbing desirable aspects of modernity. The dis-tinction between culture and civilization was clearly, in my view, what Gökalp understood to be his own substantive contribution to the debates of his day. After witnessing that his early efforts for publicly unfolding this distinction had fallen mostly on deaf ears—despite his paradoxically unparalleled influence among the elite—Gökalp lamented, "Among us, those who have grasped the significance of culture are few, and an interest in international civilization is yet to be born."[4]

My goal is to examine the identity and significance of Gökalp's thinking with regard to Turkish national identity, Islam, modernity, culture, and civilization in what we might call the secularization problematic of modern political thought.[5] Bryan Wilson has defined this as the "significance religion has for the operation and organization of the social system." Wilson writes that the "essen-tial question" of secularization theory concerns "just what part religion plays in the functioning of society." This was the question behind Gökalp's thinking about the place for religion in modern life. Wilson notes further:

> It is not necessary to rehearse yet again the functions, now lost, which religion once fulfilled for other social institutions, save to recall that religion once provided legit-imacy for secular authority; endorsed, at times even sanctioned, public policy; sus-tained with a battery of threats and blandishments the agencies of social control; was seen as the font of all "true learning"; socialized the young; and even sponsored a range of creative activities. The loss of these functions is the core of the secularization thesis.[6]

As we shall see, Gökalp distinguishes between civilization and culture in these developments in the late Ottoman-Islamic and early Turkish-laicist context. He believed that the contemporary age was marked, in part, by the loss of religion's nearly exclusive grip on the institutional and ideational spheres of global and local life. In this context, he argued that the loss of religion's universal significance did not entail a complete loss of its significance in certain social and carefully defined public spheres. At the same time, he maintained that the separation between religion and politics was fundamental for the states of the member nations of modern civilization.

My study includes an analysis of two sets of texts. The first are the major interpretations of Gökalp's thought from the English-language political science literature. These include studies widely cited as authoritative as well as short but extended discussions of Gökalp's ideas. The second are Gökalp's writings that have been translated into English. These writings are the basis for my interpretation. I will stick closely to the writings that an English-language audience shares and offer an alternative interpretation of those texts rather than import other texts. My view is that no matter how incomplete the translated selections are as a portion of Gökalp's corpus, they are sufficient for an alternative interpretation of Gökalp's thought on the present subject matter.[7]

Gökalp's thought, as we shall see, is a perfect field in which to examine the relation between secular modern prejudices and noninterpretive modes of political inquiry. Without being secular as such, the frame in which he clarified Turkey's options at the turn of the century expresses an awareness of the fundamental nature of the dynamic that we have called the secularization process. But Gökalp never thought of it explicitly in these terms and offered a tripartide set of ideals that tried to synthesize religion and modernity. As such, his thought is constituted by both religious and nonreligious meanings, which are open to many interpretations. I do not seek to close the interpretive circle as much as to offer a more compelling interpretation of Gökalp's understanding of the significance of religion in modernity than exists in the literature.

Unless Gökalp's texts are approached from an interpretive perspective, the identity of Gökalp's thought and its significance in Turkish political thought about the secular dynamics of modernity can easily be missed. We find Gökalp's understanding of the relation between religion and modernity judged as inadequate because it deviates from the standards at work in the secular and modern prejudices that I have criticized above. This judgment alone is not a problem, but it sometimes substitutes for explanation when it should be subjected to reflection in the process of understanding. I will thus show how the understanding of secularism and secular modern possibilities may be enriched through an interpretive encounter with Gökalp's interpretation of Turkey's options in modernity.

With respect to interpreting Gökalp, not his interpreters, the major claim in my account is that some of the existing studies inadequately interpret the identity and significance of Gökalp's understanding of religion in modernity because they fail to understand one context that was significant to him. This context is best described as the concerns included in the secularization problematic. Unless interpreters of Gökalp see the centrality of these concerns in Gökalp's thinking, they will fail to capture both the identity and the significance of his thinking on the place of religion in modernity.

What I mean by emphasizing the secularization problematic is not that Gökalp intended to address the secularization problematic. I am also not saying that this was the only issue of significance for Gökalp. It clearly was not. He was, after all, engaged in giving substance to the meaning of Turkish national identity in the modern age. What I am saying is that the conceptual frame in our language that most adequately enables us to capture the significance that Gökalp's understanding of religion in modernity had for him is the outline of the secularization problematic and the realization it expresses that the place of religion is undergoing a radical, historical alteration. As I have described in the chapter on interpretive inquiry, coming to understand the horizon in which another's horizon is to be adequately understood is how understanding happens. Thus, when I say that previous interpreters have failed to grasp the significance of Gökalp's thinking in what I call the secularization problematic, I am saying that they have failed to grasp the identity of his own conceptual frame for understanding an issue of significance to him. The failure to locate the significance of Gökalp's political and social thought in the secularization problematic, therefore, while it may produce alternative understandings, does not help to bring about enough understanding of the identity of his thought as a whole.

What was evident in Gökalp's thinking, and what makes the study of his ideas so relevant to thinking about secularization today, is that in the final analysis, he shared the belief with modernists in the West that social structural changes were leading to an increasingly differentiated and possibly freer world. But what is obvious from an interpretive approach to understanding Gökalp was unrealizable from within the noninterpretive literature that sustained narrow secular modern prejudices. Perhaps Gökalp's understanding of the processes of modernity that were shaping Turkey might have been meaningful, significant, and hence true for Gökalp and also within the conceptual and political context to which he contributed. The shortcomings of existing interpretations of Gökalp's understanding of the relation between Islam and modernity—the merits of their different insights notwithstanding—is related both to the understanding of modern political history that constitutes political science and to hermeneutic inquiry.

In the literature that I will examine, this dual failure is observed in two distinct places. It is observed in different evaluations of the emphasis that Gökalp placed on Islam in his trinity of Turkism, Islamism, and modernism. It is also observed in the situating of Gökalp's thinking in the context of the laicist politics that succeeded him. He did not live to see the unfolding of laicist politics in Turkey. Interpretations of Gökalp's thought usually include suggestions for how Gökalp fits into the broader context of secular political thought and practice in Turkey. I accept this as a concern and will offer a different evaluation of the place of his ideas in the history of secular politics in Turkey than we find in the existing literature.

INTERPRETING GÖKALP IN THE
SECULARIZATION PROBLEMATIC

To understand claims made about Gökalp's understanding of the relations among Islam, Turkism, and modernism, we must first understand how his nationalism has been differently construed in the literature. It would be difficult to understand claims that are made about Gökalp's view of the relation among Islam, nationalism, and modernism without understanding claims made of its core nationalist component. An account of the debate over Gökalp's nationalism also illustrates the vastly different estimations of Gökalp's political aims and interests that one finds in anglophone studies and provides the necessary backdrop for understanding the four distinct evaluations of Gökalp's view of Islam in Turkey's modernity that I describe in the next section.

Two major works on Gökalp's thought exist in the political science literature. They present remarkably contrasting accounts of Gökalp's political and social thought. The two works are Uriel Heyd's *Foundations of Turkish Nationalism: The Life and Teachings of Ziya Gökalp* (1950) and Taha Parla's *Social and Political Thought of Ziya Gökalp, 1876–1924* (1985). The former was *the* authoritative interpretation of Gökalp in social science literature until Parla's appeared thirty years later.

Heyd's Gökalp obfuscates matters of nation and of spirituality. To Heyd,

Gökalp is "by nature a collectivist" who laid the "spiritual foundations of the Kemalist revolution" by assigning a supreme and divine moral status ("all divine qualities") to the Turkish nation. As such, Heyd views Gökalp's political vision as an "instructive example of modern nationalist thought in an Eastern society" that is neither particularly original nor admirable. He sees in Gökalp both a denial of the individual's absolute moral status and a refusal to respect international obligations and norms.[8]

Heyd acknowledges that Gökalp advocated national democracy, parliamentary and constitutional government, and the independence of science, religion, art, and academia from politics. But this apparent liberality, to Heyd, is overshadowed by tendencies similar to the "German and other Central European" nationalisms which tend toward the "irrational, collectivistic, and exclusive." Revealing the standards of "political science" on which his judgment is founded, Heyd explicitly juxtaposes this kind of nationalism to the nationalism of "Western Europe . . . based on the contemporary philosophy of Enlightenment with its rational approach and its individualist and Universalist outlook." Gökalp's distinction, on which "there can be little doubt," asserts Heyd, is that his "conception of society, the elite, and the Leader prepared the ground for Atatürk's authoritarian regime."[9]

In nearly total contrast to Heyd, Parla sees Gökalp as a fundamentally democratic, pluralist, tolerant, nonelitist, nonexpansionist, rational, egalitarian, feminist, internationalist, non- and antiracist, nonchauvinistic, humanist thinker. Parla argues that Gökalp's nationalism must be seen as an alternative to the illiberal, elitist, and pretotalitarian ideologies that were shaping early twentieth-century Western Europe.

> Gökalp stands out as a democratic and rational analyst of leadership in an age when theories of charismatic leaders, plebisitarian dictators, duces, Feuhrers, "electric currents between the chiefs and the people," and iron laws of oligarchy were in the making in European political and social thought. At a minimum, faith in the rationality of the citizen and the effectiveness of parliaments was in decline; ascendant was the belief in the irrationality of the masses and the necessity of dirigist elite and leaders. With his skeptical optimism in human reason, Gökalp did not travel that path to such extremes.[10]

To Parla, Heyd's error was twofold. First, it derived in part from an insufficient understanding of the ideological context that was required to interpret Gökalp's thinking. Parla agrees that Gökalp was not a political liberal, but he perceptively notes that Gökalp's options were not limited to those represented in the individualist/anti-individualist dichotomy on which Heyd bases his critique. In the ideological context of early twentieth-century European thought, Gökalp could criticize liberalism without sliding into irrational collectivism. Situated in this context, Parla argues that Gökalp's political vision is best characterized as solidaristic corporatism: "The system as a whole took the shape of idealistic positivism: the method was scientific in the positivistic sense, and the ideology was solidarism, a variant of corporatist capitalism, as opposed to Marxist socialism or liberal capitalism. Gökalp labelled it social idealism (*iç-timaî mefkûrecilik*)."[11]

Gökalp believed that the egoistic and utilitarian individualist ideals found in some western societies should never be the basis for building altruistic, tolerant, and public-oriented social norms in Turkey. Individualism was a bankrupt social and political philosophy, a "threat to equilibrium and harmony of society but also to the individual himself"; directly addressing interpreters like Heyd, Parla writes:

> [Gökalp's system] is pure and simple solidaristic morality which values the individual without negating its prerogatives, according to his service to social solidarist and public institutions. . . . The individual gains meaning only in society without being negated by society let alone by the state. . . . [and] is defended against the incursion of the state precisely by the occupational groups and their corporations, which serve as a buffer between the state and the individual. What facile liberal clichés cannot capture is that, in solidaristic corporatism, even the occupational groups which collectively constitute civil society, exist for the free development of the individual personality, which, however, has to be "social"; but still within a framework of cultural and philosophical liberalism.[12]

Parla argues that, in addition to not grasping the correct ideological context, the interpretation of Gökalp as the "direct source" of the "chief-system," tutelary elitism, authoritarian single-partyism, and the "quasi-totalitarian statism of the Kemalist period of 1920–1940" derives also from a "failure to appreciate the moral and theoretical reservations Gökalp entered on these issues, and [from] an irresponsible conversion of some of his slogans into representations of his central ideas."[13]

With regard to Heyd's text, Parla is correct. Heyd declares his chief aim to be to "trace Gökalp's development as a thinker" in a "comprehensive," "objective," "systematic," and "scientific" manner. But the reader quickly learns that Heyd's attempt to "sift through all [Gökalp's writings] in order to discover his ideas and weave them as far as possible into a connected system of thought" excludes Gökalp's "numerous articles on theoretical sociology." Heyd justifies this decision on the grounds that "Gökalp did little original thinking and merely accepted and paraphrased theories of Western, particularly French, sociology." Instead of attending to the sociological writings, Heyd gives "greater attention to Ziya Gökalp's views on religious problems" and the place of Islam in Turkish life, which he suggests have been insufficiently examined even by Turkish scholars. Doing so, he believes, is important for "understanding the religious development in modern Turkey and the secular trend in the Muslim world in general."[14]

Heyd's choice of topics reflects a tendency in social science during the late 1940s and early 1950s to study Islam in contemporary Turkish politics and thought. But the decision to exclude Gökalp's writings on sociology has serious consequences for Heyd's interpretation of Gökalp's system of thought generally and for his interpretation of Gökalp's views on religion in particular. Parla is correct. No portion of Gökalp's thought can be understood adequately apart from the sociological writings wherein Gökalp expresses the fundamental premises of his thought (in addition to theoretical reservations of the type that Parla mentions). This is true especially with regard to his views on religion in modernity. These writings were more than mere topical excursions for Gökalp. They express the conceptual groundwork in which his political vision took shape.[15]

We may even say that his sociology *was* his political contribution. Gökalp never participated in practical politics in the "usual sense," as Parla describes it, but he did apply his sociological judgments to the political debates of his day. And he did so as a member of the political and intellectual elite wherein he enjoyed wide influence as a political adviser, lecturer, and educator for new recruits to the Turkish movement. His middle-period writings (1911–1918) are exemplary in this regard for they illustrate the deep connection between his sociology and his Turkism.[16] Thus Heyd interprets Gökalp's political thought outside the context of Gökalp's judgments about the sociological trends that he believes were setting the context for Turkey's new identity.

By excluding some of Gökalp's important texts, Heyd relies mostly on Gökalp's poetry and some essays on the nature of Turkish nationalism. Because of this, Heyd's interest in Gökalp's view of religion is more than simply an interest in Gökalp's views on Islam. To Heyd, Gökalp's religion is not Islam but Turkish nationalism, the "central ideal of Gökalp's thinking." The "deified" nation is the "source and model for all ethical values." It has, in short, "become a religion." To illustrate this interpretation, Heyd frequently appeals to Gökalp's poetry, in which he finds a justification for a strong elite leadership, "glaring patriotism," and "hatred against the West." Therefore, when Heyd says that Gökalp can claim to have laid the spiritual foundations for the

Kemalist regime, he makes a point about the nationalism of the regime, not its posture with regard to Islam.[17]

Finally, Heyd's critique of the political vision that he sees in Gökalp slides rapidly and frequently into a critique of what he sees as Gökalp's irrationalism (which can only be assumed if Gökalp is a proto-totalitarian thinker). One cannot turn the pages of Heyd's analysis without seeing Gökalp as essentially a "sloppy" thinker. Heyd uses the following language to characterize Gökalp's thinking: "emotional and biased," "subjective," "unscientific," "naive," "extreme," "exaggerating," "vague," "contradictory," "inexperienced," "unreliable," and perpetually inconsistent. By highlighting Heyd's critical frame, I am not denying either that some of these critical judgments may be deserved or that they made sense to Heyd (and others) in the immediate aftermath of the Second World War. But overall Heyd does not seem to think that Gökalp's thinking and standards might be different, and possibly coherent, both on their own terms and relative to the standards that Heyd himself employs. This is a highly anti-interpretive posture, especially when one has excluded from consideration numerous texts that might evidence more coherence than appears at first sight. To Heyd, Gökalp's ideas are nothing but an "old mentality in European dress."[18]

The more hermeneutically sensitive study of the two, Parla's interpretation rescues Gökalp from Heyd's noninterpretive account by showing the coherent solidarist-corporatist identity of Gökalp's nationalist thought. Significantly, only after Parla reconstructs this aspect of Gökalp's thinking does he subject it to a critique from a Marxian perspective. Parla criticizes Gökalp's view that capitalism could be the economic foundation for a democratic society. But in this sense Gökalp is more a foil to criticize the basic corporatist ideological center of Turkish politics than the single object of Parla's critique. Parla's hermeneutic approach illustrates his respect for Gökalp's intellectual integrity even if he disagrees with a core component of his system. Unlike Heyd, he views Gökalp's thought as "realistic," "well-considered," internally consistent, and eminently rational. "In fact," writes Parla, "the respect for theoretical reason over practical action starts and ends with Gökalp in Turkey in the twentieth century . . . [where] the Kemalist maxim 'doctrine follows action' has pervaded political life and academia alike."[19]

To be fair, Heyd's dilemma was that he believed he was interpreting Mussolini. In the texts that he analyzed, he saw himself as face-to-face with twentieth-century chauvinistic irrationalism. The problem, however, is that he did not push his inquiry of Gökalp's conceptual context where it needed to be pushed—namely, and deeply, into his theoretical writings. The identity and significance of Gökalp's views on nationalism cannot be understood adequately apart from his theoretical writings.

In this respect, Parla's analysis is superior to Heyd's, and, on the whole, correct. Where Parla's interpretation falls short, for my purposes, is in not seeing aspects of Gökalp's political theory within the frame of secularization where I think they must be seen in order to fully appreciate them. Parla situates Gökalp in the ideological skeleton of corporatist capitalism and, as such, illuminates more about the identity of Gökalp's thinking than any previous interpreter. There is, however, still more to say within the specific problematic of secularization.

INTERPRETING GÖKALP ON THE QUESTION
OF RELIGION IN MODERNITY

In addition to Heyd's and Parla's attempts at explicating Gökalp's thought, several other major contributors to the social science literature on Turkish politics have discussed Gökalp's ideas and their significance for the laicist politics of the republic. These are Masami Arai, Niyazi Berkes, and C. H. Dodd. In this body of commentary, four accounts of Gökalp's understanding of religion in modernity can be espied. All of these accounts indicate that Gökalp sought to synthesize Islam and modernity. In this broadly shared understanding, several aspects of Gökalp's thought and practice form common reference points.

The first is Gökalp's rejection of the dominant Islamic jurisprudential view that the sources of Islamic law (*şeriat*) should be found solely in divine revelation. Gökalp believed that the *nas,* comprised of the Koran and Sunna (the "sayings" and "doings" of the Prophet), were inadequate on their own as sources of legal judgment in Islamic law. He argued that the *örf,* or mores of different Islamic societies, should also be considered sources of law. Conduct, opinion, customs, traditions, and collective judgments should be a kind of social *şeriat.* While the *nas* derived from the "absolutes" of the religion—a shared text and understanding of the significance of the Prophet—and could never be subject to change, the *örf* derived from the ever-changing and variable circumstances of different Islamic communities. In his arguments on these matters, Gökalp consistently appeals to several Islamic jurists to justify this view, and he argues that this view sufficiently accounts for the historical experience of Islam in different settings.[20]

Gökalp thus saw within both the theory and the practice of Islam an inherent ability to accommodate changing contexts. If it had lost this ability, it was due to misunderstanding and to its exploitation by political regimes. Gökalp's position is consistent with the tradition that is known as Islamic reformism. Following these premises to one of their conclusions, he even advocated interpreting the *nas* through the lens of the *örf.* The mores of society could be a basis for applying the divine revelation.

The second common point of reference is Gökalp's belief that the full separation of religion and politics, or complete disestablishment of religion, is a fundamental legal requirement for modern states. This view is evident in many of Gökalp's writings, but it is well stated in his summary of the democratic legal goals of Turkish nationalism in "The Program of Turkism" (1923):

> The aim of Turkism in law is to establish modern (*asrî*) law in Turkey. The most fundamental condition for our success in joining the ranks of modern nations is the complete cleansing of all branches of our legal structure of all traces of theocracy and clericalism.
>
> Theocracy is the system in which laws are made by Caliphs and Sultans who are regarded as the Shadows of God on earth. Clericalism refers to the acceptance of traditions, claimed to be originally instituted by God, as unchangeable laws and of the belief that these laws can be interpreted by spiritual authorities, believed to be the interpreters of God.
>
> The state that is completely freed from these two characteristics of the medieval state is called the modern state. In the first place, in a modern state the right to legislate and to administer directly belongs to the people. No office, no tradition, and no other right can restrict and limit this right. In the second place, in a modern state all members of a nation are regarded as equal to each other in every respect. No special privilege is recognized for any individual, or family, or class. States that fulfill these conditions are democratic; that is, they are governed by the people. The first aim of Turkism in law is to create a modern state . . . *all traces of theocracy and clericalism should be completely eliminated.* [emphasis added][21]

A third point of reference, related to the second, is Gökalp's role as an advocate of several institutional reforms that were carried out by the Young Turks. Gökalp is said to have authored a memo that spelled out reforms that were eventually undertaken by the leadership. While there is little doubt that he supported these reforms, his sole authorship of the memo remains in question. The reforms included the elimination of the highest Islamic official in the Ottoman Empire, the *Şeyh-ül-İslâm,* from the Ottoman cabinet; the transfer of the religious courts to the jurisdiction of the Ministry of Justice; and the transfer of the administrations of the *medrese* schools (part of the religiously authorized educational institutions) to the jurisdiction of the Ministry of Education. These were early movements in the Turkish nationalist process of subordinating religious institutions and officials to lay control.[22]

Gökalp also advocated ending the independent financial and political authority of the Islamic foundations (*evkaf*) that he considered to be a "state within a state." At the same time, however, he supported the continuation of a network of religious institutions that would function autonomously from politics to provide a common institutional base for all Muslims.

Finally, all of his interpreters commonly refer to Gökalp's view that the character of modern civilization was increasingly becoming nonreligious (*Ladini*). He saw the acceptance of Japan and Turkey within the orbit of modern civilization as proof. With these common reference points in mind, we may now examine the four accounts of Gökalp's understanding of religion in modernity in the literature. First, although Gökalp tried to achieve a synthesis between Turkish nationalism, Islam, and modernity that gave equal weight to each, he failed. The first (nationalism) and third (modernity) categories were much more significant to him than the second (Islam), which is the weakest element in the system. His interest in Islamic reform, for example, was weaker than his interest in fostering the development of a modern Turkish nationalism. There are two articulators of this thesis in the literature: Uriel Heyd and Niyazi Berkes (although Berkes has explicitly disagreed with aspects of Heyd's interpretation). Both Heyd and Berkes argue that Gökalp diminished the value of Islam even as he attempted to maintain it in the trinity of Turkification, Islamization, and modernization. This interpretation further situates Gökalp in the history of twentieth-century Turkish secular thought. Because his interest in Islam is seen as the weaker part of his system, he is seen as a forerunner of Kemalism's "more complete secularism" that was even less interested in synthesizing Turkish nationalism and Islam.[23]

Heyd's analysis exhibits the methodological problems discussed above; still, he makes several serious claims about Gökalp's understanding of Islam in modernity. These claims are situated in the conceptual frame of what Heyd takes to be Gökalp's central aim—the deification of the nation. Thus Heyd argues that Gökalp's attempt to distinguish nation and religion by suggesting that religion was part of national culture was meant to "diminish Islam as a cultural factor" (in favor of the nation), something he "did not admit" for political and strategic reasons. Because Gökalp hoped for the nation's ideals to be superior to all other ideals, Islam assumed a less significant place in the system of Gökalp's thought.[24]

As with the rest of his analysis, some of Heyd's claims are only criticisms of the conclusions that he believed Gökalp had reached regarding religion's place in modern Turkish nationalism. Heyd both discounts Gökalp's argument that Islam is no longer (that is, in modernity) properly considered to be the civilization of the Turks, and suggests that Gökalp's argument lacks substance.

> In Gökalp's synthesis of Turkish culture and Western civilization there is no proper place for Islam as a third element. As far as Islam belongs to the sphere of civilization it has to be superseded by modern European values. . . . Although Gökalp is at a loss to find the roots of Islam in Turkish national traditions, he does not suggest the development of a specifically Turkish Islam. His "religious Turkism" is one of the weakest points in his programme for the cultural revival of his nation, consisting merely of the demand to introduce the Turkish language into the religious service. It is significant that Gökalp never tries to expound his concept of Islam as a purely ethical religion. For him, it is only important to state what Islam does *not* imply any more, and what has to be eliminated because of its incompatibility with the major factors of Turkish culture and Western civilization. . . . Gökalp's system does not allow religion any separate existence.[25]

It is not clear that Gökalp sought the "roots of Islam in Turkish national tradition," or that his advocacy of Islam as an ideal "consisted merely of the demand to introduce the Turkish language into the religious service," or that he never tried to expound on his view of "Islam as a purely ethical religion," or that "it is only important to state what Islam does *not* imply any more."

Compared to his treatment of Gökalp's attempt to reconcile Islam, Turkism, and modernity, however, Heyd's analysis of Gökalp's advocacy for the separation between religion and politics is much more compelling. Heyd describes Gökalp's insistence that religion and state must be separate in the modern state. What is interesting is that Heyd sees this separation fulfilled in the policies that were undertaken by Atatürk to abolish the Caliphate (1924), to eliminate from the constitution the statement that Islam is the religion of the state (1928), and to declare the state "secular" in the constitution of 1937. As a result of these changes, Heyd suggests the "separation of religion and state was complete": Turkey "has become an entirely secular state."[26]

As I discuss in the next chapter, this is a complex claim. It is not clear if the state and religion were separated in Turkey, or, if they were, if they were separated in the structural sense that Gökalp believed was necessary. The collective judgment of most scholars is that the state was never structurally separated from religion in Turkey, even if many (including outside observers like Heyd) believed this to be true (see the "control account" below for a full discussion). In other words, Heyd's claim that the policies following Gökalp's death were fully consistent with Gökalp's thinking about the need to separate religion and state may not be true because Turkish political elites never achieved it, but not because Gökalp did not advocate it.

But there is another point that I think Heyd makes, that Berkes also agrees with. This is that Gökalp would have approved of the specific form that laicist politics took in Turkey even though aspects of his articulated political vision were at odds with some laicist practices. Gökalp's thinking is understood to have provided an intellectual basis for the Kemalist "revolution"; where his ideas suffered, they did so from not being enough like the ideas of Kemalism that eliminated Islam from the ideological core of Turkish nationalism, because Islam was, from Heyd's view, the weakest element in Gökalp's trinity. As the weakest part of his system, Islam is something that Gökalp should have been able to part from. This is clearly Berkes's view:

> [Gökalp's] ideas with regard to the particulars of Islamic reform suffered most during the ensuing period of drastic secularism. However, I believe that if he had lived longer he would have been able to reconcile himself to the Atatürk policy because his ideas on the caliphacy were already at variance with the logical consequences of his Westernist nationalism, being rather fanciful utopias designed to lay a basis of internationalism to Turkish nationalism. Furthermore, we know that the constitutional clauses on secularism and the freedom of conscience and thinking were from his pen as he was a member of the committee which prepared the new constitution in 1924.[27]

This first account raises two questions: first, was Islam the weakest part of Gökalp's trinity of ideals? Second, how does his understanding of the place and significance of Islam relate to the laicist politics that succeeded him? By "weakest," I mean that Gökalp's emphasis on Islam was *not enough* relative to his emphasis on Turkism or modernism; the Islamic component could ultimately be jettisoned.

The second understanding of the relation of Islam, Turkish nationalism, and modernity in Gökalp's thought that is found in the political science literature is expressed by C. H. Dodd in his short but intelligent overview of Gökalp's thinking in his 1979 book, *Democracy and Development in Turkey.* In contrast to the previous interpretations, Dodd reads Gökalp's emphasis on Islam in his trinity as too strong. This claim is closely related to the first account, but differs in one important way. Rather than reading Gökalp's understanding of Islam as something that he could have abandoned without altering his primary goals, Dodd sees the Islamic component as overemphasized. As such it remains less secular than the understandings of those who implemented laicism, but for a different reason. To Dodd, Gökalp assigned too much room for religion in his vision of the modern state.

The problem was, as Dodd sees it, that Gökalp wanted to limit religion to private conscience (as distinct from "temporal or social" relevance) even though he "found its vitality" in society. Thus while trying to distinguish national identity (based on language and culture) from religious identity, he never fully separated them. The result was a nationalism that was too connected to religion. Dodd refers to Gökalp's inability to separate the two as the "snag in Gökalp's thinking." "He equated society with nation and insisted in language as the necessary route to the national soul. This created a dislocation between religion and nation, at least between Islam, with its waning Arab connection, and Turkism. Gökalp appeared to believe that he had limited religion to a spiritual dimension but in fact he found its vitality in a notion of society he could not square with his concept of a nation. To this day Islam fits warily and unsatisfactorily in the Turkish national context, if at all." Dodd's analysis is thus distinct from those of Heyd and Berkes, who suggest that the emphasis was less pronounced.[28]

But similar to Heyd and Berkes, Dodd believes that Gökalp's understanding of the place of Islam in modern Turkish nationalism was less secular than that offered by Kemalism.

> [His] concern for religion was rather too great for the many Westernists found in the Atatürkist regime. They did not wish to find a place for the Caliphate or for the education in religious ideals which Gökalp advocated, and they were prepared to go to the West for more than just the civilization Gökalp found there.
>
> Atatürkist official ideology proclaimed Turkey to be republican, nationalist, secularist, statist, populist, and reformist. Its nationalism abandoned the Pan-Turk, or Turanian ideals which strongly colored Gökalp's nationalism for a long period of time, *and it also became more secular.* [emphasis added][29]

The upshot of the final claim is important, as well as its resemblance to the first account of the significance of Gökalp's political thought relative to laicist politics in Turkey. In both accounts, Gökalp's understanding of the place of religion in modern Turkish culture and politics is viewed as less secular than that of the Kemalists who followed him and created, as Heyd termed it, an "entirely secular" Turkey. The difference is that while the first account couples this claim with a critique of Gökalp's thinking on Islam as his weakest element, the second joins it with an evaluation that Gökalp's thinking was too religious.

In this regard, note that in Dodd's comments quoted above, the first paragraph describes the Kemalist view of Gökalp's understanding of religion. The second paragraph describes Dodd's interpretation of the Turkish state after Gökalp. Thus, both Heyd and Dodd seem to agree that the place that Gökalp gave religion in modern Turkish social and political life was less secular than the place that the Kemalists gave it.

Like Dodd, Masami Arai, who offers a third perspective, suggests that the Islamic component of Gökalp's thought was a strong component of his nationalism. Unlike Dodd and the others, however, Arai does not suggest that Gökalp's thinking in this regard is properly situated in the frame of secularization. To the contrary, after a historical analysis of the journal *İslâm Mecmuası* in which Gökalp published his most important essays on Islam, Arai claims that Gökalp and his colleagues were not interested in secularization at all. Their primary interest was in Islamization in the frame of a modern, reformist Islam.

Despite the fact that Arai's analysis is limited to Gökalp's works before 1919, it is an important one. The reason for this is that Arai is, for the most part, interpreting the same arguments as the others above, including Gökalp's argument on Islamic reform. The important exceptions to this overlap are Gökalp's positions on matters brought to the fore by Kemalist laicism (for example, Gökalp's position on the Caliphate). But this should not be seen to weaken Arai's point because Arai intends his claims about the identity of Turkish nationalists in this period to challenge accounts of the kind that I have reviewed thus far. His claim is that Gökalp's thinking on Islam cannot be subsumed entirely in the secularization currents of Turkish national thought. He writes, "Contrary to the received wisdom, Turkish nationalists did not necessarily pursue secularization or Westernization; they were rather in favor of Islamization and modernization. They searched for a means of regaining the original truth of Islam, and a way of modernization other than Westernization."[30]

The bulk of evidence that Arai marshalls for this claim comes from his analysis of *İslâm Mecmuası,* to which Gökalp contributed seventeen articles. The journal was published in sixty-three issues between 1914 and 1916. Out of twenty-eight contributors, Gökalp was the sixth most prolific. The journal was established by the Central Committee of Union and Progress (*İttihat ve Terakki Cemiyeti*), the main political organization of the Young Turks, to show that "nationalism was not contrary to Islam." The issue originated as a debate in *Türk Yurdu,* considered the "most prominent and influential nationalist periodical in the Young Turk era." *İslâm Mecmuası* was established to focus on Young Turk support for Islamic reform. "Its watchword was 'Life with Religion, Religion with Life.'" Arai believes that "this leads to the assumption that the periodical's aim was not secularization, but the revitalization of Islam."[31]

When his claim about the identity of Turkish nationalist thought in general is applied this specifically, it is difficult to contest. Contributors to *İslâm Mecmuası* believed that a period of degeneracy had begun in the world of Islam. And they believed that the way to forestall this process was to counteract all of the causes for decline. This meant that western civilization, invading from all directions, should be criticized for its excesses, not adopted in full; more importantly, it meant that the autocratic and superstitious Islamic tradition should be reformed by a return to Islam's original truths. To this end, the editors argued that the gates to *ijtihad*—the authority to interpret the şeriat—should be opened. More importance should be placed on changing social conditions ("the advocate of this view was, needless to say, Ziya Gökalp"). Finally, the emancipation of women should be undertaken in accordance, they argued, with the original truths of Islam. To overcome what they saw as Islam's "backwardness," the editors of *İslâm Mecmuası* published a translation of the Koran to make the truth more accessible to the people of the Turkish nation.[32]

Arai wants to go farther than simply suggesting that *İslâm Mecmuası* was an Islamist journal. He believes that the commitment expressed in this journal captured the thought of these nationalists on the significance of Islam in Turkish national identity. Quoting from his study at length will help us to appreciate the contrast between Arai's interpretation and those that I have already discussed. In the concluding section of the chapter on *İslâm Mecmuası*, entitled "Modernization and Islamization," Arai places Gökalp at the center of attention:

> As is well known, the CUP government accomplished, on the advice of Ziya Gökalp, many reforms of secularization, which can be regarded as forerunners of those by Atatürk. In 1913, *ulema*s and their religious courts came under State control, they were forced to admit the authority of the secular appeals court. The Ministry of Justice began to supervise over religious courts and their employees. Then, the State began to interfere in religious education: a State-operated *medrese* was set up in Istanbul and even a state examination was given; *medreses* came under the control of the Ministry of Education, which sent directors to *medreses* to effect reforms in the curriculum and teaching staff. A Council of *Şeyhs* was organized to supervise all the dervish monasteries and lodges.
>
> These reforms are of the kind normally associated with secularization. However, articles included in *İslâm Mecmuası*, whose leaders were closely connected with

the CUP, saw these reforms as religiously motivated. As we have seen, the leaders asserted with emphasis that the original truth could be regained if alien elements and superstitions could be removed; Islam could thereby restore the clarity it enjoyed in Prophet's days. One of the means of so doing was to establish the "social base of the Law," since change and social evolution were, according to them, a manifestation of the will of Allah. It is worth mentioning that many of these works were entrusted to *ulema*s. They were responsible, according to *İslâm Mecmuası,* for the degeneration of Islam; at the same time, however, they were expected to rescue it. The Young Turks' policy of interfering in religion, establishing State-controlled *medrese*s, for example, can be regarded as a measure of revitalizing Islam, a means of substituting superstition with true religion. That is, *according to them, the policy was not that of secularization but that of Islamization.* [emphasis added]

This hypothesis is valid for the issue of emancipation of women too. As is well known, in the Young Turk era, reforms in education and law, and the codification of a family law in particular, led women to gaining a foothold in society. . . . In *İslâm Mecmuası,* however, the emancipation of women was asserted in terms of original Islamic truth; it could therefore only proceed as far as Muslims could allow. If one supposes that such reforms aimed at westernization, they certainly seem insufficient and half-hearted. They did not aim at westernization, however. They could discern the nature of western civilization while learning many things from the West. They were not so superficial as to insist—and rest content—that Islam was a basis of western civilization. The leaders of *İslâm Mecmuası* perceived the violent and religiously fanatical aspect of western civilization. Christian barbarism and fanaticism were victimizing many Muslims every year under the slogan, "Civilizing savageness." *İslâm Mecmuası* consequently criticized superficial westernization, or a mania for western ways. Their position was, needless to say, very delicate since they knew well that they had to learn many things from the West; Ağaoğlu Ahmet felicitously expressed their position as follows: Oriental ignorance, western injustice (*Şarkın cehaleti, Garbın da adaletsizliği*). They might pursue a way of modernization other than westernization. At the very least, one must interpret Ziya Gökalp's idea of "Turkification, Islamization, Modernization" in such an ambivalent context.[33]

Arai makes two claims that need to be considered. The first is that Gökalp's ideas lent support to the policy of state "interference and control" with religion (as part of his insistence on the separation of state and religion); the second is that this policy was not seen as secularization but as Islamization.[34]

The upshot of the first three interpretations reviewed here is that either Gökalp's thinking was not secular enough or that it was not secular at all. There is a fourth understanding in the literature that suggests that Gökalp's views on the significance of religion in modernity were something else altogether. This view is found in Taha Parla's book, which characterizes Gökalp as a secular thinker.

I have already noted that I find Parla's interpretation compelling, and also that I find it inadequate for the secularization problematic. Recall that Parla's primary goals were to resituate Gökalp in the appropriate ideological context of solidaristic corporatism, to rescue him from distortion, and to subject Gökalp, and by consequence the entire tradition of corporatist-capitalist thinking in Turkey, to a Marxian critique. Parla's evaluation of Gökalp's secularism must be seen within this context. For although Parla says that Gökalp's thought is far more secular than religious, he does not discuss the issue in any detail.[35]

The reason that Parla considers Gökalp's thinking to be more secular than religious is twofold. First, Parla sees the social function of Islam as a national, corporative subunit to be Gökalp's primary interest in Islam. Parla writes that the "social function of Islam, not its theology, interested Gökalp." Presumably a less secular thinker would be interested in the theology of Islam rather than its functions. Second, Gökalp's thought was more secular than not because he upheld the need for all cultural institutions, religion among them, to be separate from politics.[36]

Despite Parla's emphasis on a secular element in Gökalp's thought, there is one way that his analysis bears resemblance to the accounts of Heyd and Berkes, which view Islam as the weakest element in Gökalp's system. Parla intimates that another reason that Gökalp's thinking is secular is that Gökalp's interest in reorganizing the spiritual institutions of Islamic authority waned over time. After discussing Gökalp's Islamic advocacy of the Unionist reforms, Parla writes:

> Under Unionist rule, Gökalp expressed his anti-monarchical feelings in poems and endorsed the abolition of the Sultanate and its separation from the Caliphate in 1922 in the opening years of Kemalist rule. Nor did he object to the abolition of the Caliphate in March 1924, shortly before his death. Much, however, has been made of Gökalp's lack of explicit condemnation of the institutions of the Caliphate. His critics used this as evidence for his religious communitarianism (*ümmetçilik*) and thus for his alleged opposition to the nationalism (*milliyetçilik*) of the Kemalists as the driving principle of social and political organization. What led to such allegations, however incompatible with the universal acceptance of his credentials as the father of modern Turkish nationalism, was the position and organization Gökalp tried to give to religion as a moral and cultural institution. He envisioned a religious organization on the national scale ranging from local mosques (*mescids*) headed by *imams* to large mosques (*cami-i kebirs*) in towns headed by *müftüs*, to a national office of head *müftüs* as the highest religious authority. The *head-müftü* of all Islamic

nations would select a caliph as the head of the entire Islamic community of nations. Such a religious organization, which resembled the Roman Catholic Church, did not, however, in any way intersect with the secular political institutions of the nation. With its conferences and congresses, such as "ethical corporation" represented solely a spiritual authority. At any rate, this idea was not among the central tenets of Gökalp's system, for *his writings on the subject consisted of a few articles only, dating back to his second phase and progressively losing their strength.* [emphasis added][37]

The idea that Gökalp's concern for the independent spiritual institutions lost its strength over time resembles the view that the Islamic component of his system was the weakest element. A question to consider is whether the weight that Gökalp gave the idea of institutional organization of the Islamic *ümmet* can be separated from the "position he tried to give to religion as a moral and cultural institution." Parla suggests that the latter was an idea that faded.

But the big question regarding Gökalp's understanding of the place of religion in modernity remains. I believe that the truth lies between the existing views. This can be seen even by limiting our scope to Gökalp's writings during the period that Arai uses to illustrate Gökalp's interest in Islamization. There is a consistency in Gökalp's major judgments about these issues. To be sure, his thought changes as it develops. But the central issues related to Islam in modernity remain relatively consistent from 1911 through 1924. I focus here on the writings before 1919 (concurrent with Arai's time frame). I use the footnotes to show continuities and I explain any important developments in Gökalp's thinking on these matters where discontinuities exist.

AN ALTERNATIVE ACCOUNT

The key to grasping Gökalp's thinking on religion in modern Turkish life is in understanding how fundamentally the secularization problematic shaped his framework. Before describing the significance of religion in modern life for Gökalp, one must understand this as a central element of his overall sociological base. One must also understand that this is situated in the conceptual schema of internationality/civilization and nationality/culture. Arriving at an adequate understanding of Gökalp's understanding of religion and its significance in life requires seeing the overall frame of his social and political thought.

Gökalp was a student of French sociology, and was highly influenced by the thinking of Emile Durkheim. Like Durkheim and the sociological school of structural functionalism, Gökalp believed that all societies evolve from primitive societies that are based on mechanical solidarity to organic societies that are based on social solidarity and an advanced division of labor. Following this logic, Gökalp argued that the morphological, demographic, political, economic, and industrial changes of the contemporary age were bringing about increased structural and functional differentiation in the world at two levels of human organization. The first was in culture-nations (Durkheim's term for societies) where the advanced division of labor was creating an occupational group structure in which individuals were incorporated. In the most highly developed societies, these occupational groups (for example, family, professional) would function independently yet reciprocally to effect harmony in society. The second level was that of civilization, which Gökalp saw as the supranational grouping to which different nations belonged and in which they related.[38]

Gökalp also followed Durkheim in believing that the real engines of history were ideas, or what Durkheim called collective representations. Each group in the differentiated structures of the modern world—from the family to the civilization—is manifested in its ideals. These ideals are conditioned ("dependent upon certain social causes for their rise, growth, decline, and disappearance") by changes in the constantly evolving social structures.[39]

Betraying his positivist-idealism, Gökalp maintained that both the processes that are associated with social-structural evolution and the ideals that developed in those processes were amenable to scientific study. Indeed, this is the fundamental premise that underlies all of Gökalp's social and political judgments. He approached the sociological objectives of explanation and prescription with relentless attention to the social-structural and idealistic possibilities contained in contemporary civilization. He estimated that an objective reading of the conditions under which the Turks found themselves—as Turkey continued to transform from a multinational empire to a culturally independent nation-state—made possible an articulation of the ideals that were expressed in those conditions. Moreover, he believed that Turkey's national sociologists ought to combine a thoroughly positivist study of the objective conditions of social reality (including an explanation of factors accelerating or retarding growth) with a prescription for a conceptual apparatus for living in them. It was the national sociologists' duty to "discover the elements of national conscience in the unconscious level and to bring them up to the conscious level" and thus best adapt culture to its place in civilization. Gökalp believed that he had fulfilled his duty by identifying the objectively realistic path for Turkey, one that accounted for the various and constantly evolving structural and ideational transformations and the needs of the Turks.[40]

Gökalp's interpretation of the social-structural conditions of life was that three collective representations or ideals were necessary for Turkey to negotiate its way through this period of change: Turkism, Islamism, and modernism. These collective representations or ideals, Gökalp believed, were the ones most suited to the Turkish nation under the conditions that it faced in the teens and early twenties. According to his interpretation, the two major sociological phenomena setting the context for these ideals were: (1) the differentiation of multiethnic, multilinguistic, and religiously legitimated empires caused by the intensification of nationalism and (2) the eclipse of religious-based internationalism by a new internationalism that was founded on modern science.

Gökalp did not need to argue the first point. It was readily apparent to him and to his Turkist colleagues that nationalism had undercut the coherence of Ottoman multinationalism and cosmopolitanism. Nationalism had become a primary (though not the only) collective representation of the time: "Today the West as well as the East shows unmistakably that our age is the Age of Nations. The most powerful force over the mind of this age is the ideal of nationalism." By nation, Gökalp meant a homogeneous linguistic and cultural grouping "composed of institutions in harmony with each other." He explicitly rejected racial, ethnic, and religious criteria as the determinants for national identity, arguing frequently and forcefully that national identity is determined by socialization, not blood, ancestry, or religious belief.[41]

The rise of nationalism is related to the eclipse of religious universalism. To understand how Gökalp saw this, we must first examine his concepts of culture and civilization.[42]

Culture is the "complex of rules of language, politics, religion, morality, aesthetics, law and economy, which exists on an unconscious level in the life of the nation." The sense of rule is not strong here; when compared to other expressions of the meaning of culture, it is better understood as "ethos"; "accepted norms" regarding "belief, moral duty, aesthetics, and ideals"; or even "tastes and manners." These are "unique to each nation." If there are similarities among nations, they exist either because the nations belong to the same social type (and are consequently evolving similarly) or because one of the nations is "copying," a phenomenon that Gökalp warned against if cultural integrity is to be preserved.[43]

Indeed, because culture and nation are related concepts, Gökalp considered the preservation of Turkish national culture within modernization as one of his primary normative concerns. Culture has its own dynamic that makes a nation what it is, and this dynamic should be preserved rather than undercut as modernization takes place. "The culture of a nation is not something to be imposed or instituted." It is transmitted in the culture's living institutions, especially in education. Those things national constitute interlocking systems—religious, moral, legal, aesthetic, linguistic, economic, and technical.[44]

It is impossible, however, to understand fully Gökalp's understanding of culture apart from its twin concept, civilization. Gökalp always discussed these concepts together, and he strongly claimed that the two concepts must be understood in their relation: "One can understand the significance of civilization to the extent to which he grasps culture."[45]

A civilization group encompasses culture groups to which the latter belong. "A civilizational group is a society above societies, made up of culture groups or nations." It is the "whole that is common to various nations," which share and transmit civilizational commonalities. These commonalities comprise those things that are international and common (or "shared"). The existence of civilization "indicates that nations do not live in isolation, that they are parts of larger groups."[46]

Thus, during a period of nationalism, culture and civilization provide two reference points for each member of civilization, two related groupings to which all individuals belong. In this way, a cultural consciousness is wed to a civilizational consciousness: "As civilization consists of the sum total of the common features of several national cultures, each national culture would naturally distinguish itself from others, and then seek the international features it has in common with other cultures." Or, in the terminology of parts-whole relations, "A nation considers modern civilization a whole and itself a unit of it."[47]

Now, for Gökalp, just as the nature of culture in our time is primarily determined by the rise of nationalism as a historical phenomenon among collectivities, civilization too has been undergoing a historic, substantive transformation. He maintained that to understand the relation between culture and civilization, one must understand the historical tendencies represented by civilization. As did many others of his time, Gökalp argued that the commonality that modern nations shared was increasingly based on modern science. Modern civilization is the "product of the positive sciences, their methods and techniques." As such, "scientific truths, hygienic and economic rules, practical arts pertaining to public works, techniques of commerce and agriculture" are the new commonalities shared by diverse nations in modernity. They are the most encompassing truths to which nations with different cultures, languages, and even religions are aspiring.[48]

Gökalp's understanding of modernity can be understood only in the context of the new character of civilization. On this point Gökalp was very explicit: being modern meant becoming scientifically equal to the most scientifically and technically advanced nations of modern civilization. He considered these to be the nations of Europe, whose cultures, like all other cultures, needed to be distinguished from the civilization groups to which they belonged. "The ideal of modernity necessitates only the acceptance of the theoretical and practical sciences and techniques from Europe."[49]

Gökalp emphasized this point. Modern civilization meant the civilization common to the nations or cultures of Europe (the West), but in no way was it reducible to their cultures. Gökalp could distinguish between the two because, as a positivist sociologist, he believed that the concepts of civilization were objective relative to the concepts that constituted the national ethos. The objective nature of modern scientific knowledge made it independent of cultural specifics, sharable across societies, and—when integrated properly into those societies—beneficial to the integrity of specific cultures. He believed that modern science constituted not simply a new or different rationality, but rather a "true internationality." Its truth was evident both in the practical value of its technological fruits and in contrast to the historically antecedent ideal of religious-based internationality. He wrote in 1913: "A true internationality based on science is taking the place of the internationality based on religion."[50]

Gökalp was thinking of what he believed to be a major trend underlying the process of social evolution occurring in the Turkey of his time. In particular, he evaluated the development of social evolution from the mid-nineteenth century when Ottoman bureaucrats undertook the *Tanzimat* reforms that were aimed at reordering (to many, "modernizing") the military and bureaucratic structure of the empire. By Gökalp's time, these reforms had given life to modern institutions and ideas across many different social and political spheres in Turkey. They had also given life to the ideal of modernization (*muasırlaşma*) among the nationalist elite. Thus, Gökalp did not simply advocate a turn to the West. He thought that the social structural changes around the world—created in part by growing economic interdependence and scientific exchange—were creating the basis for a new, effective collective ideal. This ideal was the "concepts and techniques of modern science." Just as groups at the cultural level were organizing around new, national identities, different nations and different religious peoples around the world were commonly acting on the basis of a new, and now "true," internationality.

As evidence for this development, he pointed to the "participation of Japan, on the one hand, and Turkey, on the other, in Western civilization." He also cited the rise of the "separate" and "autonomous" disciplines of ethics, law, and philosophy as evidence for their departure from religion. And he observed that religious education was suffering from a decreasing lack of interest, while interest in the positive sciences increasingly strengthened. Such phenomena confirmed, from Gökalp's view, that "the area of *ümmet* is differentiating itself from the area of internationality increasingly." In this process, different peoples were looking beyond their own culture to learn new things from what also turned out to be a new civilization. The term that he used to describe this new internationality was "*la-dini,*" a French-derived term meaning nonreligious.[51]

The conceptual frame described thus far is the starting point for understanding Gökalp's evaluation of the dynamic present among nationalism, modern science, and religion under contemporary conditions caused by social evolution. In the language of the secularization problematic, Gökalp saw national identity replacing multinationalism as the hegemonic ideal at the level of culture, and science replacing religion as the hegemonic ideal at the level of civilization. It is important to note in this context that the Ottoman-Turkish concept for nation, *millet,* had previously indicated one's religious-community affiliation in Ottoman social and political life, meaning that Ottoman multinationalism was founded on the plurality of religious identities. If one were asked to what millet he or she belonged, one would say Muslim, Christian, or Jew (and so on). After the rise of nationalism, the Turkists would have another answer: "I am a Turk." The rise of nationalism marked a moment when community identities would be more than only religious. "Nation," like "internationality," was becoming differentiated. Thus, the secularization problematic is Gökalp's unmistakable starting point.

Gökalp believed that his concepts and conclusions should be taken as a professional social scientist's contribution to the development of the nation, and he sought tirelessly to challenge the conclusions of others that were based on unscientific grounds. In an essay published shortly after he made his claims regarding the new "true internationalism," for instance, Gökalp criticized the "formalism" of both radicalism and conservatism—forever appealing, he added, to "we Turks." He wrote that "neither attempts to question the origin and growth of the old or the new, or the way in which norms adapt themselves to different environments at different times. Both believe that the rule, or convention, is something above time and space, that it exists by itself . . . as a fixed and inflexible entity . . . a lifeless skeleton." In contrast, Gökalp believed that serious sustained research was needed for "tracing the historical continuity of our Turkish and Islamic traditions, and . . . the origins of the advancements which characterize our age."[52]

In this article, he characterized the living cultural institutions of the nation as traditions, which "mean creativity and progress" as well as "continuity and harmony." He wrote, "We must, first of all, know the traditions and historical growth of the institutions peculiar to the Turks." This meant those things that were true of the Turks independent of their religious or civilizational identification: their literature, archaeology, folkways, mythology and local arts—all the things found "in the life of their words, proverbs, folk-tales, and folk-epics." "Yet," he averred, "at the same time, the Turks have to study the traditions and the history of our Islamic institutions. They have to know the history of Islamic theology, mysticism, and jurisprudence." And finally, stressing the need to think clearly (as a sociologist, as it were) about the Turk's historical evolution in the modern era, he asserted:

> When the development of these [Turkish and Islamic] institutions and the manner in which they have accommodated themselves to manifold circumstances in terms of time and space become clear, then it will be evident which elements of contemporary civilization will be adopted and how they will develop in the future. . . .
>
> As tradition requires continuity and harmony, it becomes necessary to find the connection between the pre-history of the Turk and the metaphysics of religion, and by doing so to develop an Islamic-Turkish philosophy of history. And, thirdly, it is necessary for us to study the historical development, the conditioning social circumstances, and applications of technology and science, and the methods and philosophies of our age in order to use them.[53]

The critique of formalism in conservatism and radicalism evolved into a general critique of those who failed to understand that evolution is the essence of life, and thus failed to understand the nature of the changes (both structural and ideational) underlying Turkish national identity. Again, it is important to always keep in mind that these were the conclusions that Gökalp reached as a sociologist. They were his scientific premises for the study of the ideals that were best suited for his nation. From them, he criticized equally both those who followed the old internationality and believed that Islam remained the basis for Turkish civilization, and those who followed Europeanization to its cultural roots. The former group ignored actual changes while the latter were, to him, purely imitationist vis-à-vis Europe. The ideals that they advocated did not consider fully the social-structural or ideational realities of Turkey's situation. The Turkish nation needed neither to rehabilitate "fossils" nor to imitate the latest fashions in Europe. It needed to secure the development of its own living rituals and continue to integrate itself with the new civilization that was based on modern science. The rituals included both non-Islamic (changing) national traditions as well as the (historically variable) tradition of Islam that had over time, in different forms, become part of the Turkish national identity. Gökalp's was, as we have heard from others, an attempted synthesis of what he thought were three important social processes shaping Turkey's modern identity.[54]

However, Gökalp saw that just as there were Turks who believed incorrectly that their civilization was still defined according to their Islamic religion, there were also Europeans who believed that their civilization was defined according to their Christian religion. In a passage perhaps chillingly relevant to the unconscious ideational realities of our own day, he wrote, "The Balkan wars demonstrated to us even today the European conscience is nothing but a Christian conscience." It is evident that although there are new ideals, religious internationality as a consciousness has a "lasting life"—for peoples of all nations. This was problematic because it signaled to Gökalp that the major member nations of modern civilization—the Europeans—were not able to admit the Turks into what should be thought of as a nonreligious international commonality. (They evidently saw the world in terms of a Judeo-Christian (or simply Christian)/Muslim dichotomy.) It was also problematic because it led to a rise in Islamic civilizational sentiments in Turkey, the basis of which he could not contest.[55]

> The events of our time show eloquently that there are as many internationalities and humanities as there are religions. For a European, humanity is nothing but Christendom. It is true that there are principles of justice and right, brotherhood and kindness in the West, but their application extends only as far as the boundaries of the Christian religion. And, again, it is true that there is morality, philosophy, and civilization in the West, but on all of them there is the implicit or explicit stamp of the cross. It is evident that certain things not colored by Christianity are not lacking entirely in Europe. Science, technology, and industry are universal and common to all humanity. We as Muslims, under the guidance of our own style of social life, divide European civilization into two levels, and accept the "civilization of society" because it is common.[56]

Gökalp's recognition that events such as the Balkan wars thwarted the emergence of the proper collective ideals throughout the world contributed to his view that for modern nations of different religious backgrounds to participate in a civilization that was true to the objective criteria of modern science, they must secure their deeply held national and religious ideals as well as share new ideals with others. Relating culture to civilization so that all nations, but especially scientifically subordinate and culturally different nations such as Turkey, could become parts of a shared civilization without religious ideals getting in the way became a central issue of Gökalp's thinking. More generally stated, the nature of the relation between culture and civilization in the newer social structures occupied much of Gökalp's thinking after he outlined the social-structural and ideational processes shaping his judgments. It is also one of the most complex areas of this thought. Recall that to Gökalp, there were always active tendencies inside and outside Turkey that would take Turkey away from civilization (and risk losing the opportunities of the new age) or away from culture (and risk annihilating Turkey's cultural integrity). Gökalp walked the finer line and sought a synthesis in which the commonalities that were shared by members of international civilization would be secured in a context of cultural plurality. Thus, for Gökalp, without losing the distinction, culture and civilization must be synthesized; a "serious interest in culture is absolutely requisite for the rise of a genuine interest in civilization."[57]

The language in which he expressed this synthesis is the language of "absorption." Civilization must "penetrate into the life of the people" (through education, for example) in a way that maintains the cultural ethos of that people. A nation evolves as a culture "when it puts the stamp of its own language and ethos on the institutions of international civilization and adopts [these institutions] to its own spirit." Gökalp's statements can be understood properly only within his understanding of social evolution. The substance and identity of culture and civilization are constantly "living," that is, changing in the context of social evolution. Thus, nations must learn to evolve on their own while also absorbing the elements of contemporary civilization that enable their well being. In that adoption, cultures give the concepts of civilization a culturally specific meaning. This is why he believed that a "nation does not become civilized if it has not attained cultural consciousness." Becoming part of civilization must coincide with cultural evolution.[58]

Gökalp explained this in the framework of meaning. Cultures within a civilization adopt and absorb civilizational "forms" in the national culture and thus give those aspects of civilization a unique, nationally specific cultural meaning. Gökalp wrote:

> If we take European civilization as an example, we find that among European nations there are only common words, but each one understands a different meaning by the

same word they use commonly. The word "nation," for example, has different connotations for the French and the Germans. The word "state" means different things to the British, French, and Germans. The same is true for the word "constitution" or "freedom." . . . Institutions, like language, have an aspect of form and one of meaning. Institutions common within a civilization group are common only in appearance; that is, in form. From the point of view of meaning—that is, of intimate life—each nation has its own peculiar institutions. And the sum total of such institutions of a nation constitutes a culture. . . . In short, certain concepts and institutions in words and forms, and the civilization which is the sum total of them all, may be common to several nations; but national conscience is never commonly shared.[59]

For Gökalp, this notion of national cultural specificity never slides into cultural relativity. National consciousness for Gökalp must always be interpreted in the broader differentiated frame in which meaning takes shape and that provides a commonality for all of its members. As we have already noted, he frequently was at pains to hold the two primary identities in his schema together against those who would collapse them or follow either to an extreme.

Living cultures, therefore, must adapt to modern civilization through a conscious and rational selection of the concepts, techniques, and methods of modern science. They must aim to reconcile these externally born modes with their internal cultural traditions, always seeking to preserve the integrity of the internal. Jean-Jacques Rousseau, appropriately, came to Gökalp's mind. With *Emile* apparently in mind, Gökalp asked, "Can we not apply the method of negative education—which Jean-Jacques Rousseau recommended to protect nature against civilization—in order to protect, in our case, our culture against civilization." Civilization thus comprises the "rational concepts of the nation," whose culture is always evolving. Cultural consciousness is a primary condition of all else in this scheme; it is its own protection, cultural pride the national guard.[60]

With his interest in science and in the cultural history of the Turkish nation, Gökalp devoted much of his life to education rather than activity that is normally associated with politics. Education was the forum for the dual purposive projects of acculturation and absorbing civilization. And, even in this sphere, the two processes must be combined so that their differences are appreciated. The functions of each sphere must be carefully delineated and maintained: the national ethos should be "cultivated" in one, while children must be "trained" in the concepts, methods, and techniques of modern civilization.

Cultivation was necessary for national consciousness; training to make that consciousness what it can be in modernity:

> As the educator is a representative of the nation, the trainer is the leader of modernity. As the aim of education is national cultivation, the aim of training is modernity. The professor and the teacher are both educators and instructors at the same time. Training has both educational and instructive functions. This double characteristic serves the national integration as well as modern progress.
>
> Let me, therefore, conclude my discussion in the following way: while we are not in need of Europe from the point of view of culture and education, we badly need it from the point of view of techniques and learning. Let us try to acquire everything in techniques from Europe, but let us find our culture only in our own national soul.[61]

Thus, Gökalp's understanding of the significance of culture and civilization as a conceptual frame for modernity is quintessentially secular in a specific sense. The primary meanings for human beings in their cultural-national and civilizational-international identity contexts would no longer be religious. They would be both national and international-scientific. As we shall see, Gökalp was not a secular thinker as such. He did not offer a nonreligious interpretation of life, history, and national identity. But his thought fits in and must be seen as a contribution to the secular problematic of modern political theory. His understanding of culture and civilization is an insight on living in the modern world when nationalism and science are shaping the landscape of public life that was previously dominated by religious identity, structures, and languages. In the new world, new possibilities arise and new relationships develop. People who were separated by tribal or other local identities may unite in national societies, and people of different nations have a potential commonality that they did not have before. Moreover, these similarities are constantly evolving. Gökalp expected neither traditions nor the concepts and techniques of science to remain static. It cannot be emphasized enough that these commonalities can only be understood in the context of the evolution of nonreligious collective ideals on a global scale. What Wilson calls the central concern of secularization theory is central in Gökalp's social and political thought.

The international-humanitarian consequences of this logic are developed best by Parla in his critique of Heyd and of others who have associated Gökalp with chauvinistic nationalism. Against such "distortions" of Gökalp's thought, Parla brings Gökalp's international, democratic, and egalitarian perspective to the fore. Parla is less successful in connecting Gökalp's understanding of the international commonalities to his fundamental interest in the nonreligious character of this new internationality. Gökalp's internationality must be seen in the context of the secularization problematic to appreciate fully the new basis for civilizational solidarity. To Gökalp, global dynamics had created a new basis for common identity and interaction among different nations. This is not a rote statement about the end of the theological stage of history, often found in the ideological tracts of positivism. And it is not only a functional view of religion in the frame of Gökalp's solidarist corporatism. It is, again, a point about the nature of identity and ideals in modernity. In cultures that absorb civilization (and not the reverse!), while preserving their traditions, humans develop multiple identities. Gökalp's political vision cannot be sufficiently appreciated outside of the conceptual context of secularization.[62]

Still, the question remains: where has religion gone and what is its significance? In exposing the centrality of national culture and modern civilization in Gökalp's thought, it is easy to lose sight of the significance of Islam. As discussed above, some see not much weight relative to his nationalism (e.g., Heyd); others see too much relative to his nationalism (e.g., Dodd); and others, an overwhelming amount within this nationalism (e.g., Arai).

Gökalp's answer, I think, is that religion remains central to national culture, and thus within the personal, social, and spiritual needs of human beings. Though no longer as significant as it once was at both the international and the national level, within Gökalp's description of the sociological trends, religion is a key element of national culture. It may even be the basis for common ties of a spiritual kind among coreligionists of different nations. In this way it remains an international ideal, but it is not the most encompassing one for modern Turkey. Moreover, as I discussed above, he attached a condition to all of this— religion must be separated from politics. We have now the appropriate frame in which the previous interpretations may be evaluated and in which Gökalp's understanding of the significance of religion in modernity may be understood.[63]

The place that Gökalp assigned to religion in the frame of modern Turkish identity and society resulted from two primary considerations. The first is from reasoning about the consequences of structural differentiation in national society, and the second is from considerations of Islam as an ethical ideal with lasting significance in national culture as part of Turkish cultural history. The two are related. The first generates a detailed analysis of the functional role of religion as an ideal or ethical norm in modern nations generally, and in the

Turkish nation in particular. The second led Gökalp to discussions of the intrinsic value that faith has for human beings despite its overwhelming functional role in society. The two considerations work together: Gökalp's is a rational (or, in his terms, scientific) understanding of the essential place that religious sentiments play in modern (differentiated) life and conscience.

The functional value of religion may be seen throughout Gökalp's writings. In "The Social Function of Religion" (1915), he developed the essence of this view at length. With its rituals governing human ethical conduct and defining one's relation to the absolute deity, religion performs two important functions for the nation. The first is that it "silence[s] the bestial ego" of the individual toward acquiring an "audience with [one's] deity," making individuals into social beings instead of the self-oriented egoistic creatures that they might otherwise be. The second function is that Islam as a religion serves the larger national ethos. Since Islamic practice depends on public spaces for fulfilling its positive rituals, people of the nation congregate in shared social spaces to fulfill their covenant with God. The spaces that enable religious fulfillment also work functionally to incorporate geographically dispersed groups into the national whole and to reinforce their common language and culture. National language thus becomes one of the languages of the living, national rituals of Turkish Muslims.[64]

> In short, the social function of ritual expresses itself as the renunciation of individuality, and the social function of positive ritual as the fulfillment of nationality. Religion is the most important factor in the creation of national consciousness as it unites men through common sentiments and beliefs. It is because of this that genuinely religious men are those who have national fervor, and that genuine nationalists are those who believe in the eternity of faith.[65]

In addition to the national identity, Islam as a religion helps to reinforce a common identity across nations. Islamic international identity is reinforced by the gathering at Kaba and Arafat during the pilgrimage to Mecca (*Hijra*). At the international level it reminds believers of their common ties among all Muslims, however partial those ties appear from the perspective of modern civilization.

We have already seen that Gökalp developed a social evolutionary view of the bases of Islamic law. The practices of Islam should evolve along with the culture of the Turkish nation. With respect to religion, he wrote that a "law which does not live and give life cannot be a regulator of life." In this frame he had no hesitations, for example, teaching Islam as an ideal in Turkish national education. In his essay on Islamic education, published in *İslâm Mecmuası*, he declared that the "religion of Islam is one of our [national] ideals" alongside Turkism and modernism in Turkish national education. He advocated religious education consisting in the fundamentals of the faith and ritual that he believed existed in the culture of the Turks (Koran reading, pronunciation, rhythm, catechism, Islamic history, Arabic, and Persian).[66]

The negative language of "no hesitations" does not capture Gökalp's overall positive understanding of Islam as a living institution of the Turkish national ethos. It was, after all, part of the Turkish culture for which he sought to provide a language of preservation under conditions of world historical change. "Living rituals" like the Mevlid ceremony should not be preserved simply for consistency; they should be preserved because they are part of the Turkish culture. Being a Muslim is one aspect of Turkish national identity, and it should remain so.[67]

Now, Islam should remain part of Turkish culture under two conditions: one is that its laws (social *şeriat* as distinct from the fundamentals of faith) evolve, and the second, which amounts to a condition of the first, that it—like all other cultural institutions—be independent from the formalizing powers of the state. Gökalp believed that the state tended to freeze and formalize any of the institutions of culture to which it was attached. Thus, the vitality of cultural institutions is related to the degree to which they are "independent" and "autonomous" from politics and state institutions. Gökalp believed that such independence was necessary for all cultural institutions because it corresponded to the sociological trends of structural differentiation and to the need for dynamic religious, artistic, and academic practices in the cultural lives of different nations.[68]

Looking back, Gökalp asserted that the "attachment of religion to the state in our country has not been to its advantage, but rather to the extreme detriment of religion." The consequence of this attachment was that Islam lost its vitality as a spiritual force. In an essay published in *Türk Yurdu* (before *İslâm Mecmuası* was established), Gökalp described the impact of the Ottoman undifferentiated world on religion. The themes of structural separation and religious vitality merge with Gökalp's argument for reform in Islam. He also contrasts the entire scheme with the enemies of living traditions—that is, legalization and formalization:

> The state is a legal machinery; it tends to legalize and formalize any social force upon which it touches. It is because of this fact that Islam started to lose its vitality from the moment it began to be fused with the political organization and began to be formal-

ized as a system of law closed against all *ijtihad*. The religion that the state recognizes officially today and the shari'a which it formally holds is nothing but the *fikh* (jurisprudence). But the *fikh* did not exist until one and a half centuries after the *Hijra*. Until that time religion and shari'a consisted of the Kur'an and Sunna. The state today officially recognizes only one shari'a, that of the Hanafi schools. Thus, a sect that has only a scholastic value is held prior to religion which is the main thing. The situation is different in those places where Islam is independent. As religion is understood to be a religious life in these countries, the shari'a finds its sources only in the Book and the Sunna, on the one hand, and in the social life, on the other, and is increasingly becoming a social shari'a.[69]

The point that relates the independence of religion from politics to the processes of structural differentiation cannot be underemphasized. A key element of Gökalp's thinking on religion in modern life was that those holding power in religious and political institutions must now comply with these structural realities. This is to some extent what it means to be a modern, civilized nation. "The separation between religion and state is a goal sought by all civilized nations." The religious leadership as well as the political must comply with the requirements of structural differentiation that evolution has dealt them if they want to have a living religion in a living national culture. Religion must occupy its "own sphere"; its elite must abandon their claims to politics, just as politicians should ensure the autonomy of religious practice and institutions.[70]

It is fundamental to understanding Gökalp's frame for the place of religion in association with cultural and civilizational change—or, better, the significance of Islam in Turkish national life—to see that Islam, like other religions in modernity, belonged to culture. This meant several things. One is that religion was no longer the basis for civilizational identities, even if people continued to think so. The other is that religion need not—and should not—fade into history or the private realm. Both ideological options were available to Gökalp, and he rejected them both. To him, losing one's religion or adopting the ideal of a "personal" religion were ideals that were specific to the individualist cultures of Europe, whose ethical structures and ideals he believed were unsuited to the living traditions of the Turks. Religion in Turkey should remain a corporate subunit of the national culture. In this sense, it had a continuing function as an institution of personal and "semi-public" fulfillment. Religion is not simply a private matter; it remains a primary component of Turkish national culture.

Gökalp was not so naive as to think that the process of differentiation would not alter Turkish culture, or that modernization posed no risks of cultural dissolution. "We do not claim that our old culture will remain intact once we enter European civilization. . . . the make-up of national personality, culture, civilization, and state affect each other. Therefore, the innovations to take place in our civilization and state will certainly pave the way for several changes and developments in our cultural life."[71] But it is at this point that his idealism intervened; with the right collective representations, Turks as Turks could survive and even thrive under modern conditions. This is why maintaining the conceptual distinction between culture and civilization is so crucial. Turkish culture will transform rapidly as political and economic elites increasingly and inevitably seek to adopt the sciences, concepts, and techniques of modern civilization. An examination of the deeper social-structural realities suggests that religion can survive as a corporate institution of semi-public significance. Gökalp intended to provide a conceptual frame in which the preservation of culture, which included a general category of religion *independent from politics,* could be achieved during global transformation.

Thus by placing religion in culture, Gökalp elevates (or at least stresses) the significance of religion in the larger context of its loss. Islam to him was part of Turkish identity and history—in short, of Turkish culture—that must endure in modernity. To conceptualize Islam as such does not diminish its significance, even though the frame includes a recognition that religion will never be as significant as it once was. There is no evidence in Gökalp's extensive writings on this topic that his goal was anything other than to find a secure, vital place for Islam within Turkish nationalism.

Questions of emphasis are difficult to sort out in a qualitative manner. But we have seen that the first account, which suggests that Gökalp's emphasis on Islam was weak, was founded on several claims. Among the most important are that his nationalism was overwhelmingly significant relative to his Islamism, that he was not seriously interested in developing what this Islamism entailed, and that his general orientation was westward anyway. The thrust of the first account is that Gökalp could have easily parted from the ideal of Islamism. We have also seen that the second account, which suggested that his emphasis on religion was too great, was founded on a critique of Gökalp's inability to completely separate religion from national culture. If these are the bases for the emphasis-related claims of the first two accounts, the conclusion that we must reach from my interpretation is that Gökalp's emphasis on Islam in his ideational trinity was proportionate to its due given Gökalp's understanding of the larger forces shaping the ideals of modern Turkish nationalism. But this does not settle matters entirely either.

In contrast to the first account, I think that Islam was not the weakest part of his system. While recognizing that Islam would not be the hegemonic ideal at the level of either civilization or culture, he still sought to preserve a vital place for it in national culture. (The concept of vitality is crucial here.) Thus, he seems to elevate Islam's significance, rather than diminish or finesse it for political or strategic reasons. His nationalism consisted significantly in a belief that the living traditions of Turkish national culture—both religious and non—should remain vital. This is hardly a "westernist nationalism," as Berkes calls it. It was, to Gökalp, a Turkish nationalism, appropriate to the conditions that the Turkish nation faced (although its general conceptual frame could be fruitfully applied to other nations at similar stages of social evolution). Moreover, the emphasis and development of Islam as an ideal, as well as the attention given to it as a system that is in need of reform, must be considered sincere. It seems to obfuscate the identity of his thought to say that it was "only important" for Gökalp to "state what Islam does *not* imply any more, and what has to be eliminated because of its incompatibility with the major factors of Turkish culture and Western civilization" (Heyd).

I also disagree with the second account, which sees Gökalp's emphasis on Islam as too much. Dodd writes that in attempting to situate religion among the ethical ideals of culture, Gökalp reached a "snag" in his thinking. The snag was apparently there because Gökalp could not provide an adequate place for religion as a matter of nontemporal or nonsocial relevance. But Dodd's critique expects Gökalp to relegate religion to the private sphere instead of situating it in the national-social sphere, when one aim of Gökalp's theory was to provide a place for it within the the the larger social matrix of Turkish culture. Gökalp's views illustrate less how "Islam fits uneasily in the Turkish context" than how it might have, for him and for the Turkish nationalists of his time, fit more easily. According to Gökalp, Islam may be properly considered a living, nonprivate part of Turkish national culture, performing several functions as all religions do. The snag appears to be more in Dodd's thinking about the place of Islam in Turkish national life and society than in Gökalp's. Perhaps awaiting the privatization telos of modern political history, Dodd undervalues Gökalp's conviction that Islam could and should evolve with Turkish culture. And, rather than reaching a snag, it appears that Gökalp tried to work that snag out!

Dodd, like Heyd, also implies that the place to which Gökalp assigned Islam in Turkish life and society made his thought less secular than that of the Kemalists who "were prepared to go to the West for more than its civilization," and who also, unlike Gökalp, declared themselves to stand for secularism. It remains an open question in this study whether Gökalp's position, which seeks to secure a vital nonpolitical sphere for the practices of religion in both private and social life—and which connects it logically to its public philosophy without letting it define that philosophy—is less secular than the Kemalist position that religion needed to be subordinated to state supervision and control as aspects of European culture (qua "civilization") were brought to Turkey (see next chapter). The implication was that the emphasis on religion in Gökalp's thought was too great for the future secularists in Turkey.

It is here that the particular hindering secular and modern prejudices that I discuss in the previous chapter are evident in the interpretation of Gökalp's thought. Both Dodd and Heyd seem to have engaged more in showing the validity of their judgments on religion in modernity than in capturing the identity of Gökalp's. Gökalp could not live up to their secularism (as he also could not with respect to the Kemalist laicists). In this way, Dodd and Heyd were engaged in what Charles Taylor has called "norm-setting." They set the norm for secularism as the extent to which religion was eliminated from politics and relegated to the private sphere. Gökalp agreed with the first part without assenting to the second, and for this reason was seen as less secular than those who attempted to comply with this particular modernist conclusion; in Heyd's words, the Kemalists "eliminated" the Islamic component as they created an "entirely secular" state. It is significant that Gökalp did question this and was relegated to the status of a forerunner of the real secularists, despite his unqualified commitment to the separation of religion and politics in modernity. His critical relevance to the history of Turkish laicist and secular political thought is missed.[72]

As we have seen, Gökalp's view on the need to sustain independent ethical institutions for Islam with the Caliph at their head has also been contested in the literature. Gökalp's belief that a modern nation-state should separate religion and politics undergirded his optimism with regard to the survival of the Caliphate as the spiritual leader of the Islamic umma. Gökalp believed that the elimination of the sultanate made possible the spiritual independence of the Islamic organization—from the local to the international level. The Caliph as its head would "no longer be subject to politics of any nation." Genuine Islam, then, could be institutionalized to be compatible with the modern state.[73]

Whether he could have accepted the abolition of the Caliphate by the Kemalists is, of course, debatable. The abolition would not have been entirely inconsistent with his Islamic reform premises. He may have come to terms with the outcome of the Kemalist policies, but to Berkes's charge that an independent religious institutional structure was a "fanciful utopia designed to lay a basis of internationality to his Turkish nationalism" in the context of his otherwise "Westernist" nationalism, it must be asked, which is more utopian: denying common religious institutional affiliations on the basis of nationality or integrating them in a nonpolitical sphere to enrich that nationality? Even if his belief in creating such ethical institutions waned in print (as Parla notes), who is to say that his interest in the vitality of religious institutions was also jettisoned? The implication of both Parla's and Berkes's analyses is that the vitality of religion as faith connected to an institution waned over time. This does not follow. Indeed, the view that Islam should be an aspect of culture separate from the state suggests the reverse. The vitality of religion as well as the social-structural bases of this vitality were fundamental concerns for Gökalp. This is a continual theme, rather than a waning one, and should be differentiated from whether or not he thought the Caliphate could be saved under the Kemalists and an ethical Islamic corporation could be established.

For Gökalp the choice was clear: the Turks can have religious vitality in their living culture, or they can have religious laxity, fanaticism, and hypocrisy. The former is established through the separation of religion and politics (it is at least a necessary condition), the latter through their connection. Interestingly, he believed that the justification for their differentiation did not rest on the social structural conditions of modern life alone. It could also be found in Islamic history, despite several historical deviations from the norm. In the Ottoman past, for instance, "Institutions assumed several functions at the same time, in spite of the fact that Islam, from the beginning, had differentiated matters of piety (*diyanet*) from the affairs of jurisprudence (*kaza*)." But he argued that "piety and judicial judgment are very different things." Restoration of their original differentiated status is correctable, he thought, with certain structural changes such as organizing both matters under a Ministry of Pious Affairs.[74]

Situated in Gökalp's larger frame of political and social thought, it is difficult to believe that he saw such a reform—or those undertaken by the CUP—as "Islamization," which is Arai's strong implication. The need for a radical reorganization of Turkey's social and political life derived much more from Gökalp's sociological judgments, which both preceded and succeeded his writings on Islamic reform in the journal that Arai examines. It is also hard to accept Arai's claim that the policy of state "interference" and "control," is what Gökalp advocated. ("As is well known, the CUP government accomplished, on the advice of Ziya Gökalp, many reforms of secularization, which can be regarded as forerunners of those by Atatürk. In 1913, *ulema*s and their religious courts came under State control.") He may have said that certain interferences in the old order were necessary to establish separation, but characterizing the essence of his political counsel as establishing "State control" over religion and religious institutions is a distortion of his thinking.

Hence, with regard to religion's function in modern corporate bodies, Gökalp followed Durkheim closely with an appreciation of the lasting significance of religion in modernity. Religion is fitted into a social evolutionary view where it becomes a pillar of organic solidarity. The loss of religion's significance at the international level did not entail its complete loss. Not simply a matter of private conscience, religion occupies a place in the public life of individuals where public means something other than "political." (It is difficult to employ a philosophically liberal private or public categorization to a corporatist conception of the public, nonpolitical sphere.) Religion neither disappears nor becomes merely a private matter. In modernity, religion is a cultural phenomenon that fulfills several functions in the collective soul of the nation.[75]

Gökalp's understanding of the functional place of religion in modern societies was also undergirded by an appreciation for its lasting significance as an intrinsically valuable element of human life and history. Here, his understanding of religion and its significance in modern life has less to do with the nature of social structural change and national solidarity than with the nature of belief for rational creatures and the need to express that belief in more than private ways. This point is necessary to understand why Gökalp's contribution to the secularization problematic is not easily considered a secular one.

To understand this dimension of Gökalp's thought, one must consider his religious background in Sufi Islam and that he was educated and socialized in an Islamic milieu. Indeed, his political thought found expression, as Arai's study illustrates, in a milieu still heavily constituted by a discourse in which references to and understandings in Islamic history were shared by many. Gökalp was known as a mentor, or *mürşid,* in this context.[76]

The point is that Gökalp understood religion as more than a system of societal-functional value. He also had a sense for its "living" value, that is, for the value of Islam in the late Ottoman and early Turkish context in the everyday life of Muslims in Turkey. Some of his early writings express an interest in the philosophical dimensions of this role, especially as they relate to the nature of social ideals. More often, however, one espies this perspective (in the translated essays) in discussions of religion's functional value. Consider Gökalp's understanding of what he calls "sacred power." In a discussion of the "positive rituals" of religion, Gökalp offers an interpretation of human beings as creatures of both reason and belief and an understanding of the role of religion in life beyond collective aims:

> [Positive rituals] simply bring together at certain places and at certain times individuals who, because of the necessities of life, have to live scattered and make them convene with each other for a holy aim. As all kinds of meetings produce a sense of holiness in souls, so the meetings with a holy purpose certainly generate the same feeling in a much more intensified manner. The feeling of holiness is such an elixir that we may aptly call it "sacred power." Any idea touched by it turns into belief, any sentiment into a conviction. It turns the sad person into a cheerful one, the pessimist into an optimist, the skeptic into a believer. The "sacred power" makes the coward courageous, the slothful industrious, the sick healthy, the immoral virtuous, the indifferent an idealist, the weak determined, the egoistic altruistic. Men who in ordinary times and places seek different gods are brought together at national times and places by these gatherings to experience the national life.[77]

There is no simple estimation of the function of religion in one's life. What we see is an interpretation of the human conscience and the power of religious belief. Gökalp has offered a perspective on being human with the potential to act on ideals, where one of those ideals is determined by the "sacred power" of religious belief. "Men without ideals," he once noted, "are egoistic, self-seeking, pessimistic, faithless, and cowardly; They are lost souls." Human beings with ideals—including religious ones—are capable of the highest forms of activity and achievement. As a thinker who understood the profound nature of the secularization process, Gökalp never underestimated how religious belief or "sacred power" could significantly continue to constitute the activities of individuals in the Turkish cultural context, and he believed that others should not either.

It seems, moreover, that his elevation of Islam's significance in Turkish national culture is founded on this overall appreciation of religion's significance in life—modern or not. When he compared the Turkish Renaissance to the Italian Renaissance, he criticized the latter, which, in turning against the Age of the Church, "turned against the spirit of religiosity, then devoid of effective vitality, and unjustly extended its attacks to the still living parts of religion." His interest in the "still living parts of religion" is evidence for his stronger appreciation than most secularists for religion (without implying that all secular theses are hostile to religion).[78]

It is less important to my study of Gökalp's contribution to the secularization problematic to develop Gökalp's understanding of the intrinsic value of religion to human beings in his thinking than it is to show that he never seriously diminished or exaggerated its importance within Turkish national life, as others have argued. Rather, he provided a comprehensive analysis of what he considered the necessary place of religion under conditions of contemporary civilization. He saw what we would call secularity occurring at the two primary organizational levels of the world: international civilization and national culture. He believed that religion had truly lost the significance that it once had. But for him this did not mean that it has entirely lost its significance, even under the secularizing and democratizing conditions of modern politics. To the contrary, from Gökalp's "objective" determination of the conditions for contemporary collective ideals, he gave religion a privileged place in the national culture that he sought to preserve as Turkey continued its integration with the West. Culture is not a secondary category for Gökalp. He observed Islam's diminished relevance at the international level, but secured its importance at the national level. He did so by advocating the establishment of institutions, unconnected to politics, that would ensure its continual vitality as the broader processes of social-structural differentiation continued apace in the modern world. His appreciation for the vitality of religion was sincere, and it was enmeshed within a broad concern for the function of religion in modern societies and its intrinsic value for human beings.

It may be said that I have inadequately represented the ideals to which Gökalp aspired after the end of the Young Turk period, or that I have generalized from a reading of what Parla calls Gökalp's second phase. As such, I fail to consider an alteration in Gökalp's thinking from the early days when he was declaring a need for a Turkish-Islamic civilization to the later days when these are separate ideals, and when he gives greater emphasis to nationalism.

My response is threefold. First, the evidence for the continuity of Gökalp's view on the separation of religion and politics is a matter of consensus in the literature. His unequivocal rejection of theocracy and clericalism in 1923 was only a crystallization of ideas that he had expressed at least ten years earlier. Second, regarding the significance of Islam in Turkish identity, my view is that an interpretation of his thought that shows a greater interest in Islam in his earlier writings should not ignore the continuities that I articulate here. Moreover, the early rhetoric of a Turkish-Islamic civilization must be understood in a context in which Gökalp's major conceptual frame, including his distinction between culture and civilization, was still developing. That he drops this rhetoric for the more refined distinction between culture and civilization—which he clarifies on conceptual and political-ethical grounds—does not entail that Islam as an ideal becomes less important.

Overall, what we observe in Gökalp's thought over time reflects less a change of emphasis than the gradual working out of his own sociological judgments (especially the understanding of social structures and the distinctions among culture, religion, and civilization). Thus, by 1923 he wrote with sharper conceptual precision, and certainly no loss of emphasis:

> As soon as such representations as "we belong to the Turkish nation," "we are of the *ümmet* of Islam," "we are a part of Western civilization," become distinct representations in the common consciousness of the Turks of Turkey, every aspect of our social life will begin to change. The more we say "we are of the Turkish nation," the more we shall be able to show originality and personality in terms of the Turkish taste and values in language, in art, in morality, in laws, and even in religion and philosophy. As we say "we are of the *ümmet* of Islam," we shall behave in accordance with the belief that the Kur'an is our sacred book, Muhammad our sacred prophet, the Ka'ba our sacred place, and Islam our sacred religion. As we say "we are of Western civilization," we shall behave as do the European peoples in science, philosophy, techniques, and in all other aspects of civilization.[79]

This is hardly a dismissal of the Islamic component. And it is also not an exaggeration of that component in what, in the context of his corpus, is a fairly refined and intricately defined whole.

Gökalp was constantly focused on those in Turkey who shared his "yearning for a synthesis" (in opposition to those yearning for other forms of sociopolitical change). And to their inquiry, "How ought we live?" he suggested consistently that changes in the world have come to mean that Turks must live as members of the Turkish nation, as believers in the Islamic religion that is part of the national culture, and as reasoning beings benefiting from the concepts and techniques of modern science. At the conceptual level, he argued that the proper way for the members of the Turkish nation to proceed was to think of themselves in a threefold matrix of identity, to absorb civilization to culture, and to restructure the place of religion in that nexus. They should drop the "fiction of [multinational] cosmopolitanism" and embrace nationalism while simultaneously grasping the "significance of culture" and an "interest in international civilization." Losing sight of any of these dimensions, Gökalp believed, was a recipe for stagnation and missed opportunity in the changing conditions of the contemporary age. If Turkey failed to adopt the right ideals, it would lose the opportunity for freedom, cultural survival, and rationally governed success in the modern world. The reality of the contemporary age suggested that Turks, like all others, must learn to live in a world in which the primary identities of human beings were no longer singularly defined in reli-

gious terms. The identity of society, like the identity of the world, was changing, and individual members of different cultures and civilizations would need
to learn how to live in these new contexts. With the correct understanding of
evolution, and some guidance concerning ideals, they might live in harmony
with others.[80]

One more issue remains to be resolved: the place of Gökalp's understanding
of Islam in modern Turkish life and society relative to the subsequent history of
secular thought and practice in the Turkish republic. If the Kemalists did not
institutionally and symbolically separate religion and politics, Gökalp cannot
be said to have supported or even to have laid the groundwork for a policy that
was intended to control religion (or any other cultural institution). He fully
advocated complete disestablishment. If the Kemalists did not achieve this,
they may have had their reasons. But no justification for the state control of
religion is evident in Gökalp's writings. He demanded the complete autonomy
of political and religious spheres for the sake of both. Contra Heyd, Berkes,
Dodd, and Arai (and following Parla), Gökalp's position, which sought to
secure a vital, nonpolitical sphere for religion in both private and social life—
and which connected Islam logically to Turkey's public philosophy without
letting it define that philosophy—offers an alternative but not necessarily less
secular interpretation of secularism in Turkey.

I say this without implying that Gökalp was a secularist. But this does not
mean that his contribution to the secularization problematic is any less valuable. Throughout the world today, including in Turkey, there are secularists and
nonsecularists, as well as laicists and anti-laicists still seeking a conceptual frame
for granting religion a prominent place in public life without it becoming the
sole determinant of that life. Some of us are still seeking a language for the
freedom of conscience in the global multireligious context when that means
free to be religious or nonreligious (in a variety of ways). Gökalp's cul-
ture/civilization conceptual frame with its evolutionary backdrop is more appealing than more popular accounts that collapse religion with civilization and
offer no historically grounded way to a more secular, common future.[81]

Chapter 4 Interpreting
Turkey's Secular Model

Since beliefs about social institutions are partially constitutive of social
institutions, it is impossible to identify the institution except in terms of
the beliefs of those who engage in its practices.
—Alasdair MacIntyre

How far is the self-designation "secular state" still appropriate, either as a
description or as a political principle in modern Turkey?
—Richard Tapper

The hermeneutic imperative has recently gained wider currency in
comparative political studies. In a new study called *Rethinking Middle
East Politics*, Simon Bromley endorses Geoffrey Hawthorne's version
of this imperative that "to grasp the politics of any Third World
country and thereby to make illuminating comparisons between the
politics of several is to understand how those in power (and those who
seek it) have framed the common ambition to capture and define
social and political space and economically to develop; how they (or
their predecessors) have framed constitutions and formal institutions
to realize these ends; and the ways in which, imaginatively and prac-

tically, these and other more or less institutionalized institutions have been used."[1]

Our attention to the frameworks of political life is certainly a positive step in the study of any politics, "Third World" or "advanced." Yet bringing alternative frameworks into our language of explanation is difficult, and delicate, work.

In his discussion of Turkey's secular politics, Bromley highlights the "draconian" character of "Kemalist opposition to religious intrusion into public life," asserts that "Kemalism was the exemplary instance of modernization *against* Islam" (emphasis in original), and concludes, "In fact, the militant secularism of the state amounted to rigid state control over religious life, and a strict laicism in public affairs, rather than the institutional separation of Church and State, or the decline of personal belief."[2]

As such, he joins many others who have distinguished secularism in Turkey—a translation of the laiklik "arrow" or "trajectory principle" of Kemalism that was announced in the 1931 party program of Mustafa Kemal's Republican People's Party (RPP)—from secularism in the West on the basis of the former's Erastian, control-oriented character. "The religious establishment," wrote Dankwart Rustow in an influential essay, "has never been separated from the state." "The separation of religion and state was never attempted in its Western sense," observes Binnaz Toprak. Islam was "put under control and made subservient to state authority." In the Kemalist reforms, the state may have been freed from religion, but the reverse was not true. On what we may call the "control account" of Turkey's laiklik politics, the relevant terms to describe laiklik are "control" and "supervision as subordination," not "separation."[3]

Much of the control account is difficult to contest. But if our project is to be hermeneutic, then the inadequacies of this account must be appreciated. The contrast between "control" and "separation" must be removed, for it was in the original constitutive meanings of Kemalist laiklik, and it continues to be as the dynamics of laiklik politics unfold in Turkey. In this chapter I clarify the separation dimensions of laiklik, identify their significance in laik politics past and present, and offer a hermeneutic contribution to the unending quest of comparative inquiry to better understand alternative, existing relations between religion and politics in the modern world.

An understanding of the separation dimensions of laiklik is noticeably absent in many debates over laiklik in Turkey (even though they are sometimes discussed) in addition to the social science literature on the topic. There are reasons for this absence in both contexts. In Turkey, a retraditionalization of political life has slowly taken place since a multiparty electoral system was established in the late 1940s. (It has been subject to review and change by the military—in 1960, 1971, and 1980—which, when not exclusively in power, continue to influence state policies, including those that are associated with laiklik.) This retraditionalization—inaugurated and sustained by laik parties as well as religiopolitically interested ones—has been undergirded by a critique of laiklik that is based on the control account. In the anglophone social science literature, the absence of an adequate discussion of the separation dimensions of laiklik politics results from nonhermeneutic tendencies to explain political practices without due consideration of their constitutive understandings.

My project is not to displace the control account but to offer a fuller interpretation of the control relations from a hermeneutic view. My interpretation involves rehabilitating dimensions of separation in the original field of laiklik politics that are inadequately captured by the conceptual base of the control account.

Several risks accompany this effort, not least of which is the mistaken view that hermeneutic inquiry is relativist, conservative, uncritical, and suited for understanding as opposed to explanation. This essay contributes to an expanding area of inquiry that demonstrates otherwise and that shows the indispensability of hermeneutic political explanation in our collective efforts to speak authoritatively about the political lives of others.

There is also the risk that my account will be understood as a defense of Kemalism—it is not. My goal is to offer a more compelling interpretation of laiklik than can be found in the existing literature. I clarify dimensions of the political frames that previously have not been adequately considered. The authoritarianism of the Turkish state, not unlike that of many other states, has created much trouble (including problems associated with the arbitrary application of state power) for many people with many different interests. Aspects of these problems originated in the Kemalist experience. But I see no need to endorse an interpretation by one group over another; there is a need for disentangling the web of interests and concepts that the state has effectively tangled over the past seventy years.

My political hope is for laicism to be seen as an element of secularizing politics in which historically important types of separation between common political matters and less common religious matters may occur *in some senses*—types of separation that are significant in the debate over laiklik in Turkey. Aside from the risk of being misinterpreted, the risk is even greater that reinterpretations of laicism and secularism in Turkey and elsewhere—exercises led largely by nonhermeneutic forces—will produce an even less secular outcome than laiklik because they fail to see laiklik within historical attempts to create and maintain a separation between religious and political life. Indeed, to argue that there is a need to reinterpret laiklik is to presume that there is some shared understanding of that which is to be reinterpreted. My project, therefore, is to describe the original field of laiklik about which there remains much controversy.

NEITHER SEPARATION
NOR DISESTABLISHMENT

To understand the significance and the limitations of various control accounts of laiklik politics, these accounts must be seen as critiques of two other, related accounts, which also appear in various forms. The first of these two is what I call the separation account, and the second is what I refer to as the disestablishment account.[4]

When Rustow wrote that the "religious establishment has never been separated from the state," he was correcting the views of what he called the "casual Western observer with some knowledge of recent Turkish history who is likely to credit Atatürk with making Turkey over from a traditional Muslim society into a modern Western nation, and in that process, separating the religious establishment from the state." Rustow may have known of certain celebrity "casual observers" in anglophone social science. It was the relation between religion and politics in Turkey that defined Turkey's relevance to modernization theory's founding father, Daniel Lerner. In his seminal work, *The Passing of Traditional Society: Modernizing in the Middle East*, Lerner wrote, "Turkey is not yet a Modern society in our sense, but it is no longer a Traditional society in any sense." The reason for this, he maintained, was that the "Muslim institution has been separated from the secular state."[5]

Lerner, however, was not the first to see secularism in Turkey as institutional separation. Earlier and more recent observers of Mustafa Kemal's reforms— among them social scientists, political historians, and journalists—have seen in laiklik the separation of church and state or the "complete displacement" of the religious institutions. In the course of the reforms, Ahmad has suggested that the "state cut its formal ties with Islam."[6]

Subscribers to the control account have also taken issue with the concept of disestablishment as applied to Kemalist laiklik. Disestablishment connotes an attempt to deprive religion of state connection and support by removing its institutions from a position of union, patronage, or control in a political structure. Because it means withdrawing religious control or removing religion from an established position of political power, disestablishment is close in its meaning to separation. Bernard Lewis, whose book *The Emergence of Modern Turkey* is perhaps the most widely read introduction to modern Turkish political history, argues that the purpose of laiklik was to disestablish Islam and make it a "strictly private affair." Laiklik sought to "end the power of [Islam's] exponents in political, social, and cultural affairs, and to limit it to matters of belief and worship." Lewis's influence is discernible in the social science literature—for instance, in the interpretations of the political scientist Walter Weiker, whose work also focuses on modernization in Turkey. He consistently cites Lewis on this point, noting that Turkey accomplished the "formal disestablishment of Islam, and formal-legal separation of mosque and state." Weiker also endorses the applicability of the concept disestablishment while acknowledging the debate over Kemalism's severity: "Whether it was necessary for Atatürk to be as drastic as he was in disestablishing Islam is still debatable."[7]

Because of nuances of meaning for all of these concepts, adjudicating the disestablishment account is complicated. Kemalist laiklik clearly exhibits anticlerical tendencies, aiming to "destroy [religious] control," as Mardin has put it. Mustafa Kemal and his political allies launched a conscious effort to deprive Islam of a "considerable share of its controlling influence both in public and in private life." But whether the reforms sought to dismantle Islam, to "drive it out of official favor and out of the collective consciousness of the people," or to achieve "virtually total exclusion of religious influence from public life" "ending forever" the "formal power of religious functionaries"—all things that are implied by disestablish—is *still* debatable.[8]

The disestablishment account usefully connotes the exercise of political power to achieve laiklik. For instance, the abolition of the Caliphate on March 3, 1924, was not merely an inexorable outcome of nationalism's rise in Turkey. The abolition of the Caliphate was one of the first shots fired in a political battle in which the anticlerical Kemalists sought to consolidate power by depriving their opposition of a rallying point that they believed, as Mustafa Kemal later stated, might be used to limit Turkey's independence and sovereignty vis-à-vis other Islamic countries.[9]

Disestablishment, however, would entail ending the established status of Islam and ending control—at least of religion, if not of lay control over religion—in the state. According to the control account, this did not happen in Kemalist laiklik politics.

The abolition of the Caliphate together with the abolition of the cabinet-level Ministry of Religious Affairs was followed by the founding of two new institutions: the Directorate-General (*Reislik,* which is also translated as "Presidency") of Religious Affairs (*Diyanet İşleri*) and the Directorate-General of Pious Foundations (*Evkaf*). The latter administered the religious endowments, upkeep of mosques, and, after 1931, cleric remuneration. The *Diyanet İşleri Reisligi* in Turkish laik politics continues to generate controversy. It became the highest religious office in the new Turkish republican state. Its head was to be "appointed by the President . . . on the recommendation of the Prime Minister," to whose office it was to be attached (Article 4). Its function was the "dispatch of all cases concerning the Exalted Islamic Faith which relate to beliefs (*itikadat*) and rituals (*ibadat*)." These included the "administration of all mosques . . . and of dervish houses within the boundaries of the territories of the Republic of Turkey as well as with the appointment and dismissal of all *imam*s, *hatib*s (orators), *vaiz*s (preachers), *şeyh*s (leaders of dervish houses), *müezzin*s (callers to prayer), *kayyım*s (sextons), and all other employees of a religious character" (Article 5). The law also stipulated that the "Directorate-General of Religious Affairs is the proper place of legal recourse" for the jurisconsults (*müftülük*) of Islamic law (Article 5). This entailed responsibility for distributing "model" sermons (*hutbe*), and "translating, editing, and publishing authentic religious works for the public."[10]

In short, the abolition of the Caliphate by the Republic was followed by the establishment of other religious institutions that were thought to be more compatible with the Turkish national project. In their original conception, these institutions were linked with the government to control religion within the state. Toprak underscores this linkage by noting how the "organization and personnel of Islam" became "paid employees of the state." In the early thirties, Allen suggested that the sample sermons that the *Diyanet* distributed were "designed to encourage obedience to God and the Republican government." Expressing the control dimensions, Mardin writes, "The Directorates were to be attached to the Prime Minister's office so that the state would control all training for religious offices as well as salaries and appointments of all religious officials." He further suggests that these relations that have been maintained and extended over time comprise much of Turkey's "official Islam."[11]

From the viewpoint of the control account, therefore, the existence of the *Diyanet İşleri Reisliği/Başkanlığı* is counterevidence to any claim that Islam was disestablished through laiklik. To the contrary, the new state's religious institutions were "designed" largely, as Keyder has stated, to "control from above all aspects of religious life." This dynamic lies behind Mardin's remark that "in

Turkey, laicism amounted to more than official disestablishment of religion." Interpreters of laiklik might want to downplay the status of these offices, for example by identifying the head of the *Diyanet* as a "mere director-general of a department," but they cannot discount the reality of the control relations in which it exists.[12]

THE CONTROL ACCOUNT UNPACKED

To understand further why laiklik was more than disestablishment and less than institutional separation, the explanations in the literature concerning laiklik as control are helpful. The essence of the control account is that the policies, practices, relations, and institutions associated with laiklik must be understood within a set of state-religion authority relations that were true of the Ottoman imperial past. The ultimate supremacy of the state over religious institutions and officials characterized these relations. In the control account of Turkey's laiklik politics, the Kemalist-nationalist faction of the nationalist alliance exploited the pre-existing sovereign supremacy over religion to eliminate, subjugate, and pacify opponents to their "Republican-nationalist" project of cultural, political, and economic change. These two features—the institutional context and the drive for power by the Kemalist faction—are two crucial dimensions for explaining laiklik as control. A third important component of the control account is the cultural impact of the RPP's politics and of the reforms associated with laiklik.

Persisting institutional authority relations: The Republican regime inherited and exploited a long-standing tradition of institutional relations between the state and religion in the Ottoman Turkish context. The characteristic features of this relation were integration and subordination. Religion was integrated into the state but ultimate sovereignty and authority, including over the scope of religious power, rested with Ottoman palace officials. Integration was achieved in several ways, none of which should be thought of as mere instrumentalization; indeed, some see the Ottoman Empire as "probably the most perfect Islamic state ever to come into existence." The *ulema* "were integrated within the apparatus of the state." "Through their control of education [in the extensive mekteb and medrese system], of the judiciary [as qadi jurists], and of the administrative network, they acted as agents of the state." The Ottoman palace officials in turn "saw [their] duty as the preservation of the state and the promotion of Islam." The Sultans, claiming not lineage but divine selection, assumed the title of Caliph, named their armies the "soldiers of Islam," ensured the implementation of the şeriat (Islamic law), and consecrated a Sheikh of Islam (*Şeyh-ül-İslâm*)—from whom religious approval (*fetwa*) would be sought for legislative purposes. This integration of Islam and Ottoman power was "expressed in the formula *din-ü devlet* (*din wa dawla*), or 'religion and state.'"[13]

Nonetheless, structurally it was not Islam that was sovereign but the House of Osman. The crux of the relation was always determined according to the "viability of the state," not the viability of religion—even though the two were "organically" connected in institutional and legitimation terms. "In the sense that the state was necessary to keep religion flourishing, it had priority over religion." By will, command, and in circumstances of necessity, the Ottomans developed their own public law (*örf* and *kanun*) outside the stipulations of Koranic law (the şeriat). "The members of the religious institutions were appointed and could be dismissed by the Sultan," and *fetwa* rulings were subject to tacit and displayed influences under patrimonial rulership. In short, "Islam in the Ottoman polity was never an autonomous force or power *vis-à-vis* the state."[14]

Along with state hegemony over society came immense structural leverage for defining that relation. Thus, it was due to the tradition of state priority that the "Ottoman statesman of the Tanzimat [reordering] could consider the translation of the French Civil Code into Turkish without flinching." The new laicist Republic availed itself of this position by promulgating new laws to define its state structure. For example, a new Penal Code was adopted in 1926 that was "based almost entirely on the Italian Criminal Code of 1889." And, extremely important to the policies of laiklik, a new Civil Code based almost entirely on the Swiss Civil Code was adopted for matters of civil law (October 4, 1926).[15]

Interpreters who see laiklik as "control" frequently refer to state priority over religion, a continuity in the "system of power . . . and the whole system of relations between state and society," as a structural underpinning of laiklik. With no independent Ottoman-Islamic religious institution to speak of, therefore, the Republican nationalists who assumed control of the state could hardly be said to have secularized Turkey's state structures like the "church and state" separation in the West.[16] The new *institutional* relation is better described in İlkay Sunar and Sabri Sayarı's phrase as "state-dominant monoparty authoritarianism," reflecting the new regime's interest in exploiting the traditional relations of power. Applying Hawthorne's concept of "frames," the political space that was captured by the Kemalists was characterized by state hegemony, and this structural relation, though redefined, was not altered fundamentally once its inhabitants changed. The state-society relation instituted by the Kemalists might be even better described as party-dominant state authoritarianism. Indeed, a precondition for laiklik in Turkey was for the Kemalists to occupy by themselves the hegemonic position in the state.

Thus, the tradition of state hegemony over religion is one reason why the separation and disestablishment accounts (with their privatization addendum) fall short in capturing the frame of structural political power in which laiklik was effected. Modernization prejudgments (Gadamer), expecting secularism as structural differentiation qua separation between the political and the religious spheres inadequately capture the institutional frame of power that shaped Kemalist possibilities. Due to existing institutional conditions, subscribers to the control account suggest that interpreters of laiklik should "expect control, not separation," despite the temptation to equate modernity with unfolding differentiation between spheres—to see perhaps a "liberal evolution" as Robinson saw; interpreters of Turkey should expect "transcendental state hegemony."[17] The Kemalists' drive for political power to control the state itself is another feature of this still-incomplete picture.

The political battle: Beyond institutional conditions, the control account also points us toward examining the political struggle that culminated in laiklik politics. To fully understand laiklik and the control account, we must go beyond the structural background to look at the power politics that shaped it. In particular, we must consider the struggle for control over the fledgling Turkish state after Turkey's War for Independence, in which the faction of the nationalist movement that was led by Mustafa Kemal consolidated its power and implemented its version of Turkey's modernity, including its understanding of the relation between Islam and politics.[18]

The national struggle: It must be remembered that the principle of laiklik was not declared in the constitution of the Turkish Republic until 1937. Between 1922, when the last Ottoman Sultan left Istanbul in the custody of the British navy, and 1928, the constitution of the Republic declared the religion of the state to be Islam (Article 2) and the state to be the executor of the şeriat (Article 26). The şeriat was no longer formally enforced by 1926, when the Ottoman Imperial Code and the şeriat were replaced with a modified Swiss Civil Code. Even when the "religion of the state" clause is dropped in 1928 (April 10), laiklik, however, does not appear in the Constitution.[19]

Significantly, laiklik makes its first "official" appearance in October 1927 as part of "The President Gazi Mustafa Kemal His Excellency's Declaration of the General Principles agreed to in harmony at the Republican People's Party [3rd]

Congress." In this document, the Party declares itself to be "Republicanist, *lâyık*, populist, and nationalist" (*Cümhuriyetçi, lâyık, halkçı ve milliyetçidir;* *"Lâyık"* is an older spelling of *laik*, the adjectival form of laiklik).[20]

This party—whose members and subsequent inheritances are usually referred to as the Kemalists, and their ideology as Kemalism—emerged from a geographically diverse national independence coalition that was organized by prominent CUP members, led by the elected head of a representative committee, Mustafa Kemal, and founded to "safeguard the Sultanate, the Supreme Caliphate, and the integrity of the country against foreign pressure." The British occupation of Istanbul and arrest of prominent nationalists (March 15–16, 1920), the subsequent dissolution of the Ottoman legislature (final session, March 19; formally dissolved by Sultan, April 11), the political and territorial designs set for Turkey in the Treaty of Sèvres, and the Ottoman Sultan's capitulatory condemnation of both Mustafa Kemal and the Anatolian-based movement initiated a national struggle (*milli mücadele*) to defend the sovereignty of the nation (*millet*) as declared in Article 1 of the provisional constitution of January 2, 1920.[21]

The language of the struggle was constituted as many before it by an Islamic idiom. The Turkish Grand National Assembly (TGNA) began on April 23, 1920, in Ankara with a prayer at the Hacı Bayram mosque whose Mufti pronounced a counter-fetwa (religious decree) to "do all to liberate the Caliph from captivity." The TGNA followed by passing a Law Against High Treason forbidding, inter alia, the "misuse of religion for political purposes" (April 29, 1920). A conference in Sivas of July 1921, attended by religious dignitaries such as the Bediüzzaman Said Nursi, affirmed its support for the struggle and helped mobilize the population to "free Islamic lands" by expelling the "infidel invaders." In battle, those who fell were constituted as *şehit*, and, on September 19, 1921, the victorious leader Mustafa Kemal was hailed as *Gazi*, both terms meaningful in the Islamic conceptual "cluster" of struggle. Şehit connotes a martyr for the faith; Gazi, meaning fighter for the faith, was historically bestowed on the most courageous Ottoman warrior heroes. The identity of the national struggle as a struggle for Islamic freedom waged by Ottoman patriots was so profound that at the war's end in October 1922, "many now became convinced that the Sultanate could be abolished and a constitutional system essentially Islamic in character maintained at the same time."[22]

But the reality was that in the national coalition, there were deeply different visions of the structure and aims of the new state. Turkish political sovereignty was yet undecided, especially regarding the relation between Turkish nationalism and Islam. Of the many contestants over Turkey's new constitution, two groups emerged inside the TGNA to debate the conceptual bases of modern Turkish sovereignty. Though it is difficult to capture all orientations—there were multidimensional secularists, westernists, and Islamists—the groupings adequately describe the general tendencies within the TGNA that coalesced as political developments unfolded. There were others outside, such as a group led by Enver Pasha, as well as other "left" and local liberty-oriented opponents to the national movement. To subdue *this* opposition, the TGNA—increasingly dominated by Kemal and his loyal supporters—passed a law on July 31, 1923, creating Independence Tribunals empowered to execute on the spot those who committed "crimes against the nation."

The "First Group" (*Birinci Grup*) was originally organized by Mustafa Kemal as the Defense of Rights Group. This name reflects Kemal's attempt to portray his group as the legitimate successor to the national movement. Many of the group's members were, like Mustafa Kemal, products of the military and civil service training schools that were created during the Ottoman state's modernization efforts, the Tanzimat, and the extension of these made by the Committee of Union and Progress in the early nationalist milieu. Ideologically, they were also anchored in a quasi-positivist version of Turkish nationalism that saw "degenerate" Islam as responsible for the nation's "decay," and science as the "truest guide to life." As such, they sought to use the institutions of the state in a tutelary fashion to effect a far-reaching political and cultural transformation program to lift the Turkish nation to the level of "contemporary civilization," as Mustafa Kemal was fond of saying.[23]

The "Second Group" (*Ikinci Grup*) was established in direct opposition to Mustafa Kemal and his First Group's claim to speak on behalf of the entire nation. Comprised of diverse ideological tendencies, the Second Group coalesced after Kemal began a narrowly based and personalistic style of decision making. Members of the Second Group, for instance, objected when the decision to declare the Republic was taken at a meeting of Kemal's party—while the Second Group members were out of town—rather than in the Assembly. Among the members of this group were former CUP members who variously favored stricter constitutionalist rule and greater political and economic liberty, defended the less-constitutionalist Ottoman past, and advocated an ulema-dominated Assembly. In most accounts, this group's dwindling influence in the TGNA was offset by its support from the majority of the population. Important for my account is this group's view that Islam "was not opposed to science" and thus that political and cultural reforms should take place in a frame of respect for Turkey's Islamic traditions. Countering criticisms of the First Group, it denied any opposition to change and declared its allegiance to the "national spirit."[24]

Portions of the Second Group evolved into a political party on two occasions during Mustafa Kemal's rule. However, both the Progressive Republican Party (*Terakkiperver Cumhuriyet Fırkası,* hereafter PRP, founded November 17, 1924), whose leaders had "played a role in the national struggle only second to that of Mustafa Kemal himself," and the Free Republican Party (*Serbest Cumhuriyet Fırkası,* hereafter FRP, founded August 12, 1930), who were "hardly distinguishable from the RPP in terms of social background characteristics," had the misfortune of becoming successful in focusing opposition on the governing party and on Mustafa Kemal's increasingly personal rule. Fewer than nineteen months after its founding, the PRP was charged with abetting "obscurantist reactionarism" (*irtica*) by the Independence Tribunals that were established during the Kurdish rebellion of 1925 and dissolved (along with other forms of opposition, including members of the media). The FRP leadership dissolved that party themselves just four months after its founding, after it was accused of treason for contesting the tightly controlled elections of 1930 when Mustafa Kemal and the RPP perceived the growing challenge that the opposition parties posed to their power. In 1926, after discovery of a plot on Mustafa Kemal's life (June 15), leaders of the PRP were put on trial. Some were incarcerated; seven were executed. As Rustow points out, "only few . . . had any prior knowledge of the plot," while the "charges that the Progressive Party had abetted the Kurdish uprising" were "even flimsier." These were purges of a viable political opposition.[25]

If the abolition of the PRP and the FRP proved that the Kemalists would not tolerate any opposition in the state governing center, the regime's militant response to the Kurdish rebellion and the Kubilay (or Menemen) incident (1930–31) demonstrated its determination to eliminate its rivals on the periphery. Enabled by the community organization and authority relations of the religious Sufi orders (*tarikat*), both protestations were constituted greatly in an Islamic idiom.[26]

Indeed, like the *tarikat* leaders, the "Kemalists also recognized the significance of religion in the Kurdish revolt and the vital role played by popular Islam in the lives of the masses." They responded by declaring martial law and securing extensive power to crush their opponents. These powers were codified in the Law for the Maintenance of Order that, among other things, renewed the power of the Independence Tribunals to execute enemies of the regime without the Assembly's sanction. That June, the PRP was dissolved and the revolt was crushed. Some of its intellectual and military leaders were hanged, and six months later (November 30), all *tarikats* were outlawed, and their meeting houses (*tekke, zaviye*) and other sacred sites (including the *türbe*, or sacred tombs) closed.[27]

A similar response followed the Kubilay incident. This incident—really a violent protest—was considered unique by the officials because it signified to the Kemalist faction the power of "savage reactionaries" in Western Anatolia, where Kemal was assumed to be widely recognized as a liberator. Martial law was imposed, followed by a new set of institutional reforms that were designed to propagate the Kemalist view of the Turkish national project. Not necessarily in direct response to the incident, but certainly as part of their "nation-building" effort, the regime opened the People's Houses (*Halk Evleri*) in rural towns in 1932, and the People's Rooms (*Halk Odaları*), in the villages. Both were successors to the unsuccessful Turkish Hearths (*Türk Ocakları*). The Kemalists thought of these institutions as replacements for the local mosque as a place for social gathering and forums to propagate their view of the Turkish national project. According to the control account, these places had one aim: "Propagating culture in the Western mold." I return to aspects of cultural control in these accounts shortly.[28]

In the highly charged and increasingly less-contested atmosphere that was created by Kemalist authoritarianism, the RPP constituted itself deliberately as a cadre party under the leadership of the charismatic president, His Excellency Gazi Mustafa Kemal. (It was not until November 26, 1934, that the TGNA, fully consolidated under Mustafa Kemal's rule, bestows on him the surname "Atatürk," meaning literally, the "ancestral father of the Turks.") The Kemalists believed that they must forge their new "legitimacy" in this fluid situation—by force if necessary—if their version of modernization was to proceed. "The essence of the Turkish revolution," writes Özbudun, "is that it concentrated on the extension and consolidation of the precarious beachhead . . . to make it secure beyond all possible challenge." Mustafa Kemal and the party's publicists activated Kemal's charismatic image and all institutions that it could find or create to define its new legitimacy as well as the formal concept of Turkish citizenship that it would require. Özbudun expressed the substance of the control account by saying that the RPP conceived of all six arrows of Kemalism—its central ideological tenets—"as a means of strengthening the state (or the center)"—that is, of strengthening the RPP's control over the state. This political power dynamic is at the core of the control account of laiklik.[29]

THE KEMALIST VISION
OF THE CENTRAL REFORMS

In his *Speech* of October 1927, spanning six days and nearly forty hours, Mustafa Kemal offered his account of the intentions and purposes guiding the RPP's struggle. The speech has not been systematically studied in anglophone literature; therefore, some of what follows represents my own attempt to deepen the control dimensions of laiklik. Kemal was the chief ideologue of the regime, so his declarations provide central insight on the meanings and purposes undergirding laiklik.

Kemal expressed two significant dimensions of laiklik. The first concerns its relation to the other "arrows" of Kemalism, especially republicanism, nationalism, "people-ism," and transformationism. Mustafa Kemal's asseverations suggest that the meanings that constitute laiklik politics cannot be entirely separated from the meanings that constitute these other terms in the Kemalist frame. This applies especially to the so-called cultural reforms associated with laiklik that I will introduce in this context. These reforms were intended, as Mustafa Kemal said, to raise Turkey to the level of "contemporary civilization." The second feature of his speech that is relevant here relates to crucial statements that Mustafa Kemal made regarding his own understanding of Islam and its relation to political power. These assertions are significant because they partly illuminate the conceptual frame of the new religious policy in which the Kemalists controlled religion.

The speech was delivered following the RPP's overwhelming victory in national elections for the Assembly. (All of the candidates were handpicked by Mustafa Kemal, so his RPP naturally did well.) It also technically coincided with the period during which the Law for the Maintenance of Order, imposed during the Kurdish rebellion, was still in effect. Just sixteen months prior, opponents of Kemal who were implicated in an Izmir assassination attempt were executed. Furthermore, the speech came on the heels of the previous year's adoption of several significant reforms that are associated with laiklik. Important among these in this context are: 1) the implementation of the new Turkish Civil Code replacing Islamic law (discussed further below), and 2) a Penal Code outlawing "political associations on the basis of religious or religious sentiments" and reaffirming the Law Against High Treason concerning the "misuse of religion, religious sentiments, or things that are religiously considered as holy, in any way to incite the people to action prejudicial to the security of the state" (January 1926). In this setting, Mustafa Kemal's rhetoric expresses confidence that the RPP's interpretation of the Turkish national project would proceed undeterred by political opposition; this includes policies associated with laiklik.[30]

In the speech, Mustafa Kemal rejected as "absurd" and "erroneous" suggestions that Turkish sovereignty be based in Islamic concepts and structures of legitimacy. Turkey's "national salvation," he asseverated, required tearing up the old foundations, replacing them with new ones (he was not one to stress continuities), and, in the process, securing respect for Turkey's "unlimited independence" from foreign design. Articulating the premise behind the Kemalist "populist" arrow, Mustafa Kemal declared that the new source of legitimacy should be "the people," whose collective interests should be represented by a new leadership that would usher in a new era and a new consciousness.[31]

As for the old sources of legitimacy, the Assembly had already declared the Ottoman Empire to have "passed into the dustbin of history . . . in perpetuity" on the day that the British took over Istanbul (November 1, 1922). Concerning the institutions of Islam, Mustafa Kemal believed the goal of maintaining the Caliphate as a temporal head of the international Islamic community to be both a threat to "national sovereignty" and unrealistically utopian. His strong implication was that it would be unreasonable for other Muslims if they were to surrender the definition of their interests over to a Turkish Caliph. "Neither common sense nor reason," he stressed, "will ever admit that any individual Muslim will confer on any man the authority of guiding and administering the affairs of the whole Muslim world," regardless of the "beauty" of the idea. Those Turks and non-Turks who propose it expose the Muslim world to exploitation as well as risk Turkey's political sovereignty. Kemal averred that they are "ignorant" and "blind" to political realities.[32]

Part of this ignorance, Mustafa Kemal maintained, was founded on the failure of his adversaries to appreciate the need to gain respect in the "eyes of the civilized world." This concept, along with its converse regarding the need to rout the "ignorant forces of the uncivilized," appears as a primary justification for many reforms associated with laiklik. Just as the Ottoman Empire lacked the authority that is accorded to modern states based on the sovereignty of "the people," the Caliphate would have been only a "laughing stock in the eyes of the really civilized and cultured peoples of the world."[33]

Indeed, living up to the standards of the "really civilized and cultured peoples of the world" reaches far into the politics that are associated with secularization in Turkey. Regarding the Hat Laws, for instance, Mustafa Kemal said (in a passage that is sometimes favorably quoted in the literature): "It was necessary to abolish the fez, which sat on our heads as a sign of ignorance, fanaticism, or hatred to progress and civilization, and to adopt in its place the hat, the customary dress of the civilized world, thus showing, among other things, that no difference existed in the manner of thought between the Turkish nation and the whole family of civilized mankind."[34]

The sartorial reforms have a complex background history that is not always mentioned by those who find them significant as indications of the regime's interest in westernization. This history represents well Mustafa Kemal's understanding of national aims vis-à-vis international civilization expressed in his speech as well as the conflict that those aims would engender inside Turkey, wherein different conceptions of the civilization to which Turkey should belong continued to assert themselves.

Sartorial styles appear to have had politically symbolic importance even prior to the nationalist period. During the previous century, Sultan Mahmud (1808–1839) adopted the fez "from current Venetian fashion as a brimless compromise between the Muslim turban and the Christian hat." According to Rustow, this act "implied a death sentence on the bastard Levantine culture that pervaded Istanbul" as well as Kemal's home of Salonica. It also coincided with efforts—in architecture and the arts—to maintain a unique Ottoman identity while also adopting a Europeanization program. Almost a century later, Turkish national sympathies led some to adopt the *kalpak,* a black lamb-skinned cap worn by the Turan peoples of Anatolia and Central Asia.[35]

Mustafa Kemal also believed that Turks should dress differently, but he rejected the kalpak because it was not representative of the "international civilization," which he believed that the Turks should emulate. Toynbee captures the core of Kemal's view: "The galpaq [sic]," he wrote, "no less than the fez, marked off its wearers from the Western people who wore hats and had inherited the earth." Thus, the RPP "deliberately set itself to remove this symbolic banner." In speeches throughout Anatolia, Mustafa Kemal also pointed out that the hat was less expensive than the fez and that Turkish dress was already multifaceted due to Byzantine cultural diffusion. But the justificatory conceptual thrust remained: the Turks must dress in the "ordinary clothes in use among the civilized peoples of the world."[36]

The first law on dress in the Republic referenced the head gear of public servants who were not otherwise required to wear special dress (September 21,

1924). Under this law, all hats and veils were prohibited in state institutions. In May of the following year, the Turkish navy adopted the German Naval cap. A law passed in November 1925 extended these policies, declaring that all men who covered their heads must do so with a brimmed cap. Head covering for women was never prohibited except for women working in state institutions, but it was greatly discouraged to promote social equality among all members of the nation and greater social liberty for women.[37]

The regulations on dress were met with immediate resistance. General Nurettin Pasha, a deputy from Bursa, "sought to prove the law unconstitutional, and pleaded that, whatever regulations might be imposed on officials, all other governments—both in Europe and Asia—allowed private citizens to wear the head-gear they pleased," a recurring theme in some quarters of the nationalist movement. Other opponents claimed that the hat brim constrained prayer (which requires the touching of the forehead to the ground), or that it illustrated once again that Turkish "modernizers" were interested less in national development than in imitating the West. Protests that followed the regulations precipitated more Independence Tribunals and a forceful response, including executions, by the government in parts of Anatolia (Sivas, Erzurum, Rize, and Giresun). The series of incidents that were related to the Hat Laws are illustrative of laik politics in Turkey because many of these dynamics and themes never disappear within the conceptual frame of modernization in Turkey. The Kemalist goal of becoming civilized would forever be contested as unconstitutional, imitationist, or hostile to the religiocultural ways of the Turkish people.[38]

Regardless, the RPP continued with its program and its ambition to align Turkey with the political, cultural, social, and economic flow of the West, sloughing off its "repressive past of ignorance, fanaticism, and backwardness." This understanding is a component of all of the so-called cultural policies associated with laiklik politics. These include the adoption of the Gregorian calendar (January 1, 1926), the adoption of Aramaic numerals (May 24, 1928) and the prohibition of public use of Arabic script (November 3, 1928), the elimination of Arabic and Persian from school curricula (1929), the adoption of the metric system (1933), the abolition of all titles and hereditary positions (November 27, 1934), the adoption of last names (January 1, 1935), the prohibition of religious clothing outside of places of worship (1934), the adoption of the Saturday-Sunday weekend (May 1935), the conversion of the Hagia Sophia to a museum (1935), and the encouragement of western literature and arts as well as the creation of new "modern Turkish" ones. The declaration of the state as laik, translated for westerners as secular, was itself a signal that Turkey was becoming westernized. To the Turks it was clear that their new leadership was demoting the Islamic past in favor of a "westernized" future.[39]

DIFFERING INTERPRETATIONS OF ISLAM

As I discuss above, the demotion of Islam occurred structurally as well as with the creation and subordination of the Presidency of Religious Affairs. Mustafa Kemal's discussion of the abolition of the Caliphate was a significant moment in his *Speech*. He claimed that this decision was a result of a recognition among the elite "that it is indispensable in order to purify and elevate the Islamic faith, to disengage it from its condition of being a political instrument which it had been for centuries through habit." This utterance is considered to be telling in some accounts of laiklik because it is interpreted as evidence for the disestablishment account or as evidence that Kemal (and hence his policies associated with laiklik) sought a form of secularism that respected religion. The utterance insinuates a distinction between Islam as a "pure" faith and Islam as a political tool.[40]

There are different interpretations of the RPP's attitude toward Islam even in the literature of the control account. For example, Binnaz Toprak asserts that "Islam was equated with reactionary and obscurantist political views which stood in the way of reform, development and progress," and Dodd claims that "there was no truck with religion." Bromley further suggests that Kemalism was quintessentially a form of "modernization against Islam." My view is that the Kemalists distinguished between "Islams," and that they supported one and actively opposed the other.[41] Those who sought to use Islam as a political tool (for purposes other than those of Kemalism) were seen by the Kemalists as "obscurantist" and would always meet opposition from the new laik state; whereas those who viewed Islam as a matter of faith would find the laik republic hospitable.[42]

This point is not incidental to a control account of laiklik. Toprak, who obscures the distinction in the above comment, makes this clear: "Because Islam is something more than a religious belief system, the problem of secularization also becomes something more than formal separation [between the state and religion]." The problem is one of authority, and whatever else the early Kemalists may have wanted to do with religion, they were not willing to relinquish supremacy to divine sources. This was clearly true after March 1924. Previously, as Parla has discussed in his study of the Six Arrows, Mustafa Kemal "entertained an idea of a Turkish-Islamic (-Western) synthesis" while still maneuvering through the early sovereignty debates. As early as 1922–1923, he asseverated a concern that his group's politics "lacked certain things in terms of religion." He praised Islam as the most reasonable (*makul*) and natural (*tabii*) religion and articulated a desire to purify it from its degenerated and superstitious forms.[43]

For those interpreters who distinguish between different interpretations of Islam in Turkey, Kemal's support for Islam "in all its plain trueness" becomes evidence for the RPP's support for freedom of religion, if not for Islamic reform. Thus, even while it instituted new controls over religion, the Kemalist regime is seen to have ensured the fulfillment of Islam as a faith. Rustow interprets the situation:

> The official pronouncements of Kemal's Republican People's Party commonly stressed that its secularism stemmed from a desire to rescue religion from its traditional entanglement with worldly affairs and thus to see it assume an even stronger position within its proper sphere of personal conscience. There is no doubt that from the lips of many Kemalists such statements were perfectly sincere. Nothing could have been more alien to the spirit and practice of Kemal's policy than any systematic persecution or molestation of clerics. The mosques remained open, and parents remained free to bring their children up in the precepts of Muslim ethics and in the practice of worship. The two highest festivals—the *Kurban Bayramı* [feast of the sacrifice] and the *Şeker Bayramı* [feast after Ramazan]—were recognized . . . cannons and drums continued to sound during Ramazan; and boys at the time of the circumcision continued to parade in the streets in their blue caps and colorful sashes.[44]

It may also be pointed out that the abolition of the medrese system did not entail removal of state-sponsored religious training and instruction for the state's religious establishment. The medrese of the Süleymaniye complex in Istanbul was to be replaced by the Faculty of Divinity at the nearby University of Istanbul administered by the Ministry of Education. In 1928, a committee of the Faculty issued a report stating that "religious life must be reformed, like moral and economic life, by means of scientific procedure and by the aid of reason." It proposed that prayers and Koran recitation be offered in Turkish rather than Arabic. (This was not the first call for Islamic reform in Turkey. As I discuss in the previous chapter, some Young Turk ideologues had already been publishing translations of the Koran so that it would be accessible to non-Arabic speakers.) The report also suggested far-reaching reforms of the mosques, including the introduction of vocal and instrumental music, Imam's missions, pews, cloakrooms, and the wearing of clean shoes. Although these were never adopted, aspects of the reform project were accepted in 1932 when, "under the initiative of Atatürk, the Qur'an was intoned in the mosques in Turkish" and an edict from the *Diyanet* required that all calls to prayer (*ezan*) be issued in Turkish. The edict did not reference the language of prayer, which remained Arabic.[45]

The significance of these policies that are directly or indirectly associated with laiklik politics in Turkey is that they demonstrate the *laicism* of Kemalist laiklik. This is in contrast to attempts in the literature to describe Kemalist state support for religion as secularism.

LAICISM NOT SECULARISM

If "secularism" as a political concept connotes anything, it connotes a political sphere that is not influenced by religion. This conception accommodates control relations between a secular center and religion but little room for public policy directly interested in religion or religious considerations more generally. Laiklik did not entail ending state interest in religion. Therefore, an understanding of laiklik in Turkey would incorporate the concept of laicism, or lay governance into our explanatory frameworks.

In a religious frame, *lay* persons—literally "the people"—can be religious believers too. Laiklik is no exception (though I do not mean that all supporters of laicism were practicing Muslims). The institutional relations that were established in its course reflect a concern of the Kemalists to support—with varying degrees—a version of their interpretation of "pure" Islam, which adopted aspects of the Islamic reformist ideas seen in Ziya Gökalp's Turkish nationalist thought. The elimination of the Ottoman ulema was followed by the elevation of "lower-level religious personnel" to a similar role for the Republic. Their knowledge of what Mardin terms the "religious sciences" might not have been as thorough as their predecessors, but this does not alter the fact that laiklik included what Berkes aptly named a "new religious policy." The state's efforts to cultivate a new clerical class, thus "enabling many more laypersons to be vocal in religious affairs"—should not be disregarded in our account of the original conception of laiklik politics.[46]

Generally stated, laicism entails institutionally elevating lay people to a superior position to those who occupy positions as members of a religiously wise strata. This is the path that the Kemalists pursued, largely as a way of implementing their "Turkish transformation." Supporters of laicism may be devout or not; they may even be clerics who oppose, for instance, the excessive entanglement of religion and political power.

Thus, although laicism in the Turkish context expresses an anticlerical purpose to some extent (some state clerics remained), it was not necessarily antireligious. In one dimension, laiklik entails giving priority over religious matters to those who believe in the Kemalist version of religion. The Kemalist supporters in this case included clerics as well as lay persons who accepted the Kemalist interpretation of the place of Islam in politics.[47]

This point helps to make sense of Kemalism. It also clarifies confusion among interpreters of laiklik who see laiklik as secularism and who might be less aware of the different interpretations of Islam in Turkey's laiklik politics. The confusion is caused, in part, by monolithic conceptions of Turkish Islam and, in part, by descriptions of RPP authoritarianism that ignore its religious policy.[48]

I do not mean to suggest that all of the ambiguous areas that are involved in interpreting Kemalist laiklik are resolved by seeing it as a form of laicism. The range of its commitment to its own religious policy continues to be debated. I maintain that the shift in our comparative, explanatory language from secularism to laicism helps to clarify the politics that are associated with the original conception of laiklik. I shall return to this theme later.[49]

THE CONTRIBUTION OF ŞERIF MARDIN: KEMALIST POSITIVISM AND THE "STRANGLEHOLD OF FOLK CULTURE"

To Kemal's critics, especially those whom he considered reactionary, the association between his party's politics and the program for political and cultural westernization became so close that even the latter became authoritarian relative to Islam. Thus, notwithstanding the RPP's defense of its agenda, modernization in Turkey, in some versions of the control account, would be seen as modernization by a secular elite at the center imposed on or against Islam of the periphery (*modernleştirmek* as opposed to *modernleşmek*). The foremost interpreter of this dynamic in Turkey is Şerif Mardin, whose paradigmatic notion of a center-periphery cultural gap has had a profound influence on interpretations of modern Turkish politics.[50]

Mardin's work has consistently stressed how Atatürk's "cultural Westernization" program, with its underpinnings in Comtean positivism and Mustafa Kemal's own disposition against the "stranglehold of folk culture," manifested in an effort to "chase out of modern Turkey" the Islamic "mythopoetic forms" of Turkish folk culture that were central to Turkish identity during the Ottoman period. Islam, Mardin writes, "was a rich store of symbols and ways of thinking about society." It "defined for many individuals the means by which they handled their encounters with daily life, served to crystallize their identities and regulate their psychological tensions, and provided modes of communication, mediation, and community leadership." In short, Islam constituted an integral element of self and society.[51]

Positivism, by contrast, provided for the Kemalists the vision that the theological stage of history is over, and that its remnants are a sign of historical backwardness in need of enlightenment through education that is based on the modern sciences. In this frame, reason and theology are at odds, and the role of the new secular state was to "eliminate the power of religious ideas and laws, customs and arrangements" to bring the people to a higher rationality. This would be done by cleansing their minds of anachronistic superstition and "purifying them in light of true science."[52]

For Mardin, Kemalism's emplacement in positivism was its fundamental flaw in sociopolitical terms, especially in the Turkish-Islamic context. Based in an "uncompromising materialistic problem-setting mode" that manifested in a "clear distaste for religion," Kemalism, in Mardin's account, offered only a cognitive directive as a foundation for modern Turkish identity. It therefore created an "ethical vacuum" with profound consequences in a society whose "cultural knapsack" was rooted in the metaphorical dimensions of religion. The "inability of Kemalism to provide a social ethos that appealed to the heart as well as the mind was more disorienting than would appear at first sight."[53]

Coupled with a program designed to alter the cultural dynamic of Muslim Turks in line with the West, Kemalism amounted to an assault on the integrity of Turkish society: "Depriving a person of his ability to use the set of symbols which shape his individual approach to God may be a more distressing blow to him than depriving him of other values. It may be easier to take defeat on the battlefield than to be deprived of the means of personal access to the sacred, especially if this access is one of the processes that make for mental equilibrium, personal satisfaction, and integration with the rest of society."[54]

But it was not only positivism that undergirded this blow to Turkish folk culture. Mardin argues that an additional impetus derived from Mustafa Kemal's "disgust with the forms of social control which sprang from folk culture." A common denominator of all of the "secularist reforms" is the "liberation of the individual from the collective constraints of the Muslim

community." "Mahalle Islam" (roughly, neighborhood Islam) in Turkish culture "snuffed out personality." It constituted a "stranglehold," requiring that
"final legitimation" be "obtained in terms of religious values." To Atatürk,
"Western society which received its legitimation from science, was more open
and therefore more inventive." It would be necessary through reform, to "wrest
the individual away from" the "idiocy of traditional community-oriented life."
"Could a civilized nation," Mustafa Kemal had asked, "tolerate a mass of people
who let themselves be led by the nose by a herd of *sheikhs, dedes, deids, tschelebis,
babas,* and *emirs;* who entrusted their lives to chiromancers, magicians, dice
throwers, and amulet sellers?" Mardin notes how Kemal's interest in integrating
male and female relations stems from this attitude and could be seen only as an
attack on local notables. "In fact, Atatürk's thrust to establish women's rights
may be conceptualized as a concentrated effort to smash what to him appeared
as the most stifling, and dark aspect of the *mahalle* ethos, namely the restraint it
placed on contacts between men and women in the day-to-day routine of
life."[55]

All of these factors, Mardin suggests, show how Kemalist claims that laiklik
was *not antireligious* could hardly have been convincing to all of its opponents.
Islam as a "personal value" could not meet the everyday ethical demands of a
culture in which Islam was a principle of social cohesion. From this angle, all of
the "secularist" reforms that were intended to "modernize" Turkey were more
than disestablishment because they imposed control by a Western-oriented
elite that was intent on carrying out an ethically limited and contextually
inappropriate political and cultural program.[56]

Each cultural reform, Mardin suggests, can be seen as a devaluation of Islam's
"rich symbolic fund." The adoption of the Gregorian calendar, for instance,
signaled the alien "time dimension of the Republic." By erasing the "metaphor
of Islamic time," this reform caused a "void in the structure of time." New
schools that "tried to bring students into contact with Western culture, literature, music, and even social thought" failed to address esoteric but familiar
peripheral themes, such as the "unity of God, the limits of man's freedom and
the danger of the times though which they were living." For some the "village
institutes (People's Houses and People's Rooms) were dens of iniquity because
they shared the influence of Marxism; for others, because the students were
exposed to the teachings of Freud." A turn to the West in favor of "opera, ballet
and Western polyphonic music (oriental music in public being banned for a
time)," Kemalist modernism with laiklik symbolized the oppression of local

culture. (Turkey became fertile ground for the future reception of postmodernism.)[57]

SUMMARY: THE CONTRIBUTIONS OF THE CONTROL ACCOUNT

The unfolding of laiklik politics within the frame described in control accounts indicates how interpreters of Turkey's laiklik politics explain them, as Bromley does, as "rigid state control over religious life" and "modernization against Islam." From these dynamics Kemalist laiklik earned its reputation as strict, firm, militant, staunch, and determined—in addition to rigid, the English word that comes closest to the Turkish concept of *katı*. The consequences of Kemalist political authoritarianism, combined with the Kemalist cultural reforms, suggest an institutionalized pattern of control as part of the identity of secularism in Turkey.

There is no single control account. We have seen differences among them. For instance, Mardin sees aspects of laiklik as "galling to the Muslim population of Turkey" (the singularity of the "Muslim population" is important), while others, like Rustow, see laiklik as perfectly consistent with the religious needs of modern Turks.

Despite the differences, however, these control accounts explain how the policies of laiklik, founded on the Ottoman-Turkish tradition of sovereign hegemony, were carried out within a context of political contestation in which the Kemalists gained political power and utilized it to effect their version of the "Turkish transformation." This allows us to consider one control account from diverse versions. It persuasively describes the power relations between the center of the sovereign state and the religious institutions within it, and it captures the sociological dynamic between that center and its periphery. To those who saw secularization as institutional separation, proponents of the control account suggest control, not separation. To those who believed that modernization in Turkey confirmed the elimination of religion from the public sphere, the control account suggests supervision through institutionalized power relations, not privatization.

An implicit critique of two of modernization theory's historical expectations for modernity is thus at work in the control account. The control account posits that secularism in Turkey did not result in a structural differentiation as separation between political and religious spheres. And the control account suggests that religiopolitical forces in modernity did not, in Turkey, inevitably assume their place in the private sphere. Some of them were crushed in the exercise of political power by the state as the Kemalists articulated a new interpretation of Islam and constructed new institutions for that interpretation. As a result, Islam has never been fully privatized in Turkey. Clerics who accepted the Kemalist terms of laicism were allowed to assume a new place within the state's religious institutions. The control account suggests that the separation and privatization theses of modernization must be open to reconsideration in the study of laiklik.

Both of these theses indicate the narrowing secular-modernist prejudgments about the character of modern political history that I criticize in Chapter 1. In Gadamer's terminology, such assumptions constitute hindering prejudgments that should be reevaluated in a hermeneutic engagement with this field of interpretation.

In effect, in the history of anglophone interpretations of Turkish politics since the founding of the Republic, the control account functions as a "counter-historiography" relative to attempts by social scientists to portray laiklik as "secularism in a western sense." Importantly, this is true in the Turkish political context as well, where expositions of the control dynamics that constitute laiklik—from a variety of viewpoints with a variety of interests—have profoundly impacted the critique of "official history" and, consequently, laiklik politics after the one-party period. Early republicans defended laiklik, like the other reforms, as an achievement to make Turkey a modern state in the western sense. Mardin calls the "idea of a secular state" the "foundation myth of the republic." A close reading of the control accounts in the literature on Turkey or on Turkish politics reveals an attempt to distinguish secularism in its western sense from secularism in Turkey. Where the state wished to assert commonality, interpreters of the state's claims have asserted difference. As Toprak writes: "What the control account argues is that what early republicans did was to call a relation of control, 'separation'; that this was not true; that originally there was no separation; that what the state did was to control religion in order to relegate it to marginality in public affairs. Hence the control account questions, or is critical of, the official Kemalist claim that there was a separation. Hence, the control account is, in a sense, a counter-historiography to official history."[58]

SEPARATION DIMENSIONS OF LAIKLIK

Without losing sight of the persuasive claims of the control account, it is not clear that its conceptual thrust adequately captures the character of the power frames that constitute laiklik. For example, the distinction between Islam as a faith, moral message, and set of rituals, and Islam as a counterrevolutionary (Kemalist) religiopolitical force intimates that it is incorrect to consider secularism in Turkey as hostile to religion. The conceptual thrust of the control account is not adequate to describe some practices that are associated with laiklik. The original practices that were associated with laiklik may have been hostile to certain forms of Islam, but the general claim that they were hostile to all aspects of Islam is not compelling, as argued by some subscribers to the control account.

Similarly, a thorough look at some of the separationist claims about laiklik made by those who established it indicates that the term "separation" does not simply reference the institutional power relations that the control account scrutinizes. The existence of certain separationist claims does not alone constitute counterevidence to the control account. The hermeneutic imperative to gauge conceptual frames is not so facile. It suggests identifying the different aspects of the constitutive matrix of meanings and considering which of them are most powerfully true in the understandings of participants in power relations. These meanings must influence our account of their political lives. We might say, for instance, that actors are wrong about separation in one sense, while truthful about it in another; but to say that they are wrong at all must be grounded in an accurate account of aspects of their conceptual frame that are true for them.

In this context, the control account gets a hermeneutic boost when we examine the broad contours of debate over laiklik after the one-party period. Although normative evaluations differ, all participants agreed that control was a central constitutive element of Kemalist laiklik. Defenders of a religiopolitical ethic or of the Ottoman-Islamic past saw religion tied to a state that sought to impose atheistic (or communist) designs on an essentially religious people. (This argument became a demand for greater religious freedom as true secularism requires.) Some descendants of the Second Group saw laiklik as a heavy-handed attempt to interfere with the Muslim identity of the Turkish people. ("The Turks are a Muslim people and will remain Muslim"—"we will not try to change this aspect of your identity"—became familiar among this group's leaders.) Kemalists, who continued to deny accusations of atheism—even pointing out their support for religious reforms—argued that some control over some forms of religiopolitical expression were necessary to minimize "reactionaryism" in politics. All three understandings have conceptual constituencies. The constitutive control dimensions of laiklik are expressed in the control account. Relative to claims about separation between religion and the state, the control account is more accurate than alternative separation accounts.[59]

What, therefore, are the possible dimensions of separation that are true of laiklik in the single-party period? There are several, evidenced by specific constitutional, educational-sociocultural, and legal reforms. These separation dimensions are expressed in the most definitive descriptions of laiklik made by the RPP's leading ideologues and stated in party documents during the project's formative years, especially 1923–1931. Is is essential to identify true, separation-constitutive dimensions of laiklik politics to arrive at a hermeneutically sound explanation of them.

Evidence of non-institutional separationist understandings: In addition to claims to have separated religious institutions from the state, the early historical dialogue indicates other separationist claims. For example:

(1) In the rationale for the draft bill of the Turkish Civil Code, Minister of Justice Mahmut Esat (Bozkurt), a member of the ruling cadre's inner circle, asserted that the "principle distinguishing characteristic of states that belong to the civilization of the present century"—a group that Turkey was, according to the RPP leadership, in the process of joining—"is their considering religion and the world separate."[60]

(2) Similarly, the 1927 RPP statutes—issued when the RPP, in Mustafa Kemal's declaration noted above, officially and publicly described itself as *lâyık* for the first time—mentioned a separationist purpose to laiklik. It read, "The party, [so that it may] rescue matters of belief and conscience from politics and from various complications of politics, and [so that it may] realize all political, social, and economic laws, institutions, and needs according to principles and forms secured by the positive, experimental knowledge and sciences of contemporary civilization, counts among the most urgent principles the complete separation of religion (*tamamen birbirinden ayırmayı*) from the world in matters of state and nation" (Article 3).[61]

(3) Şerif Mardin notes that in a parliamentary debate in 1928, laiklik was defined as the "separation of religion and worldly concerns."[62]

(4, 5) The 1931 and 1935 programs of the RPP reiterate the decision of the party to make all laws, rules, and regulations according to the requirements of the present century and the methods, knowledge, and sciences of contemporary civilization. Both then state: "As the conception of religion is a matter of conscience, the party considers it to be one of the chief factors of the success of our nation in contemporary progress to maintain as separate (*ayrı tutmak*) ideas of religion from politics, from the affairs of the world and of the state."[63]

The existence of the word "separation" does not imply that any real separation occurred. What it does imply, however, is that the concept of separation is a feature of laiklik in its original conception in Turkey. Now, how *might* this be true? Or, within the context of the preceding discussion: given that the control account offers an explicit rejection of other separationist claims, to what extent or in what ways these utterances may be constitutive of the actions, policies, practices, relations, and institutions associated with laiklik?

Before answering this question directly, four aspects of the statements documented above must be noted. First, separation is *not* conceived in *institutional* terms alone. The claims reference separating religion or religious ideas and matters of belief and conscience from politics, the world, or affairs of the world in matters of state and nation. Thus, the emphasis is on separating religious theory and practice from the theory and practice of the state. (I include "practice" here, because the documents mention both religious ideas and religion in general.) Second, this separation is seen to have several aims, ranging from "rescuing" religious matters from political conflict (a theme in Mustafa Kemal's speech) to defining religion's proper realm as the realm of conscience (*vicdan*). Third, each explication of laiklik mentions the Turkish nation's goal of progress and success in self-government according to the positive sciences, methods, and knowledge of contemporary civilization. Finally, the sense of separation is active in these claims. In 1927, the party considers it urgent to create a division. By 1931 and 1935, it seeks to maintain a separation presumably already achieved.

The active, contextual meanings of separation: Some accounts of laiklik in the anglophone social science literature capture this active sense of the concept of separation. For example, Metin Heper describes the effort "to free politics from religion"; Feroz Ahmad sees an effort "to cut" the state's formal ties with religion. The distinction between an active sense of separating and a descriptive claim that asserts a de facto separation is important: laiklik may not have accomplished a complete separation between religion and politics, religion and the world, and so on. But actors who participated in laiklik may have intended to separate one from the other to some extent from a previous position of interrelation in some specific areas of state activity. Indeed, certain Kemalist practices that are associated with laiklik express this purpose. Salient among them are the constitutional changes of April 1928: the abrogation of articles declaring the religion of the state to be Islam and guaranteeing the execution of Islamic law (Articles 2 and 26 of the 1924 constitution, respectively); and the substitution of "I swear on my honor" for "I swear before God" in the declarations of allegiance to the Turkish Republic that are taken by Assembly deputies and the president (Articles 16, section 2; and 38, section 3).[64]

To emphasize these declarations, they should also be seen against the historical background of the relation between the state and religion during the Ottoman period. The 1876 Ottoman constitution that was nominally in place in the final years of Ottoman rule expressed well this relation. Article 3 of the Constitution stated, "The Ottoman sovereignty which is united in the person of the sovereign of the supreme Caliph of Islam belongs to the eldest of the princes of the dynasty of Osman." Articles 4, 5, and 7 further elucidated the Islamic identity of the Sultan: "(4) His majesty the Sultan is by the title of the Caliph the protector of the Muslim religion. He is the sovereign and the Padishah of all Ottomans. (5) His majesty is irresponsible. His person is sacred. (7) His majesty the Sultan counts among the number of his sovereign rights the following prerogatives . . . his name is pronounced in the mosques during the prayers . . . he causes to be executed the dispositions of the şeriat (sacred law) and the laws." And Article 11 declared that "Islam is the religion of the State," guaranteeing protection and privileges for all recognized religions.[65]

The 1921 Constitution eliminated the imperial dimensions of these articles, but maintained Islam as the state religion. Given the historical relation between the Ottoman state and Islam, the 1928 abrogations and amendments overturn a profound tradition of state-religion interdependence. The constitutional changes fit squarely in the expressed project of actively separating or disentangling religion from its previous interrelation with state affairs in these particular contexts.

Therefore, rather than seeing the concept of separation as a de facto descriptive account of laiklik's achievements, it should be understood as a purpose of laiklik in a particular historical context. No matter to what extent the political and religious spheres remained interrelated after the Kemalist reforms the ruling cadre sought to ensure that they would be less intertwined than before. A separating of the two was necessary—not in a complete and institutional sense, but in other senses related to the political, social, cultural, and economic ends of the Kemalist project.

The political, social, and cultural objectives of Kemalism have already been discussed in some detail. I will now relate the political, social, and cultural objectives of Kemalism that I have discussed to the project of laiklik and its character as a central principle of the Kemalist transformation. One preliminary caution: the control dimensions of these goals should always be kept in mind when considering the concept of separation. The concept of separation here does not mean complete separation; it means certain separations in a context of overall control. This is why my account of the separationist dimensions of laiklik is an effort to strengthen the control account, which I later discuss.

Separating affairs of the world: Many documents discuss the project of laiklik explicitly after the major reforms have been undertaken. There are few that do so during the reforms, prior to the constitutional changes. Among the former, one of the most authoritative statements is Recep Peker's 1931 (October 16) "Explication" of the RPP reforms at a colloquium sponsored by Istanbul University. Peker (1888–1950) was a member of the RPP inner circle and general secretary of the Party three times between 1923 and 1936. An excerpt from his "Explication" in which he describes laiklik illustrates how the RPP leadership understood affairs of the world. After quoting the full text of the party definition of its laiklik arrow (quoted above), Peker names the abolition of the medrese school system and the Islamic law courts as the two definitive accomplishments of laiklik. These two actions and the totality of educational and legal policies and practices that comprised them are vital areas in which the Kemalists understood their project as one of separating affairs of religion and those of the world. Matters related to education and law are cornerstones of the specifically Kemalist laik project of separating religious theory and practice from worldly affairs.[66]

Education: The Unity of Education Law (*Tevhid-i Tedrisat Kanunu,* March 1924) exemplifies this conceptualization. It brought all educational and scientific institutions under the control of the Ministry of Education—all religious schools (*medreses* and *mekteps*) as well as the budgets of the Sheriat and Vakf Ministry that managed them. (Recall that the Caliphate was abolished and that the Presidency of Religious Affairs was established on the same date.) The purpose of the law was to unify previously dichotomous educational tracks between religious and nonreligious education, thus bringing education under the control of the party-controlled state. The RPP installed an educational system that would teach the ideals of the RPP, especially those related to the study of the explicitly antitheological and antitheocentric positive sciences.[67]

This goal was not achieved in 1924. Religious classes continued to be offered in the primary schools. In 1927, they were offered by parental request. It was not until RPP consolidation over the state was complete in 1928 that the RPP implemented national education excluding religious theory and practice expedited (especially after the constitutional reforms): "The Ministry of Education took steps to drop classes in religion from the school curricula." Lessons in Arabic and Persian were abolished in 1928, and instruction was "left to specialized departments at the university level"; classes in religion were dropped in the urban primary schools in 1930 and in middle schools in 1931; the change was effected in the village schools in 1933. 1928 marks the moment of consolidation; just as religious theory and practice were separated in constitutional clauses, they would be separated from education in the contemporary sciences as national education, as Mustafa Kemal called it, would take hold.[68]

The Kemalist view was that "religious superstition" held the nation back. It induced lethargy that impeded "national progress and development." Thus religious theory in public education was incompatible with the progress that was necessary to reach contemporary civilization. The RPP's 1931 program stated that the "foundational stone" of its "public educational policy is the abolition of ignorance" (1931 Program, "National education and instruction," section 5A). Peker describes the schools as "far from superstitions" of the religious traditions that dominated the nation's past. Regardless of the control dimensions that were entailed by such a policy, the RPP conceptualized their policies related to unifying education as designed to separate religion from worldly proceedings.[69]

An explicit statement of the attitudes that are necessary for success that would be cultivated in the new educational system appears in the second clause of the fifth section of the party's 1931 educational program. It states an interest in cultivating "republican, nationalist, and *lâyık* citizens" who would respect or honor the "Turkish Grand National Assembly and the Turkish state." A short statement of the need to develop a national character that respects the historical past of the Turkish nation (as opposed to Ottoman traditions) is followed by a statement recurring throughout the literature on laiklik: the methods and knowledge that are pursued in education are to be molded to "secure success in material life for its citizens." This statement follows one that explicates the nationalist character of the new educational program. Presumably it is intended as further commentary on its *layik* character. This assumption is supported by such repeated themes in the definition of laiklik in the party's official program. The Kemalist view is that education must be freed from religious beliefs as a precondition for success in the material world. Deep in the Kemalist understanding of state, national, and international affairs is the idea that material success depends on the division of religion and education.[70]

The significance of this calls for a brief detour. As Parla has shown, the declared intent to create republicanist, nationalist, and laik citizens for purposes related to material success links dimensions of the laiklik project with goals of national economic development. Although I do not deal directly with the Kemalist state's solidarist-corporatist policies that are related to economic development, there is an intersection between these "worldly" affairs and laiklik. From its inception, the RPP considered economic development as a top priority. Its 1923 statement (September 9), "Nine principles of the People's Party," which declared the intention of the first group to become the People's Party, "set forth as certain conditions the securing of national, economic, and administrative independence." The first four goals deal with national sovereignty of the state and its institutions, the irrevocability of the abolition of the Sultanate, the survival of the Islamic world's Caliphate that will support new national institutions, internal security, and the creation of new courts. Immediately following these, the Party lists ten measures for economic and social betterment. Among them are new tax policies; support for tobacco, agrocommerce, and industrialization, and so on. Moreover, the sentence in the 1927 document that declares the RPP to be *lâyık* (see above) reads: "The RPP is Republicanist, *lâyık*, populist, and nationalist and *counts as first order of importance the securing of national economic interests*" (emphasis added). There is a conceptual association between the removal of religion from national education and the creation of the educational/sociocultural/attitudinal conditions for national economic development. The earliest official conception of Turkey's laik politics reveals the goal to create nationally loyal and *lâyık* citizens who will "achieve success in the material world."[71]

The conceptual links between laiklik and national economic development illuminate what the Kemalists believed would be the benefits of the knowledge and methods of the positive sciences: the road to progress required the development of a nonreligiously influenced instrumental rationality. As the Party documents have shown, developing citizens with a positivist rationality was an explicit goal of laiklik policies. Thus, aspects of the educational policies that were associated with laiklik should be understood as related to policies connected to national economic development. The relation becomes sharper upon considering the policies that were designed to integrate Turks culturally (for example, dress, script, etc.) with the West.

Separate religious schools: Elements of the Kemalist laik interest in controlling religious as well as nonreligious education, discussed in the control account, also appear in the Unity of Education Law. This law has been interpreted as "eliminating all religious educational institutions." Some maintain that all religious education was forbidden by the reforms.[72]

According to the law, however, neither of these appear to be the case. Article 4 empowers the Ministry of Education to establish a Faculty of Divinity at the Darülfünun (later Istanbul University) "with the duty of training officials, such as preachers, for the performance of religious services." It also empowers the Ministry to open separate mekteps (*ayrı mektepler*) to serve as lower-level religious schools for the same purpose.[73]

True, dwindling enrollments and interest led to the transformation of the Faculty into the Institute of Islamic Research in the Faculty of Letters in 1933, and the cessation of the mekteps in the same year. The falling interest largely coincided with the post-1928 consolidation. But the law, which later empowered the revival of these institutions on a scale well beyond the intent of the RPP, established a role for the RPP in all education, religious as well as nonreligious. In 1934, the *Diyanet İşleri Reisliği*—"attached to the Prime Minister's office"—initiated Koran courses, partly as replacements for the mekteps. "The number of teachers and students grew steadily after 1934."[74]

There does not appear to be a complete cessation of the state's interest in religious education. If a unified nonreligious education was meant to cultivate a new citizen who was loyal to RPP ideals, the purpose of the religious education was to meet the religious needs of the nation; to "engage in research and to foster the new religious outlook," as Howard Reed describes it. That the Unity of Education law was promulgated simultaneously with the abolition of the Caliphate underscores its status as an expression of RPP purposes to secure hegemony for its version of lay governance. It was not inconsistent with this view that the state should support some religious education. It is significant, however, that in the conception of these founding educational policies, the nonuniversity-level religious schools and their purposes would be considered separate (*ayrı*) from the newly unified national educational system and its republican, national, and laik goals.[75]

Civil affairs—the rationale of the Turkish Civil Code: Beyond education, there is perhaps no policy more fundamental in the history of laiklik practices in Turkey than the abolition of religious law to govern civil affairs, and its replacement with a modified version of the Swiss Civil Code. Peker's juxtaposition of this reform to those related to education in his 1931 "Explication" underscores its significance. Mardin notes that the adopted civil code stands "like a rock in a sea of change" during laiklik's erosion in the post-single party period. There is perhaps no better single speech act of the pre-1927 period that states clearly the objectives of RPP policies that are associated with separating religion and state than Mahmut Esat (Bozkurt)'s "Rationale for the Draft Bill [of the civil code]." The "Rationale" was delivered as the Assembly was presented with a draft of the new code. It appears as a preamble to the code, which was adopted February 17, 1926, and implemented in October of the same year. The text should occupy a seminal status as an expression of laiklik's purposes, but it has not received the attention that it deserves. In it, Mahmut Esat explains the reasons behind the dismissal of religious laws in civil and commercial relations.[76]

As Minister of Justice and representative of the committee that prepared the bill, Mahmut Esat states unequivocally in the beginning of the preamble that the main failing of the Ottoman Imperial Code (the Mecelle) for the requirements of contemporary civilization is that religion is its main principle. Religion in contemporary legal codes is incompatible with the times and consequently, as he explains, "irreconcilable with Turkish national life." Significantly, he never mentions Islam. He conceptualizes the issue in general terms of religion, mores, customs, and traditions. And, although the new civil code contributed greatly to women's emancipation in Turkey because of the increased conjugal rights for women that it provides (for example, male monogamy, prohibition of divorce by repudiation, rights over surname after divorce, inheritance and property claims), the "Rationale" does not raise this issue. It emphasizes the need for a legal system consistent with the ruling party's definition of the interests of the Turkish nation and the patterns that were established by contemporary civilization. All else derives from these two goals.[77]

What were the real interests of the Turkish nation according to Mahmut Esat? There are several stated in the text, which related directly to the separation of religion and the world. They are stated in four different arguments that suggest how understanding the purposes of the civil code is crucial to understanding the purposes in the original conception of laiklik.

The first argument is that religion and the state must be separated because religions are incapable of change, "whereas life marches on." States that derive their legal codes from religion and that usually serve the interests of the "mighty and the oppressors" rather than the people condemn the communities in which these codes are applied to living in a medieval status. The implementation of such codes in the Turkish context is a hindrance to progress and inconsistent with the Turkish "revolution":

Those states whose laws are based on religion cannot satisfy . . . the demands of the country and the nation, for religions contain [express] immutable judgments. Life marches on; needs quickly change; religious laws cannot express any value, any meaning beyond form and dead words in the face of inexorably changing life. Not to change is a necessity for religions. . . . Laws that derive their principles from religions unite the communities in which they are being implemented with the primitive ages from which they have descended and constitute one of the major factors and reasons impeding progress. It should not be doubted that our laws that receive their inspiration from the immutable judgments of religion and are still linked [in continuous contact] to divine law are the most powerful factor in tying the Turkish nation's destiny to the stipulations and rules of the Middle Ages, even during the present century. The Turkish Republic's remaining deprived of a codified civil code which is the regulator of national social life, a code that should be inspired only by that life, is irreconcilable with the meaning and the conception required by the Turkish revolution.

Mahmut Esat generalizes this argument such that it applies not only to religions but to all mores embedded in local and regional legal codes. If the Turkish nation is backward in any sense, he asserts that this is due to the "medieval organizations and religious laws that unnecessarily besiege it." He declares, "To stay absolutely loyal to beliefs inherited from grandfathers and ancestors in the face of truths is incompatible with reason and intelligence." The implementation of the new Turkish Civil Code is thus rational and intelligent.

The second, related argument is that the previous legal system, in which the laws of religious communities (millets) governed the civil relations of residents suffered from "irregularities and persistent disorder." As such, these "primitive" codes fail to satisfy the interests of what Mahmut Esat calls political, social, economic, and national unity.

The experiences of Germany, France, and Switzerland, including the struggle of the French to deny the Church its power in civil relations, are invoked to demonstrate that Turkey's needs are similar to those of other states belonging to the "family of nations" of the "present century." Member states of this family, which was created as a result of "continuous social and economic contacts," find it necessary to unify their legal systems by eliminating local juridical diversity. Local and regional, linguistic and methodological, jurisprudential heterogeneity based on religious laws and mores breeds legal irregularity and disorder. Since it places the fate of the people on chance rather than a definite and stable principle of justice, such disorder is not conducive to the real interests of the nation. Mahmut Esat discusses the situation in the Republic:

[With some exceptions] judges of the Turkish Republic are adjudicating by extrapolation and inference from slapdash *fıkıh* [Islamic codes of jurisprudence] and religious principles. The Turkish judge is not bound in his judgements by any specific precedents, binding rulings and principles. Therefore, the judgement reached in a case in one locality of our country and the judgements arrived at in a similar case that is being adjudicated under the same conditions in other localities of the country are usually different from and contradictory with each other. Consequently, in the administration of justice, the people of Turkey are being exposed to irregularities and persistent disorder. Fate of the people does not depend on a definitive and stable principle of justice, but on medieval *fıkıh* rules that are coincidental, change-dependent, and mutually contradictory. To rescue Republican Turkish justice from this chaos, deprivation and very primitive situation, it has become indispensable to create quickly and legislate a new Turkish Civil Code that is fitting to the requirements of our transformation and of the civilization of the present century.

In contrast, jurisprudential homogeneity brings great benefits. He expresses the indispensable prerequisite for such benefits as follows: "The fundamental point of these laws [of the states of the present century] that we respect is the separation, in the absolute sense, of religion and state. Switzerland, Germany and France strengthened and fortified their political and national unities, and their economic, social salvations and developments by promulgating their civil codes." Esat asserts that the alternative situation of legal heterogeneity relying on local religions and traditions in the European context "was not desired, could not be desired, and could not have even been imagined." The will of the leadership in this matter is resolute. The need to achieve unity—to strengthen Turkey's political unity—by abolishing backward and confusing legal codes requires, in Mahmut Esat's words, the separation of religion and state. Of course, given the ties that linked religion to the state in laiklik practices, even though Mahmut Esat says religion and state, what he means here is religion and the legal system of the state.

Mahmut Esat's third and forcefully stated argument is that religion, once removed from legal power, resides in the "inviolable and secure" realm of conscience. This is a theme in all of the documents of the RPP leadership that I have discussed. To the Kemalists it was a corollary of separating religion qua religious theory and practice and the state qua matters of the world, politics, and nation. Religion's relegation to the conscience was also, as Mahmut Esat said, "one of the principles of the contemporary civilization that distinguished the old and the new."[78]

The second and third arguments are summed up in the following passage:

There is no doubt that the purpose of laws is not to arrive at any stipulation which derives from mores or tradition or from any religious rules which should be only matters related with the conscience, but rather with providing and satisfying at any cost the political, social, economic, and national unity. The principal distinguishing characteristic of states that belong to the civilization of the present century is their considering religion and the world separate. The opposite of this results in the domination of the conscience of someone who does not agree with the accepted religious foundations of the state. The understanding of states of the present century cannot accept this. Religion is to be revered and would be immune as long as it remains a matter of conscience from the point of view of the state. Intrusions of religion into laws as articles and stipulations have always during history resulted in serving the arbitrary will and desire of rulers, the mighty, and oppressors. In separating religion from the world, the state of the present century saves humanity from these bloodstained afflictions of history and allocates religion to the conscience as the real and eternal throne for it. Especially in states that contain subjects belonging to various religions, in order to acquire the ability of carrying out a single law in all of the community, this severing of relations with religion is a requisite for the sovereignty of the nation. This is because if the laws will be based on religion it becomes necessary for the state that is faced with the necessity of accepting freedom of conscience to make separate laws for its subjects belonging to various religions. This situation is totally opposed to the political, social, economic, and national unity that is a fundamental condition in states of the present century.

This passage also hints at the fourth justification for separating religion and the legal system of the state in the comment, "Especially in states that contain subjects belonging to various religions, in order to acquire the ability of carrying out a single law in all of the community, this severing of relations with religion is a requisite for the sovereignty of the nation." This suggests that the RPP considered Turkey's religious heterogeneity a reason for separating religion and the state. But, this comment might also allude to other considerations that influenced the RPP leadership's decision to pursue and to declare a policy of separating religion and state.

These considerations involve promises by Turkey to the occupying powers during the negotiations at Lausanne between November 1922 and July 1923. In the "Rationale," Mahmut Esat mentions the issue only briefly, but in an essay presented on the fifteenth anniversary of the Turkish Civil Code entitled "How the Turkish Civil Code was prepared," he notes that the legal position of foreigners as well as "subjects of different religions" came up at Lausanne.

To understand these concerns some background is necessary. Previous to the Republic, the Ottoman empire allowed foreign powers to gain special economic and legal privileges over both the latter's own subjects residing in the Ottoman lands and over residents of religiously similar millets. The former were manifested in the famous capitulations treaties. The consequences stemming from the Treaty of Küçük Kaynarca, described by Shaw as "one of the most fateful documents of Ottoman history," illustrate the latter. In this treaty, Russia and the Ottomans agreed to Crimea's independence. In return for some territorial concessions the "sultan had to give the czarina the right to build and protect an Orthodox Church in Istanbul. [This was] subsequently interpreted to signify Russian protection over all Orthodox Christians in the empire . . . thus enabling Russia to intervene in Ottoman internal affairs for its own advantage in the century that followed." Although the Turks at Lausanne were not negotiating with the Russians, they knew this history and were determined to gain recognition of Turkey's sovereignty over the territory that the new state now encompassed.[79]

The Lausanne Treaty eventually abolished all special legal institutions and codes for the non-Muslim and non-Turkish residents in Turkey. Turkey declared its obligation to protect their constitutional rights through judicial reform. Part of that obligation was fulfilled in the adoption of the Swiss Civil Code.

It is clear that the Kemalist leadership sought to signal their compliance with the terms agreed on at Lausanne. In his commemorative essay on the code, Bozkurt asserts:

> When the topic of abolishing the capitulations was raised, foreign states rejected our just wishes, pointed out our legal system's backwardness and reliance on religious foundations. They were saying that laws should be *layık* is a requirement of the idea of a modern state. As for yours [they said], they are taken from religious foundations. We cannot give up our subjects to the principles of the Muslim religion. Let alone that although we are Christian, we have abrogated the Christian legal system even in our own countries. You can apply religious laws to your own subjects. But you cannot impose these on your subjects who belong to other religions. The twentieth century cannot accept this kind of understanding. Conscience should be free.[80]

These comments express the conceptual link between the goal of attaining respect for Turkey's legal and national sovereignty and the purposes of separating religion and state in legal affairs. Immediately following them, Bozkurt asserts that such demands by the western powers were the only ones that were relevant to the adoption of the new civil code. Moreover, he quickly interprets the demands of others regarding the separation of religion and the state within the goal of achieving national unity. His language is quite revealing about the frame in which the leaders of the RPP understood their new position as the hegemonic powers in the Turkish state:

> They said many other things. But there is no need to consider them here. This is the one of interest to our topic.
> What would be the character of this organ of justice to which foreigners as well should bow (*baş eğmek*)? What possible form would it take?
> We may say this in one word: *Layık*.
> We know that this is the important attribute that distinguishes modern states from those of the past.[81]

Considerations of religious and national ("foreign") heterogeneity must also lie behind the statement in the 1927 RPP program declaring the need to "rescue matters of belief and conscience from . . . various complications [conflicts] of politics" (quoted above). Indeed, the negotiations at Lausanne and conflicts with religiopolitical and religionational oppositions reviewed above in the control account suggest that the potential areas of conflict that are considered in the program emerged from outside of Turkey as much as from inside.

Beyond these considerations, the historical record shows that the Kemalists considered the many different interpretations of Islam (and of religion in general), including its own, extant within the borders of Turkey at the time. The 1925 rebellion and objections to the cultural and institutional reforms in the name of freedom of religion provide some evidence for this. At a general doctrinal level, there are also significant contrasts between Alewite, some forms of Sufism, and religiopolitical forms of Sunnite interpretations of Islam; the Alevis, whose adherents have always formed a significant portion of the population (estimates are as much as twenty percent of today's population), along with segments of some schools of folk Islam in Turkey, have generally favored the anticlerical tendencies of Kemalist laiklik.

Thus, we may sum up some of the worldly affairs from which religion must, within the Kemalist laiklik frame, be separated and the purposes of that separation as follows: In accordance with the RPP's reading of the requirements of contemporary civilization; and to secure the RPP's hegemony and definition of national aims in legal, social, educational, cultural, and economic matters; and to gain respect for national sovereignty in the internal and external political circumstances in which the national movement existed; religion was removed from its previous position of power, separated in this sense, overdefining the theory and practice of legal, social, cultural, and economic spheres wherein it was seen as a fetter, causing arbitrary, confused, primitive, and medieval governance, lethargy, and harmful ills to the people of the Turkish nation. In this conceptual frame, some of the separationist claims that were related to separating religious theory and practice from affairs of state and nation expressed by the actors who implemented the new policies, practices, and institutions of laiklik must be seen as true characterizations of the RPP effort to disentangle religious affairs at least partly from their previous interrelation. In short, religion was to some extent separated from the state in Kemalist laiklik.

Furthermore, the remaining themes that we have already explored above derive from this frame of laiklik politics. Religion—"rescued" from politics (a theme in the major speech acts of the time, namely the Rationale for the Civil Code, Mustafa Kemal's *Speech,* and the official party programs)—finds a secure home in the conscience, which the government will ensure and protect, actively as did the Religious Affairs Presidency. Laiklik, therefore, is not atheism, as expressed by the major actors and party publicists; laiklik is, in their conceptual and power frame, a progressive, civilized, forward-looking principle of national development whereas anti-laiklik principles are uncivilized and regressive. Finally, religion separated from the mundane and remaining within the conscience is consistent with the progressive ends of laiklik.

In essence, the laiklik politics that separated religion from worldly affairs in constitutional, educational, sociocultural, and legal spheres of state activity cannot be wholly decoupled from the RPP's efforts to bring state and society, and to a certain extent the sphere of conscience, under its control. The meaning of separation in Kemalist laiklik is inescapably situated within RPP governance.

A HERMENEUTIC CONTRIBUTION:
CONSTITUTIVE TENSION AND OVERLAP

As I argue in Chapter 2, it is impossible to explain the various dimensions of political life adequately without accounting for the subjective and the intersubjective, shared and contested meanings that constitute those dimensions. Without offering an interpretation of these meanings in all of the natural hermeneutic limits that I have described, we cannot be sure that we are explaining others' political lives or our own. An adequate account of politics must describe the meanings and significance of politics—its identity—for participants.

Separation as well as control constitute the actions, policies, relations, and institutions associated with laiklik politics in Turkey. The separationist meanings that constitute the separation dimensions of Turkish laiklik overlap with the control meanings that make up laiklik's control dimensions. The conceptual area that they share is also, however, fraught by conceptual tension, given that some of the separationist claims that were made by party publicists announcing the complete separation of religion and state appear as attempts to gloss over the control dimensions. Interpretively stated, insofar as these separationist claims occlude the control dimensions, they may be corrected and set aside. There is ample evidence to refute them, such as the intersubjectively understood control meanings associated with laiklik's power relations. Both interpretively and institutionally, the new state was involved with religious responsibilities. One of the merits of the control account is that it successfully debunks the institutional separationist claims for the accomplishments of laiklik that were made both by participants and observers of laiklik politics.

The tension between separation and control thus lies in two analytically separable but practically related aspects of laiklik: that actors who established the control relations that are associated with laiklik politics actually understood some of the most important dimensions of these relations as relations of separation; and that some of the policies of separation that are legitimately considered as having achieved certain forms of separation between religion and state affairs were undertaken within the context of RPP control such that they enhanced that control.

Educational policies are a good example of the first kind of tension. Preexisting religious schools (medreses and mekteps) were abolished as religious theory and practice was removed (read separated) from a newly unified national educational system under the direction (read control) of the party. At the same time, the law empowered the Ministry of Education to open separate and new religious schools for the party's newly defined religious educational policy. The control relations in these institutional structures were partly understood as relations of separation. The civil code is an adequate example of the second kind of tension: religion was removed from legal affairs in the interest of legal uniformity (national unity) and recognition of the new government by outside powers; that is, to enhance the control of the new authorities in Turkey.

In short, the concepts of separation and control are not totally separable. But this also means that neither is eliminable. We must understand the practical dimensions of separation within the relations of control such that we understand both a) that even these control relations were meaningfully constituted as relations of separation and b) that the relations of separation played a role in enhancing the control structure. From a hermeneutic perspective, the policies and practices that are associated with laiklik would not be what they were without those understandings.

Thus, the dimensions that were intended to effect a separation are not adequately considered or disclosed by the control account. It is in this sense that my account of the separationist dimensions of laiklik seeks to deepen the control account by beginning to fill in its (non)hermeneutic gaps. Laiklik is not adequately explained by the concepts of the control account.

My account of laiklik is not that laiklik contains some contradictions. That may be true in some ways, but my goal is to grasp the relation between the self-understandings of the Kemalist laicists and particular power dynamics, not simply to describe extant meanings in those dynamics. Moreover, at the meta-empirical level I explain in detail how certain policies, practices, and institutional relations are what they are because of, not despite, a conceptual tension between separation and control in their very conception. We might even say that the tension constitutes laiklik in Turkey's politics: certain policies, practices, relations, and institutions associated with Turkey's laiklik politics have achieved separation within an overall structure of control such that specific aspects of this structure were seen by the participants in those structures, at least in part, as ones of separation. This is what I mean by constitutive overlap. What have been seen in the literature as mutually exclusive poles concerning the power relations between religion and the state were not distinct in the self-understandings of the agents of those relations. The meanings of separation and the dimensions of laiklik that were constituted by the conceptual frame undergirding the purposes of separation are inextricably related to the meanings of control and the dimensions of laiklik that were constituted by the purposes of control.[82]

This finding has important significance. For example, it is impossible to account for the history of the subsequent politics within Turkey's laiklik politics without understanding both the separation and the control dimensions of laiklik. The conceptual tension between separation and control has provided the dynamic focal point for the debate over laiklik in Turkey since 1923. Depending on how the tension is resolved (which has historically depended on political-ideological commitments as well as nonhermeneutic postures), the achievements of Kemalist laiklik are interpreted differently by many participants in laiklik politics as well as nonparticipants trying to understand them. The basic point is that the RPP's authoritarian political tendencies overlap with its laicist separationist politics just as control and separation do. Some opponents of RPP authoritarianism frequently collapse the distinction, while defenders of RPP reforms stress separation over control.[83]

It is no coincidence that many reforms associated with laiklik were considered by Recep Peker to be at the center of the the Turkish transformation. In his 1931 explication of the transformation principle of Kemalism, he included reforms that he had described previously within laiklik as being almost as important to the Republic's new identity as the foundation of the Republic itself: "The most grand and most valuable foundation of the transformation is the republic. However, along with this grand foundation [are] the implementation of the new civil code and laws of justice, the closing of the Islamic law courts and medreses, the emplacement of a single court and school system, the prohibition of dervish orders, the closing of the tekkes and türbes, the wearing of the cap and lastly the new Turkish alphabet." Peker's sequence underscores the centrality of the reforms associated with laiklik—both those that define its control dimensions and those that define its related separation dimensions—in the RPP's political struggle for its Turkish transformation.[84]

With this in view, the inadequacies of the control account in describing the identity of laiklik now seem considerable. Some of what the ruling cadre saw as its primary achievements in the Turkish transformation are those features of laiklik that are inadequately explained by the control account. We might even say that the achievements of the Turkish transformation lie in the dimensions of laiklik that should be conceptualized, at least partly, as separation, not as control. Without seeing this, it is not possible to see how the actors saw their accomplishments as a transformation.

SHARED UNDERSTANDINGS IN KEMALISM
AND ANGLOPHONE SOCIAL SCIENCE

Kemalist laiklik, then, contains within it constitutive dimensions that are open to various interpretations. The reception in the social science literature concerns us as well, and, indeed, the RPP's western anglophone social science jury ruled in favor of the Kemalist reforms and impact (without adequately understanding them). Research in the history of social science literature on Turkey since 1925 evidences a dominant view among influential observers of Turkish politics, expressing a shared understanding with the Kemalists, of the identity and significance of laiklik politics. RPP policies in this area have been viewed as fundamental in advancing Turkey's maturity from one civilization (old, traditional, fatalistic, and dominated by Islam) to another (new, modern, active, and dominated by science).[85]

The view was based in an understanding of Islam (in anglophone circles) as incompatible with progress and therefore in need of relegation to the past (or private sphere). In addition, accounts in the literature openly endorsed the aims, interests, and sources of the RPP legitimacy claims, and named the period between 1920 and 1935 as one of the greatest revolutions in history, or a radical break from the past. Mustafa Kemal was seen as the catalyst or pragmatic alchemist for a process that had its own internal modernizing dynamic. Two insightful observers of politics in the Middle East, Alan Richards and John Waterbury, have said that the western modernization and nation-building literature of the 1950s and 1960s "could, in spirit, have been written by Atatürk."[86]

Indeed, judging by the interpretations of Turkey's secular politics in the literature, Atatürk and the RPP leadership appear to have judged correctly that all of the ideas, symbols, and so on that were associated with Islam, if established in a position of political power, would not earn Turkey favor and respect in the western world. Hans Kohn saw the "complete change in structure of the state" as marking an "epochal transition." The RPP, he wrote, "is imbued with the spirit of secularism and liberalism which is making such headway today in all the countries of the East, fulfilling everywhere the same task as it did in Europe a century and a half ago, the task of overcoming the darkness of the religious and feudal Middle Ages. . . . It is as in a stuffy room the windows were suddenly thrown open." Daniel Lerner declared that the Turks, as transitionals, were entering history out of traditional holes. He predicted that the Turks would soon have opinions on public matters, tradition being "none of [the Modern's] business." Walter Weiker, striking a note that pervades his work, wrote in 1963 that "certainly it must be agreed that many of Atatürk's reforms of the 1920s and 1930s were sine qua non for much of the achievement in the social and economic betterment of the Turkish people that has taken place under the Republic." And Rustow writes: "In sum, the Atatürk revolution, combining continuity of leadership with radical change of direction, used Turkey's defeat in World War I and its victory in the War of Independence as a grand opportunity to transform a decaying, traditional, dynastic-theocratic empire into a vibrantly modern nation-state."[87] As a result of these estimations, Turkey's political evolution has been taken as a model for secularism in the Muslim world, modernization of Islam, and westernization in a non-western context (as well as postwar democracy, economic growth, and rapid sustained recovery).[88]

When, during the multiparty period, there were signs of Islam's presence (or persistence) in public life, Turkey became a test case for the harmonious fusion of civilizations (Lewis) and amalgamated forms of tradition and modernity (Rustow). Indeed, well before the Turkish-Islamic synthesis gained currency in Turkey during the 1980s, it was discussed by anglophone interpreters who had sympathetically received the Kemalist project. Expressing Kemalist laicist understandings—indeed, as discussed above, ones that Mustafa Kemal considered—Lewis wrote in 1951:

> So far the basic social and cultural reforms are intact, but an extension of religious revival might well endanger them, with far-reaching consequences for the whole future of Turkey. Some restoration of Islam is probably necessary if the Turkish people is to recover its balance after the revolutionary changes of the last thirty years and achieve a harmonious fusion of its inherited and its acquired values. If the people and rules of Turkey today can achieve such a synthesis, they will render a service not only to Turkey but to the whole world of Islam. Unfortunately there is little sign of such a synthesis yet, and many of the leaders of the Islamic revival profess a reactionary and xenophobic faith which, if it becomes dominant, could undo much of the work of the last thirty years or longer.[89]

Given these estimations of Kemalism's significance, it is not so surprising that some influential interpreters would join the Kemalists by announcing the separation of church and state in Turkey. Their understandings of the historic significance of the Kemalist project bear remarkable resemblances to those of enthusiastic Kemalists, due in large part to their shared positivist methodological and historical posture to the world on these matters. It is not incidental that the Kemalist justification for changing the script and language of the Turks was repeated in the literature (on the devaluation of the constitutive relation between politics and language, see Chapter 2). Mustafa Kemal's evaluation of Arabic script as a set of incomprehensible signs was quoted and endorsed by Lewis as "not without foundation." Arabic, Lewis wrote, is "ill-suited for Turkish sounds," "difficult to teach," and "troublesome to print." By contrast, Latin is "clear, simple, and phonetic" and likely to enhance literacy rates and cultural expansion. Similarly, Dodd wrote of the "more cumbersome Arabic" and asseverated that the language reforms "both broke a powerful connection with the Islamic and Arab heritage and made it easier to extend literacy."[90]

The question for us is, does the shared understanding between anglophone interpreters of Turkey and the Kemalist political forces in Turkey thus vindicate the secularization as institutional separation accounts of the former? And, therefore, are we to credit the outside interpreters of laiklik with capturing the identity and meaning of its separation dimensions (in ways not captured by the control account)? I have argued that separation is one understanding that constitutes laiklik's institutional control relations. What must be considered is to what extent the anglophone interpreters of laiklik were right in declaring the separation or disestablishment of state and religion.

While it is indispensable to a full account of laiklik to understand that control relations between the state and religion are understood as relations of separation within the constitutive frames of laiklik politics, it is a mistake to credit anglophone subscribers to a "secularism as institutional separation" account with explaining that dimension in laiklik politics. The shared sense of the significance of laiklik between anglophone interpreters and regime partisans was not an explanatory guide, although it often comes within an explanatory frame as a contribution to the objectivist discourse of social science. If statements like Lerner's that declare institutional separation were explanatory in intent, they were explanatory as descriptions of the structural relations rather than of the constitutive understandings of those relations.

The exclusive relation between language and politics manifested by such descriptions is the distinguishing characteristic of nonhermeneutic approaches to the study of political institutions. Moreover, in the recent period of modern political science, these approaches have sustained historical expectations for particular outcomes of modern political history, such as the separation of religion and politics. My thesis is that hermeneutic approaches cannot sustain this or any other singular view of political modernity. History is, and should be considered, more open than the narrow version of secular modernism that is found in the anglophone literature and is imposed as a standard in comparative studies. The failure to account for the constitutive understandings is the definitive product of nonhermeneutic tendencies in the social sciences that engage in political explanation. Nonhermeneutic approaches will always fall short of understanding the particular characteristics of the subject matter as well as their significance in the political and historical dynamics in which they participate. This is true of the study of laiklik in Turkey.

There are counterexamples in this anglophone literature to my sweeping claims. For instance, Walter Weiker suggested in 1963 that secularism in Turkey "was interpreted to mean virtually total exclusion of religious influence from public life." This characterization comes close to one of the constitutive senses of separation that I describe above. The word "virtually" is significant in this way. Weiker leaves room for the possibility that the Kemalists did not totally exclude religion from politics, but Weiker does not indicate the constitutive control meanings at all. A form of the separation account is left as a description of the achievements of laiklik. The same habit of explanation can be found in

Rustow's most recent characterization of "Atatürk's principle of secularism." He writes, "A half- century ago, the defenders of the Ottoman theocratic establishment deeply resented secularism as an attack on religion itself whereas Atatürk insisted that his policy of separation of religion and politics and of secular education did not imply any enmity toward religion."[91] It should be said that Rustow, whose seminal 1957 control account added much understanding to laiklik, at least accounts for the meaning of secularism when he addresses the matter. By contrast, Weiker's 1963 analysis, wherein he describes a policy debate on Islam and secularism, the concept of secularism is frequently used without any conceptual unpacking—a tendency throughout the literature to leave the concept undefined. Still, that Weiker and Rustow have highlighted the separation concept apart from the more powerful constitutive control concept betrays the kind of nonhermeneutic approach that could be fruitfully deepened by hermeneutic engagement.[92]

Interestingly, the compelling control account within hermeneutics still falls short. As I discuss, its advocates offer a compelling description of the control relations between state and religion in Turkey, but these are not always hermeneutically interested ones either. Frequently they are nonhermeneutically guided structural accounts. This is evident in the expressed interest in re-describing separation as control, thus identifying the power relations between state and religion. But this is done without due attention to the constitutive institutional separation dimensions as well. My account fills this gap in the understanding of laiklik.

The separation account falls short because the primary institutional and interpretive dynamics between state and religion were understood as control relations that implicated the Kemalists in religious matters. An office of religious affairs, entrusted to manage doctrine and practice in the name of Islam is not privatizing matters, of Islam or of conscience in general. The control account also falls short, but for a different reason. The relations of control were partly understood by actors as relations of separation, in the sense of separating religion from its previous interrelation in certain spheres. Without that understanding those relations would not be what they are.

Therefore, a compelling account of laiklik politics in Turkey must account for both the control and separation dimensions expressed therein. It is insufficient to identify only one. Both mutually and complexly comprise the matrix of meanings that constitute the power relations, political history, sociological impact, and geopolitical realities associated with laiklik in Turkey. To miss these complex dimensions, moreover, is to unduly narrow our vision of Turkey's political history and future possibilities within the laiklik dynamic. As indicated above, when the one-party period ends, both the control and separation conceptual streams must be followed. They comprise the major themes of the unfolding dynamic. We are poorly equipped to understand laiklik if we begin our analyses without due recognition of both to these constitutive frames.

A CRITICAL, COMPARATIVE, EXPLANATORY
CHANGE: LAICISM NOT SECULARISM

To close, I identify one final advantage of hermeneutics in studying Turkey's laiklik politics, which is generalizable to the study of all secular modern possibilities of modern politics. In Chapter 2, I argue that the chief aim of accounting for the political lives of others is to bring their concepts into our own (within all the natural limitations and exchanges that this involves). Understanding occurs, following Gadamer and Taylor, when we fuse horizons such that we become able to say something that is true of the other. This process involves what Taylor calls the central demand of hermeneutic political theory, "that we confront our language of explanation with the self-understandings of our subjects." In this confrontation, our (the "explainer's") conceptual languages and hence our understanding of political possibilities, is expanded beyond our original language (and remains open to further enlargement).

In this chapter, I have tried to show how the constitutive meanings of separation in the politics of laiklik in Turkey must be brought into our account of those politics, that is, into our language for understanding laiklik. To close, I suggest that this bringing into our language something that is true of the other must be done with the concept of laiklik itself.

For years, along with inadequate analyses of the constitutive dimensions of laicist practices, interpreters have not paid enough attention to ambiguities that arise in the translation of laiklik into secularism in the anglophone context.

The concept of laiklik is derived from the French *laïque* and *laïcité* (compare Spanish *laicidad,* Italian *laicità*), and can be translated into English as laicism (French, *laïcisme*). The concept is not entirely foreign to the anglophone vocabulary. The core meaning of laicism, drawn from the French experience by the Kemalists, implies lay control over religion.[93]

By contrast, secularism, at least in anglophone contexts, does not connote exactly the same meaning. The concept of lay is not entirely synonymous with the concept of secular. The former implies "the people" as distinct from the religious-wise strata ("clergy" in Christian contexts, "rabbinate" in Jewish contexts, "ulema" in Islamic contexts). A lay person, for instance, may be religiously devout. By contrast, secular may imply nonreligious, irreligious, or even antireligious. Indeed, secularism is frequently associated with nonreligious moral doctrines in contradistinction to religious moral doctrines. In addition, in English-speaking contexts, the term "secularism" as a constitutional concept may imply the separation between religion and the state, whereas, laicism may mean lay hegemony over the state. Finally, secular political practices, as distinct from the constitutional concept, might be thoroughly antireligious, while lay religious practices might be anticlerical and antireligious in some senses, but not necessarily as antireligious as secular practices. These are only a few differences among many.[94]

Most interpreters discuss laiklik in Turkey as synonymous and perfectly interchangeable with secularism. For example, Philip Robins, who refers to laicism, calls Atatürk's state formally secular. Walter Weiker (among many others) refers to Kemalist secularism; and Cağlar Keyder calls the center of lay control exclusively secular. Furthermore, characterizations of the multiparty period that translate laiklik as Atatürk's policy of secularism abound. Many of these are not simply descriptive statements; they discuss the unfolding of secular politics in Turkey. Rustow describes critical conversations about laiklik during the RPP's 1947 congress as the "quest for a redefinition of secularism"; Kemal Karpat refers to the RPP's "understanding of secularism" as having undergone extensive criticism. As a result, the RPP is said to have relaxed secularism while the opposition Democrat Party de-emphasized secularism. Both parties were said to have "compromised the question of secularism for political purposes" resulting from their support for religiously interested policies. Weiker asserts that despite these retreats, secularism was firmly established in Turkey—several years after he had averred that "it is generally agreed that secularism *per se* is no longer an issue." Richard Tapper disagreed with this, seeing debate during the 1980s over "strict traditional secularism" (meaning Kemalist secularism). He suggested that it was being redefined yet again. Marguiles and Yildizoğlu, perhaps aware of an additional distinction between laiklik and secularism, disagreed. They suggested that prior to the 1980s "the concept of secularism was not open to question."[95]

The following two comments, by Rustow and Ergun Özbudun respectively, exemplify the usual portrayal of laiklik:

Since Atatürk's day, secularism has been deeply embedded both in the constitution and laws of the country and in the political consciousness of the elite.

For more than a half a century Turks have been living under a secular, national republican state clearly based on a Western model.[96]

My study shows that even if secularism as separation constitutes laiklik, calling Turkey a secular state, without unpacking the meaning of this term in an anglophone context, might not capture the history and identity of laiklik politics. This is especially true with descriptions of "Kemal Atatürk's secularism" and suggestions like Dodd's that the reforms "secularized political life," or Jacob Landau's that "Atatürk's goal was a modern secular state." Even if the end was secularism, which it was not according to my account, it is an obfuscation to ignore laicization as the means. In sum, expressing the identity of laiklik by translating it as secularism perhaps has part of the meaning right, but not enough of it. In fact, it increases our perplexity.[97]

Some recent interpreters of Turkey's secular state have found some of its not-so-secular dimensions in contradiction with its reputation. The emergence of a new account of Turkey's laiklik politics expresses a skepticism of Turkey's claim to be secular. Best named the "so-called account," some of Turkey's interpreters see a "so-called secular state." The skepticism of this account is expressed well by David Barchard who describes the *Diyanet İşleri Reisliği* as a "department of the supposedly secular Turkish state." The question posed by Tapper portrays the same skepticism: "How far is the self-designation 'secular state' still appropriate, either as a description or as a political principle in modern Turkey?" This skeptical thrust is evident as early as the late 1940s inside Turkey. One of the few outside observers to notice it was Howard Reed, who noted that critics of laiklik saw the use of their taxes to pay Imam's salaries as "hardly secular."[98]

The hermeneutic imperative to bring other concepts into our explanatory language is particularly relevant in this quandary of potentially misleading concepts. This is tricky, however, because the word "laiklik" is translated into English as "secularism." In the Turkish-speaking context the two concepts are often fused. Mardin, for instance, "refers to the constitutional principle of laicism or secularism." Almost universally, texts, seminars, journalistic writings, and conversational uses of the term "laiklik" are translated as secularism. Thus, what from the outside appears to be a fundamental distinction between separation and control is collapsed in the Turkish concept of laiklik as well as in Turkey's laiklik politics. Even French speakers use English to describe the Republic's "strict secularism." This linguistic situation reflects the constitutive meanings within Turkey, but it raises a dilemma for all interpreters—participants in Turkey's laiklik politics as well as outside speakers of various languages who try to understand that participation. The dilemma is implied in this comment by one of the few laiklik interpreters to attend to the distinction: "In Turkish, secularism is not equivalent to the American term, which generally refers to the separation of church and state. Rather, it is a concept based on the European notion of laicism, according to which religious practice and institutions are regulated and administered by the state." This comment partly occludes aspects of laiklik that I describe above. First, it occludes the fact that religious institutions are in the state, not simply subject to its administration. They are not fully independent institutions. Second, these aspects of regulation and administration are understood as control with some aspects of separation.[99]

But beyond these occlusions, the dilemma is clear: should we choose, with English speakers of Turkish, to translate laicism as secularism? Or, alternatively, do we choose to translate laiklik as laicism? If we chose the former, we may accept the Turkish case as one alternative form of secularism; if we choose the latter, we should describe it as one form of laicism. Both are available within the hermeneutic frame, but perhaps one is preferable to the other.

The choice is not merely a matter of semantics. As I discuss, laiklik in Turkey consists of certain political power relations that institutionally connect and interpretively implicate the state in religious matters. Laiklik, therefore, might be better understood by English speakers if the concepts were not subject to potential misunderstanding. For this reason, laiklik should be translated as laicism and discussed as such. If we must bring the concept of secular in somewhere, the constitutive meanings are available to describe laiklik as laicism with some tendencies toward secularism, as well as some tendencies toward nonsecularism.

In the simplest terms, following the hermeneutic imperative will better convey the declared principle of the Turkish state. But it will also help us to better understand some of the most pivotal moments in Turkey's laicist politics. Alas, the members of the RPP did not reinterpret secularism during the 1947 Congress; they reinterpreted laicism (a reinterpretation which coincided with, inter alia, an increase in their support for forms of religious education in the state's unified schools). The Democrat Party's reforms did not redefine secularism as much as they did laicism (thus, the party went even further in their support for state-sponsored religious education). İlkay Sunar and Binnaz Toprak's description of the DP's impact on laicism in Turkey is exemplary: "The DP criticized the RPP for interfering with the religious practices of the citizenry, stating that laicism did not stop simply at separating religion from politics but meant in practice [under the RPP] interference with and a negative attitude towards religious observance."[100] Of course, a negative attitude toward religious observance would be a secular attitude. But, as my discussion shows, it is not clear that this was generally true of Kemalist laiklik, even though it was true regarding some forms of Islam in Turkey.

As Sunar and Toprak's statement intimates, conceptualizing laiklik as laicism also enables us to understand the contested dimensions between control and separation, a contest whose roots trace back at least to Ziya Gökalp's insistence that a modern state separates religion and politics (one kind of secular thesis that can be found in Turkey's political history). Throughout the twentieth century, the Turkish lay elite has quarreled over the structure and government of the religious institutions and life of Turkey. This is not a surprising fact if we think of laiklik as a form of laicism, but it might startle some who think of it as secularism.

No anglophone interpreter of Turkey has suggested that Turkey be consistently considered a laicist state. Bernard Lewis tried to inject the concept into anglophone understanding by writing: "The basis of the Kemalist religious policy was laicism, not irreligion; its purpose was not to destroy Islam, but to disestablish it—to end the power of religion and its exponents in political, social, and cultural affairs, and limit it to matters of belief and worship. In thus reducing Islam to the role of religion in a modern western, nation-state, the Kemalists also made some attempt to give their religion a more modern and more national form." Further to his credit, Lewis consistently brings the concept of lay, as opposed to secular, into his historical descriptions of the Atatürk experience. But Lewis's account falls short even as it surpasses others in these respects. It is not clear that the purpose of laicism was disestablishment, especially with regard to ending the power of religion and its exponents in political affairs. The same may be said about limiting religion to matters of belief and worship, or the ambiguously stated notion of reducing it to the role of religion in a modern, western nation-state.[101]

Switching translations from secularism to laicism is not enough. The constitutive content of the politics must also be clarified. This is Simon Bromley's error in the account that I represent at the beginning of this chapter. Juxtaposing control to separation, Bromley states, "In fact, the militant secularism of the state amounted to rigid state control over religious life, and a strict laicism in public affairs, rather than the institutional separation of Church and State, or the decline of personal belief." Lewis makes a similar error when he suggests that *laicité* in Turkey—which he defines as the principle of separation between religion and state—"was accomplished by Atatürk in a series of radical measures, including the disestablishment of Islam."[102]

Some have tried to explain the uniqueness of the Atatürk experience by stressing its militancy in building a state in which secularism, as Rustow states, "is more stringent" than "the separation of church and state in the West."[103] Such accounts hedge slightly on the authoritarian dimensions of structural, political, and cultural control. The usual way that the distinction is conveyed is illustrated in the control accounts above: Turkey's secular state is "different from secularism in a Western sense," assuming that there is one western meaning for secularism (which there is not).

Toprak has made the interesting suggestion that we can perceive Turkey's uniqueness by thinking of it as a semi-secular state: "If we accept the principle that the separation of church and state by definition excludes state interference in religious life, we have to agree with [Bülent] Daver that the Turkish Republic is a semi-secular state. Its brand of secularism is rather unique and should be understood as such."[104]

The problem with suggestions like this is that they all seem to imply that the state center that was created by laiklik was nonreligious or that religion became thoroughly private. In some senses this may be true, but it is not descriptive enough of the overall realities of laiklik.[105]

The concept of secular indubitably implies nonreligious, and to some extent privatization of religious belief; does it make sense to speak of a semi-nonreligious state center? Or, is it, alternatively, more accurate to speak of a lay center? I prefer the latter. Toprak's reasons for choosing "semi-secular" seem to be based on an interest in understanding Turkey's uniqueness relative to other contexts. My reading of the "semi" claim is that semi is intended to represent the control dimensions of laiklik's institutional relations, in contrast to their absence in states that entirely separate the two realms. This concept, however, partly occludes that these control dimensions are structurally and conceptually integrated within the state umbrella, not under it in a semi-autonomous subordinate sense. The use of the concept of secular, without placing it within laicism, fails to capture adequately the identity of laiklik.

The conceptualization of laiklik as secularism in all of the accounts of Turkey's laiklik politics betrays the persisting influence of the kind of secular-modern prejudgments that I criticize in the first chapter. Interpreters insist on seeing secular outcomes wherever theocracy does not exist. This is true of the literature on Turkey's laiklik politics (leaving aside the question of whether the Ottoman Empire was a theocracy), and I suspect that it is largely true in other contexts. The judgment that secularism immediately (naturally? necessarily?) succeeds theocracy leads to some confusions in political explanation; that is, it blinds us to identifying variations in nontheocratic politics, of identifying the range of non- and posttheocratic possibilities for structuring the relation between religion and matters of conscience and politics. Therefore, as the separation account of laiklik politics in Turkey betrays nonhermeneutical analytical dispositions that are supported by prejudgments about certain secular and modern outcomes of modern political history, the control account does so as well, albeit in a slightly different way.

To call laiklik laicism may not be exact—we might, for instance, see that Turkey's laicism, unlike France's laicism, was anticlerical only to a certain extent (the *Diyanet İşleri Reisliği* remained inside the state). But to see it as anticlerical to some extent—with the clear implication that the state was not necessarily hostile to its own institutionalized religion—we get closer to the identity of laiklik than most of its interpreters do. There was, for example, "no deliberate and extended experiment with pure secular westernization" under the Kemalist regime. Similarly, to see laiklik as constituted by control relations, as well as by aspects of separation, we arrive at a more precise account of Turkey's "uniqueness." The structures and intention exist to use religion in politics (in what elites believe is the interest of the state) as well as to disengage it (for the same reason).[106]

Referring to the contemporary functions of Islam in Turkish politics, İlter Turan speaks about how "religion provides a framework within which political power may be exercised, is an element of social control which includes values such as being respectful of governmental authority and of public servants, and compliance with the government's commands . . . [for example] is one of the several ways through which obedience to political authority is secured; is a source of symbols, ideas, and meanings that are used to elicit positive political behaviors from society; . . . [and in sum] is a resource which may be mobilized for 'purposes of state' whenever it is found useful or necessary." None of this should surprise an observer who understands laiklik as one form of laicism. We also see that the hat reforms may not have been intended to change the contents of the head in their entirety (I borrow the phrase from Philip Hitti).[107] In short, we see laiklik as laicism. To do so is to be able to explain better the frames of laicism in Turkey's political life and to understand what it would be like to participate in the policies, practices, relations, and institutions that constitute this aspect of it. It is at least a beginning.[108]

Finally, for all interpreters of Turkey's version of laicism to learn more about distinctions that are related to secular politics in the global context through a study of the Turkish experience, we are no worse off. There is little to credit in the anticipatable objection that laicism is a poor explanatory concept for audiences that are not aware of its existence. That the Kemalists chose to describe their project of laicism in terms of the French anticlerical experience is a hermeneutic fact of indispensable importance in the comparative study of power relations between politics and religion. Through an interpretive engagement with political life not only is our understanding of Kemalist laiklik enhanced, but also our perception of global conceptual and practical possibilities within secularization politics. Furthermore, the entire exercise emphasizes the inseparable critical and genuinely comparative dimensions of the hermeneutic project's mission of political understanding.

Conclusion Toward a Critical, Comparative, Secular Hermeneutics

The purpose of this study has been to make sense of perplexity about contemporary theopolitics by establishing the indispensability of the hermeneutic approach to explaining modern political possibilities. By indispensable, I mean that an account of the concepts that constitute political life is a necessary condition of any claim to have understood or explained it. I have scrutinized the unifying claim of hermeneutics in political inquiry, what an account should look like with regard to various dimensions of politics, and how the hermeneutic approach can contribute to broader critical, comparative interests in the study of modern politics. I have also argued that the analytical imperatives of hermeneutic political inquiry enable us to explain our subject better, and by disposing us to think in terms of alternative and contested rather than singular outcomes, to expand our conceptual framework—our prejudgments, in Gadamer's terms, of which we can be conscious—within which we seek to explain modern politics.

Dissatisfied as many are by an argument from abstract theory alone, I have demonstrated the indispensability of hermeneutic political inquiry for studying aspects of modern politics that are drawn from

Turkish secularizing thought and practice, aspects that are complexly constituted by a matrix of meaning within the range of the secular and the religious.
Providing histories of the interpretations of Ziya Gökalp's thought and the
practices that are associated with Turkey's secular politics, I have argued that
nonhermeneutic explanatory dispositions and "secular modern" prejudgments
about the character of modern political history have shaped anglophone social
science's explanatory engagements with these two significant features of Turkey's experience within the secularization problematic.

The work of Gökalp, significant for his attempt to articulate the political,
cultural, and scientific preconditions for a secular future in Turkey, was chosen
to illustrate the hermeneutic approach with regard to interpreting speech acts.
Turkey's secular model, better understood as Turkey's laicist politics, was chosen
to illustrate the indispensability of hermeneutics in the explanation of political
practices, relations, policies, and institutions (indeed, the domain that comparative political science is usually occupied with).

In both cases, I have indicated how hermeneutic inquiry elicits a better
understanding and explanation of their identity and character than has previously been achieved in the anglophone literature. I have also described their
significance within Turkish politics and within the theoretical and practical
concerns of comparative political theory and politics. My study of Gökalp's
thought regarding the ability of Islam to endure under conditions of modernization and nationalism, for example, illustrates how the hermeneutic move enables
a critical confrontation with the view that religion as such must either enter the
private sphere or fade altogether under conditions of modern politics. My study
of the constitutive dimensions of the original conception of laicism in Turkey
shows how institutional possibilities within the secularization problematic are
more plural than encompassed by the "secularization as structural separation"
judgments that are found in political science literature on modernity.

The two studies demonstrate how hermeneutics allows one to delve into
more of the subtleties and nuances that make the historical, theoretical, and
political contest that is associated with secularism in Turkey what it is. Gökalp's
ideas display an underappreciated ability to relate secularizing, sociological
realities, happening largely unnoticed by ordinary people, to their lived traditions; realities that he conceptualized as retaining a vital sense of integrity under
conditions of expansive change. A product of both prenationalist Ottoman
realities and the nationalist milieu, he described a future for Turkey that would
allow for the development of the evolutionary potential of the nation and its
culture within the increasingly common field of civilization. That he could

imagine the separation of politics and religion in a frame that valued religion as the ethical system of the Turks and placed priority on the evolution of culture, and then make this separation a prerequisite for Turkey's national development, is testimony to his status as a theorist of secularism in Turkey.

Moreover, his insistence that a modern state separates religion and politics as it aspires to absorb international civilization within a framework of cultural integrity stands in contrast to Kemalism's laicist politics that institutionalized state control over religion to implement its version of cultural modernization. (Indeed, had the political and social scientists who studied Gökalp's thought considered Gökalp's view on the public relevance of Islam as an ethical system within a Turkish culture evolving within modern civilization as reasonable, they would have had a critical vantage point to examine the nature and ends of Kemalism's laicist politics of control.)

Taken together, the constitutive meanings that are expressed in Gökalp's thought, and in politics that are associated with the Republican Peoples Party's laicism form the conceptual borders in which the processes of laicization have unfolded in Turkey. The Kemalists took the separation of religion and the state seriously enough to incorporate reforms that were intended to effect a separation between aspects of public affairs and the theory and practice of religion. But these dimensions of separation were not enough to weaken fundamentally the control character of Kemalist laicism. In its original conception, laicism never escaped the politics of Kemalist authoritarianism that shaped it.

The Kemalists institutionalized a structure of governance and oversight with regard to Islam. No separation between religion and the state ever occurred under Atatürk—only partial areas of separation developed within a structure of state and society control and, in some dimensions, enhanced state control. "Disestablishment" does not capture the mechanisms of reestablishment. Indeed, every label needs a qualifier; almost all existing accounts of the topic do not explain the constitutive complexity adequately: control, but not only control; separation, but within a structure of control; disestablishment, and then reestablishment; anticlerical, but only to a certain point; privatization encouraged, but not institutionally or ideologically sustained; and so on. The policies, practices, relations, and institutions associated with laiklik in Turkey were conceptualized within the project of gaining control over the state and over the definition of the Turkish national future. Only a hermeneutic engagement is suited to clarify these dimensions. And, indeed, further work on laicism in Turkey directed toward explaining aspects of these constitutive dimensions in greater conceptual detail remains necessary.

In the history of interpreting Gökalp and laiklik, it is evident that hindering prejudgments of particular narrowly conceived secular modern expectations supported by nonhermeneutic modes of inquiry have cooperated to present an inadequate explanation of the identity of these two crucial features of secular thought and practice in Turkey.

Criticisms of either nonhermeneutic approaches or narrow-secular modern judgments—both in general political science inquiry and within Middle East studies—are found in the existing literature. As I have argued above, however, I am inclined to disagree with some formulations of both. For example, in the Turkish context, criticisms of studies lacking apparent hermeneutic credentials have blossomed. These critiques follow a recognition of the need for language training in the study of Ottoman-Turkish history. In the early 1970s, one of the interests for such training in political science studies was to take research beyond social-background analyses (relying on so-called objective indicators such as family, education, profession, etc.) to value-studies that would examine closely attitudes, socialization, and general cultural, behavioral, and political norms. With regard to explaining Turkish political life, much of this switch was contained within nonhermeneutic political inquiry.[1]

The shift from nonhermeneutic tendencies occurs with Şerif Mardin's reorientation of political and sociological studies from the center to the periphery. Mardin's works constitute an explicit rejection of what he refers to as the positivist and secular orientations of research in and on Turkey that, he says, are conspicuous in making no attempt to understand Islam's sociological dynamic. Tapper has added that studies on Islam's role in Turkey, focusing solely on political parties, elections, and state-centric variables, do not adequately account for the meaning and importance of Islam in the lives of Turkish people.[2]

In addition to these criticisms, observers of Turkish politics have long criticized the expectations of some early researchers awaiting the replacement of tradition by modern. Rustow argued for an amalgamate approach to tradition and modernity based on his studies of the Turkish case. Binnaz Toprak followed this with a study of the complex relation between Islam and political development in Turkey. Similarly, Huri İslamoğlu and Keyder have criticized the failure of stagelike modernization theory to theorize the impact of capitalist penetration and the Ottoman-Turkish context's peripheral status vis-à-vis the world economy. They object to Bernard Lewis's 1961 book, once hailed as a "complete and satisfactory explanation of the phenomena of the Turkish republic," as exemplary of "superstructural analysis" that is overloaded with the "political and ideological emphasis found in most modernization literature."[3] My study contests both forms of criticism.

Unlike those who criticize the nonhermeneutic inadequacies in Turkish studies, I submit that the hermeneutic approach is indispensable not simply for the study of traditions, in a (neo)conservative sense of the word, at the periphery. It is relevant in the study of all traditions, including those within which political phenomena at "center" participate. The hermeneutic engagement cannot completely support one reading of history—narrowly secular or religious. Some hermeneuticists argue that tradition in the conservative sense is history (or civilization, or culture, or homeland, or economy, or geography), forgetting the critical opening of all alternatives that hermeneutics must expose. The critical edge of hermeneutic inquiry is still in need of further theorizing; but it goes further than where it is assumed to. Mardin's comment that Islamic studies taken up by "many young laypersons" in Turkey "can be termed a hermeneutic exercise for enriching their Muslim culture" is, from the perspective of the interpretive approach I articulate, representative of this limited theorizing. The hermeneutic exercise cannot be placed on only one side of the tradition/modern dichotomy. Rather than reproducing that dichotomy, it opens both prongs.[4]

My view is that positivism and other forms of non- or antihermeneutic approaches to the study of political life have, within political explanation, marginalized all traditions, not simply conservatively understood ones. Thus, we are as much in need of hermeneutic studies of secular politics—its meaning and importance in the lives of people generally—as we are of studies of religious and theopolitical life. As I argue in Chapter 1, too frequently hindering secular modern judgments about modernity are perceived as the truth of secularism and modernism, rather than as one possible—and contestable—account of them within these two traditions. Concepts and practices associated with both secularism and religion must be hermeneutically engaged. The blinding, bifurcating divisions must be broken down. There is more in the range of post- and nontheocratic possibilities for conceptualizing and organizing the relation between politics and religion or between the political and all matters of conscience than is captured by these categories. Practicing hermeneutics enables a deeper evaluation of the range of possibilities within the secularization politics before us.

My argument differs from the literature that criticizes historical expectations associated with modernization theory in my insistence that the problem is not simply with ideology. To conceive of the interpretive problem in such terms alone will not enable avoiding it in the future. The problem is with interpretive prejudice that is constitutive of much political science research on modernity and supported by nonhermeneutic approaches. Thus, the difficulty of assuming historical necessity cannot be solved simply by looking at other variables or with a different ideological emphasis. It requires a shift in our posture toward inquiry; such a shift will entail a deconstruction of the inadequate, over-generalized categories of tradition and modernity, will effect a broader vocabulary for the study of political change, and will entail a genuinely altered sense of historical possibility.

The uniqueness of this study within Turkish studies and general political science considerations on interpreting theopolitics lies in my attempt to join a critique of conceptions of secular modernity with a critique of the methods that are employed to understand it, to illustrate their combined untoward influences within political explanation, and to demonstrate the indispensability of hermeneutics for overcoming those influences to arrive at more complete and compelling explanations of politics in modernity.

This argument is significant to understanding theopolitics and our perplexity with it, in Turkey and elsewhere. Many theopolitical movements—including so-called fundamentalist ones—are on the rise because they share, with many of their interpreters, the view that modernity had brought in the secular. Now, the secular has failed, they say, so theopolitics—even fundamentalism—makes sense. It is the "way." But, what if what we believed to be clearly secular turns out not to be so—it turns out to contain secularizing tendencies, but, as with Turkey, given the interest in and control over religion, not properly secular.

The rise of theopolitics in Turkey and in other contexts does not therefore mark the failure of the secular; it expresses a debate between those who have different interpretations of religion and who seek to institutionalize them, or, put more crudely and taking strategy into account, those who have used Islam in one way (such as Turkey's laicist founders, who sought to pursue some secularizing dimensions of politics), and those who seek to use it in another. The secular political system envisioned by secularization theorists—both religious and nonreligious—has not yet arrived. The grounds on which our perplexity was founded were not what we thought they were. The rise of the theopolitical is not nearly so odd as much as is the idea that religion had faded from political relevance.

We need a broader conceptual framework for organizing our understandings of possibilities within the secularization problematic of modern politics. If we seek genuinely comparative theories of secularization, we must, for example, bring Ziya Gökalp's thoughtful distinction between civilization and culture as well as the concept of laicism to our language. To do so will reveal a more complex picture of the phenomena that we have held securely in our consciousness of the historical inevitability of secularization. This is the indispensability of hermeneutics in interpreting theopolitics in a so-called secular age. The examples that are drawn from Turkey's experience with laicist thought and practice illustrate how hermeneutic inquiry can literally free us of narrow forms of historical necessity. Therefore, against those who see the problem only in terms of method, I argue that the errors lie in the constitutive historical judgments of modern political inquiry. And, in response to those who see the problem as one of ideology, I call for a fundamental rethinking of the understandings constitutive of political inquiry, and thus our posture toward political explanation.

Obviously, Turkey's status as a model to other countries aside, the problems of relating the demands of different religions to politics are not unique to Turkey. Understanding experiences within this problematic in other contexts requires that we adopt the hermeneutic approach to more adequately delineate the conceptual and historical contours of modern politics in the secularization problematic. As political and economic programs spread rapidly around the globe, students of modern politics must improve their skills for understanding the constitutive dimensions of those politics. A better ability to participate in another's conceptual field might open the door to more negotiated and participatory, as opposed to imposed and hierarchical, futures. If it does, it will demonstrate the viability of one version of secular politics that seeks to identify a common frame among differently situated inhabitants of common public spheres. (Alternative outcomes are, of course, always in the realm of possibility. But at least the error will not lie solely in not having tried to understand better.)[5]

There are many who would take issue with my claim that secularism remains a viable option for modernity, and is even still worth studying. The reasons for dismissing secular politics vary. Some dismissals stem from an arbitrary narrowing of the meaning of secularism to "solving problems in the affairs of the world." Consequently, it is argued that secularism is nothing unique, and, because many different religions are as interested in the flow of everyday life, secular politics can easily be replaced by secularly oriented religions. Other dismissals stem from the reductive claim that secularism relegates ethical issues of politics to a lower priority than material issues. As such, it is argued that secularism contributes little to the ethical-political dilemmas of our time. Still others reject the relevance of secularism because, especially in the so-called developing world, secular projects have been tied to authoritarian politics. Gayatri Spivak, for instance, thinks that we can take for granted the "connection between imperialism and secularism." Claims like this are present in the Turkish context; carelessly equating one authoritarian form of laicism with secularism, one rejects secularism's relevance to contemporary ethical-political matters.[6]

Against such conceptualizations, hermeneutic political inquirers must be prepared to clarify the content and viability of secular and secularizing political and ethical traditions in modern politics. This is not so improbable a need as it sounds. The concept of secularism has lost its force in comparative political inquiry in part because it has been stripped of its concern with creating (context-specific) conditions that will ensure the fullest expression for the human conscience. Theopolitical discourses, aided by pluralist academics who have sometimes carelessly accepted these discourses unquestioningly, have seen secularism as threatening because it poses the possibility that such freedom will entail abandoning religion. Their interpretation has gained veritable proof from authoritarian regimes whose interests lie far from ensuring the conditions for the free exercise of conscience, yet claim to be secular.[7]

There are more dimensions of this conceptual situation, a situation that is not easily reversed. Nonetheless, it must be stated that authoritarian politics is inconsistent with the conception of secularism that frees itself from the purposefully obfuscating critiques of it emerging from theopolitical discourses. The conceptual block that pervades discussions about secularism should not interfere with the need to theorize democratic, secular conditions that can replace existing barriers to the exercise of freedom of conscience, whether the matters of conscience be religious, non- or antireligious, or political in ways having nothing to do with religion.

Therefore, along with the need for fuller, hermeneutically sensitive accounts of the range of politics within the secularization problematic comes the need to develop a language and capacity to think broadly and critically about alternative, existing relations between politics and conscience in modernity. A reinvigorated, historically informed, context-specific, politically responsible, and philosophically defensible secular disposition toward modern politics might be the political-ethical wing of the hermeneutic commitment in political inquiry.

Appendix

THE RATIONALE FOR THE DRAFT BILL (OF THE TURKISH CIVIL CODE)

There is at present no codified civil code of the Turkish Republic. What exists is the Mecelle [Ottoman code] that deals with only a small portion of contracts. It contains 1,851 articles. The writing of it was begun on 8 Muharrem 1286, and completed and put into force on 26 Şaban 1293.[1] It can be said that only 300 articles of this code can fulfill the needs of the present. The rest cannot be implemented because they are nothing but some primitive principles that cannot answer our country's needs. The rule and main principles of the Mecelle are religion. While on the contrary, human life is subject to major changes every day and even every moment. It is not possible even to arrest and stop life's march and changes. Those states whose laws are based on religion cannot satisfy before long the demands of the country and the nation, for religions contain [express] immutable judgments. Life marches on; needs quickly change; religious laws cannot express any value, any meaning beyond form and dead words in the face of inexorably changing life. Not to change is a necessity for religions. For this reason, that religions should remain only matters of conscience is one of the principles of the civilization of the present century and one of the most important elements that distinguish the new civilization from the old. Laws that derive their principles from religions unite the communities in which they are being implemented with the primitive ages from which they have descended and constitute one of the major factors and reasons impeding progress. It should not be doubted that our laws that receive their inspiration from the immutable judgments of religion and are still linked [in continuous contact] to divine law are the most powerful factor in tying the Turkish nation's destiny to the stipulations and rules of the Middle Ages, even during the present century. The Turkish Republic's remaining deprived of a codified civil code which is the regulator of national social life, a code that should be inspired only by that life, is irreconcilable with the meaning and the conception required by the Turkish revolution. Another characteristic which distinguished the state of the present century from primitive political organizations is that, in the latter, the rules implemented in the destiny of the community are not laid down in statutory law. In nomadic periods, rules are not codified as such. The judge adjudicates by custom and tradition. With the exception of the 300 articles of the Mecelle, on the subjects of the Turkish Civil Code, judges of the Turkish Republic are adjudicating by extrapolation and inference from slapdash *fıkıh* [Islamic codes of jurisprudence] and religious principles. The Turkish judge is not bound in his judgments by any specific precedents and binding rulings and principles. Therefore, the judgment reached in a case in one locality of our country and the judgments arrived at in a similar case that is being adjudicated under the same conditions in other localities of the country are usually different from and contradictory with each other. Consequently, in the administration of justice, the people of Turkey are being exposed to irregularities and persistent disorder. Fate of the people does not depend on a definitive and stable principle of justice, but on medieval *fıkıh* rules that are coincidental and change-dependent and that are mutually contradictory. To rescue Republic Turkish justice from this chaos, deprivation, and very primitive situation, it has become indispensable to create quickly and legislate a new Turkish Civil Code that is fitting to the requirements of our transformation and of the civilization of the present century. To this end, the Turkish Civil Code that has been prepared has been received and excerpted from the Swiss Civil Code which among the civilized laws is the most recent, most perfect, and in the interest of the people. This duty has been performed by a special commission consisting of our country's distinguished jurists working under the directives of the Ministry of Justice.

There are no major differences among the needs of the nations that belong to the family of nations of the present century. Continuous social and economic relations [contacts] have transformed into a family a large and civilized mass of humanity and continues to do so. It is not valid to claim that the draft bill of the Turkish Civil Code would, upon its being put into force, become irreconcilable with the needs of the country because its principles have been received from a foreign country. In any case, it is known that the Swiss state comprises German, French, and Italian races who belong to various histories and traditions. It is beyond doubt that such a code which has shown the flexibility of application in a context that is heterogeneous even culturally is capable of implementation in a state like the Republic of Turkey that contains a race which is ninety percent homogeneous. Conversely, the viewpoint that a progressive code of a civilized country would not be capable of implementation in the Republic of Turkey is considered invalid. Such a thesis would be tantamount to the logical reasoning implying that the Turkish nation lacks the innate ability for civilization. On the contrary, the facts of reality, both in the present and past, totally contradict this claim. Having as witness the history of the Turkish renovation, it can be said that the Turkish nation has not been exposed to any of the reasonable and sound innovations which are concurrent with reason and intelligence, and which have been created according to the requirements of the present century. Throughout the course of our history of innovation, the innovations created out of a concern for the public interest have been opposed only by those groups whose interests were threatened who have mislead and corrupted the people in the name of religion and wrong and superstitious beliefs. The decision of the Turkish nation to accept unconditionally the contemporary civilization and the whole of its principles should not be forgotten. The most obvious and dynamic [lively] evidence for this is our transformation itself. If some of the elements of contemporary civilization are seen to be irreconcilable with the Turkish community, this is not because of a deficiency in the Turkish nation's ability and aptitude, but because of the medieval organizations and religious laws which unnecessarily besiege it.

As a matter of fact, the stipulations of the Mecelle are doubtlessly irreconcilable with contemporary civilization. But it is also obvious that the Mecelle and similar other religious regulations are not reconcilable with Turkish national life. The Ministry of Justice deems the Swiss Civil Code, which is the most recent and most perfect of its kind, as a civilized work that will satisfy the boundless intelligence and ability of our nation, which has heretofore been restricted, and serve as fertile soil for it. No single point can be imagined in this code that would be disagreeable to our nation's sentiments [emotions].

It is important to point out as well that the Turkish nation, which marches with the decision to receive and adopt contemporary civilization rather than graft contemporary civilization onto itself, is bound to keep in step with the requirements of contemporary civilization at all costs, rather than the other way around, that is, by adopting the contemporary civilization to itself. The draft bill we have prepared contains the more important parts of these requirements. The idea of absolute loyalty to custom, to traditions and mores, is so dangerous a doctrine that it cannot take humanity even one step further than its most primitive condition. No civilized nation has succumbed to such a doctrine, but rather has, acting in conformity with the requirements of life, not hesitated often to lay waste to customs and traditions that constrain it. (To stay absolutely loyal to beliefs inherited from grandfathers and ancestors in the face of truths is not compatible with reason and intelligence.) As a matter of fact, revolutions have been used as a very influential means to this end.

Prior to the implementation of the German Civil Code, Germany followed, in its central parts, the Roman law codified by the Byzantines 1500 years prior. To this law, both the texts of the national law and those of the localities were added. In the east and north, there was a mixed situation of Prussian law with Roman law and local codes. In the remaining parts, French law was valid. Of the German population, 33 percent were subject to Roman law, 43 percent to Prussian law, 7 percent to Saxon law, and 17 percent to France's. Before the implementation of the German Civil Code, there were Latin, French, Greek, and local German languages in the German law. In Bavaria alone, there were between 70 and 80 methods pertaining to marriage contracts. There was no possibility for a judge to be informed separately of all of those regulations [texts]. Before the publication of the German Civil Code, there was no possibility of knowing to which code a person in a given circumstance would be subject. With this civil code, the German jurists suddenly rescued their country from laws of a thousand and one kinds handed down through the centuries and created a single code for all of Germany.

The law was promulgated on 3 July 1896 and ratified unanimously by the National Assembly. According to custom and the traditionalists, the draft bill of the German Civil Code was a bit theoretically abstract; and from a practical perspective it was regarded as quite worthless. Nevertheless, they themselves could not even see the possibility of excluding a single principle from the law.

The French Civil Code is also a production of a transformation. It, too, brought forth new principles by trampling over old codes, customs, and traditions. Among the most evident innovations of the law were the annulment of class and land privileges and the taking charge of family law from the church. Before the promulgation of the Civil Code, France was administered with very different local and written customs: in the south with the law that remained from Roman times; in the north there were regulations coming from Germanic sources. Moreover, each region had a civil-relations code peculiar to itself. The Civil Code that was an overwhelming blow to superstitious beliefs erased all relics and declared in their place new codes and regulations. The most intractable adversary of the French Civil Code was the Church. This is because this law denied domination of Catholicism in civil relations and especially in matters of family law.

Switzerland, before the publication of the Civil Code, possessed as many laws as the number of cantons. The Swiss Code suddenly totally abrogated all of the laws that contained various customs and traditions and in their place put a really different, single code. These three big movements were the latest crushing defeats of the "Historical School" that wanted to tie all of life to dead traditions. Our purpose in giving these examples is to show in a dynamic way that nations, according to the necessities of the times and the requirements of civilization, do suddenly abandon their customs and traditions and that this farewell is not something that brings harm and danger, but entails, rather, great benefits. The fundamental point in these laws that we respect is the separation, in an absolute sense, of religion and the state. Switzerland, Germany, and France have strengthened and fortified their political and national unities and their economic, social salvations, and developments by promulgating their civil codes. In view of these vital needs, in none of these states—even in a state like Switzerland where public opinion prevails in the most expansive sense—was the prolongation of old mores, local and customary relations, and religious habits desired, capable of being desired, or even capable of being imagined.

There is no doubt that the purpose of laws is not to arrive at any stipulation which derives from mores or traditions or from any religious rules which should be only a matter related with the conscience, but rather with providing and satisfying at any cost the political, social, economic, and national unity. The principle distinguishing characteristic of states that belong to the civilization of the present century is their considering religion and the world separate. The opposite of this results in the domination of the conscience of someone who does not agree with the accepted religious foundations of the state. The understanding of states of the present century cannot accept this. Religion is to be revered and would be immune as long as it remains a matter of conscience from the point of view of the state. Intrusions of religion into laws as articles and stipulations have always during history resulted in serving the arbitrary will and desire of rulers, the mighty, and oppressors. In separating religion from the world, the state of the present century saves humanity from these bloodstained afflictions of history and allocates religion to the conscience as the real and eternal throne for it. Especially in states that contain subjects belonging to various religions, in order to acquire the ability of carrying out a single law in all of the community, this severing of relations with religion is a requisite for the sovereignty of the nation. This is because if the laws will be based on religion it becomes necessary for the state that is faced with the necessity of accepting freedom of conscience to make separate laws for its subjects belonging to various religions. This situation is totally opposed to the political, social, economic, and national unity that is a fundamental condition in states of the present century. It is necessary to remember that the state is not only in contact with its subjects, but also with foreigners. In this case it becomes necessary to accept special stipulations for them under the name of capitulations. This point has been the most important aspect of the rationale used by foreigners for the preservation in our country of the capitulations that are abolished in the Lausanne treaty. Besides, from the time of Sultan Mehmet the Conqueror until recent times, this religious situation especially was the cause for the legal exemptions that were adopted regarding non-Muslim subjects. In point of fact, during the preparation of the draft bill of the Turkish Civil Code, all those minorities who are present in our country have informed the Ministry of Justice that they give up all the rights that were recognized to themselves in the Lausanne treaty.

We wish to note right here an event that was valuable in our history of renovation. Ali Pasha had once proposed an identical adoption of the French Civil Code to Sultan Aziz. But upon the intervention of Cevdet Pasha this great enterprise came to naught and the Mecelle was substituted in its stead. As a matter of fact, the Sultan's administration whose whole concern consisted of personal interest and which had adopted hypocrisy as its guiding [major] principle, did not even make its principle of decision the requirements of the real interests of the nation.

The Turkish nation, by demanding unconditionally from the world of civilization all the laws that have been given to civilized nations by the present century, has imposed on itself, by this proclamation, with its own hand, all the civilized duties required by these laws. This is one of the meanings of the draft bill. The day the Turkish Civil Code, which is being submitted for the approval and ratification of the Grand Assembly that is the supreme representative of the

Turkish nation, is put into force, our nation will have been saved from the faulty and confusing beliefs of 13 centuries that are enveloping it and, closing the doors of the old civilization, will have entered the contemporary civilization that grants life and light. By preparing this law, the Ministry of Justice harbors no doubts that, before history and our transformation, it has fulfilled its national duty and expressed the real interests of the Turkish nation.

Minister of Justice
Mahmut Esat

Notes

INTRODUCTION

Epigraph: Eric Hobsbawm, "The Crisis of Today's Ideologies," *New Left Review* 192 (1992): 58; John Dunn, *The Political Thought of John Locke* (Cambridge: Cambridge University Press, 1969), 3.

1. By "we" I refer to those political inquirers and observers who see themselves as "secularly oriented" on political matters.

2. Taylor, "Interpretation and the Sciences of Man," in *Philosophy and the Human Sciences,* 32.

3. On "prejudice," see below and Gadamer, *Truth and Method.* Hereafter this text will be referred to as TM. For "high expectations," see Ross, *Origins of American Social Science,* 7.

4. For alternative secularizing possibilities, see Chadwick, *Secularization of the European Mind.*

5. An account of this sort always develops within a variety of hermeneutic limits, which I detail in Chapter 2. For Taylor's account of this aim, see Taylor, "Comparison, History and Truth," 42; "Understanding and Ethnocentricity," in *Philosophy and the Human Sciences,* 125–29; "Theories of Meaning," in *Philosophy and the Human Sciences,* 281; "Interpretation and the Sciences of Man," in *Philosophy and the Human Sciences,* 28.

6. In distinguishing between interpretive and noninterpretive approaches to po-

litical explanation, I am not denying that noninterpretive approaches require interpretation. I am distinguishing between hermeneutic and nonhermeneutic understandings of the practice (and possibilities) of political explanation. Throughout the book, I
use the terms "interpretive inquiry" and "hermeneutics" interchangeably.

7. TM, 299.

8. The Prime Minister's claim is partly intended to undermine the Turkish military's
similar counterclaim, and testifies to Turkey's emplacement in a set of general political
problems associated with democratization, such as the relations between the military
and the state, authoritarianism, and nationalism, all experienced in other contexts, East
and West. A context that resembles Turkey's secularization politics is India; see, e.g.,
Madan, "Secularism in Its Place"; Nandy, "Politics of Secularism"; and discussions in
Van Der Veer, *Religious Nationalism,* esp. 12–26 and 197ff.

9. While I distinguish between the substantive-theoretical and the methodological dimensions of any explanatory posture for my analysis, I view the two as *always* fundamentally
related. I do not mean to imply any dichotomy between theory and method. My
concern is with their relation.

10. Parla, *Social and Political Thought of Ziya Gökalp,* 1. Hereafter this text will be referred to
as SPTZG.

11. See Dryzek and Leonard, "History and Discipline in Political Science"; Farr, "Political
Science and the Enlightenment of Enthusiasm"; Gunnell and Easton, "Introduction" in
Development of Political Science, 2, 30.

12. My history is therefore "linked to agendas for disciplinary identity," Dryzek and
Leonard, "History and Discipline," 39; see also Gunnell and Easton, "Introduction" in
Development of Political Science, 1.

13. These questions conform to the suggestions that are made by Dryzek and Leonard in
their conception of postempiricist histories of political science: "[Political science] histories should, above all else, attend to the episodes of political science in context. Practices,
approaches, research traditions, theories, and methods should be apprehended and
judged for their success and failure according to how well they understood and resolved
the problems they confronted" ("History and Discipline," 43). Cf. James Farr, "From
Modern Republic to Administrative State: American Political Science in the Nineteenth
Century," in Easton, *Regime and Discipline,* 132–33; and John Gunnell, who raises some
of these matters in his reflections on the historiography of the discipline ("The Historiography of American Political Science," in *Development of Political Science,* 15, 27, 29;
David Easton, John G. Gunnell, and Michael Stein, "Introduction," in Easton, *Regime
and Discipline,* 5–8).

14. By "traditionary" text, Gadamer means a text understood as authoritative over time (we
might say a "classic"). A critical evaluation of our prejudices does not take place at any
time. Notice, however, how his statement does not limit the occurrence of a provocation
to this context.

15. TM, 299.

16. Gadamer, "Problem of Historical Consciousness," 137.

17. Gadamer is interested in the thesis that history and truth ultimately exceed all self-
conscious understanding (Weinsheimer, *Gadamer's Hermeneutics,* 200).

18. Quotes from Weinsheimer, *Gadamer's Hermeneutics,* 1985, 199; TM, 272.

19. TM, 306.

20. TM, 299.

21. Gadamer, "Problem of Historical Consciousness," 137.

22. Weinsheimer, *Gadamer's Hermeneutics,* 180; TM, 295–96, 300ff.

23. TM, xxviii.

24. TM, xxviii, 197; Terence Ball, "Deadly Hermeneutics; or SINN and the Social Scientist" in *Idioms of Inquiry,* ed. Terence Ball (Binghamton: State University of New York Press, 1987).

CHAPTER 1: INTERPRETING ALTERNATIVE MODERNITIES

Epigraph: J. G. A. Pocock, "Modernity and Anti-Modernity," 47. Agnes Heller, "Moses, Hsüan-Tsang, and History," in Deutsch, *Culture and Modernity,* 536.

1. All quotations from Halliday, *Iran: Dictatorship and Development,* 31. In 1963, the Shah launched the White Revolution, opposed by the radical (i.e., not all) clerics who had been recently reorganized under the leadership of Ayatollah Ruhollah Musavi Khomeini, following the death of Ayatollah Abol-Qasim Kashani in 1962. Khomeini's criticisms of the modernizing policies of the Pahlavi regimes date back to 1943. See Abrahamian, *Khomeinism: Essays on the Islamic Republic.* Khomeini was exiled by the government in 1964.

2. Bill, "Power and Religion in Revolutionary Iran," 27, 46–47.

3. Anderson, "Policy-making and Theory Building," 73.

4. Hereafter, my references to a "secular modern" prejudice are intended only to cover the particular form of it that I unpack and criticize here. As I discuss in detail below, I do not think of secular-modernism, or the conceptual and historical possibilities within it, in monolithic terms.

5. Sewell, "Three Temporalities," 5.

6. Henry Maine is quoted in Collini et al., *Noble Science,* 218.

7. Mayer, *Redefining Comparative Politics,* 212–13; see also Eickelman and Piscatori, *Muslim Politics.*

8. All quotations in this paragraph are from Huntington, "Goals of Development," 25–26.

9. Table from Huntington, "Goals of Development," 24.

10. He varies on the other culture categories, with the exception of Latin or Nordic, which is not surprising since they are the essential criteria for the entire teleological schema; see Huntington, "Clash of Civilizations," 22–49.

In terms of religion and modernization, what is important is Huntington's own conceptual looseness in a discussion that he characterizes as about "culture" and not "principal religion." Huntington's argument would be much different if he called on political scientists to take religion seriously. For examples of those in the policy sciences of those who do, see essays in Johnston and Sampson, *Religion.*

11. See Krishna, "Secularism," 548, 553; and Smith, "Retrospective Thoughts," 16–17.

12. See Eickelman and Piscatori, *Muslim Politics,* 23; Esposito, "Study of Islam," 3; Hudson, "Islam and Political Development," 3.

13. All quotations from Hudson, "Islam and Political Development," 2.

14. See Smith, "Retrospective Thoughts," 16; Hudson, "Islam and Political Development," 2–3.

15. Halliday, *Iran,* 34; on the removal of religion from politics, Halliday writes: "The struggle of European liberals and revolutionaries from the Middle Ages onwards against clericalism and the Christian religion were necessary to remove religion and the invocation of supernatural authority from political life, and the same applies to Islam, Judaism, or Hinduism" (34).

16. Quotations from Schabert, "Modernity and History I: What is Modernity?" 17–18.

17. Isaac, "Why Postmodernism Still Matters," 118–222. See also White on "post-modern modernity" (*Political Theory and Post-Modernity,* 4). Isaac's interlocutor, Marshall Berman, responds to him by arguing that modernism does not ignore limits but believes that "we are forced to continually remake the world in order to maintain these limits, to keep them from turning into empty forms, to preserve their human meaning" ("A Response to Jeffrey C. Isaac," *Tikkun* 4, no. 4 [1990]: 123). Berman does not fault the Enlightenment with twentieth-century barbarism; such violence, he suggests, is transhistorical. "If the peoples of the world learn to live with each other rather than blow each other up, it will be because we have caught up with that old Enlightenment modernism just in time" (123).

18. Harding, "Representing Fundamentalism," 374, 392.

19. Asad, "Religion and Politics," 3, 11.

20. See Ross, *Origins,* 7.

21. Pocock, "Modernity," 47–48.

22. For discussion of "essentially contested concepts," see W. B. Gallie, *Philosophy and Understanding* (New York: Schocken, 1968); MacIntyre, "Is a Science of Comparative Politics Possible?"; MacIntyre, "Essential Contestability," 1–9; Gray, "Contestability of Social and Political Concepts," 333–48; William Connolly, *The Terms of Political Discourse* (Lexington: Heath, 1974).

23. See Osbourne, "Modernity is a Qualitative Not a Chronological Category," 73.

24. Habermas, *On the Logic of the Social Sciences,* 42; Schabert, "Modernity and History I," 9.

25. Eisenstadt, *Origins and Diversity of Axial Age Civilizations,* 2; cf. *Origins* with Eisenstadt, "Cultural Tradition," 443–505.

26. Pocock, "Modernity and Anti-Modernity," 48–59.

27. Pocock, "Modernity and Anti-Modernity," 49.

28. Pocock, "Modernity and Anti-Modernity," 50.

29. Bacon and Bodin are quoted in Schabert, "Modernity and History I," 13, 11.

30. Schabert, "Modernity and History I," 15.

31. Schabert, "Modernity and History I," 16–17.

32. Gay, "Enlightenment in the History of Political Theory," 377.

33. Pocock, "Modernity and Anti-Modernity," 52–53.

34. Pocock, "Modernity and Anti-Modernity," 53.

35. See Farr, "Political Science and the Enlightenment of Enthusiasm," 65; Taylor, "Introduction," in Taylor, *Human Agency and Language;* and Hawthorne, *Enlightenment and Despair;* see ch. 2 for a fuller discussion of positivist and neopositivist forms.

36. Binder, "Natural History of Development Theory," 7.

37. On historical transitions, see Sewell, "Three Temporalities," and Tilly, *Big Structures*. For an exposition of the replacement dynamic in "nation-state" building, see Migdal, *Strong Societies and Weak States.*

38. Pocock, "Modernity and Anti-Modernity," 56. Literature that debunks the "old" assumptions includes: Rustow, "Near East"; Rustow, "Turkey" and *A World of Nations;* Bendix, "Tradition and Modernity Reconsidered"; Rudolph and Hoeber Rudolph, *Modernity of Tradition.* On neopatrimonialism and patrimonialism, see, e.g., Christopher Clapham, *Third World Politics: An Introduction* (Madison: University of Wisconsin Press, 1985). See also Randall and Theobald, *Political Change and Underdevelopment,* Chs. 1 and 2.

39. Max Weber, "Domination by Economic Power and Authority" in Lukes, *Power,* 32. In terms of systemic change replacing the old, the same would apply if we were to think in terms of modes of production or social formations: cf. Ernesto Laclau, "Feudalism and Capitalism in Latin America," *New Left Review* 67 (1971); Perry Anderson, *Lineages of the Absolutist State* (London: Verso, 1979); Laclau and Mouffe, "Post-Marxism Without Apologies."

40. See Terence Ball, "The Picaresque Prince: Reflections on Machiavelli and Moral Change," *Political Theory* 12, no. 4 (1984): 521–37.

41. Heller, "Modernity's Pendulum," 1.

42. See Springborg, "Politics, Primordialism and Orientalism," 185–211.

43. Tilly, *Big Structures,* 12; Eisenstadt, *Origins and Diversity,* 10.

44. Tilly, *Big Structures,* 12. As the editors of the journal *Thesis Eleven* have written: "Modernization should no longer be seen as a synonym for development with its own preconception cast from the moulds of either Parsonian evolutionism, historical materialism, or Leninist practices. Rather, it is indicative of a multidimensional set of experiences and world-orientations or cultures which often clash with one another in the present, as well as with the past" (33 [1992], iii).

45. Deutsch, "Preface," in Deutsch, *Culture and Modernity,* xiii–xiv. Thus, we do not need to eliminate responses like Jeffrey Isaac's discussed above from the politics of modernity. His postmodern sensibility is a uniquely Western view of the relation between religion and life in modernity.

46. Rorty, "Philosophers, Novelists and Intercultural Comparisons," 4, 14; Larry Wolff, "Review" (of Adam Michnick's *The Church and the Left*), *New York Times Book Review,* 21 March 1993; Martin Jay, "Lyotard and the Denigration of Vision in 20th Century French Thought," *Thesis Eleven* 31 (1992): 35; Joe Barnhart, "The Incurably Religious Animal" in *Religious Resurgence and Politics in the Contemporary World,* ed. Emile Sahliyeh (Albany: State University of New York Press, 1990), 31.

47. See Ellis Goldberg, "Smashing Idols and the State: The Protestant Ethic and Egyptian Sunni Radicalism," *Comparative Studies in Societies and History* 33, no. 1 (1991): 3–35; Said Amir Arjomand, "Religion, Political Order and Societal Change," in *Current Perspectives in Social Theory,* ed. S. G. McNall (London: JAI Press, 1985), 1–15; Saad Eddin Ibrahim, "Anatomy of Egypt's Militant Islamic Groups: Methodology and Preliminary Findings," *International Journal of Middle East Studies* 12 (December 1980): 423–53. For

discussions of constituent class dynamics, see Manfred Halpern, *The Politics of Social Change in the Middle East and North Africa* (Princeton: Princeton University Press, 1963); Richards and Waterbury, *A Political Economy of the Middle East;* on Islam more generally, see Esposito, *Islam,* and Eickelman and Piscatori, *Muslim Politics,* 1996.

48. Sharabi, *Theory, Politics and the Arab World,* 2; El-Affendi, "Studying My Movement," 89.

49. Skinner, *Foundations of Modern Political Thought,* 243; "exclude in advance," Richard Rorty, "Cosmopolitan Without Emancipation: A Response to Lyotard," in *Modernity and Identity,* ed. Scott Lash and Jonathan Freedman (Cambridge: Basil Blackwell, 1992), 59; and Putnam, "French Revolution and the Holocaust," 310. On making relevant substantive and philosophical distinctions, Abrahamian's analysis of the complexities of Ayatollah Khomeini's ideology is a good example of the kind of study that we need; see Abrahamian, *Khomeinism.*

50. Ibrahim, "Special Report" 304.

51. "Movements of secular cultural criticism . . . " Sharabi, *Theory, Politics and the Arab World,* 2.

52. Arendt, *Between Past and Future,* 94.

53. Guillermo O'Donnell and Philippe C. Schmitter, "Introducing Uncertainty," in O'Donnell et al., *Transitions from Authoritarian Rule,* 1.

54. See Ross, *Origins,* 7.

55. Taylor, "Inwardness and the Culture of Modernity," 92.

56. Taylor, "Politics of Recognition," 93.

57. Taylor, "Understanding and Ethnocentricity," 132. Hillary Putnam has written: "The clash of traditions and conceptions of the good will certainly continue. If that clash is not accompanied and tempered by the effort to understand the values and conceptions of the good which are not our own and the willingness to compromise, our worst fears will certainly come true. Writing of the very failing I have been discussing, the failure (James calls it a 'blindness') to understand the 'values and meanings' of others, James writes: 'No one has insight into all ideals.' No one should presume to judge them off-hand. The pretension to dogmatize about them in each other is the root of most human injustices and cruelties, and the trait in human character most likely to make the angels weep" ("French Revolution and the Holocaust," 311). Similarly, White implores: "Our creative bringing into presence in language must be joined with a preserving of the sense of otherness" (*Political Theory and Post-Modernity,* 60).

CHAPTER 2: THE INTERPRETIVE COMMITMENT IN POLITICAL SCIENCE

Epigraph: Alasdair Macintyre, "Is a Science of Comparative Politics Possible?" 339; Aristotle, *Nicomachean Ethics,* Book I iii, (New York: Penguin, 1953), 64–65.

1. Gadamer stresses this point against philosophers of understanding who believe that it is possible to regulate understanding by method—namely, Wilhelm Dilthey, Friedrich Schleiermacher, and Emilio Betti. See selections by the first two in Mueller-Vollmer, *Hermeneutics Reader,* and by Betti in Bleicher, *Contemporary Hermeneutics;* cf. Weinsheimer, *Gadamer's Hermeneutics,* ch. 1; and Bauman, *Hermeneutics and Social*

Science, 46–47. In one essay, Gadamer makes the suggestion that what is needed is a "scientific approach that is disciplined by phronesis," where the possibility of a "phronesis that is supposed to be scientifically governed" is decisively rejected (Gadamer, "A Letter by Professor Hans-Georg Gadamer" in Bernstein, *Beyond Objectivism and Relativism*, 263).

2. Weinsheimer, *Philosophical Hermeneutics and Literary Theory,* x; "counterposing," in Dunn, "Elusive Community: The Political Theory of Charles Taylor," in Dunn, *Interpreting Political Responsibility,* 184; Taylor, "Interpretation and the Sciences of Man," in *Philosophy and the Human Sciences,* 53.

I employ "commitment" to avoid the implication of methodologism carried by most available alternatives in political science, such as paradigm, research program, theory, research tradition, method, program, and mode of inquiry. Stance, approach, or disposition might fit here as well. These terms identify an interpretive practice that understands itself as not governed by method but still aims to achieve certain explanatory ends. Given the powerful institutionalized methodological demands in political science, any attempt to avoid methodologism is doomed. What all interpretive political inquirers must do is to avoid falling into the habit, well established in most political science texts, of situating interpretive inquiry in the field of alternative methodologies in political science. It is an alternative approach, but not an alternative method. Here, I am again following John Dunn, who has criticized Charles Taylor's use of the concept of science on similar grounds ("Elusive Community," 184).

3. Dunn, "Practicing History," 174.

4. Dunn, "Practicing History," 175.

5. See Bauman, *Hermeneutics,* 7; Mueller-Vollmer, *Hermeneutics Reader,* 1. Bauman defines *hermeneutikós* as related to explaining: "'explaining' is used here in the sense of 'clarifying', of rendering the obscure plain, the unclear clear" (7).

6. There are several different claims associated with methodological naturalism and positivism. When I mention positivism in this work (what many in political science also term behavioralism), I mean the practices of political inquiry that are committed to the model of explanation detailed in the next paragraph of the main text. Many people committed to these practices eschew the label of positivism.

7. See Ernest Nagel, *Structure of Science,* 4, 21ff.

8. Weinsheimer, *Philosophical Hermeneutics,* 23. See introduction to Fred Dallmayr and Thomas McCarthy (*Understanding and Social Inquiry* [Notre Dame: University of Notre Dame Press, 1977]) for an overview of this background. "Observation" in methodological naturalism connotes the gathering of "sense-data," what is "immediately given" (as the philosophers of the Vienna Circle said it) without the interference or distortion of pretheoretical frameworks or values.

9. The implications of Wittgenstein's thought reached a large English-speaking audience through the work of Peter Winch, whose classic *The Idea of a Social Science* was first published in 1958. As Dallmayr and McCarthy note, "it is not necessary to look to Germany for significantly different theories of interpretive understanding" (*Understanding,* 137). They point to the writings of Michael Oakeshott as well.

10. Cf. Hollis and Smith, *Explaining and Understanding in International Relations,* Ch. 4;

Little, *Varieties of Social Explanation,* 71. Ironically, Michael Gibbons's edited reader on interpreting politics includes but one reference to the work of MacIntyre as a footnote to an essay by Winch; see Gibbons, *Interpreting Politics.*

11. Ball, "Introduction" to Ball, *Idioms of Inquiry,* 2. On the narrow thinking about political science practices, consider that the following introductory texts still in use contain no substantive discussion on interpretive inquiry: Robert A. Bernstein and James A. Dyer, *An Introduction to Political Science Methods,* 3rd. ed. (Englewood Cliffs: Prentice Hall, 1992); Richard I. Cole, *Introduction to Political Inquiry,* 4th ed. (Pacific Grove, Calif.: Brooks/Cole, 1985); Janet Buttolph Johnson and Richard A. Joslyn, *Political Science Research Methods* (Washington: Congressional Quarterly Press, 1986); and W. Phillips Shively, *The Craft of Political Research,* 3rd. ed. (Englewood Cliffs, N.J.: Prentice-Hall, 1990). These texts are expressive of noninterpretive, method-driven approaches in political science.

12. See Taylor, "Neutrality in Political Science," 58–90.

13. See Gunnell, *Between Philosophy and Politics,* 29, 91; *Descent of Political Theory,* 2, 8. For a critique of Gunnell's reading of the self-alienating tendencies of political theorists who criticized positivism, see Sheldon Wolin, "History and Theory: Methodism Redivivus," in *Tradition, Interpretation, and Science: Political Theory in the American Academy* (Albany: State University of New York Press, 1986), 50–51.

14. Dunn, "Elusive Community," 183. On living positivist assumptions, cf. David Easton "Political Science in the United States: Past and Present," in Easton et al., *Development of Political Science,* 284, 288.

15. See, e.g., David Paris and James F. Reynolds, *The Logic of Political Inquiry* (New York: Longman, 1983); Alan Zuckerman, *Doing Political Science: An Introduction to Political Analysis* (Boulder, Colo.: Westview, 1991), and Little, *Varieties.* Paris and Reynolds draw mostly on literature from outside political science (Wittgenstein, Schultz, Winch, and others). Zuckerman has a section on anthropological approaches but contains no recognition of statements in political science literature. On thinking problematically about what interpretation involves, or ignoring the significance of interpretive inquiry when no such set of methods seems available, see Easton, "Political Science," 287–88; Louis J. Cantori, "Future Directions in Comparative Politics," in *Comparative Politics in the Post-Behavioral Era,* ed. Louis Cantori and Andrew Ziegler Jr. (Boulder, Colo.: Lynne Reiner, 1988), 408.

16. Easton, "Political Science," 289.

17. Taylor, "Interpretation," 32; Dallmayr, *Language and Politics,* 1, 9. For further discussion on language, see Dallmayr, *Language and Politics,* 53ff.

18. Quotations from Taylor, "Language and Human Nature," 110–11.

19. Most quotations from Taylor, "Theories of Meaning," in *Human Agency and Language,* 248–92; Taylor, "Language," 114.

20. See Taylor, "Theories of Meaning," 264, 269–71; Taylor, "Language," 114.

21. MacIntyre, "Mistake," 62–63; "Indispensability of Political Theory," 19–20. In most cases when I speak of meaning in this sense, I intend meanings, understandings, and dimensions of significance. Continually writing all three in one sentence becomes burdensome for the writer as well as the reader.

22. Taylor, "Language," 122.

23. Taylor, "Language," 122–123; Ball et al., *Political Innovation and Conceptual Change,* 1.

24. Taylor, "Introduction," in Taylor, *Human Agency and Language,* 8, 73; Taylor, "Self-Interpreting Animals," in *Human Agency and Language,* 45; Taylor, "The Politics of Recognition," in *Multiculturalism and the Politics of Recognition,* ed. Amy Gutmann (Princeton: Princeton University Press, 1992), 33.

   Throughout this essay, the reader might wonder about the extent of my claims regarding the constitutive thesis. Do I mean "entirely" constituted? Do I mean "partly"? I do not mean entirely, but I do not mean partly either. I mean constituted more significantly than is generally appreciated. (I cannot claim to have solved this problem.)

25. Taylor, "Politics," 36.

26. Taylor, "Language," 117.

27. Taylor, "Interpretation," 40.

28. Taylor, "Interpretation," 36.

29. Shklar, "Squaring the Hermeneutic Circle," 473, cf. 457–58; on "freedom," see Taylor, "Interpretation," 45.

30. Taylor and Bogdan, *Introduction to Qualitative Research Methods,* 8.

31. Taylor, "Comparison, History, and Truth," 39. Cf. Bauman: "Historical texts are activated (indeed, brought into being) by the beams of light cast by our historical practice, and then they are part of the current flow of history" (*Hermeneutics,* 44).

32. Holt and Richardson, "Competing Paradigms in Comparative Politics," in Holt and Turner, *The Methodology of Comparative Research,* Ch. 1; Rose, "Comparing Forms of Comparative Analysis," 462.

33. Outhwaite, *New Philosophies,* 71. See also Taylor, "Language," 147, and Geertz, "From the Native's Point of View," 147. Dialogical inquiry might, furthermore, expand the horizons of our interlocutors. But this need not happen, because their interest may not be what ours is—namely, to make sense of others. Their interest might be to help us make sense, and, in this process, if conversation takes place, they may understand differently as well.

34. Taylor, "Theories of Meaning," 281; Taylor "Comparison," 41.

35. Geertz, "From the Native's Point of View," 145; Bauman, *Hermeneutics,* 16; Taylor, "Comparison," 46.

36. Taylor, "Politics," 67.

37. Taylor, "Understanding and Ethnocentricity," 125, 129.

38. Quentin Skinner, "Reply to My Critics," in Tully, *Meaning and Context,* 251–52; "that we can . . . ," MacIntyre, "Relativism, Power, and Philosophy," 393.

39. Skinner, "Language and Political Change," 7–8.

40. See Taylor, "Understanding," 120–21; Taylor, "Comparison," 40.

41. Taylor, "Comparison," 42.

42. I draw this example from MacIntyre, and extend it slightly. See MacIntyre, "Mistake," 70.

43. MacIntyre, "Ideology, Social Science and Revolution," 324–25.

44. Taylor, "Interpretation," 24.

45. MacIntyre, "Mistake," 61; Skinner, "Reply," 246. Cf. Farr, "Resituating Explanation."

46. Martin Jay has referred to Skinner's influential essay entitled "Meaning and Understanding in the History of Ideas" as the "manifesto of a militant contextualist movement," in "Textualist Approach to Intellectual History," 8. I rely heavily on Skinner's "statement of what I actually believe" ("Reply," 235) in my discussion. My view is that some of his points may have been stated with different emphases in his many articles, but that this statement is the best account of them.

47. Collingwood, quoted in Dunn, *Political Obligation in Its History Context,* 2, 3; Dunn, "The Identity of the History of Ideas," in Dunn, *Political Obligation,* 161.

48. Austin, quoted in Skinner, *Meaning and Context,* 83; on illocutionary force, see Skinner, "Reply," 261–62; see also Dallmayr, *Language,* 89–92.

49. Skinner, "Motives, Intentions, and the Interpretation of Texts," in Tully, *Meaning and Context,* 99; Dunn, "Identity," 16; Skinner, "Reply," 99.

50. Skinner, "Reply," 271. His focus is primarily on intentions as distinct from motives. The former, he argues, are inside the text-act, while the latter are antecedent to and prompt it. "Motive" is close to what Austin called the perlocutionary force, which informs what a speaker was doing *by* doing something, as distinct from *in* doing something. Skinner's interest in intent makes sense, because he has been concerned with understanding what an author was doing in saying something rather than what the audience was doing in or by receiving it.

51. Quotations from Skinner, "Reply," 233, 247.

52. See Skinner, "Reply," 247, and *Foundations,* x.

53. On prejudice, see "Reply," 254, 280–81; on epistemological individualism, see 206–9; on continuous interpretation, 285; on method, 236, 280–281. Note that others, like James Tully, speak of Skinner's approach as a procedure (with five steps) or a technique, Tully, "Pen is the Mighty Sword," 7, 10.

Skinner's acceptance of the ever-present role of prejudice must be read as a concession when compared with some of his previous, more militant anti-anachronistic writings. In one, he suggested not "bowing to" a "limitation," he associated with Gadamer that "we are likely to be constrained in our imaginative grasp of historical texts in ways that we cannot even be confident of bringing to consciousness" ("The Idea of Negative Liberty: Philosophical and Historical Perspectives," in *Philosophy in History,* ed. Richard Rorty, J. B. Schneewind, and Quentin Skinner [Cambridge: Cambridge University Press, 1984], 201). Surely Gadamer does not speak *only* of "constraints." We should recognize Skinner's considered judgment: "We inevitably approach the past in light of contemporary paradigms and presuppositions" ("Reply," 280–81); "It would be a quixotic form of self-denying to insist that our language of explanation must at this point match whatever language the people in question applied or might have applied to themselves. If we wish to furnish what we take to be the most powerful explanations available to us, we are bound to employ what we believe to be the best available explanatory theories and the concepts embodied in them. As a result our vocabulary of appraisal and explanation will be almost certain to include a number of concepts that would have been incomprehensible to the people to whom we are applying them" (254).

54. Skinner, "Reply," 280.

55. All quotations from Skinner, "Reply," 246.

56. Taylor, "Interpretation," 36.

57. MacIntyre, "Is a Science of Comparative Politics Possible?" 11–12.

58. Taylor, "Theories of Meaning," 280; Taylor, "Interpretation," 28.

59. Taylor, "Interpretation," 32; Taylor, "Theories of Meaning," 271.

60. "An anti-hermeneutic science can retain its epistemological respectability only by the consistent refusal to say anything about what we are *doing* and why we are doing it" (Dunn, "Practicing History," 151).

61. See also Farr, "Understanding," 36.

62. Taylor, "Interpretation," 56; MacIntyre, "Epistemological Crises," 56–58; MacIntyre, "Ideology," 331; MacIntyre, "Is a Science of Comparative Politics Possible?" 10.

63. Taylor, "Interpretation," 18.

64. Ferejohn, "Rationality and Interpretation," 283.

65. Taylor, "Interpretation," 24.

66. "We can," Skinner, "Reply," 285.

67. Dunn, "Practicing History," 167–68, 170; cf. MacIntyre, "Indispensability," 20.

68. Taylor, "Understanding," 124.

69. Dunn, "Practicing History," 170.

70. "Understanding is inseparable from criticism, and this in turn is inseparable from self-criticism," Taylor, "Understanding," 131; cf. Moon, "Political Science and Political Choice," 245.

71. Taylor, "Comparison"; Peter Winch, "Understanding a Primitive Society," 106; Ball, *Political Innovation,* 2; Bruns, *Hermeneutics,* 7; Taylor, "Interpretation," 53–54. Some interpretive theorists hope that this will lead to "a greater degree of understanding, and thereby, a larger tolerance for various elements of diversity" (Skinner, "Reply," 287); or even the "emancipatory effect of opening up the unidimensional discourse in whose terms our political and cultural conversations have for too long been conducted" (Ball, *Political Innovation,* 14). With a good deal of "charity of attitude" (Dunn, "Practicing History," 160) from others as well as on our own part, these hopes might be fulfilled.

72. Farr, "Understanding," 29. On the history of political consciousness, see, e.g., Skinner, *Foundations;* Dunn, *The Political Thought of John Locke* (Cambridge: Cambridge University Press, 1969); and works by Pocock. On conceptual histories, see Ball et al., *Political Innovation.* On comparative histories, see, e.g., MacIntyre, "Is a Science of Comparative Politics Possible?"; Dunn, *Modern Revolutions: An Introduction to the Analysis of a Political Phenomenon* (Cambridge: Cambridge University Press, 1972); "Introduction" to Farr et al., *Political Science in History,* 137–38. On the general point, cf. Kavanaugh, "Why Political Science Needs History," 479–95, esp. 491ff.

73. Skinner, "Reply," 287; J. A. W. Gunn, "In Praise of Whiggism and Other Good Things," in *Regime and Discipline: Democracy and the Development of Political Science,* ed. David Easton, John G. Gunnell, and Michael Stein (Ann Arbor: University of Michigan Press, 1995), 86–87. Gunn quotes Dunn's view that the writing of the history of ideas "needs to be Whig as to subject matter, just as, like all history, it must be Tory as to truth," and comments that Dunn provides a "manageable distinction that can be rendered as that between why we visit the past and what we do when we get there" (89). But Gunn also

criticizes the Gadamerian approach to this dilemma: Dunn's distinction, Gunn believes, "has a common-sense quality for which one looks in vain in the more apocalyptic visions that compete in modern scholarship. Even of the positions that are presented as mediating between extreme alternatives, most fail to convey much that is readily intelligible. Who has ever made operational Gadamer's 'fusion of horizons'?" (89). Cf. J. W. A. Gunn, "After Sabine, After Lovejoy: The Languages of Political Thought," *Journal of History and Politics* 6 (1989): 1–45.

74. Skinner, "Reply," 287. Taylor, "Interpretation," 53–54. On the relation between concepts and changing practical institutional relations in the world, see Dunn, *History of Political Thought* (Cambridge: Cambridge University Press, 1996), 33–34.

75. My goal has been to identify some general theses about interpretation shared by different kinds of interpretive projects. Any project of this sort risks displeasing someone within its intended scope. I recognize that much remains to be discussed. I have not, for example, identified in any detail what these alternative projects look like; I have not discussed explicitly various questions of power or truth involved in interpretation. While I have made some attempt to account for points of difference between interpretive inquiry and other modes, I have not addressed all of them (cf. Tully, "Wittgenstein and Political Philosophy," 172–204).

76. Richards and Waterbury, *Political Economy of the Middle East*, 347. I write "said to" because the quote is from Bernard Lewis's highly influential *Emergence of Modern Turkey*, in which his translations generally favored a modernization perspective on crucial terms such as "revolution," "mentality," "truth," and so on. Lewis's translations are not usually problematic, but they may be contestable. It is significant that Lewis included this passage and brought it to our attention.

77. Quoted in Lewis, *Emergence*, 410.

78. Mardin, "Turkey, Islam, and Westernization," 212, 216.

79. "Religiously anchored," Sunar and Sayari, "Democracy in Turkey: Problems and Prospects," 170; "modern nation . . . the positive sciences," Gökalp, "Towards Modern Science," 279.

80. Webster, *Turkey of Atatürk*, 288; Lerner and Robinson, "Swords and Ploughshares: The Turkish Army as a Modernizing Force," 24.

81. Harris, *Turkey: Coping with Crisis*, 3. On Kemalist history, see, e.g., Akural, "Kemalist Views on Social Change," 132, 147–148; Akural suggests that "Kemalist historians refrained from exploring the many contours of history; instead, in an unduly present-minded way, they sought a single element, theme or hero. Official republican history therefore emerges as the very flattened account of a march from darkness to light. . . . They tended to consider all existing Ottoman institutions as 'antiquated,' 'medieval' or 'decrepit.' It did not occur to the Kemalist historians that in attributing the Ottoman decline to pan-Islamism and pan-Ottomanism Atatürk was looking for a rationale to support his regime rather than for the causes of the empire's decline." For a statement of the need to examine Kemalism in a historical context, see Özbudun and Kazancıgil, *Atatürk: The Founder of a Modern State*, 2–3.

For examples from the Turkish anglophone literature of ongoing interpretive debates, see, e.g., Ersin Kalaycıoğlu, "The 1983 Parliament in Turkey: Changes and Continuities," in Heper and Evin, *State, Democracy, and the Military: Turkey in the 1980s;* Mardin, *Religion and Social Change in Turkey;* Parla, *Social and Political Thought of Ziya Gökalp.* Non-Turkish contributors to the new history include: Arai, *Turkish Nationalism in the Young Turk Era* and Zürcher, *Turkey.* Zürcher writes, "If the author of this book thought existing general histories of modern Turkey entirely satisfactory, this book would obviously not have been written" (327). The works of these historians should be seen, in part, as fulfilling earlier calls for such critical historical research by prominent historians in the American social sciences; see Kemal Karpat, "Introduction," in Karpat, *Ottoman State and Its Place in World History;* Shaw, "Ottoman and Turkish Studies in the United States."

CHAPTER 3: SECULARIZATION AND MODERNIZATION IN TURKEY: INTERPRETING THE IDEAS OF ZIYA GÖKALP

Epigraph: Gökalp, "An'ane ve Kaide" ("Tradition and Formalism" hereafter referred to as TF), 92; Gökalp, "Türkçülük Nedir?" ("What is Turkism?" hereafter referred to as WITR), 288. Unless otherwise noted, all of Gökalp's citations below are from Berkes, *Turkish Nationalism.*

1. Quotations from Arai, *Turkish Nationalism in the Young Turk Era,* 42. Hereafter this text will be referred to as TNYTE. The writer quoted by Arai ("a time of revolution") was Ali Canip, who, with Ziya Gökalp and Ömer Seyfittin, was a major contributor to the journal *Genç Kalemler.*

2. Berkes, "Ziya Gökalp"; Parla, *Social and Political Thought,* 22. Hereafter this text will be referred to as SPTZG.

3. On Namık Kemal, see Mardin, *Genesis of Young Ottoman Thought.* For further detail on the background context, see Berkes, *Development of Secularism;* Lewis, *Emergence of Modern Turkey;* Shaw and Shaw, *History of the Ottoman Empire;* and Zürcher, *Turkey.*

4. WITR, 287. See also Berkes, who understands Gökalp's objective to have been to "revolutionize the sociological and political language of the Turkey of his time" ("Ziya Gökalp," 378); and Parla, who states that Gökalp "both included aspects of Young Turk thought—transcending the latter, however, by incorporating it into a new synthesis, the totality and the logic of which was entirely different" (SPTZG, 20).

5. Gökalp did not employ the concept of a "secularization problematic." I do so here as a heuristic guide for considering his thinking about religion in modernity.

6. Wilson, "Reflections on a Many-Sided Controversy," 199–200.

7. For a review of the debate in Turkish interpretive circles see SPTZG, 120–22. Major original works worth examining that I do not analyze here include Gökalp's letters, historical writings, and poetry. Selections from his historical writings appear in Devereux's volume. I discuss the substance and significance of Gökalp's poetry below.

8. Heyd, *Foundations of Turkish Nationalism,* ix, 56–57, 123–24, 149, 163, 164, 170. Hereafter cited as FTN. On respecting international obligations and norms, see FTN, 58–59, 123, 124, 169.

9. For Heyd's acknowledgments on national democracy, etc., see FTN, 136–39, 140, 164, 169.

10. SPTZG, 94.

11. STPZG, 26, 54. When Parla declared the need for a "systematic and critical analysis of the meaning and influence of Ziya Gökalp's political theory," he had in mind both Heyd's "slanted" treatment and the "abuses" to which his ideas were put in Turkish political history (124). In the context of Turkish political discourse, "distortions of his thought were equal to if not greater than, his direct influence and accepted proposals." The "Left have accused him of racism and totalitarianism, while the right, have praised him for the same, wrong reason" (122). Kemalists consider Gökalp to be an "exponent of religious conservatism" while the right Islamic radicals think of him as an "uncritical advocate of Westernism, insensitive to the prerogatives of Turkism and Islam in history" (121; cf. Berkes, "Ziya Gökalp," 377). Even in academic circles, Gökalp's reputation is mixed, with some hailing him as a "sociologist as great as Durkheim, or perhaps even greater," while others "have described him as no more than an imitator" (120). Still, among the former, there are those who pay "lip-service to Gökalp's being the founding father of academic sociology in Turkey" (122). Compare Berkes's short remarks to this effect ("Ziya Gökalp," 377). On Gökalp and Durkheim, see Birtek, "Turkish Adventures," 17–146.

12. Parla, SPTZG, 67–69; see Gökalp, "Milliyet Mefkûresi" ("The Ideal of Nationalism," hereafter TIN), 81–82; esp. "İktisadî Türkçülük," 310–12; "Millî Dayanışmayı Kuvvetlendirmek" ("Strenthening National Solidarity," hereafter SNS), 64–67; and "Vatanî Ahlâk" ("The Programme of Turkism—Morality"). Keep in mind that "when Gökalp says [advocates] modernization, certainly meaning Westernization, this is not the liberal West, but it is the corporatist West," that he has in mind (SPTZG, 90).

13. SPTZG, 93.

14. FTN, x–xi. On Gökalp's relation to French sociology, cf. Berkes, "Ziya Gökalp," 376, 383n7; SPTZG, 8–9, 21, 42ff; TNYTE, 92.

15. Regarding the milieu of Turkish studies in the 1940s and 1950s, see Birge, "Islam in Modern Turkey"; John A. Kingsbury, "Observations on Turkish Islam Today," *Muslim World* 47, no. 2 (1957): 125–33; Bernard Lewis, "Recent Developments in Turkey," *International Affairs* 27, no. 3 (1951): 320–31, and "Islamic Revival in Turkey"; Howard A. Reed, "A New Force at Work in Democratic Turkey," *Middle East Journal* 7 (1953): 33–44, "Revival of Islam in Secular Turkey," "Religious Life of Modern Turkish Muslims," and "Secularism and Islam in Turkish Politics"; Rustow, "Politics and Islam in Turkey, 1920–1955"; Smith, "Turkey: Islamic Reformation?"; Stirling, "Religious Change in Republican Turkey"; Lewis V. Thomas, "Recent Developments in Turkish Islam," *Middle East Journal* 6 (1952): 22–40, and "Turkish Islam," *Muslim World* 54 (1954): 181–85; A. L. Tibawi, "Islam and Secularism in Turkey Today," *Quarterly Review* 294 (1956): 325–37.

16. On this background, see FTN, 31–33; TNYTE, 45; SPTZG, 13–15, 50–53.

17. See FTN, 57, 123, 125, 135–36, 160–63. To maintain my focus on the substantive aspects of dispute in the literature, a full discussion of Heyd's use of poetry is beyond the scope of this book. Briefly, Berkes and Parla agree that selective reliance on Gökalp's poetry has led "to his ideas being understood partially or inadequately" (Berkes, "Preface" to *Turkish Nationalism and Western Civilization*, 7; SPTZG, 34–35). Berkes notes that for Gökalp poetry was only a hobby that he practiced to popularize some of his ideas. Gökalp also believed that it might contribute to the development of modern Turkish national litera-

ture. Moreover, "placed in its proper context," writes Parla, the poetry "reveals nothing but personal and political integrity and intellectual, if pedantic, consistency." The proper context is that of the Balkan and First World wars when Gökalp idealized the Turkish nation to "reinforce popular morale and solidarity." According to Parla, the nationalism that is expressed in the poems is neither racist nor irredentist as some have suggested. It is an expression of the defense of national cultural values, consistent with the standards that Gökalp expresses in his theoretical writing. But Heyd largely excludes a discussion of those writings. This is one reason why Heyd's and Parla's interpretations of Gökalp's work are vastly different. The poetry that Heyd extensively relies on completely ceases after 1915 (SPTZG, 35).

18. See FTN, 51, 66, 78, 81, 112–99. Oddly, despite such a devastating critique of Gökalp's analytic capacities, Heyd is still able to complement Gökalp for having "had beneficial influences in developing the scientific study of sociology in Turkey" (153). Heyd presented his study in antonymous terms to those that he used to characterize Gökalp's thinking (scientific, objective, etc.). Heyd's interpretation expresses an unequivocal dichotomy between Heyd's own rationality and his subject's irrationality. A good example is Heyd's view that Gökalp "exaggerates the deficiencies" of the Tanzimat reforms, and "in general does not appreciate the importance of this period which, in spite of all its imperfections, was a necessary stage in the modern development of his nation" (77–78). Cf. Gökalp's careful but critical treatment of the Tanzimat's attempt to "extend the process of Europeanization even to the most intimate sources of our national personality. That was their greatest mistake" (Gökalp, "Asrî Aile ve Millî Aile" ["Modern Family and National Culture," hereafter MFNC]), 249. Gökalp says, "Doubtless we would not have been able to survive at the age without accepting and assimilating European civilization unconditionally. Since the leaders of the *Tanzimat* realized this and put it into practice, we are deeply indebted to them. Under the circumstances of their age, their understanding of a renaissance could not have been otherwise. But to think in this way today would be unpardonable" (249). Heyd's sympathies lie with the Tanzimatists, for he does not accept the value of Gökalp's distinction between culture and civilization either, characterizing it mistakenly as an "antithesis" (FTN, 64; cf. Berkes, "Ziya Gökalp," 384). Similar examples can be found throughout Heyd's analysis.

Despite its shortcomings, Heyd's view of Gökalp became the orthodox view in the social sciences for many years. Although the relation between Heyd's analysis and similar judgments is difficult to trace, we can say that Heyd's interpretation was often cited as, for example, the "best study on Gökalp in English" (Tachau, "Face of Turkish Nationalism"). It was the only study on Gökalp in English until Parla's. We can also say that the judgment that Gökalp's nationalism was "autocratic, totalitarian, [and] leader-worshipping," as Kemal Karpat said in his introductory text to Turkey's politics, was a shared one (Karpat, *Turkey's Politics*, 27, 252–60, 455). Karpat accepted Heyd's argument, suggesting that Gökalp's nationalism "denied the individual freedom," "unlike liberal nationalisms in Western Europe" (26, 252). Furthermore, he lamented that Gökalp symbolized the lack of a "tradition of political thinking in Turkey [that] . . . prevents politics from concentrating on ideas and issues" (456, cf. 260). Karpat asserts that a central question that has yet to be addressed is, "Does the need for modernization arise from a desire for advanced comfort and prestige, or is it the expression of an inner urge for broader views on the human being and his society?" (456). This is the question with which Gökalp grappled.

19. See SPTZG, 22, 64, 86–93, 105–20.

20. See Gökalp, "İslâm Terbiyesinin Mâhiyeti" ("Nature of Islamic Education," hereafter NIE); "Örf Nedir?" ("What are Mores?"); "İçtimaî Neviler" ("Classification of Social Sciences"); "Dinin İçtimai Vazifeleri" ("Social Functions of Religion," hereafter SFR); "Millî Terbiye" ("National Education," hereafter NE). I describe Gökalp's Islamic reformism as well known because even passing comments and references to Gökalp in the literature tend to relate his name to Islamic reformism in Turkey (see, e.g., Webster, *Turkey of Atatürk*, 156–57, and Rustow, "Near East," 369–530). One of Heyd's lasting contributions to understanding Gökalp is in making this point clear. In a passage that is cited by both Parla and Dodd (Dodd in *Democracy and Development in Turkey*, 81), Heyd wrote, "But for the anti-Islamic attitude of Atatürk, Gökalp might have become the initiator of a fruitful scientific investigation of Islam in Turkey and perhaps even the father of an interesting religious reform movement" (FTN, 82). (Whether Atatürk's view of Islam was fully "anti" is a matter of great debate, a point that I address in the following chapter.)

21. Gökalp, "Hukukî Türkçülük" ("Turkish Programme—Law," hereafter TPL), 304.

22. See, e.g., Berkes, *Development*, 1964.

23. Heyd makes several claims regarding this issue. But given the methodological problems associated with his interpretation I do not deal with all of them. Others are: he suggests that most important about Gökalp's Islam was how the Islamic concepts of equality, fraternity, and jihad were intended to strengthen his patriotic sentiments (123) and then illustrates this claim by quoting from Gökalp's poetry. And, he suggests that it was "in the last years of his life" that Gökalp "strongly emphasized the importance of Islam as a moral factor and attaches particular value to the religious education of youth." To illustrate this claim, Heyd quotes from a 1922 essay. What is missing, however, is an acknowledgment that Islam is a moral factor both in life and in education in Gökalp's writing at least as early as 1915 (see esp. SFR, 184–93). In my reading Gökalp's logic is similar to the following: because religion is part of culture, and no longer a civilization, and because culture is the basis of education, religion ought to be part of education as well. Compare also Heyd's reading of Gökalp on the rituals of Islam (FTN, 84) with Gökalp, SFR, esp. 188ff.

24. FTN, 98.

25. FTN, 98–99.

26. FTN, 88–92, 94, 158.

27. Berkes, "Ziya Gökalp," 376.

28. Dodd, *Democracy*, 83–85. Dodd writes, "Islam should rightly be regarded a spiritual, not a temporal or social religion," 84. To see the contrast with Berkes's view, consider Berkes's claim that Gökalp "mobilized all his energies to demolish the theocratic conception of nationality" by seeking to distinguish between Islam as an international religious community and the nation as a distinct sociological entity ("Ziya Gökalp," 385).

29. Dodd, *Democracy*, 85.

30. See TNYTE, 91–92, 97.

31. See TNYTE, 48, 83–90. Arai also analyzes the content of two other journals to which Gökalp contributed, *Genç Kalemler* and *Türk Yurdu*. In addition to showing the Islamist orientation of these periodicals, Arai stresses their relation to the government of the Committee of Union and Progress and the development of their nationalism in cooperation with immigrant Turkish intellectuals from Russia.

32. TNYTE, 90.

33. TNYTE, 95–96.

34. One of his less important claims should be addressed here, however. My reading of the essays that are translated by Berkes suggests that Gökalp's critical appreciation of the West can be found in articles dating from 1913 in the journal *Türk Yurdu;* see, e.g., "Üç Cereyan" ("Three Currents of Thought," hereafter TC), 74–75, "Cemaat Medeniyeti" ("Civilization of Community and the Civilization of Society," hereafter CCCS), 101–2.

35. Parla's emphasis is clear in one of his introductory remarks. "In constructing his synthesis of Turkism, Islamism, and Modernism, Gökalp's genius was able to do justice to all of these elements. He could handle the dichotomies of tradition-modernity, continuity-change, nationalism-internationalism, and Islamism-secularism much better than his contemporaries. What has not been duly appreciated in Gökalp's thought is the fact that, in his synthesis, the emphasis has always been on the second terms of these dichotomies. That fact, I think, will emerge clearly from the present study. In this sense, Gökalp's thought is more modern than traditional, and more universalist than nationalist, however surprising at first sight this may sound to ears accustomed to cliché interpretations of Gökalp" (SPTZG, 22). Notice how the issue of secularism drops in favor of Parla's primary contexts of relevance.

36. SPTZG, 38–40. Parla also notes Gökalp's view that Sufi Islam could provide an ethical ideal for Turkish society. But the emphasis, Parla suggests, was society first, then Islam. Sufism "was a prop for solidarism, not the reverse." Like other Durkheimians, Gökalp viewed religion generally as something that "helped hold society together" (SPTZG, 38).

37. SPTZG, 40.

38. On occupational groups functioning harmoniously, see Gökalp, "Hars Zümresi, Medeniyet Zümresi" ("Community and Society," hereafter CS), 98–100; "Bir Kavmin Tetkikinde Tàkibolunacak Usul" ("The Scientific Study of Communities," hereafter SSOC), 121; CS, 98. On civilization, see, e.g. CS, 100–101. Consider: "The law regulating the life of the culture-groups is the differentiation and multiplication of the primitive groups from an undifferentiated and multi-functioning unit to a state in which special groups come into existence to perform specific functions" (CS, 101). For continuity, see also "Hilâfetin Hakiki Mahiyeti" ("Caliphate," hereafter TC1), 224.

39. On collective representations, see TIN. "Dependent upon . . . disappearance," Gökalp, "Tarihi Maddecılık ve İçtimaî Mekkûrecilik" ("Historical Materialism and Sociological Idealism," hereafter HMSI), 65. For continuity, see Gökalp, "Medeniyetimiz" ("Our Civilization," hereafter OC), 275ff.; "Millî Vicdanı Kuvvetlendirmek" ("Strengthening the National Consciousness," hereafter SNC), and SNS.

40. Gökalp, "Millî İçtimaaiyat" ("National Sociology," hereafter NS), 173. See also NE, 237–38; Gökalp, "İçtimaî Neviler" ("Classification of Social Sciences," hereafter CSS),

149; SSOC, 114; CS, 100. He contrasted his own work with that of the "utopian who fails to see that nature is an ordered system governed by uniform laws, and thinks that he can impose over nature whatever he likes" ("İçtimayat ve Fikriyat" ["Manifestations of the National Ethos," hereafter MNE], 165). Unlike the utopian, the "evaluation and creation of new values, or idées forces" "must take real trends into account" ("Bugünkü Felsefe" ["Philosophy of Today"]). For continuity, see Gökalp, "Pîrimin Vasiyeti" ("Testament of My Spiritual Guide," hereafter TSG).

41. On Ottoman multinationalism and cosmopolitanism, see TIN, 81; "Today the West . . . is the ideal of nationalism," TC, 72; "composed of institutions . . . each other," NE, 238. For continuity on the ideal of nationalism, see Gökalp, "Millet Nedir?" ("What Is a Nation?" hereafter WIN); see also CS, 81–82; MNE, 158.

42. The meanings of these two central concepts take shape over time in Gökalp's writings, especially between 1911 and 1919. After 1917, however, Gökalp's thinking about them is relatively consistent. Compare the concept of sentiments ("Yeni Hayat ve Yeni Kıymetler" ["New Life and New Values," hereafter NL]) with "living vernacular of the people" (TC, 74), with "civilization of the people in" (CCCS), and with the "sum total of value judgements" (NE, 246, 168). He later admits to a "confusion" in 1911, renounces the chauvinistic tendencies in his discussion of the Turkish civilization (in NL) and restates the distinction (WITR, 284).

43. "The complex of . . . of the nation," MNE, 166; "accepted norms . . . and ideals," CS, 97; "tastes and manners," MFNC, 248. On the preservation of cultural integrity, NE, 247; NS, 173; WIN, 134.

44. MNE, 166. For continuity on this theme, see Gökalp, "İnkılapçılık ve Muhafazakarlık" ("Revolutionism and Conservatism," hereafter RC), 266. "Interlocking systems," SSOC, 121. For continuity on this theme, see WIN, 135–37; OC, 269; and "Hars ve Tehzib," ("Culture and Refinement," hereafter CR).

45. WITR, 287. For continuity, see esp. Gökalp, "Hars ve Medeniyet" ("Culture and Civilization," hereafter C and C).

46. Gökalp, WITR; MFNC, 248; WIN, 132, 134.

Like the concept of culture, Gökalp's understanding of "civilization" developed over time: used without precision—in Gökalp's own estimation—in NL, "Halk Medeniyeti" ("Civilization of the People"); clarified later (see above notes on culture)—full clarity in TC and CS, 101. The concepts remain consistent thereafter. For continuity, see HMSI, 269, and CR.

47. WITR, 287; WIN, 133.

48. WIN, 134. See also MFNC, 248; WITR, 288; CS, 97.

49. TC, 75. See also NE, 245. Gökalp's Turkish term for what has been translated as "modern" is *asrî,* which may also be translated as "contemporary" or "of the age," but should not be translated as "secular" as Berkes does on occasion (see, e.g., TPL, 305).

50. TC, 76–77. On the objective nature of civilizational concepts relative to the national ethos, see WITR, 287. On the distinction between European civilization and culture within Gökalp's frame, consider as well: "Yes we shall accept European civilization unconditionally. But because of our national culture, we shall still remain distinct from the other European nations" (WITR, 289). "We have to be disciples of Europe in

civilization but entirely independent of it in culture," MFNC, 250. Compare NE, 235. For continuity, see "İlme Doğru" ("Towards Modern Science," hereafter TGS); OC; RC, 268; CR, 281.

51. TC, 76–77. Gökalp later drew attention to the participation of the "Jews," OC, 269–70, 277. On separate and autonomous disciplines, see TC, 74; CCCS, 102. On the decreasing lack of interest in religious studies, see NE, 234; WIN, 133. On "la-dini" as "non-religious," see TC, 76–77.

Readers of the history of Turkish studies will find passing comments about Gökalp's understanding of Islam in modern Turkey that suggest that la-dini meant irreligious, and hence awakened the ire of the religious conservatives. This evaluation is found in Adnan-Adivar, "Interaction of Islamic and Western Thought," 126; and repeated by Lewis, *Emergence,* 403. The former writes: "Gökalp's most unfortunate mistake was the erroneous translation of the word '*laic*' as '*ladini*' (irreligious), an error that did much to lead the Muslim clergy, with Shayh al-Islam at their head, into a hostile attitude." I think that Adnan-Adıvar is mistaken. Gökalp could have chosen the word laic rather than la-dini. But he chose la-dini because it captured the non-religious character of the new civilization, rather than excited the ire of the conservatives. It is interesting that laic as well as the practices associated with it had exactly the latter effect. This is clarified in Ch. 4.

52. TF, 92–94; cf. NL. For continuity see especially "Dehaya Doğru" ("Towards Genius," hereafter TG), 279. Gökalp's challenges to the nonscientific conclusions of others began as early as NL, 58.

53. All quotes in this paragraph are from TF, 94–96. Although we see the conceptual distinction between culture and civilization at work here, this essay preceded his clarity on these two concepts. It was also one of the essays in which Gökalp confused the concepts of civilization and culture in a truly chauvinistic fashion. He had called for a contemporary "Turkish-Islamic civilization" (95). He later admitted the error in terminology (based on his political-ethical views), but he never rescinded the conceptual point that I think stands and is one of his most eloquent early statements of the new ideals to which Turks should aspire in the context of social evolution.

54. For Gökalp's critique of the imitationist tendencies of the former group, see NS, 178; NE, 237; MFNC, 252; WITR, 287. For continuity, see especially "Halka Doğru" ("Towards the People," hereafter TOWP), C and C, RC, and OC. Unlike those he criticized, the national sociologists use, among other things, the right methods (of "convergence" and "conciliation"); see NS. This would pave the way toward ideational integration. See NS, 171ff; cf. MNE, 167.

55. "The Balkan wars . . . Christian conscience," TC, 75. "A lasting life. . . ," CCCS, 102. Consider also, "In spite of the growth of several ideals, it is still religion that exercises the most powerful force over our minds" (CCCS, 102). He cited the United States and Switzerland here as well. For continuity, see SNS, 64.

56. CCCS, 101–2.

57. WITR, 287; cf. SPTZG, 33.

58. On "absorption," see WITR, 288. "When it puts the stamp . . . its own spirit," SSOC, 120. "A nation . . . cultural consciousness," WITR, 288. For continuity, see TG; TGS,

264; OC, 270; TPE; "Lisanî Türkçülük" ("Turkist Programme—Language"); TOWP; C and C, 108–9, 289.

59. MNE, 168.

60. MFNC, 247, 252. On cultural consciousness as the primary condition of all else, see WITR, 288.

61. NE, 247; see also 240. On Gökalp's political activities, see FTN, 1–15; SPTZG, 10–15.

62. On the theme of internationality (mentioned in the beginning of this paragraph), Gökalp's political vision offers a view of a newly shared rationality among individuals of all nations: "Every person is first of all a member of a nation and then of an international community" (WITR, 287). "Human culture is nothing but a synthesis of national culture and international civilization . . . humanity is heading towards an international society by the federation of free nations" (WITR, 288). "In short, civic morality consists in loving and respecting, first our fellow countrymen, then our coreligionists and, finally, all human beings. One of the obligations imposed by civic morality is not to violate the lives, property, freedom and dignity of any of these human beings" (SNS, 62). "People cannot live by only one ideal. As the ideal of nationalism is imperative, the ideals of inter-community life, of international life, and inter-religious life are equally acceptable. With respect to ideals we are pluralist" (CCCS, 103).

63. On Gökalp's estimation on the relation between religion and culture as part of his sociological analysis, see esp. TIN, 82, and abovementioned citations on the meaning of culture. For continuity, see esp. C and C, 289; TPR.

64. SFR, 190–91. Consider, "Prayers should furthermore be performed in places which are consecrated, that is separated from ordinary places," such as the *mescit,* "the social sphere where the people of a neighborhood or village get together"; the mosque (*cami*), "the one where the people of a district or country form the congregation"; the great mosque (*cami-i keir*), "the one where people of a big city or province form a religious collectivity"; and, finally, the "Kaba and Arafat . . . [that] bring a huge collectivity every year from among the able-bodied members of the *ümmet* of Islam. All nationalities within Islam attend these gathering through their representatives" (SFR, 191–92). For continuity, see TC1, "Hilâfefetin İstiklâli" ("Independence of the Caliphate," hereafter IC), "Hilâfetin Vazifeleri" ("The Caliphate," hereafter TC2).

65. SFR, 192–93. For continuity, see TC1, 224.

66. NE, 242; NIE, 233.

67. On "living rituals," see NS, 172. For continuity, see esp. RC, 267; "Dinî Türkçülük" ("The Turkist Programme—Religion"), 108. Consider also: "The Turkists are those who aim at Western civilization while remaining Turks and Muslims," C and C, 290. While it may be tempting to interpret this as a statement that decouples Turkish national identity and Islam, one must remember that there were among the political elites of Gökalp's day those who would gladly drop the Islamic component. Gökalp is not decoupling the two as much as he is asserting their relation.

68. See NS, 180–81, 185; TC, 73; and CCCS, 102. For fuller discussion, cf. SPTZG, 90.

69. All quotes in this paragraph are from CCCS, 102–3. On the "harm" of the historical attachment between religion and state, see SFR, 185, and NIE, 234. For continuity, see SNC, 61.

70. "The separation between religion," CCCS, 102–3; see also WIN, 132; SSOC, 121; SFR,

184. For continuity, see TC1, 224–26; IC; TC2, 232; and TPL, 304–5. "Own sphere," SFR, 185. Consider also, "One of the greatest tasks of religion in organic society is to leave other institutions free within their own spheres" and cover "only those ideas and sentiments which have to remain spiritual and sacred," SFR, 185, 186.

71. MFNC, 249–50.

72. On "norm-setting," see Taylor, "Understanding and Ethnocentricity," in *Philosophy and Human Sciences,* 132. "Eliminated," FTN, 151. Would the emphasis on separating religion and politics be too great for the Kemalists, whose laicist practices are interpreted by authoritative social scientists in Turkey as having never fully achieved separation between religion and politics? Or did Gökalp misunderstand the power relations necessary for disestablishment? Gökalp may be rightfully criticized for ignoring politics as a phenomenon with an importance beyond sociological speculation, but is this criticism applicable here?

73. TC1, 226. On the relation with the modern state, see IC, 228. After the abolition of the Sultanate, Gökalp wrote, "We are deeply grateful to the Grand National Assembly and its famous president for their success in giving the office of the Caliphacy a character that is compatible with the principles of popular and national sovereignty, which is the foundation of modern states and through which genuine Islamic unity in religious life can be achieved," TC1, 227; TC2, 231–32.

74. Gökalp, "Diyanet ve Kaza," 200–201.

75. For continuity on religion as a pillar of organic solidarity, see OC, 268.

76. On Gökalp's reputation as a *mürşid,* see Berkes, "Ziya Gökalp," 376.

77. SFR, 192; on religion as a social ideal in his early writings, see, e.g., "Muhiddin-i Arabî."

78. Gökalp, "Tevfik Fikret ve Türk Renesansı" ("Turkish Renaissance and Literature,") 145.

79. HMSI, 62–63. See also OC, 276–79.

80. "Yearning for a synthesis," WITR, 287; "fiction of [multinational] cosmopolitanism," NL, 58; TC, 71; WITR, 287. For continuity, see TOWP; RC, 266–68, and his "testaments," Gökalp, "Babamın Vasiyeti," "Hocamın Vasiyeti," and TSG.

81. I have in mind Samuel Huntington's sketch of "The Clash of Civilizations?" as well as "criticisms" of Huntington that reiterate the core of his conceptually problematic— from the more refined Gökalpian perspective—understanding of the concept of "civilization." See Huntington, "Clash."

CHAPTER 4: INTERPRETING TURKEY'S SECULAR MODEL

Epigraph: MacIntyre, "Is a Science of Comparative Politics Possible?" 12. Tapper, "Introduction" in *Islam in Modern Turkey,* 2. I dispute some assumptions in Tapper's question.

1. Hawthorne, "Waiting For a Text?" 42; quoted in Bromley, *Rethinking,* 3.

2. Bromley, *Rethinking,* 125-26. Bromley relies greatly on John L. Esposito's account of the reforms associated with laiklik (see Esposito, *Islam and Politics*).

3. Rustow, "Politics and Islam in Turkey," 70; " Toprak, "The State, Politics and Religion in Turkey," in Heper and Evin, *State, Democracy and the Military,* 120. See also Toprak, "Religion and Turkish Women," in Abadan-Unat, *Women in Turkish Society;* Nermin Abadan-Unat, "The Impact of Legal and Educational Reforms on Turkish Women," in

Keddie, *Women in Middle Eastern History*, 193–94; Dalacoura, "Turkey and the Middle East in the 1980s," 208; Keyder, "Class and State in the Transformation of Modern Turkey," 201–2; Paul Dumont, "The Origins of Kemalist Ideology," in Landau, *Atatürk and the Modernization of Turkey*, 38; Reed, "Religious Life of Modern Turkish Muslims," 147–48; Rustow, *Turkey*, 29. The six arrows are republicanism, nationalism, étatism, populism, laicism, and transformationism. The concept of "Erastian"—referring to attempts to sever a church/state connection by subordinating the religious establishment to lay control—is offered by Lewis in *Emergence*, 271, 412.

4. I recognize that the categories adequately capture differing attempts in the literature to characterize the original identity and purposes of laiklik. Still, they are somewhat more fluid than simple classification allows.

5. Rustow, "Politics and Islam in Turkey," 69. Lerner, *Passing of Traditional Society*, 111.

6. Ahmad, "Politics and Islam in Modern Turkey," 6. For evidence that earlier and more recent observers have seen the "separation of church and state," see, e.g., Dodd, *Democracy and Development in Turkey*, 82; Earle, "New Constitutions of Turkey," 85; George Harris, "The Role of the Military in Turkish Politics, Parts I and II," *Middle East Journal* 19, nos. 1 and 2 (1965): 65; Lenczowski, *Middle East in World Affairs*, 115; Webster, *Turkey of Atatürk*, 127–29; *Economist*, "Turkey Survey" (December 14, 1991): 4.

7. "Disestablish . . . a strictly private affair," Lewis, "Islamic Revival in Turkey," 38; Lewis, *Emergence*, 412–13; Lewis, "Europe and Islam," 121. Weiker, "Turkey, the Middle East, and Islam," 27, 29–30; Weiker, *Modernization of Turkey*, 110. For Lewis's influence elsewhere in the literature of political science, see, e.g., Ellen K. Trimberger, *Revolution From Above* (New Brunswick, N.J.: Transaction, 1978), 67–68; Mehmet, *Islamic Identity and Development*, 119, which cite him explicitly on this point. Cf. Lewis also with Webster, *Turkey of Atatürk*, 229; and Landau, "Introduction" in *Atatürk and the Modernization of Turkey*, xii.

8. "Of a considerable . . . in private life," Kohn, "Ten Years," 146; "to drive it . . . of the people," Tachau, *Turkey*, 27; cf. 30–31; "virtually total . . . religious functionaries," Weiker, *Modernization*, 110–11. Cf. Dodd, *Politics and Government in Turkey*, 21; Sunar and Sayarı, "Democracy in Turkey," 168–69.

9. See Berkes, *Development of Secularism in Turkey*, 450–51; Atatürk, *Speech*, 593–95; Toynbee, *Survey of International Affairs* 1925, 55–56; Zürcher, *Turkey*, 173–75; Dumont, "Origins," 38; Keyder, "Class and State," 210; Toprak, "State, Politics," 120.

10. See Reed, "Atatürk's Secularizing Legacy and the Continuing Vitality of Islam in Republican Turkey," 322. The DIR was created by law number 429 *Şer'iye ve Evkaf ve Erkanıharbiyei Umumiye Vekaletlerinin İlgasına Dair Kanun*. English text in Toynbee, *Survey*, 572–74; Allen, *Turkish Transformation*, 176–77.

11. Toprak, "Islam and the Secularism in Turkey," 91; Allen, *Turkish Transformation*, 221ff; Mardin, "Turkey, Islam, and Westernization," 179, 191; Mardin, "Religion in Modern Turkey," 287; cf. Sunar and Toprak, "Islam in Politics," 426.

12. Keyder, "Class and State," 210; Mardin, "Religion and Secularism in Turkey," 191; "mere . . . department," Rustow, *Turkey*, 29.

13. "Probably . . . into existence," Kemal Karpat, "Presidential Address—MESA 1985: Remarks on MESA and Nation and Nationality in the Middle East," *Middle East Studies*

Association Bulletin 20 (1986): 9–10; "were integrated . . . the state," Mardin, "Religion and Secularism," 194; "saw . . . promotion of Islam" and "expressed . . . " Mardin, "Religion and Politics in Modern Turkey," 139. The Ottoman Sultan laid claim to the Caliphate in 1517 after Selim I conquered Egypt. See also İnalcık, "Nature of Traditional Society"; Heper, *State Tradition and Turkey,* 24–27; Keyder, "Class and State," 207; Mardin, "Power, Civil Society, and Culture in the Ottoman Empire."

14. See Mardin, "Religion and Secularism," 194; Mardin, "Religion and Politics," 139; Heper, *State Tradition,* 24–27. There is a debate as to whether one should consider this a theocratic relation. Cf. Karpat, *Turkey's Politics,* 288; and Lewis, *Emergence,* 212; who suggest that it was theocratic, with Rustow, "Middle East," 174, e.g.

15. The "Ottoman statesman . . . without flinching," Mardin, *Religion and Social Change in Turkey,* 18; "based almost . . . Code of 1889," F. Gölcüklü, "Criminal Law," in Ansay, *Introduction to Turkish Law,* 179.

16. "System of power . . . society," Sunar and Sayarı, "Democracy in Turkey," 169; "secularized . . . the West," Berkes, *Development,* 480.

17. See Robinson, "Lesson of Turkey," 424–38; Heper, *State Tradition,* 87–88.

18. Throughout this and the following section, I draw on documentary material that was published extensively in two studies on the Kemalist single-party period, in Turkish. They are Mete Tunçay's *T.C.'nde Tek-Parti Yönetimi'nin Kurulması (1923–1931) (The Founding of the Single Party Regime in the Turkish Republic)*, and Taha Parla's *Türkiye'de Siyasal Kültürün Resmî Kaynakları (The Official Sources of Turkish Political Culture)*. Both studies are original contributions to the literature on the single-party period. I frequently cite only the original documents that are reproduced in these works.

19. Cf. "The founding of the secular Turkish republic in 1923 . . . ," (Sunar and Sayarı, "Democracy in Turkey," 168–69), and "A further step toward equality came in 1928 when articles of the 1924 Constitution specifying Islam as the state religion . . . were replaced by articles separating religion and state and declaring the Turkish republic a secular state" (Stanford H. and Ezal Kural Shaw, *History of the Ottoman Empire and Modern Turkey,* Vol. 2 [London: Cambridge University Press, 1977], 378).

Laiklik was placed in the constitution on February 5, 1937, in law number 3115. For evidence of the significance of this point in the current dialogue, see Feride Acar, "The True Path Party, 1983–1989," in Heper and Landau, *Political Parties and Democracy in Turkey,* 198. The law of November 1, 1922, which abolished the Sultanate (Muhammad VI, Vahidettin), preserved a role for the Caliphate (Abdul Mejid, cousin of Vahidettin) founded on the "sovereignty of the Turkish state," to be "occupied by a member of the House of Osman" (English text in Toynbee, *Survey,* 50–51).

20. The *Cümhuriyet Halk Fırkası,* or RPP, was founded as the *Halk Fırkası,* September 9, 1923. *Cümhuriyet* (Republican) was added on November 10, 1924. Later, the spelling of the first term was changed to *Cumhuriyet.* It was not until May 9, 1935, that the CHF changed its name to the *Cümhuriyet Halk Partisi,* adopting the French term in place of the Arabic-derived term *fırka.* The standard reference is to the CHP (rather than CHF) or to its translated equivalent, RPP. The text quoted in this paragraph may be found in Tunçay, *Founding,* 394.

21. Mustafa Kemal called for a meeting on March 19, the day after the Ottoman legislature

met for the last time. "Millet" must be translated as nation, but should not be thought of as a strictly secular term. Previous to its incorporation in a nationalist discourse, it connoted "religious community" in the multireligious Ottoman setting. Cf. Tunçay, *Founding,* 30n.6, who quotes Mustafa Kemal's own affirmation of this religionational dimension in the mobilization context.

The Treaty of Sèvres had divided remaining Ottoman lands among the British, Greek, Italian, French, and capitulating Ottoman governments. Greece gained a mandate over Izmir, Thrace, and the Aegean islands, and the Italians over the Dodacanese and Rhodes islands. It also recognized an independent Armenia, including Erzurum, Bitlis (eastern, central Anatolia), and Trabzon (eastern Black Sea), and it envisioned a plebiscite in Kurdistan. The final borders of Armenia were to be set by the President of the United States. The Ottoman government signed the treaty on August 10, 1920.

The *Anadolu ve Rumeli Müdafaa-i Hukuk-u Milliye Cemiyeti,* the Association for the Defense of National Rights, was formed in 1919 at the Sivas Congress (September 4–11) with Mustafa Kemal as chairman. Mustafa Kemal and members of the Young Turk CUP had begun in June of 1919 to coordinate the activities of a nationalist resistance movement whose structures had been created by the CUP government before it left Istanbul (see Zürcher, *Turkey*). The nationalists' purpose was affirmed in the "National Pact" (*Misak-ı Milli*) that was drawn up at the Congress of Erzurum (July 23–August 6, 1919) and promulgated on September 13 at Sivas as a signal to the foreign powers that there was a new sovereign in Anatolia. It was endorsed by the nationalist-dominated Ottoman Chamber of Deputies on January 28, 1920, three months before the British occupied the city. (The nationalists had won a victory in the October 1919 elections.) The Congress at Sivas declared its opposition to foreign occupation and to the formation of the state of Armenia. It had succeeded the Association for the Defence of Rights of Eastern Anatolia (March 3, Erzurum), formed just after Greece made formal claims to Izmir at the Paris Peace Conference (February) and in response to the Ottoman government's capitulatory moves to cooperate with the occupying powers (formalized by March 7). On March 29, the Italians landed in Antalya (Mediterranean coast). On May 15, the Greeks landed at Izmir under British and United States naval protection. The first armed clashes between the Greeks and the Turks occur west of Aydın on May 25.

After dismissing Mustafa Kemal from Ottoman duty on July 8, 1920, the Sultan declared him an outlaw on July 11, shortly after Mustafa Kemal's activities in Amasya. Then, on April 11, 1920, the Sultan had his Şeyh ul-İslâm issue a fetwa "denouncing the nationalists as a gang of common rebels whom it was an imperative duty of any loyal Muslim to kill" (Rustow, "Politics and Islam," 75). Rustow considers this a "real turning point—the watershed between a religious past and a secular future." Had the Sultan "like so many of his generals and ministers . . . escaped to Ankara to lead the resistance movement," the conclusion of the struggle might have taken a different political form (77). On May 24, the Sultan condemned Mustafa Kemal to death, just after the Anatolian-based assembly was established.

22. "To do all . . . captivity," Rustow, "Politics and Islam," 76; "misuse . . . political purposes," quoted in Lewis, *Emergence,* 412; "free Islamic . . . invaders," Atatürk, *Speech,* 363; "many now . . . same time," Ahmad, "Politics and Islam," 6. See also Earle, "New

Constitutions," 80–81; Allen, *Turkish Transformation*, 172; Stirling, "Religious Change," 400; Mardin, "Religion and Secularism," 209; Mardin, "Turkey, Islam," 94–95; Mardin, *Religion and Social Change*, 3–4; Karpat, "Military Interventions: Army-Civilian Relations in Turkey before and after 1980," in Heper, *State, Democracy, and the Military*, 153; Toprak, *Islam and Political Development*, 64–65; Lewis, "Europe and Islam," 119–20.

23. See Atatürk, *Speech*, 41, 336. The First Group, or the Defense of National Rights of Anatolia and Rumelia (*Müdafaa-i Hukuk Grubu*) tried to inherit the standing of the previous nationalist movement. It is worth noting in this vein that the First Group was not the first group founded in the assembly (Tunçay, *Founding*, 42). It succeeded, among others, the Association for the Preservation of Sacred Institutions, founded by traditionalists out of a concern that Mustafa Kemal's financial and political arrangements with the USSR indicated a move towards communism (Zürcher, *Turkey*, 166). The reputation of the group and the Republican People's Party that followed it within the anglophone literature, and indeed within Turkish historiographical work as well, is "pragmatic" (Lerner and Robinson, "Swords and Ploughshares," 32). Szyliowicz calls Atatürk "above all a non-ideological pragmatist" Szyliowicz, "Elites and Modernization," 30; cf. Atatürk, *Speech*, 336. This view results from at least two related sources. The first is the acceptance of the actors' self-definition without question. "Pragmatism," writes Birtek, was also the "favored self-definition of the RPP" ("Turkish Adventures," 126). The second is the granting of a privileged status to the stated scientific goals of the new regime while overlooking how even these goals were contained within one particular articulation (among many others) of the Turkish nationalist thesis. Kemalism is not non-ideological and its "pragmatism" should be measured within the ideological context from which it was born. Cf. Parla, *Official Sources;* Parla argues that Kemalism's objectivist claims conceal its own status as a "Third Way" ideology.

On the historical genesis of this group, see Berkes, "Historical Background of Turkish Secularism," 62; Chambers, "Ottoman Ulema and the Tanzimat," 36; Mardin, *Genesis*, and "Religion and Secularism," 195–96.

24. See Karpat, "The Republican People's Party, 1923–1945," 46. On criticisms of Mustafa Kemal's authoritarian tendencies, see Zürcher, *Turkey*, 166. On the support for this group, see Shaw, *History*, 360–63; Karpat, *Turkey's Politics*, 36ff; Frey, *Turkish Political Elite*, 376–77; Rustow, "Politics and Islam," 76ff; Atatürk, *Speech*, 504ff; Berkes, *Development*, 448ff. A point relevant to our study is that in 1920 one fourth of the members of the TGNA had religious backgrounds (Frey, *Turkish Political Elite;* Rustow "Politics and Islam"; Lewis, *Emergence;* Toprak, *Islam and Political Development*, 64–65). By 1923, this dwindled to 7 percent, and by 1927, 3 percent.

25. "Played a role . . . Kemal himself," Ahmad, "Politics and Islam," 72; "hardly distinguishable . . . characteristics," Özbudun, *Social Change and Political Participation in Turkey*, 41–42, and Frey, *Turkey Political Elite*, 342–43; "only few . . . even flimsier," Rustow, "Atatürk as Founder of a State," *Daedalus* 97 (Summer 1968): 805. On the closure of the FRP, see Toprak, *Islam and Political Development*, 74–75; Ahmad, *Turkish Experiment in Democracy, 1950–1975*, 66–79; Özbudun, *Social Change*, 134; Rustow, "The Near East," 408; Keyder, "Political Economy of Turkish Democracy," *New Left Review*, no. 115 (May–

June, 1979): 13; Frey, *Turkish Political Elite,* 332–35; Atatürk, *Speech,* 718–21; Lewis, *Emergence,* 255.

26. I am adopting the common center/periphery parlance from Mardin, "Center-Periphery Relations: The Key to Turkish Politics?" The Kurdish rebellion is generally recognized to have been complexly constituted by both religious and nationalist dimensions of meaning, something true of the Turkish national struggle as well (see Martin van Bruinessen's work on this topic).

27. Ahmad, "Politics and Islam," 6–7; Ahmad, *Turkish Experiment,* 71–78. Martial law was declared on February 21, 1925, and was initially supported by the PRP; it remained in effect until December 23, 1927. The Law for the Maintenance of Order, or *Takrir-i Sükûn Kanunu,* was passed on March 4, 1925; it was opposed by the PRP, and remained in effect until March 1929. The law that closed the institutions of Folk Islam was number 677, November 30, 1925.

28. Mardin, "Religion and Politics," 207. Martial law was imposed on January 1, 1931, and lasted through March 8, 1931. For accelerated ideological efforts, see Lewis, *Emergence,* 382–83; Karpat, "Republican People's Party," 52, 63; Szyliowicz, "Elites and Modernization," 38–39.

29. Özbudun, *Social Change,* 43; for further discussion, see Özbudun, "Postauthoritarian Democracies: Turkey," 341; Heper, *State Tradition,* 78–79, 99. On cultivating a hero status for Kemal, note that the first statues of Mustafa Kemal were erected on October 3, 1929.

30. The translation of the law is Lewis's, from *Emergence,* 412.

31. Atatürk, *Speech,* 526, 591, 592.

32. Toynbee, *Survey,* 50–51; Atatürk, *Speech,* 595, 594, 686.

33. Atatürk, *Speech,* 489, 586.

34. Quoted, e.g., by Lewis, *Emergence,* 268; and Lewis, *Turkey,* 92.

35. Rustow, "Atatürk as Founder," 814. See also Toynbee, *Survey,* 73–74. Apparently, the Greeks of Anatolia celebrated their apparent liberation from Ottoman rule by donning the brimmed hat.

36. Toynbee, *Survey,* 73–74. On Kemal's justifications, see also Lewis, *Turkey,* 92.

37. In several widely quoted phrases, Mustafa Kemal said, "Let them show their faces to the world and let them have a chance to see the world." "A society or nation consists of two kinds of people, called men and women. Can we shut our eyes to one portion of a group, while advancing the other, and still bring progress to the whole group? Can half a community ascend to the skies while the other half remains chained in the dust? The road of progress must be trodden by both sexes together, marching arm in arm as comrades. . . . In some places I see women who throw a cloth or a towel or something of the sort over their heads, covering their faces and their eyes. When a man passes by, they turn away, or sit huddled on the ground. What is the sense of this behavior? Gentlemen, do the mothers and daughters of a civilized nation assume this curious attitude, this barbarian posture? It makes the nation look ridiculous: it must be rectified immediately" (quoted in Abadan-Unat, "Impact," 179; Lewis, *Turkey,* 44).

38. Toynbee, *Survey,* 74–75. On the recurrence of these themes in recent years, see, e.g., Olson, "Muslim Identity and Secularism in Contemporary Turkey," and Arat, "Islamic Fundamentalism and Women in Turkey."

39. One such western-centric and culturally narrow view was expressed as follows: "It is easier to think of the Turk as a normal member of the family of European nations if he wears a hat, a pair of trousers, uses the Latin alphabet, respects the integrity of women, and parades with a constitution, than the exotic characteristics he has symbolized heretofore" (Jameson, "Social Mutations in Turkey," 493).

I distinguish between these reforms and those associated with Kemalism's inward looking nationalism, intended, as Landau puts it, to "further pride in an attachment to Turkey" ("Introduction," xii). These include the Sun Language Theory, language purification, and the Turkish history thesis. The first theory held that pure Turkish was central to the development of all languages. Its thesis was institutionalized in 1932 with the founding of the Turkish Linguistic Society (July 12). The function of this institution was to purify the language by replacing all words derived from Arabic or Farsi roots with their "pure Turkish" equivalents. If none existed, a new word was to be created (see Heyd, *Language Reform in Modern Turkey*). The Turkish historical thesis suggested that Central Asia Turks were the original source of all civilization.

40. Atatürk, *Speech,* 684. The phrase that I translate as "purify and elevate" is differently translated in the literature as "cleanse and elevate" and "secure the revival of"; cf. Webster, *Turkey of Atatürk,* 280, and Lewis, *Emergence,* 264. The concepts that Mustafa Kemal employed were *"tenzih ve îlâ etmek."* It is interesting that both concepts are located within a Islamic discourse.

On the labeling of the opposition as reactionary, see Kushner, "Turkish Secularists and Islam," 92–93; Karpat, *Turkey's Politics,* 22; Rustow, "Near East," 433, and "Turkish Democracy in Historical and Comparative Perspective," 10; Turan, "Religion and Political Culture," 39–40; Heper, "Islam, Polity," 351. This is not to suggest that all those whom the Kemalists considered "reactionary" were anti-laicists. They may have been anti-Kemalists: "Kemalists associated even moderate conservative elements with the views of reactionaries blinded by religious dogmatism" (Akural, "Kemalist Views on Social Change," 132.)

41. Toprak, "Religious Right," 2; Toprak, *Islam and Political Development,* 38; Dodd, *Politics and Government,* 316.

42. For an interesting set of reflections on how the concept of an obscurantist has been fundamental to Kemalism and to perpetuating religious conflict in politics, see Toprak, *Islam and Political Development,* 122–23; Reed, "Revival of Islam," 267.

43. Toprak, *Islam and Political Development,* 25; Parla, *Official Sources,* 274–275, 276, 288. Reed also notes this as Mustafa Kemal's early position; see "Atatürk's Secularizing Legacy," 325.

44. Rustow, "Politics and Islam," 84–85; "in all," Parla, *Official Sources,* 288. There is evidence that a case was made to the RPP leadership at the time by some Islamic reformists that the Caliphate was not necessary to Islam, and that its implicating Islam in a position of political power conflicted with Islam's theological purposes. Therefore, undergirding the view that abolishing the Caliphate would "rescue" Islam may have been some Islamic reformist ideas.

45. Toynbee, *Survey,* 208; Birge, "Islam in Modern Turkey," 49. The Faculty of Divinity was created in law number 430, March 3, 1924. After the 1950 elections, the new governing

party, the Democrat Party, gave Müezzins (the callers to prayer) the option of Turkish or Arabic after 1950. "Most chose Arabic" (Ahmad, *Turkish Experiment*, 365).

46. Mardin, "Islam in Mass Society," 165; Berkes, *Development*, 484; Mardin, "Islam in Mass Society," 165.

47. Cf. "The state was not anti-clerical as long as the ulema made no overt attempts to interfere with the reforms," Shaw, *History*, Vol. 2, 387. Few utilize the full, comparative, conceptual vocabulary of state-religion relations to capture the identity of what are commonly termed secular politics in any context. "Anticlerical" is one example in the Turkish case.

48. I borrow the theme of "different interpretations of Islam" from Esposito (*Islam* [Oxford: Oxford University Press, 1991]).

49. Mustafa Kemal's pronouncement concerning true Islam would not be the last in the future of laiklik politics, as careful interpreters of Turkish politics have noted. İsmet İnönü, his deputy who succeeded him as president, defended the RPP's position of respect toward Islam, expressing the hope that the "whole world . . . will observe that the cleanest, purest, and truest form of Islam will flourish in our midst" (quoted in Reed, "The Revival of Islam," 270). Cemal Gürsel, one of the leaders of the 1960 coup that ousted the RPP's opponents from power, argued that Islam "has been explained negatively and incorrectly" and articulated a "national and progressive understanding of Islam" (in Ahmad, *Turkish Experiment*, 374); Gürsel's replacement as president in 1966, Cevdet Sunay, "made the necessary point that religion and reactionarism are not the same thing" (Dodd, *Politics and Government*, 307); RPP descendant Bülent Ecevit defended his 1974 coalition with the Islamist "National Salvation Party" by arguing: "Turks should derive their strength from the essence of Atatürk's republic 'which merges Islam and nationalism' and which opened the path for contemporary civilization and democracy" (Kushner, "Turkish Secularists," 93). The 1980 coup leaders, avowedly Kemalist, codified religious instruction in the 1982 Constitution as the duty of the state. This was defended by Prime Minister Bülent Ulusu: "As stated by the generals and government spokesmen, the purpose was to undermine the undesirable Koran courses given privately, to liberate religious education from erroneous and harmful influences, and provide, instead, for a true and enlightened understanding of Islam" (quoted in Heper, "State, Democracy, and Bureaucracy in Turkey," 188–239). Such assertions illustrate an ongoing intersubjective conceptual continuity.

50. See Mardin, "Center-Periphery Relations."

51. Mardin, "Religion and Secularism," 216; Mardin, *Religion and Social Change*, 18, 185, 197; Mardin, "Religion and Politics," 156; and Mardin, "Turkey, Islam," 180–81. See also work by Reed and Stirling.

Citing Robert Bellah's work, Mardin suggests: "Just as biblical imagery provided the basic framework 'for imaginative thought in America up until quite recent times' [Bellah], so too it was on the metaphors of the Quran that Muslims depended and still depend for imaginative creation, for self-placement and self-realization" (*Religion and Social Change*, 195–97; cf. Keyder, "Class and State," 208ff.). Mardin details one case of this phenomena with an interpretation of the life and influence of Said Nursi (1873–1960). Nursi, who suffered incarceration and internal exile under the RPP, considered the

Kemalists "European worshipping imitators of Frankish customs" (Mardin, *Religion and Social Change*, 95), and thus to Mardin represents a "reaffirmation in the concepts of the periphery" of the "norms set by the Quran in such as way as to re-introduce the traditional Muslim idiom of conduct and of personal relations into an emerging society of industry and mass communications" (13). Said Nursi's contribution to modern Islamic thinking is also noted by Kurshid Ahmad, who places him among the likes of the most influential "contemporary revivalists" in Islam (Kurshid Ahmad, "The Nature of Islamic Resistance," in *Voices of Resurgent Islam*, ed. John L. Esposito, 218–29 [New York: Oxford University Press, 1983]).

52. Abadan-Unat, "Impact of Legal," 178; Atatürk, *Speech*, 591. See also Mardin, "Religion and Secularism," 198; Landau, "Introduction," xii-xiii. The Ottoman-Turkish roots of positivism can be traced to the early Tanzimat period. See the previous chapter for details. An interesting text from this period is Auguste Comte's letter to Reşid Paşa, then Grand Vizier, urging the Ottomans to seize the positivist project. Comte suggested that Islam, with its worldly emphasis, was even better prepared to enter the positivist future than Christianity, which counseled its believers to look away from this world; see Comte, "A Reşid Paşa, ancien Grand Vizier de l'Empire Ottoman," *Correspondence Generale et Confessions* (Paris: Mouton, [1853], 1973), 38–41.

Countless interpreters stress Kemalism's rationalist and positivist underpinnings. Özbudun and Kazancıgıl write, "If it is possible to reduce Kemalism to a single dimension, it would not be wrong to single out rationalism, since it was a rationalist and positivist mentality that underlined all of Atatürk's speeches, thought, actions, and reforms" (*Atatürk*, 4); cf. Mardin, "Turkey, Islam," 198, 216, and *Religion and Social Change;* Rustow, "Atatürk," 873; Heper, "Islam," *State Tradition*, 63. "The new individual whom the Republican regime wanted *to bring out,*" wrote Karpat in a memorable line in Turkish studies, "was a rationalist, anti-traditional, anti-clerical person, approaching all matters intellectually and objectively" (emphasis added, Karpat, *Turkey's Politics*, 53; Heper, *State Tradition*, 64). Some of these interpreters, however, overemphasize the rationalist dimensions of Kemalism, choosing not to consider the problems with positivist rationality and ignoring its place in Kemalist nationalism (see Habermas, *Knowledge and Human Interests*). Heper suggests that Kemalism parallels the French ideologues for whom "science was a means for dissolving illusions," but the Kemalists were engaged in creating their own illusions. That nationalism diluted Kemalism's scientific and rationalist tendencies is evident in some of the early Kemalist historiography: the works of the "early Kemalists," Akural writes, "have a markedly ethnocentric coloration and contain many distortions of historical facts in the service of patriotic impulses" ("Kemalist Views," 143).

53. Mardin, *Religion and Social Change*, 32; "Turkey, Islam," 180; *Religion and Social Change*, 25; "Religion and Politics," 155–57. Cf. "The Republic had not been able to propagate a social ethic that was sufficiently meaningful to the rural masses to enable them to react positively to its modernization drive. This was its main failing, and it was especially galling to the Muslim population of Turkey" ("Islam and Mass," 163).

54. Mardin, *Religion and Social Change*, 21. Mardin's interest in critically evaluating the implications of Kemalism's positivism and in exploring the Islamic foundations of life in Turkish society has had a discernible impact in the social and political science studies on

Turkey, in Turkey, and elsewhere. Metin Heper, for example, draws on Mardin's work to elaborate that "Kemalism did not play any role at the level of personality development. The end result was 'the real impoverishment of Turkish culture'; among the intelligentsia this state of affairs led to a type of human relations which have been vacuous, sentimental and yet devoid of compassion. . . . Kemalism could not perform the metaphysical function of a religion . . . for at least some members of the educated elite. . . . their life must have become increasingly dissatisfying; they must have felt a need to complement it with ethical principles that could not be derived from Kemalism" ("Islam, Polity," 360–62; *State Tradition*, 90–91). Similarly, Walter Weiker, in his comprehensive study *The Modernization of Turkey*, cites Mardin and captures a widespread understanding in the Turkish state that Islam *can* and *should* play a role in Turkey's political life: after noting Mardin's point made in a 1969 essay that "there are [in Turkish folk culture] . . . many dimensions of religion among the lower classes in Turkey which are more secular than religious," Weiker writes. "Thus one of the reasons for the revived role of religious-based *institutions* ([in the multiparty period] as distinct from the revival of *religion*) was simply that in large part the Republic had not yet succeeded in replacing those services. It is widely agreed that the large number of religious-based local associations which have been organized in all Turkish communities have at least as many community functions as theological ones. Of course, one of the problems is that these associations often serve as vehicles for political influence of persons who have radically conservative orientations to social, economic, and political issues. But, on the other hand, their leaders are often fairly representative of the general social values of much of the Turkish people, and they may thus be able to serve as sources of stability and of easing the potential psychological dislocation of people who are undergoing rapid social change. . . . As hypothesized in this study, such a situation may be functional for orderly Turkish development even though some other aspects of modernization may be slowed down as a result" (Weiker, *Modernization*, 106–7; see also Tachau, *Turkey*, 87–90). In contrast to Weiker, Mardin has registered some reservations about the ability of state elites to truly understand the dynamic of Islam if they chose to use it for stabilization purposes ("Religion and Politics," 146). For a more general statement of Mardin's thesis, beyond the Turkey context, see Arkoun, *Rethinking Islam*, 20–23; Eickelman and Piscatori, *Muslim Politics*.

55. Mardin's quotes from "Religion and Politics," 216, and "Religion and Secularism," 213; "Could a . . . amulet sellers?" Atatürk, *Speech*, 722; "In fact . . . routine of life," "Religion and Politics," 216.

56. "Religion and Politics," 217, 425; cf. Lewis, *Turkey*, 92.

57. *Religion and Social Change*, 22, 195–99; "Islam in Mass Society," 163. Cf. Reed "Revival of Islam," 125.

58. Personal communication; "counter-historiography," Mardin, "Religion in Modern Turkey," 288; "the idea . . . myth of the republic," *Religion and Social Change*, 1. On the official historiography, see also Zürcher, *Turkey*, 183.

59. In defending themselves from charges of atheism, Kemalists have pointed, e.g., to guarantees in the constitution for religious freedom (1924 Art 64, sec. 5), laws against religious discrimination (Art 75, sec. 5), and penal code statues regarding blasphemy, damage to sacred sites or insults of "spiritual officials" (Articles 175–178, adopted March

1, 1926; Gürelli, *Turkish Criminal Code*, 70–71; cf. Mardin "Religion and Secularism," 210).

On the conceptual constituencies of the power concepts, see Ahmed Emin Yalman,"Islam in Turkey Today," 70–71; Reed, "Faculty of Divinity in Ankara," 290–312, 22–35; and "Atatürk's Secularizing Legacy," and "Continuing Vitality of Islam in Republican Turkey," 333; Rustow, "Politics and Islam," 92–94; Karpat, *Turkey's Politics*, 233, 274, 434; Ahmad, *Turkish Experiment*, 365–69, and "Politics and Islam," 9, 19; Toprak, *Islam and Political Development*, 77ff; Sunar and Toprak, "Islam in Politics," 429.

60. Bozkurt, "*Esabı Mucibe Lâhihası*"("The Rationale of the Draft Bill [of the Turkish Civil Code"]). This text is translated and reproduced in the Appendix. All references to Bozkurt, unless otherwise noted, are in the Appendix.

61. Original text in Tunçay, *Founding*, 382. The word that I translate as "complications" may also be translated as "disputes" or "conflicts."

62. Mardin, "Religion and Politics," 192–93.

63. Texts in Tunçay, *Founding*, 448. See also Rustow, "Politics and Islam," 84; K. H. Henrey, "Glimpses of Turkish Opinion," *Muslim World* 48 (October 1958): 318; Webster, *Turkey of Atatürk*, 307–9. The statements in the text are selected because of their authoritative status in defining the ends of laiklik. Similar statements abound in the documents, journals, and histories of the period.

64. Heper, "Islam, Polity," 305; Ahmad, *Turkish Experiment*, 369.

65. See "The Ottoman Constitution," *American Journal of International Law* 2 (Supplement, 1908): 367–87.

66. Text and interpretation in Parla, *Official Sources*, 1992, 106–23.

67. On the purposes of the law, see Berkes, *Development*, 460ff.

68. Berkes, *Development*, 476; Reed, "Atatürk's Secularizing Legacy," 330; Berkes, *Development*, 476.

69. Text and analysis in Tunçay, *Founding*.

70. Texts mentioned in the paragraph appear, with analysis, in Parla, *Official Sources*, 71.

71. Parla, *Official Sources*, 71–99, 246–47. The original 1923 and 1927 texts are from Tunçay, *Founding*, 52, 395.

72. Abadan-Unat, "Impact," 179; Birtek, "Turkish Adventures," 132.

73. Original text in Serin, ed. *Milli Eğitim Mevzuatı (National Education Regulations)*, 18. The compatibility of religious training schools with dimensions of the original conception of laiklik—an issue that has caused controversy with the ever-expanding network of such schools—is found here.

74. On the cessation of the mekteps, see Reed, "Faculty"; "The number . . . after 1934," Reed, "Atatürk's Secularizing Legacy," 330.

75. Reed, "Atatürk's Secularizing Legacy," 322.

76. Mahmut Esat Bozkurt (1929–1943) received his Doctorate of Law from Freiburg Law Faculty in Switzerland, served briefly as Economics Minister, and occupied the position of Minister of Justice from 1924 until September 22, 1930. He was one of the architects of the legal reforms. After 1935, he taught in the Law Faculty at Istanbul University where he also lectured on the topic of his book, *Atatürk's Revolution*. Like Recep Peker, Mahmut Esat Bozkurt was a prominent public interpreter of the politics of the single-party period

(see Tunçay, *Founding*, 173n.71, 185n.1). I am especially grateful to Professor Ersin Ka-laycıoğlu for recommending this text. Another discussion of the text in English can be found in Berkes, *Development*, 470ff.

77. The process of reform in the interest of female social rights arguably began during the rule of the Union and Progress Party. In 1911, a girls lycée was opened. In 1917 a new Family Law, inter alia, strengthened women's rights at the time of marriage. It also raised the minimum age requirements from twelve to seventeen for women and fifteen to eighteen for men. There is a wide literature on the question of women's rights in Turkey. Toprak's idea that Turkish women were "emancipated but unliberated" with the Civil Code is one attempt to distinguish between (limited) personal and legal rights that women gained in Turkey and freedom in a wider sense from patriarchal constraints. The civil code is thus seen as a new beginning for Turkish woman whose personal rights extended from the domestic to the political sphere with suffrage legislation during the 1930s. Women gained (or more accurately, were granted), the right to participate in municipal elections (April 14, 1933), the right to participate in electing the council of elders in villages (October 26, 1933), and the right to vote and participate in general elections (December 5, 1934) fourteen years before France, Italy, and Belgium.

Care should be taken not to exaggerate the accomplishments of the civil code since it reiterated certain patriarchal themes such as male household supremacy and male au-thority to circumscribe female economic liberties (see Lovejoy, *Turkish Civil Code of 1926*). Still, the parties of the time declared their intent to see women as equal partici-pants in the project of nation building and provided enhanced personal status and political rights to that end. Lovejoy accurately writes that the Turkish wife gained a "more equal position vis-à-vis her husband in respect to personal relations," but cautions against seeing the "assigning [of] a secular status to women" as anything more than an "ancillary motive of the reforms; indeed, a hypocritical one when considering the reformer's own personal attitudes toward women" (26). It is noteworthy that the nuptial ages were lowered from seventeen (women) and eighteen (men) to fifteen (women) and eighteen (men) in 1938 (22–24).

78. See also Bozkurt, *Türk Medeni Kanunu Nasıl Hazırlandı?* ("How Was the Turkish Civil Code Prepared?"), 13.

79. Shaw, *History*, Vol. 1, 250. Foreigners became subject to the jurisdiction of their consul-ates as a result of the Capitulations Treaties signed between the Ottoman Empire and France (February 18, 1536), England (May 3, 1590), and the Hapsburg Empire (June 20, 1685). In the first treaty with the French, in addition to French trade benefits, "French consuls were given the right to hear and judge all civil and criminal cases arising among and between French subjects in the Sultan's dominions without interference by Otto-man officials and judges, although the latter were allowed to help enforce judgments if requested to do so. Civil cases involving Muslim subjects did have to be tried in Ottoman courts according to Muslim law, but the defendants were allowed to have French consular representatives to advise them. In criminal cases, French subjects were excused from being called before Ottoman judges but instead were referred to the grand vizier or his agent, in which case the testimonies of Ottoman and French subjects were given equal weight. This was unlike the situation in the Muslim courts, where the testimony of

Muslims had to be given special credence" (Shaw, *History*, Vol. 1, 97–98; cf. 29, 163, 182, 189). Shaw suggests that the capitulations Treaties have their precedent in the fifteenth-century agreement between Sultan Beyazıt and the Venetians that allowed for special economic status for the latter.

80. Bozkurt, "How Was the Turkish Civil Code Prepared?" 9–10; cf. Bozkurt, *Atatürk İhtilâli (Atatürk's Revolution)*, 339ff. Note that the statement says "legal system" and not all aspects of religious thought and practice from the state.

81. Bozkurt, "How Was the Turkish Civil Code Prepared?" 9–10.

82. A slightly different conclusion, but closer than almost all others at expressing the interrelation is David Kushner's: "Without relinquishing state control over religious affairs, it was their aim . . . to turn religion into a matter of personal faith and rites, and to eliminate its role in shaping social and political institutions" ("Turkish Secularists," 89). I note the limits of this claim above. There is no evidence of a lasting, practical interest in fully privatizing religion, or, therefore, of "eliminating its role in shaping social and political institutions." Of course, Turkey's laiklik politics are not unique in this respect.

83. For evidence of the relevance of the concept separation in the debate see comments by Adnan Adıvar, "Ten Years"; Reed, "Revival of Islam," 279; Tachau and Ülman, "Attempt to Reconcile," 164.

84. Text and interpretation in Parla, *Official Sources*, 117–19; 120–22.

85. On maturity, cf.: "I think of Turkey as a country that is coming of age" (Webster, *Turkey of Atatürk*, 288). On civilization, cf.: "Here, before our very eyes is occurring a transition of civilizations, the abandonment of practices which originated in Arabia, based upon the union of religion and politics, the adoption of a pattern which developed in Europe, based upon the separation of religion and politics" (Allen, *Turkish Transformation*, 206). On fatalistic, especially interesting is the emphasis, found in the early political and social studies of Webster, Allen and Lerner, on the concept *kısmet*. Literally, this means "fate" or "destiny"—it is a concept that is deeply imbued with theosophic and what Mardin calls mythopoetic meanings. The aforementioned interpreters adopted *kısmet* as the starting point for the development of Turkey and indeed for the individual psychology of Turks. Webster called it "do-nothing fatalism"; Robinson discussed "dogmatic fatalism" (Webster, *Turkey of Atatürk*; Robinson, "Lesson of Turkey," 36; cf. Allen, *Turkish Transformation*, 206). On the domination of Islam, this theme is pervasive until at least the mid-1950s, especially in works that do not distinguish, as the Kemalists did, Islam as a faith from Islam as a counter-regime force. Webster called Islam "decadent" and an "incubus" (*Turkey of Atatürk*, 69). Allen noted that it might be a "dike to progress" (*Turkish Transformation*, 85). Even afterward, it remained a theme in parts of the literature. For example, in a recent study on "religion and political culture in Turkey," one political scientist writes: "Islam does not teach its followers to change society" (Turan, "Religion and Political Culture," 48). On "new . . . science," all of these come as juxtapositions to the previous concepts throughout the literature.

86. Frey, *Turkish Political Elite*, 3; Weiker, *Modernization*, 110; Webster, *Turkey of Atatürk*, 69, 240, 245ff; Richards and Waterbury, *Political Economy*, 347.

87. Rustow, "Turkey's Liberal Revolution," 10; Kohn, "Ten Years," 148, 154–55; "traditional

holes," Lerner, *Passing,* 30, 33, 70–71; Weiker, *Turkish Revolution,* 154; Weiker, *Modernization,* 110; Weiker, "Turkey, the Middle East, and Islam," 20. Cf. Tachau, "It is difficult to imagine a more radical break from tradition . . . " (*Turkey,* 38).

88. See Karpat, *Turkey's Politics,* 63, 452; Allen, *Turkish Transformation,* 63; Kohn, "Ten Years," 152; Toynbee, *Survey,* 73; Rustow, "Near East," 523; Rustow, "Turkey's Liberal," 5; Bernard Lewis, "Foreword," in Rustow, *Turkey,* xi.

This culminated (in the post-USSR scramble for control over Central Asia) with the U.S. government declaring, "we think that Turkey could be a model for countries of the former Soviet Union because it's a democratic secular state with a free market economy, which is the way we would like to see these countries moving" (Legislate briefing network, February 10, 1992). One should note that Turkey's so-named democratic secular model has been taken as a model by Western countries for non-Western ones when Turkey was interested in joining the countries to its west in the new European Union (cf. Eickelman, "Re-imagination of the Middle East," 5–6; and Wright, "Islam, Democracy, and the West," 142). The relevant policy-related discourse has now turned to "civil society" (see esp. Lewis, "Why Turkey Is the Only Muslim Democracy."

89. Lewis, "Islamic Revival in Turkey," 39. This point continues with a comment that seems to anticipate the current debate over civilizational relations: "In Turkey, as in other Muslim countries, there are those who talk hopefully of achieving 'a synthesis' of the best elements of West and East. This is a vain hope—the clash of civilizations in history does not usually culminate in a marriage of selected best elements—rather in promiscuous cohabitation of good, bad, and indifferent alike. But a true revival of religious faith on the level of modern thought and life is within the bounds of possibility. The Turkish people, by the exercise of their practical common sense and powers of improvisation, may yet find a workable compromise between Islam and modernism that will enable them, without conflict, to follow both their fathers' path to freedom and progress and their grandfathers' path to God" (39–40). Cf. Tachau, *Turkey,* 163, and Weiker, *Modernization,* 66–67, 246–47.

90. Lewis, *Emergence,* 279; Dodd, *Politics and Government,* 22. Akural criticizes Lewis, Uriel Heyd, and by inference Dodd, among many others, including Turkish "Kemalist historians," for speaking without competence on this issue: "Historians and social scientists in the field of Turkish studies, though their comprehension of methods of teaching reading is negligible, do not hesitate to cite the reforms as a foreword step towards westernization, and no questions are raised concerning the actual efficacy of the Latin alphabet for teaching and reading." Akural cites psycholinguistic research to argue that reading is a selective process in which the reader uses cue systems in the written language "to sample what is written, to predict on the basis of those cues, and then to confirm or correct that prediction according to its congruence with subsequent graphophones, syntactic and semantic information;" the "pace of learning is greatly influenced by non-linguistic factors as well, including intelligence, previous experience with books, social and political considerations, and method of instruction. Moreover, once the ability to read has been acquired, proficient reading seems to proceed as efficiently in a language like Ottoman-Turkish using Arabic script as it does in modern Turkish using Latin script" ("Kemalist Views," 135–36).

91. Rustow, "Turkish Democracy in Historical and Comparative Perspective," 10; cf. "A Democratic Turkey Faces New Challenges," 61. Weiker, *Turkish Revolution*, 4.

92. Weiker, *Turkish Revolution*, 9; note that Rustow is not entirely exempt from this critique. In 1979, he described the Turkish state as secular ("A Muslim population in a secular state") in a policy-oriented article, "Turkey's Travails," 92. I am aware that one should not always expect rigorous conceptual work in such places.

93. Some evidence of the influence of the French experience exists in the conceptualization of the Turkish founding, e.g., in the Rationale of the Civil Code. Birtek writes, "The Turkish Republic was constituted in a world in which the Third Republic prevailed as a model" ("Turkish Adventures," 112). Cf. also Keyder, "The Political Economy of Turkish Democracy," *New Left Review* 115 (May–June 1979): 3; Adnan-Adıvar, "Ten Years," 244, 251; Özbudun, "Established Versus Unfinished Revolutions," 394.

94. There is some debate within Islam regarding the existence of a clerical class. Strict orthopraxy aside: "There does exist a corps of experts in the law, theological-jurists who supervise orthodoxy and the application of religious law in conjunction with the state" (Arkoun, *Rethinking Islam*, 67).

    The difference between laicism and secularism *may* be seen as one of temporal scale. Perhaps laicism is one step in the direction of secularism. Perhaps it is the final stage of anti-clericalism. To clericalists (as opposed to clerics), it is probably a backward movement. To secularists it may be a step in the right direction. To laicists, it might be just right.

95. Robins, *Turkey and the Middle East*, 4, 11; Weiker, *Modernization*, 107; Keyder, "Class and State," 207–8; "Politics and Islam," 94; Karpat, *Turkey's Politics*, 272–73; Bahrampour, *Turkey: Political and Social Transformation*, 22; Toprak, *Islam and Political Development*, 79; Weiker, "Turkey, the Middle East, and Islam," 27; Weiker, *Modernization*, 105; Tapper, Introduction, 1; Margulies and Yildizoğlu, "Political Use of Islam in Turkey," 17.

96. Rustow, "Turkey's Travails," 92; Özbudun, "Postauthoritarian Democracies," 329.

97. Dodd, *Democracy and Development*, 48; "Atatürk's goal as a modern secular state," Landau, "Introduction," xiv.

98. "So-called secular state," Barry Rubin, quoted in "U.S. Remains Moscowcentric," *New York Times*, May 31, 1992; "department of the supposedly secular Turkish state," David Barchard, "Muslims, Be Men Not Mice," *Spectator*, (February 10, 1990): 14; "hardly secular," Reed, "Revival of Islam," 278.

99. Mardin, *Religion and Social Change*, 96; Eric J. Rouleau, "Turkey: Beyond Atatürk," *Foreign Policy* (Summer 1996): 70; "In Turkish," Abadan-Unat, "The Impact," 3–4.

100. Sunar and Toprak, "Islam in Politics," 429–30. Neither Sunar nor Toprak are sufficiently consistent in this regard. Cf. Toprak, *Islam and Political Development*, Ch. 1. Birtek and Toprak write, "Radical secularism as state policy . . . had been a fundamental aspect of the republican ethos in Turkey" ("Conflictual Agendas," 194); while Sunar and Sayarı write, "The founding of the secular Turkish republic in 1923 . . . " (Sunar and Sayarı, "Democracy in Turkey," 168–69).

101. Lewis, *Emergence*, 412; "Europe and Islam," "Islamic Revival," 121. Cf. Birtek, who defines *laicism* in Turkey as having "rigorously separated the state from religion and relegated the latter to the individual's conscience" ("Turkish Adventures," 133).

102. Bromley, *Rethinking,* 125–26; Lewis, "Why Turkey Is the Only Muslim Democracy," 46.

103. Rustow, *Turkey,* 29.

104. Toprak, *Islam and Political Development,* 47.

105. Cf. Berkes's suggestion that the goal was interpreted to "create a new and modern state and society that would be secular *in so far as possible.* It meant that there would be no room for religious considerations and there would be no difference between a Muslim and a non-Muslim. Even if these remained in their real form in principle and theory only . . . it had the unavoidable power of effecting and guiding later action" (emphasis added, Berkes, "Historical Background," 65). It is a sound idea: "secular in so far as possible"; but it does not clarify enough.

106. "No deliberate and . . . Westernization," Rahman, *Islam and Modernity,* 95. The will to use religion politically is an issue that bothers many in Turkey—of various secularizing and religiopolitical orientations—who wish to see a more secular politics in Turkey. In comparative studies of lay elites in Middle East politics, the instrumental "use of Islam" has been explained generally as an effort to enhance a regime's legitimacy (Hudson, "Islam and Political Development," 16; Turan, "Religion and Political Culture," 42). Anglophone interpreters of Turkish politics see the "use of Islam" in the multiparty period as a tool for "political advantage"—i.e., for getting votes, maintaining kinship and clientelist relations, rewarding regional cliques and tarikats and thus "as an integrative force"; for satisfying the moral needs of the Turkish people; for fighting communism and other so-called left and right, discordant and divisive, anti-solidarist partitive interests political tendencies, including Kurdish national ones; and, more generally, for outbidding competitors to power. *None of these are unique to Turkey.* Dodd has written, "The crux of the matter seems to be that in a country where the alarm against communism is now always being sounded off, religion can be seen to have its prophylactic uses" (*Political Development,* 307–9). See Sunar and Toprak, "Islam in Politics," 429; Heper, *State Tradition,* 353; Rustow, "Politics and Islam," 93; Karpat, *Turkey's Politics,* 276; Bianchi, *Interest Groups,* 105; Barchard, *Turkey and the West* (London: Routledge & Kegan Paul, 1985); Parla, *Social and Political Thought;* Kushner, "Turkish Secularists," 94; Saylan, *Religion and Politics,* 16; Ahmad, "Politics and Islam," 13, 18; Abadan-Unat, "Impact," 187–88.

The "use of Islam" has become less of a problem to some interpreters of Turkey because Islam and the concept of a "legitimate right" with "legitimate options within the system" is taken as an ingredient of Turkish democratic processes (see Üstün Erguder, "The Motherland Party, 1983–1989," in *Political Parties and Democracy in Turkey,* ed. Metin Heper and Jacob M. Landau [London: I. B. Tauris, 1991], 153). As Dalacoura put it, "Even General Evren, leader of the military coup of 1980 and later president of the Republic and head of the army . . . quoted passages from the Koran in his speeches and decided to make religious instruction compulsory in schools. Turks, after all, are a pious people. But this does not mean they want to bring down the secular state and follow Iran's example" ("Turkey and the Middle East," 216)—as stated when questions of whether Turkey and states the Middle East would follow Iran's example during the 1980s.

107. Philip K. Hitti, "Foreword" to *Near Eastern Culture and Society: A Symposium on the Meeting of East and West,* ed. T. C. Young (Princeton: Princeton University Press, 1951).

108. Turan, "Religion and Political Culture," 42. He notes a few examples (see above for their roots in the one-party period): "A person who dies in battle for the cause of religion is a *Şehit* and goes directly to heaven. Now this symbol has been borrowed from religious vocabulary, and is used to describe any public servant who dies in the course of public duty; in this way, government service is elevated to the level of God's cause. Similarly, the Friday sermons are used to invite citizens to engage in acts supportive of government. The Directorate of Religious Affairs sends out model sermons to imams (preachers) which may encourage the citizens, for example, to pay their taxes, or to contribute to foundations established to assess the armed forces" (42).

CONCLUSION: TOWARD A CRITICAL, COMPARATIVE, SECULAR HERMENEUTICS

1. Literature that expressed the need for greater language training during the seventies included: Stanford Shaw, "Ottoman and Turkish Studies," 124–26; and Rustow, "Middle East"; Frey, *Turkish Political Elite;* Tachau, *Political Elites,* 10; Tachau and Good, "Anatomy of Political and Social Change," 552; Lewis J. Edinger and Donald D. Searing, "Social Background in Elite Analysis: A Methodological Inquiry," *American Political Science Review* 61, no. 2 (1967), and Weiker, "Modern Turkish Studies," 16.

    There was always a parallel tradition in anglophone studies, initiated in the Republican period by J. K. Birge and pursued further by Howard Reed in the 1950s, that was concerned with describing the history of religion and religious change in Turkey. See works by Birge and Reed. Winder's suggestion that religious studies once formed a major part of Middle East studies allows us to place Allen's study within this class of works as well. See Winder, "Four Decades," 40–59; Allen, *Turkish Transformation.*

2. Quotations from Mardin, *Religion and Social Change,* 41; "Islam in Mass Society," 167; and Tapper, *Islam in Modern Turkey,* 2. The body of literature motivated by these concerns is growing.

3. Rustow, "Turkey"; Toprak, *Islam and Political Development;* İslamoğlu and Keyder, "Agenda," 46–47; G. Lewis, "Book Review of *The Emergence of Modern Turkey,*" *International Affairs* 38 (1962): 107.

4. Mardin, "Islam in Mass Society," 168. The full text of Mardin's remark is: "The fact that many young laypersons in the post-1980 period have been engaged in what can be termed a hermeneutic exercise for enriching their Muslim culture, and the fact that they take the Western philosophic discourse seriously, shows the other aspect of the issue [of general secularization trends in Turkey]." With reference to this comment, hermeneutics cannot be placed only on the side of religion and culture. Its interest, even in Turkey, should encompass what Mardin refers to as "western philosophic discourse" as well.

5. For a readily accessible discussion of the concept of politics that is implied here, see, e.g., Crick, *In Defence of Politics.*

6. Gayatri Spivak, *Outside the Teaching Machine* (New York: Routledge, 1993), 194. To understand the importance of Spivak's claim in the context of India, see esp. Van Der

Veer, *Religious Nationalism;* Madan, "Secularism in Its Place," and Nandy, "Politics of Secularism." Van Der Veer's discussion of the ways in which the state in India is not secular (23) is particularly important in this regard. For more general discussion of the power relations of concern here, see Nelly Richard, "Postmodernism and Periphery"; and Hall, "West and the Rest," 184–228. As this literature suggests, Spivak's concerns are not to be dismissed entirely, but they should be informed by hermeneutic inquiry. On secularly oriented religions, see, e.g., Eickelman and Piscatori, *Muslim Politics,* 53.

7. An important analysis of comparative interest in this regard is Zubaida, "Religion, the State, and Democracy," 51–63.

APPENDIX: THE RATIONALE FOR THE DRAFT BILL (OF THE TURKISH CIVIL CODE)

I am grateful to Taha Parla, Yurdanur Salman, and Ersin Kalaycıoğlu for their assistance in translating this text. Some of the sentences in the original Turkish are windy and dense. I have tried not to misrepresent this feature of the text. In addition, I have placed the English equivalents of terms that I did not translate literally in brackets.

1. Muharrem and Şaban are the names of the first and eighth months, respectively, on the Arabic lunar calender. The years listed are 1870 and 1877, respectively.

Select Bibliography

Abadan-Unat, Nermin. "The Impact of Legal and Educational Reforms on Turkish Women." In *Women in Middle Eastern History: Shifting Boundaries in Sex and Gender*, ed. Nikki R. Keddie, 177–94. New Haven: Yale University Press, 1991.

————, ed. *Women in Turkish Society*. Leiden: E. J. Brill, 1981.

Abdel-Malek, Anouar, ed. *Contemporary Arab Political Thought*. London: Zed, 1983.

Abrahamian, Ervand. *Khomeinism: Essays on the Islamic Republic*. Berkeley: University of California Press, 1993.

Adnan-Adıvar, Abdulhak. "Ten Years of Republic in Turkey." *Political Quarterly* 6 (1935): 240–52.

————. "The Interaction of Islamic and Western Thought in Turkey." In Young, *Near Eastern Culture and Society*.

Ahmad, Feroz. *The Turkish Experiment in Democracy, 1950–1975*. Boulder: Westview, 1977.

————. "Politics and Islam in Modern Turkey." *Middle East Studies* 27, no. 1 (1991): 3–21.

————. "The Progressive Republican Party, 1924–1925." In Heper and Landau, *Political Parties and Democracy in Turkey*.

Akural, Sabri. "Kemalist Views on Social Change." In Landau, *Atatürk and the Modernization of Turkey*.

Allen, Henry Elisha. *The Turkish Transformation: A Study in Social and Religious Development*. Chicago: University of Chicago Press, 1935.

Almond, Gabriel A. "Comparative Political Systems." *Journal of Politics* 18 (1956): 391–408.

———. *A Discipline Divided*. Beverly Hills: Sage, 1990.

Almond, Gabriel A., and James S. Coleman, eds. *The Politics of Developing Areas*. Princeton: Princeton University Press, 1960.

Almond, Gabriel A., and J. Bingham Powell, eds. *Comparative Politics: A Developmental Approach*. Boston: Little, Brown, 1966.

Anderson, Lisa. "Policy-Making and Theory Building: American Political Science and the Islamic Middle East." In Sharabi, *Theory, Politics and the Arab World*.

Ansay, T. *Introduction to Turkish Law*. Ankara: Society of Comparative Law and Middle East Technical University, Faculty of Administrative Sciences, 1966.

Arai, Masami. *Turkish Nationalism in the Young Turk Era*. Leiden: E. J. Brill, 1992.

Arat, Yeşim. "Islamic Fundamentalism and Women in Turkey." *Muslim World* 80, no. 1 (1990): 17–23.

Arendt, Hannah. *Between Past and Future*. New York: Penguin, 1956.

Arjomand, Said Amir. *The Turban for the Crown*. Oxford: Oxford University Press, 1988.

Arkoun, Mohammed. *Rethinking Islam: Common Questions, Uncommon Answers*. Boulder: Westview, 1994.

Asad, Talal. "Religion and Politics: An Introduction." *Social Research* 59, no. 1 (Spring 1992): 1–18.

Atatürk. *A Speech Delivered by Ghazi Mustapha Kemal, President of the Turkish Republic*. Leipzig, Germany: K. F. Koehler, 1929.

Bahrampour, Firouz. *Turkey: Political and Social Transformation*. New York: Theo. Gaus' Sons, 1967.

Ball, Terence, ed. *Idioms of Inquiry*. Binghamton: State University of New York Press, 1987.

Ball, Terence, and James Farr, eds. *After Marx*. Cambridge: Cambridge University Press, 1984.

Ball, Terence, James Farr, and Russell L. Hanson, eds. *Political Innovation and Conceptual Change*. Cambridge: Cambridge University Press, 1989.

Barchard, David. *Turkey and the West*. London: Routledge & Kegan Paul, 1985.

Bauman, Zigmunt. *Hermeneutics and Social Science*. New York: Columbia University Press, 1978.

Baynes, Kenneth, James Bohman, and Thomas McCarthy, eds. *After Philosophy: End or Transformation?* Cambridge: MIT Press, 1989.

Bendix, Reinhardt. "Tradition and Modernity Reconsidered." *Comparative Studies in Society and History* 9, no. 2 (1967): 292–346.

Berkes, Niyazi. "Ziya Gökalp: His Contribution to Turkish Nationalism." *Middle East Journal* 8, no. 4 (1954): 375–90.

———. "Historical Background of Turkish Secularism." In *Islam and the West*, ed. Richard N. Frye, 41–68. The Hague: Mouton, 1957.

———. *The Development of Secularism in Turkey*. Montreal: McGill University Press, 1964.

———, ed. *Turkish Nationalism and Western Civilization: Selected Essays of Ziya Gökalp*. New York: Columbia University Press, 1959.

Berlin, Isaiah. *Historical Inevitability*. London: Oxford (Auguste Comte Memorial Trust Lecture, No. 1, 12 May 1953, at London School of Economics and Political Science), 1955.

Bernstein, Richard J. *The Restructuring of Social and Political Theory*. Philadelphia: University of Pennsylvania Press, 1976.

———. *Beyond Objectivism and Relativism*. Philadelphia: University of Pennsylvania Press, 1983.

Bianchi, Robert. *Interest Groups and Political Participation in Turkey*. Princeton: Princeton University Press, 1984.

Bill, James A. *The Politics of Iran: Groups, Classes, and Modernization*. Columbus: Charles E. Merrill, 1972.

———. "Power and Religion in Revolutionary Iran." *Middle East Journal* 36, no. 1 (Winter 1982): 22–47.

Bill, James A., and Carl Leiden. *Politics in the Middle East*. Boston: Little, Brown, 1979.

Bill, James A., and Robert Springborg. *Politics in the Middle East*, 3d ed. Glenview, Ill.: Scott, Foresman/Little, Brown Higher Education, 1990.

Binder, Leonard. "Prolegomena to the Comparative Study of Middle East Governments." *American Political Science Review* 51 (1957): 651–68.

———, ed. *Crisis and Sequences in Political Development*. Princeton: Princeton University Press, 1971.

———. "The Natural History of Development Theory." *Comparative Studies in Society and History* 28, no. 1 (1985): 3–32.

———. *Islamic Liberalism: A Critique of Development Ideologies*. Chicago: University of Chicago Press, 1988.

Birge, John Kingsley. *The Bektashi Order of Dervishes*. London: Luzac, 1937.

———. "Secularism in Turkey and Its Meaning." *International Review of Missions* (October 1944): 462–32.

———. "Islam in Modern Turkey." In *Islam in the Modern World: A Series of Addresses Presented at the Fifth Annual Conference on Middle Eastern Affairs*, ed. Dorothea Seelye Franck. Washington, D.C.: Middle East Institute, 1951.

Birtek, Faruk. "The Turkish Adventures in the Durkheimian Paradigm: Does History Vindicate M. Labriola?" *Il Politico* (University of Pavia, Italy) 56, no. 1 (1991): 17–146.

Birtek, Faruk, and Binnaz Toprak. "The Conflictual Agendas of Neo-liberal Reconstruction and the Rise of Islamic Politics: The Hazards of Rewriting Modernity." *Praxis International* 13, no. 2 (1993): 192–212.

Bleicher, Josef. *Contemporary Hermeneutics: Hermeneutics as Method, Philosophy, and Critique*. London: Routledge and Kegan Paul, 1980.

Bozkurt, Mahmut Esat. "*Esabı Mucibe Lâhihası*" ("The Rationale of the Draft Bill [of the Turkish Civil Code]"). In Yavuz, *Medeni Kanunu* (The Turkish Civil Code), 3–10.

———. *Atatürk İhtilâli* (Atatürk's Revolution). Ankara: Altın Kitaplar, 1944 [reprinted in 1967].

———. "*Türk Medeni Kanunu Nasıl Hazırlandı?*" (How Was the Turkish Civil Code Prepared?). In *Medeni Kanunu XV Yıl Dönümü* (The Fifteenth Anniversary of the Civil Code), ed. H.-A. Yücel, 9–20. Istanbul: Kenan Matbaası, 1944.

Bromley, Simon. *Rethinking Middle East Politics: State Formation and Development.* Cambridge: Polity, 1994.

Bruce, Steve, ed. *Religion and Modernization: Sociologists and Historians Debate the Secularization Thesis.* Oxford: Oxford University Press, 1992.

Bruns, Gerald. *Hermeneutics: Ancient and Modern.* New Haven: Yale University Press, 1992.

Bucknill, J. A. S., and H. A. S. Utidnian. *The Imperial Ottoman Penal Code.* London: Humphrey Milford, 1913.

Burke, Peter, ed. *New Perspectives on Historical Writing.* University Park: Pennsylvania State University Press, 1992.

Cantori, Louis J., and Andrew H. Ziegler Jr., eds. *Comparative Politics in the Post-Behavioral Era.* Boulder: Lynne Reinner, 1988.

Chadwick, Owen. *The Secularization of the European Mind in the Nineteenth Century.* Cambridge: Cambridge University Press, 1975.

Chambers, Richard L. "The Ottoman Ulema and the Tanzimat." In *Scholars, Saints, and Sufis: Muslim Religious Institutions since 1500,* ed. Nikki R. Keddie, 33–46. Berkeley: University of California Press, 1972.

Collini, Stephan, Donald Winch, and John Burrow. *That Noble Science of Politics: A Study in Nineteenth Century Intellectual History.* Cambridge: Cambridge University Press, 1983.

Comte, Auguste. *A General View of Positivism.* Centenary ed. New York: Robert Speller & Sons, 1975 [1865].

Crick, Bernard. *In Defence of Politics,* 4th ed. Chicago: University of Chicago Press, 1992.

Dalacoura, Katerina. "Turkey and the Middle East in the 1980s." *Millennium: Journal of International Studies* 19, no. 2 (1990): 207–27.

Dallmayr, Fred R. *Language and Politics.* Notre Dame: University of Notre Dame Press, 1984.

Dallmayr, Fred R., and Thomas McCarthy, eds. *Understanding and Social Inquiry.* Notre Dame: University of Notre Dame Press, 1977.

Deutsch, Elliot, ed. *Culture and Modernity: East-West Philosophic Perspectives.* Honolulu: University of Hawaii Press, 1991.

Devereux, Robert. *The Principles of Turkism.* Leiden: E. J. Brill, 1968.

Dodd, C. H. *Politics and Government in Turkey.* Berkeley: University of California Press, 1969.

———. *Democracy and Development in Turkey.* North Humberside, England: Eothen, 1979.

Dryzek, John, and Stephen T. Leonard. "History and Discipline in Political Science." In Easton et al., *Regime and Discipline,* 27–48.

Dunn, John. *Modern Revolutions: An Introduction to the Analysis of a Political Phenomenon.* Cambridge: Cambridge University Press, 1972.

———. "Practicing History and Social Science on 'Realist' Assumptions." In *Action and Interpretation: Studies in the Philosophy of the Social Sciences,* ed. Christopher Hookway and Philip Pettit. Cambridge: Cambridge University Press, 1978.

———. *Political Obligation in Its History Context: Essays in Political Theory.* Cambridge: Cambridge University Press, 1980.

———. *Interpreting Political Responsibility: Essays, 1981–1989.* Princeton: Princeton University Press, 1990.

————. *The History of Political Thought and Other Essays*. Cambridge: Cambridge University Press, 1996.

Earle, Eduard Mead. "The New Constitutions of Turkey." *Political Science Quarterly* 40 (1926): 73–100.

Easton, David. *The Political System: An Inquiry into the State of Political Science*. New York: Alfred A. Knopf, 1953.

————. *A Systems Analysis of Political Life*. New York: Wiley & Sons, 1965.

Easton, David, John G. Gunnell, and Luigi Graziano, eds. *The Development of Political Science: A Comparative Survey*. New York: Routledge, 1991.

Easton, David, John G. Gunnell, and Michael Stein, eds. *Regime and Discipline: Democracy and the Development of Political Science*. Ann Arbor: University of Michigan Press, 1995.

Eickelman, Dale. "The Re-Imagination of the Middle East: Political and Academic Frontiers." *Middle East Studies Association Bulletin* 26 (1992): 3–12.

Eickelman, Dale, and James Piscatori. *Muslim Politics*. Princeton: Princeton University Press, 1996.

Eisenstadt, S. N. "Breakdowns of Modernization." *Economic Development and Cultural Change* 12, no. 4 (1964): 345–67.

————. *Modernization: Protest and Change*. Englewood Cliffs: Prentice-Hall, 1966.

————. "Post-Traditional Societies and the Continuity and Reconstruction of Tradition." *Daedalus* 102, no. 1 (1973): 1–28.

————, ed. *The Origins and Diversity of Axial Age Civilizations*. Albany: State University of New York Press, 1986.

————, ed. *Patterns of Modernity*. Vol. 1. New York: New York University Press, 1987.

————. "Cultural Tradition, Historical Experience, and Social Change: The Limits of Convergence." In *The Tanner Lectures on Human Values*, ed. M. McMurrin, 443–505. Salt Lake City: University of Utah Press, 1990.

El-Affendi, Abdelwahab. "Studying My Movement: Social Science Without Cynicism." *International Journal of Middle East Studies* 23 (1991): 83–94.

Eralp, A., M. Tünay, and Birol Yeşilada, eds. *The Political and Socioeconomic Transformation of Turkey*. Westport: Praeger, 1993.

Esman, Milton J., and Itamar Rabinovich, eds. *Ethnicity, Pluralism and the State in the Middle East*. Ithaca: Cornell University Press, 1988.

Esposito, John L., ed. *Voices of Resurgent Islam*. New York: Oxford University Press, 1983.

Esposito, John L. *Islam and Politics*. Syracuse: Syracuse University Press, 1984.

————. "The Study of Islam: Challenges and Prospects" (Presidential Address, MESA). *International Journal of Middle East Studies* 24 (1990): 1–15.

————. *Islam: The Straight Path*. Oxford: Oxford University Press, 1991.

Evans, Peter, Dietrich Rueschemeyer, and Theda Skocpol, eds. *Bringing the State Back In*. Cambridge: Cambridge University Press, 1985.

Farr, James. "Marx's Laws." *Political Studies* 34 (1986): 202–28.

————. "Resituating Explanation." In Ball, *Idioms of Inquiry*, 45–66.

————. "The History of Political Science." *American Journal of Political Science* 32 (1988): 1175–95.

———. "Political Science and the Enlightenment of Enthusiasm." *American Political Science Review* 82, no. 1 (1988): 50–66.

———. "Understanding Conceptual Change Politically." In Ball et al., *Political Innovation and Conceptual Change,* 24–49.

Farr, James, John G. Gunnell, Raymond Seidelman, John Dryzek, and Stephen T. Leonard. "Can Political Science History Be Neutral?" *American Political Science Review* 84, no. 2 (1990): 587–607.

Farr, James, and Raymond Seidelman, eds. *Discipline and History: Political Science in the United States.* Ann Arbor: University of Michigan Press, 1993.

Farr, James, John Dryzek, and Stephen T. Leonard, eds. *Political Science in History.* Cambridge: Cambridge University Press, 1995.

Ferejohn, John. "Rationality and Interpretation: Parliamentary Elections in Early Stuart England." In *The Economic Approach to Politics: A Critical Reassessment of the Theory of Rational Action,* ed. Kristen Renwick Monroe, 279–305. New York: HarperCollins, 1991.

Finifter, Ada W., ed. *Political Science: The State of the Discipline.* Washington, D.C.: American Political Science Association, 1983.

Flew, Antony. *Thinking About Social Thinking: The Philosophy of the Social Sciences.* Oxford: Basil Blackwell, 1985.

Foucault, Michel. *Power/Knowledge: Selected Interviews and Other Writings, 1972–1977.* New York: Pantheon, 1980.

———. "What Is Enlightenment?" In Rabinow and Sullivan, *Interpretive Social Science,* 157–74.

Fowler, Robert Booth. *Religion and Politics in America.* Philadelphia: American Theological Library Association, 1985.

Frey, Frederick. *The Turkish Political Elite.* Cambridge: MIT Press, 1965.

Gadamer, Hans-Georg. "The Problem of Historical Consciousness." In Rabinow and Sullivan, *Interpretive Social Science,* 82–140.

———. *Truth and Method.* 2nd rev. ed. Trans. Joel Weinsheimer and Donald G. Marshall. New York: Crossroad, 1989.

Gay, Peter. "The Enlightenment in the History of Political Theory." *Political Science Quarterly* 59, no. 3 (1954): 374–89.

Geertz, Clifford. "The Uses of Diversity." In *The Tanner Lectures on Human Values,* ed. M. McMurrin, 251–276. Salt Lake City: University of Utah Press, 1986.

———. "From the Native's Point of View." In Gibbons, *Interpreting Politics,* 133–47.

———. *After the Fact: Two Countries, Four Decades, One Anthropologist.* Cambridge: Cambridge University Press, 1995.

Gerth, Hans H., and C. Wright Mills, eds. *From Max Weber: Essays in Sociology.* New York: Oxford University Press, 1946.

Gibbons, Michael, ed. *Interpreting Politics.* New York: New York University Press, 1987.

Gökalp, Ziya [Tevfik Sedat, pseud.]. "Bugünkü Felsefe" ("The Philosophy of Today"). *Genç Kalemler,* no. 2 (Salonika, 1911). Translated in Berkes, *Turkish Nationalism and Western Civilization,* 46–50.

———. [Tevfik Sedat, pseud.]. "Muhiddin-i Arabî" ("The Philosophy of Idealism of Ibn

Al-'Arabi"). *Genç Kalemler,* no. 8 (Salonika, 1911). Translated in Berkes, *Turkish Nationalism,* 50–55.

———[Demirtaş, pseud.]. "Yeni Hayat ve Yeni Kıymetler" ("New Life and New Values"). *Genç Kalemler,* no. 8 (Salonika, 1911). Translated in Berkes, *Turkish Nationalism and Western Civilization,* 55–60.

———. "Üç Cereyan" ("Three Currents of Thought"). *Türk Yurdu* 3, no. 35 (Istanbul, 1913). Translated in Berkes, *Turkish Nationalism and Western Civilization,* 71–77.

———. "An'ane ve Kaide" ("Tradition and Formalism"). *Türk Yurdu* 4, no. 39 (Istanbul, 1913). Translated in Berkes, *Turkish Nationalism and Western Civilization,* 92–96.

———. "Cemaat Medeniyeti, Cemiyet Medeniyeti" ("The Civilization of Community and the Civilization of Society"). *Türk Yurdu* 4, no. 47 (Istanbul, 1913). Translated and abridged in Berkes, *Turkish Nationalism and Western Civilization,* 101–3.

———. "Mefkûre" ("The Nature of Ideals"). *Türk Yurdu* 5, no. 32 (Istanbul, 1913). Translated in Berkes, *Turkish Nationalism and Western Civilization,* 66–70.

———. "Halk Medeniyeti" ("Civilization of the People"). *Halka Doğru* 1, nos. 14–15 (Istanbul, 1913). Translated and abridged in Berkes, *Turkish Nationalism and Western Civilization,* 89–92.

———. "İslâm Terbiyesinin Mâhiyeti" ("The Nature of Islamic Education"). *İslâm Mecmuası* 1, no. 1 (Istanbul, 1914). Translated and abridged in Berkes, *Turkish Nationalism and Western Civilization,* 233–235.

———. "Fıkh ve İçtimaiyat" ("Islamic Jurisprudence and Sociology"). *İslâm Mecmuası* 1, no. 2 (Istanbul, 1914). Translated in Berkes, *Turkish Nationalism and Western Civilization,* 193–96.

———. "İçtimaî Usul-ü Fıkh" ("The Social Sources of Islamic Jurisprudence"). *İslâm Mecmuası* 1, no. 2 (Istanbul, 1914). Translated in Berkes, *Turkish Nationalism and Western Civilization,* 196–98.

———. "Örf Nedir?" ("Mores"). *İslâm Mecmuası* 1, no. 14 (Istanbul, 1914). Translated and abridged in Berkes, *Turkish Nationalism and Western Civilization,* 152–56.

———. "Kıymet Hükümleri" ("Value Judgments"). *İslâm Mecmuası* 1, no. 18 (Istanbul, 1914). Translated and abridged in Berkes, *Turkish Nationalism and Western Civilization,* 148–49.

———. "İçtimaî Neviler" ("Classification of Social Sciences"). *İslâm Mecmuası* 2, no. 20 (Istanbul, 1914). Translated and abridged in Berkes, *Turkish Nationalism and Western Civilization,* 123–25.

———. "Ahlâk İçtimaî Midir?" ("Moral Values and Society"). *İçtimaiyat Mecmuası* 1, no. 3 (Istanbul, 1914). Translated in Berkes, *Turkish Nationalism and Western Civilization,* 149–52.

———. "Bir Kavmin Tetkikinde Tâkibolunacak Usül" ("The Scientific Study of Communities"). In *Millî Tetebbular Mucmuası* (1915). Translated and abridged in Berkes, *Turkish Nationalism and Western Civilization,* 113–23.

———. "Diyanet ve Kaza" ("Religion and Law"). *İslâm Mecmuası* 2, no. 35 (Istanbul, 1915). Translated in Berkes, *Turkish Nationalism and Western Civilization,* 199–202.

———. "Dinin İçtimai Vazifeleri" ("Social Functions of Religion"). *İslâm Mecmuası* 3, no. 34 and 36 (Istanbul, 1915). Translated and abridged in Berkes, *Turkish Nationalism and Western Civilization,* 184–93.

————. "Millî Terbiye" ("National Education"). *Muallim*, nos. 1–4 (Istanbul, 1916). Translated and abridged in Berkes, *Turkish Nationalism and Western Civilization*, 235–47.

————. "Millî İçtimaiyat" ("The Methods of Cultural Sociology" and "National Sociology"). *İçtimaiyat Mecmuası* 1, no. 1 (Istanbul, 1917). Translated in Berkes, *Turkish Nationalism and Western Civilization*, 171–83.

————. "İçtimaiyat ve Fikriyat: Cemiyette Büyük Adamların Tesiri" ("Manifestations of the National Ethos"). *İçtimaiyat Mecmuası* 1, no. 2 (Istanbul, 1917). Translated and abridged in Berkes, *Turkish Nationalism and Western Civilization*, 156–71.

————. "Millet Nedir?" ("What Is a Nation?"). *İçtimaiyat Mecmuası* 1, no. 3 (Istanbul, 1917). Translated and abridged in Berkes, *Turkish Nationalism and Western Civilization*, 126–34.

————. "Tevfik Fikret ve Türk Renesansı" ("The Turkish Renaissance and Literature"). In *Muallim* (Istanbul, 1917). Translated in Berkes, *Turkish Nationalism and Western Civilization*, 144–47.

————. "Asrî Aile ve Millî Aile" ("Modern Family and National Culture"). *Yeni Mecmua* 1, no. 20 (Istanbul, 1917). Translated and abridged in Berkes, *Turkish Nationalism and Western Civilization*, 147–52.

————. "Aile Ahlâkı, Düğün Adetleri" ("The Foundations of the Turkish Family"). *Yeni Mecmua* 1, no. 21 (Istanbul, 1917). Translated and abridged in Berkes, *Turkish Nationalism and Western Civilization*, 252–55.

————. "Türkçülük Nedir?" ("What Is Turkism? A Recapitulation"). *Yeni Mecmua*, no. 28 (Istanbul, 1917). Translated and abridged in Berkes, *Turkish Nationalism and Western Civilization*, 284–89.

————. "Hars Zümresi, Medeniyet Zümresi" ("Community and Society"). In *Türkleşmek, İslâmlaşmak, Muasırlaşmak* (Istanbul, 1918). Translated in Berkes, *Turkish Nationalism and Western Civilization*, 97–101 (1959). Originally published as "Cemaat ve Cemiyet." *Türk Yurdu* 4, no. 41 (Istanbul, 1913).

————. "Milliyet Mefkûresi" ("The Ideal of Nationalism"). In *Türkleşmek, İslâmlaşmak, Muasırlaşmak* (Istanbul, 1918). Translated in Berkes, *Turkish Nationalism and Western Civilization*, 79–82.

————. "Dehaya Doğru" ("Towards Genius"). *Küçük Mecmua*, no. 1 (Diyarbekir, 1922). Translated in Berkes, *Turkish Nationalism and Western Civilization*, 262–65.

————. "İlme Doğru" ("Towards Modern Science"). *Küçük Mecmua*, no. 2 (Diyarbekir, 1922). Translated in Berkes, *Turkish Nationalism and Western Civilization*, 279–80.

————. "Hilâfetin Hakiki Mahiyeti" ("The Caliphate"). *Küçük Mecmua*, no. 24 (Diyarbekir, Nov. 1, 1922). Translated in Berkes, *Turkish Nationalism and Western Civilization*, 223–27.

————. "Hilâfetin İstiklâli." *Küçük Mecmua*, no. 25 (Diyarbekir, 1922). Translated (untitled) in Berkes, *Turkish Nationalism and Western Civilization*, 227–29.

————. "Hilâfetin Vazifeleri." *Küçük Mecmua*, no. 26 (Diyarbekir, 1922). Translated in Berkes, *Turkish Nationalism and Western Civilization*, 229–33.

————. "İktisada Doğru." *Küçük Mecmua*, no. 7 (Diyarbekir, 1923). Translated and abridged in Berkes, *Turkish Nationalism and Western Civilization*, 309–10.

———. "Babamın Vasiyeti" ("My Father's Testament"). *Küçük Mecmua*, no. 17 (Diyarbekir, 1923). Translated in Berkes, *Turkish Nationalism and Western Civilization*, 35–37.

———. "Hocamın Vasiyeti" ("My Teacher's Testament"). *Küçük Mecmua*, no. 18 (Diyarbekir, 1923). Translated and abridged in Berkes, *Turkish Nationalism and Western Civilization*, 37–39.

———. "Pîrimin Vasiyeti" ("The Testament of My Spiritual Guide"). *Küçük Mecmua*, no. 19 (Diyarbekir, 1923). Translated in Berkes, *Turkish Nationalism and Western Civilization*, 39–42.

———. "İktisadî Mûcize." *Küçük Mecmua*, no. 23 (Diyarbekir, 1923). Translated and abridged in Berkes, *Turkish Nationalism and Western Civilization*, 307–9.

———. "Millet Nedir?" *Küçük Mecmua*, no. 28 (Diyarbekir, 1923). Translated and abridged in Berkes, *Turkish Nationalism and Western Civilization*, 43–45 and 134–138.

———. "Şehir Medeniyeti, Köy Medeniyeti" ("Villages and the Commune"). *Küçük Mecmua*, no. 30 (Diyarbekir, 1923). Translated and abridged in Berkes, *Turkish Nationalism and Western Civilization*, 138–40.

———. "Köy ve Şehir." *Küçük Mecmua*, no. 33 (Diyarbekir, 1923). Translated and abridged in Berkes, *Turkish Nationalism and Western Civilization*, 140–41.

———. "İktisadî Vatanperverlık" ("The Programme of Turkism—Economy"). *Küçük Mecmua*, no. 43 (Diyarbekir, 1923). Translated and abridged in Berkes, *Turkish Nationalism and Western Civilization*, 306–7.

———. "Tarihî Maddecilik ve İçtimaî Mekkûrecilik" ("Historical Materialism and Sociological Idealism"). *Yeni Gün* (Ankara, 8 March 1923). Translated in Berkes, *Turkish Nationalism and Western Civilization*, 60–66.

———. "İnkılapçılık ve Muhafazakarlık" ("Revolutionism and Conservatism"). *Yeni Gün* (Ankara, 17 May 1923). Translated in Berkes, *Turkish Nationalism and Western Civilization*, 265–68.

———. "Medeniyetimiz." *Yeni Mecmua*, no. 68 (Istanbul, 1923). Translated and abridged in Berkes, *Turkish Nationalism and Western Civilization*, 268–79.

———. "Dinî Türkçülük" ("The Programme of Turkism—Religion"). *Türkçülüğün Esasları* (Ankara, 1923). Translated in Berkes, *Turkish Nationalism and Western Civilization*, 301.

———. "Edebiyatımızın Tahrıs ve Tehzibi" ("The Programme of Turkism—Literature and Music"). *Türkçülüğün Esasları* (Ankara, 1923). Translated in Berkes, *Turkish Nationalism and Western Civilization*, 298–301.

———. "Halka Doğru" ("Towards the People"). *Türkçülüğün Esasları* (Ankara, 1923). Translated and abridged in Berkes, *Turkish Nationalism and Western Civilization*, 259–62.

———. "Hars ve Medeniyet" ("Culture and Civilization"). *Türkçülüğün Esasları* (Ankara, 1923). Translated and abridged in Berkes, *Turkish Nationalism and Western Civilization*, 104–9 and 289–90.

———. "Hars ve Tehzib" ("Culture and Refinement"). *Türkçülüğün Esasları* (Ankara, 1923). Translated and abridged in Berkes, *Turkish Nationalism and Western Civilization*, 280–81.

———. "Hukukî Türkçülük" ("The Programme of Turkism—Law"). *Türkçülüğün Esasları* (Ankara, 1923). Translated in Berkes, *Turkish Nationalism and Western Civilization*, 304–5.

———. "İktisadî Türkçülük" ("The Programme of Turkism—Economy"). *Türkçülüğün*

Esasları (Ankara, 1923). Translated and abridged in Berkes, *Turkish Nationalism and Western Civilization,* 311–13.

———. "Lisanî Türkçülük" ("The Programme of Turkism—Language"). *Türkçülüğün Esasları* (Ankara, 1923). Translated and abridged in Berkes, *Turkish Nationalism and Western Civilization,* 290–98.

———. "Millî Dayanışmayı Kuvvetlendirmek" ("Strengthening National Solidarity"). *Türkçülüğün Esasları* (Ankara, 1923). Translated in Devereux, *Principles of Turkism,* 62–71.

———. "Millî Vicdanı Kuvvetlendirmek" ("Strengthening the National Consciousness"). *Türkçülüğün Esasları* (Ankara, 1923). Translated in Devereux, *Principles of Turkism,* 57–61.

———. "Siyasî Türkçülük" ("The Programme of Turkism—Politics"). *Türkçülüğün Esasları* (Ankara, 1923). Translated in Berkes, *Turkish Nationalism and Western Civilization,* 305–6.

———. "Vatanî Ahlâk" ("The Programme of Turkism—Morality"). *Türkçülüğün Esasları* (Ankara, 1923). Translated and abridged in Berkes, *Turkish Nationalism and Western Civilization,* 302–4.

———. *Turkish Nationalism and Western Civilization: Selected Essays of Ziya Gökalp.* Trans. Niyazi Berkes. New York: Columbia University Press, 1959.

Gray, John. "On the Contestability of Social and Political Concepts." *Political Theory* 5 (1977): 333–48.

Grondin, Jean. *An Introduction to Philosophical Hermeneutics.* New Haven: Yale University Press, 1994.

Gunnell, John G. *Between Philosophy and Politics: The Alienation of Political Theory.* Amherst: University of Massachusetts Press, 1986.

———. "Disciplinary History: The Case of Political Science." *Strategies: A Journal of Theory, Culture and Politics* 4, no. 5 (1991): 182–227.

———. *The Descent of Political Theory.* Chicago: University of Chicago Press, 1993.

Gürelli, Nevzat. *The Turkish Criminal Code.* Trans. the Judge Advocates Office of Joint United States Military Mission for Aid in Turkey. South Hackensack, N.J.: Fred B. Rothman, 1965.

Habermas, Jürgen. *Knowledge and Human Interests.* Boston: Beacon, 1971.

———. "Modernity—an Incomplete Project." In Rabinow and Sullivan, *Interpretive Social Science.*

———. *The Philosophical Discourse of Modernity.* Cambridge: MIT Press 1987.

———. *On the Logic of the Social Sciences.* Cambridge: MIT Press, 1988.

Hadden, Jeffrey K., and Anson Shupe, eds. *Secularization and Fundamentalism Reconsidered.* New York: Paragon House, 1989.

Hall, Stuart. "The West and the Rest: Discourse and Power." In *Modernity: An Introduction to Modern Societies,* ed. Stuart Hall, David Held, Don Hubert, and Kenneth Thompson, 184–229. Oxford: Basil Blackwell, 1996.

Halliday, Fred. *Iran: Dictatorship and Development.* New York: Penguin, 1979.

———. "The Iranian Revolution and Its Implications." *New Left Review,* no. 166 (1987): 24–39.

Harding, Susan. "Representing Fundamentalism: The Problem of the Repugnant Cultural Other." *Social Research* 58, no. 2 (Summer 1991): 373–93.

Harris, George S. *Turkey: Coping with Crisis*. Boulder: Westview, 1985.

Hawthorne, Geoffrey. *Enlightenment and Despair: A History of Sociology*. Cambridge: Cambridge University Press, 1976.

———. "Waiting For a Text? Comparing Third World Politics." In *Rethinking Third World Politics*, ed. J. Manor. London: Longman, 1991.

Held, David. *Models of Democracy*. Cambridge: Polity, 1987.

———. *Political Theory and the Modern State*. Stanford: Stanford University Press, 1989.

Heller, Agnes. "Modernity's Pendulum." *Thesis Eleven* 31 (November 1992): 1–13.

Henrey, K. H. "Glimpses of Turkish Opinion." *Muslim World* 48 (October 1958): 315–21.

Heper, Metin. "Islam, Polity and Society in Turkey: A Middle Eastern Perspective." *Middle East Journal* 35 (1981): 45–63.

———. *The State Tradition in Turkey*. Beverley, North Humberside: Eothen, 1985.

———. "State, Democracy, and Bureacracy in Turkey." In *The State and Public Bureaucracies: A Comparative Perspective*, ed. Metin Heper, 131–44. Westport, Conn.: Greenwood, 1987.

Heper, Metin, and Ahmet Evin, eds. *State, Democracy, and the Military: Turkey in the* 1980s. Berlin: Walter de Gruyter, 1988.

Heper, Metin, and Jacob M. Landau, ed. *Political Parties and Democracy in Turkey*. London: I. B. Tauris, 1991.

Heyd, Uriel. *Foundations of Turkish Nationalism: The Life and Teachings of Ziya Gökalp*. London: Luzac, 1950.

———. *Language Reform in Modern Turkey*. Jerusalem: The Magnes Press, 1954.

Hirschman, Albert O. "The Search for Paradigms as a Hindrance to Understanding." *World Politics* 22, no. 3 (April 1970): 177–94.

Hobbes, Thomas. *The Leviathan*. Cambridge: Cambridge University Press, 1990.

Hollis, Martin, and Steve Smith. *Explaining and Understanding in International Relations*. Oxford: Oxford University Press, 1990.

Holt, Robert T., ed. *The Methodology of Comparative Research*. New York: Free Press, 1970.

Holt, Robert T., and John M. Richardson. "Competing Paradigms in Comparative Politics." In Holt and Turner, *Methodology of Comparative Research*, 21–72. New York: Free Press, 1970.

Holt, Robert T., and John E. Turner. "Crises and Sequences in Collective Theory Development." *American Political Science Review* 69 (1975): 979–94.

Hudson, Michael C. "Islam and Political Development." In *Islam and Political Development: Religion and Sociopolitical Change*, ed. John L. Esposito, 1–24. Syracuse: Syracuse University Press, 1980.

———. "The Political Culture Approach." In *Political Liberalization and Democratization in the Arab World: Vol. I, Theoretical Perspectives*, ed. Rex Brynen, Bahgat Korany, and Paul Noble, 61–76. Boulder: Lynne Reinner, 1995.

Hume, David. *Essays: Moral, Political, and Literary*. Indianapolis: Liberty Classics, 1985.

Huntington, Samuel P. "The Change to Change." *Comparative Politics* 3 (April 1971): 283–322.

———. "The Goals of Development." In Weiner and Huntington, *Understanding Political Development*, 3–33.

————. "The Clash of Civilizations?" *Foreign Affairs* 72, no. 3 (1993): 22–49.

Ibrahim, Saad Eddin. "Anatomy of Egypt's Militant Islamic Groups: Methodology and Preliminary Findings." *International Journal of Middle East Studies* 12 (December 1980): 423–53.

————. "Special Report: Crises, Elites, and Democratization in the Arab World." *Middle East Journal* 47, no. 2 (1993): 292–305.

İnalcık, Halil. "The Nature of Traditional Society." In *Political Modernization in Japan and Turkey*, ed. Robert Ward and Dankwart A. Rustow, 42–63. Princeton: Princeton University Press, 1964.

Isaac, Jeffrey C. "Current Debate: Is Modernism Destructive? Why Postmodernism Still Matters." *Tikkun* 4, no. 4 (1990): 118–22.

İslamoğlu, Huri, and Çağlar Keyder. "Agenda for Ottoman History." In *The Ottoman Empire in the World Economy*, ed. Huri İslamoğlu. Cambridge: Cambridge University Press, 1987.

Jackman, Robert A. "Cross-National Statistical Research and the Study of Comparative Politics." *American Journal of Political Science* 29 (February 1985): 161–82.

Jameson, S. H. "Social Mutations in Turkey." *Social Forces* 15 (May 1936): 482–96.

Jay, Martin. "The Textualist Approach to Intellectual History." *Strategies: A Journal of Theory, Culture and Politics* 4, no. 7 (1991): 7–18.

Johnston, David, and Cynthia Sampson, eds. *Religion: The Missing Dimension of Statecraft*. Oxford: Oxford University Press, 1994.

Kalaycıoğlu, Ersin, and Ali Yaşar Sarıbay, eds. *Türkey'de Siyaset: Süreklilik ve Değişim*. Istanbul: Der Yayınları, 1992.

Kant, Immanuel. *Political Writings*. Cambridge: Cambridge University Press, 1991.

Kaplan, Lawrence, ed. *Fundamentalism in a Comparative Perspective*. Amherst: University of Massachusetts Press, 1992.

Karpat, Kemal H. *Turkey's Politics*. Princeton: Princeton University Press, 1959.

————, ed. *The Political and Social Thought of the Contemporary Middle East*. 2nd ed. Westport, Conn.: Greenwood, 1982.

————, ed. *The Ottoman State and Its Place in World History*. Leiden: E. J. Brill, 1974.

————, ed. *Social Change and Politics in Turkey: A Structural-Historical Analysis*. Leiden: E. J. Brill, 1973.

Kavanaugh, Dennis. "Why Political Science Needs History." *Political Studies* 39, no. 3 (1991): 479–95.

Keddie, Nikki R. "Ideology, Society and the State in Post-Colonial Muslim Societies." In *State and Ideology in the Middle East and Pakistan*, ed. Fred Halliday and Hamza Alavi. New York: Monthly Review, 1988.

————, ed. *Scholars, Saints, and Sufis: Muslim Religious Institutions since 1500*. Berkeley: University of California Press, 1972.

————. *Roots of Revolution: An Interpretive History of Modern Iran*. New Haven: Yale University Press, 1981.

Keyder, Çağlar. *State and Class in Turkey: A Study in Capitalist Development*. London: Verso, 1987.

————. "Class and State in the Transformation of Modern Turkey." In *State and Ideol-*

ogy in the Middle East, ed. Fred Halliday and Hamza Alavi. New York: Monthly Review, 1988.

Kohn, Hans. "Ten Years of the Turkish Republic." *Foreign Affairs* (October 1933): 141–55.

Kramnick, Isaac, ed. *The Portable Enlightenment Reader.* New York: Penguin, 1995.

Kratochwil, Friedrich. "Regimes, Interpretation and the 'Science' of Politics: A Reappraisal." *Millennium* 17, no. 2 (1988): 263–84.

Krishna, Daya. "Secularism: Sacred and Profane." In Deutsch, *Culture and Modernity,* 548–57.

Kushner, David. "Turkish Secularists and Islam." *Jerusalem Quarterly* 38 (1986): 88–106.

Kuyaş, Ahmet. "Book Review: *Turkey and the Middle East* (by P. Robbins)." *Middle East Studies Association Bulletin* 26 (1992): 211–12.

Laclau, Ernesto, and Chantal Mouffe. "Post-Marxism Without Apologies." *New Left Review* 169 (1987): 79–106.

Landau, Jacob M., ed. *Atatürk and the Modernization of Turkey.* Boulder: Westview, 1984.

Lapidus, Ira. "Islam and Modernity." In Eisenstadt, *Patterns of Modernity,* 89–115.

Lawrence, Bruce. *Defenders of God: The Fundamentalist Revolt Against the Modern Age.* San Francisco: Harper and Row, 1989.

Lenczowski, George. *The Middle East in World Affairs.* 4th ed., Ithaca: Cornell University Press, [1952], 1980.

Lenin, V. I. *The State and Revolution.* New York: International, 1932.

Leonard, Stephen. "The Pedagogical Purposes of Political Science." In Farr et al., *Political Science in History,* 66–98.

Lerner, Daniel. *The Passing of Traditional Society: Modernizing the Middle East.* New York: Free Press, [1958], 1964.

Lerner, Daniel, and R. D. Robinson. "Swords and Ploughshares: The Turkish Army as a Modernizing Force." *World Politics* 13, no. 1 (1960): 19–44.

Leslie, Margaret. "In Defence of Anachronism." *Political Studies* 18 (1970): 443–47.

Lewis, Bernard. "Islamic Revival in Turkey." *International Affairs* 28, no. 1 (1952): 38–48.

———. "History-Writing and National Revival in Turkey." *Middle Eastern Affairs* 4 (1953): 218–27.

———. *The Emergence of Modern Turkey.* London: Oxford University Press, 1961.

———. "Foreword." In Rustow, *Turkey,* vii–xi.

———. "Europe and Islam." In *The Tanner Lectures on Human Values,* ed. M. McMurrin, 90–139. Salt Lake City: University of Utah Press, 1991.

———. "Rethinking the Middle East." *Foreign Affairs* 71, no. 4 (1992): 99–119.

———. "Why Turkey is the Only Muslim Democracy." *Middle East Quarterly* 1 (March 1993): 41–49.

Lewis, Geoffrey. *Turkey.* 3rd ed. Cambridge: Cambridge University Press, [1955], 1965.

Little, Daniel. *Varieties of Social Explanation.* Boulder: Westview, 1991.

Locke, John. *Two Treatises on Government.* Cambridge: Cambridge University Press, 1988.

———. *First Letter on Toleration.* New York: Library of Liberal Arts, 1950.

Lovejoy, H. O. *The Turkish Civil Code of 1926 and Its Reception in Rural Turkey.* B.A. Thesis, Princeton, 1972.

Lukes, Stephen. *Power: A Radical View.* Atlantic Heights: Humanities Press, 1975.

————, ed. *Power.* New York: New York University Press, 1986.

Lustick, Ian. *For the Land and the Lord: Jewish Fundamentalism in Israel.* New York: Council on Foreign Relations, 1985.

Lynn, William S. *Geographic Ethics: Geography and Moral Understanding.* Ph.D. dissertation, Department of Geography, University of Minnesota, forthcoming, 1997.

Lyotard, Jean-François. *The Postmodern Condition.* Minneapolis: University of Minnesota Press, 1984.

Machiavelli, Niccolò. *The Prince and the Discourses.* New York: Modern Library, 1950.

MacIntyre, Alasdair. "A Mistake About Causality in Social Science." In *Philosophy, Politics, and Society,* ed. Peter Laslett and W. G. Runciman, 48–70. Oxford: Basil Blackwell, 1967.

————. "Is a Science of Comparative Politics Possible?" In *Philosophy, Politics and Society,* ed. Peter Laslett, W. G. Runciman, and Quentin Skinner, 9–26. Oxford: Basil Blackwell, 1972.

————. "Ideology, Social Science and Revolution." *Comparative Politics* 5, no. 3 (April 1973): 321–42.

————. "The Essential Contestability of Some Social Concepts." *Ethics* 84, no. 1 (1973): 1–9.

————. "Epistemological Crises, Dramatic Narrative, and the Philosophy of Science." In *Paradigms and Revolutions,* ed. Gary Gutting. Notre Dame: University of Notre Dame Press, 1980.

————. *After Virtue.* Notre Dame: University of Notre Dame Press, 1981.

————. "The Indispensability of Political Theory." In *The Nature of Political Theory,* ed. David Miller and Larry Seidentap. Oxford: Clarendon, 1983.

————. "Relativism, Power, and Philosophy." In Baynes et al., *After Philosophy,* 385-411. Cambridge: MIT Press, 1987.

Madan, T. S. "Secularism in Its Place." *Journal of Asian Studies* 46, no. 4 (1987): 747–59.

Mardin, Şerif. *The Genesis of Young Ottoman Thought: A Study in the Modernization of Turkish Political Ideas.* Princeton: Princeton University Press, 1962.

————. "Opposition and Control in Turkey." *Government and Opposition* 1, no. 3 (1966): 375–88.

————. "Power, Civil Society, and Culture in the Ottoman Empire." *Comparative Studies in Society and History* 11 (June 1969): 258–81.

————. "Ideology and Religion in the Turkish Revolution." *International Journal of Middle East Studies* (1971): 204–6.

————. "Center Periphery Relations: The Key to Turkish Politics." *Daedalus* (Winter 1973): 169–96.

————. "Religion in Modern Turkey." *International Social Science Journal* 29 (1977): 279–97.

————. "Religion and Secularism in Turkey." In Özbudun and Kazancıgil, *Atatürk.*

————. "Turkey, Islam, and Westernization." In *Religion and Societies: Asia and the Middle East,* ed. C. Caldarola. Berlin: Mouton, 1982.

————. "Religion and Politics in Modern Turkey." In Piscatori, *Islam in the Political Process,* 138–59.

————. "Freedom in an Ottoman Perspective." In Heper and Evin, *State, Democracy, and the Military: Turkey in the 1980s.*

————. *Religion and Social Change in Turkey: The Case of Bediüzzaman Said Nursi.* Albany: State University of New York, 1989.

————. *Jön Türklerin Siyasi Fikirleri, 1895–1908 (The Political Ideas of the Young Turks, 1895–1908).* İletişim: İstanbul, 1992.

————. "Europe in Turkey." In *Avrupa Nerede Bitiyor? (Where Does Europe End?)* ed. Jale Parla. Istanbul: Helsinki Citizens' Assembly, 1993.

————. "Islam in Mass Society: Harmony Versus Polarization." In *Politics in the Third Turkish Republic,* ed. Metin Heper and Ahmet Evin, 161–70. Boulder: Westview, 1994.

Margulies, Ronnie, and Ergin Yıldızoğlu. "The Political Use of Islam in Turkey." *Middle East Report* (July–August 1988): 12–17, 50.

Marty, Martin, and Scott Appleby, eds. *The Fundamentalism Project.* Chicago: University of Chicago Press, 1991–1993.

Marx, Karl, and Frederick Engels. *The Communist Manifesto.* New York: Monthly Review, 1964.

————. *The German Ideology.* New York: International, 1970.

Marx, Karl. "On the Jewish Question." In *The Marx-Engels Reader,* ed. Robert Tucker. Cambridge: Cambridge University Press, 1972.

Mayer, Lawrence C. *Comparative Political Inquiry: A Methodological Survey.* Homewood, Ill.: Dorsey, 1972.

————. *Redefining Comparative Politics: Promise Versus Peril.* Beverly Hills: Sage, 1989.

Mehmet, Ozay. *Islamic Identity and Development: Studies of the Islamic Periphery.* London: Routledge, 1990.

Migdal, Joel S. "Studying the Politics of Development and Change: The State of the Art." In Finifter, *Political Science,* 309–38.

————. *Strong Societies and Weak States: State-Society Relations and State Capabilities in the Third World.* Princeton: Princeton University Press, 1988.

Mill, John Stuart. *The Subjection of Women.* Cambridge University Press, 1995.

Mitchell, Timothy. *Colonizing Egypt.* Berkeley: University of California Press, 1991.

Moghadam, Val. *Modernizing Women: Gender and Social Change in the Middle East.* Bloomington: Lynne Reinner, 1993.

Moon, J. Donald. "The Logic of Political Inquiry: A Synthesis of Opposed Perspectives." In *Political Science: Scope and Theory (Handbook of Political Science, Vol. 1),* ed. Fred I. Greenstein and Nelson W. Polsby, 131–228. Reading, Mass.: Addison-Wesley, 1975.

————. "Political Science and Political Choice: Opacity, Freedom, and Knowledge." In Ball, *Idioms of Inquiry,* 231–48.

Mueller-Vollmer, Kurt. *The Hermeneutics Reader.* New York: Continuum, 1989.

Nagel, Ernest. *The Structure of Science: Problems in the Logic of Scientific Explanation.* Indianapolis: Hacket, 1977.

Nandy, Ashis. "The Politics of Secularism and the Recovery of Religious Tolerance." *Alternatives* 13 (1988): 177–94.

O'Donnell, Guillermo, Philippe C. Schmitter, and Lawrence Whitehead, eds. *Transitions from Authoritarian Rule: Southern Europe.* Chicago: University of Chicago Press, 1986.

Olson, Emilie A. "Muslim Identity and Secularism in Contemporary Turkey: The Headscarf Dispute." *Anthropological Quarterly* 58, no. 4 (1985): 161–71.

Osborne, Peter. "Modernity is a Qualitative Not a Chronological Category." *New Left Review* 192 (1992): 65–84.

"The Ottoman Constitution." *American Journal of International Law* 2 (Supplement, 1908): 367–87.

Outhwaite, William. *New Philosophies of Science: Realism, Hermeneutics, and Critical Theory.* New York: St. Martin's, 1987.

Öncü, Ayşe, Çağlar Keyder, and Saad Edin Ibrahim, eds. *Developmentalism and Beyond.* Cairo: American University of Cairo Press, 1994.

Özbudun, Ergun. "Established Versus Unfinished Revolutions: Contrasting Patterns of Democraticization in Mexico and Turkey." In *Authoritarian Politics in Modern Society: The Dynamics of Established One Party Systems,* ed. Samuel P. Huntington and Clement Henry Moore, 380–405. New York: Basic, 1970.

———. *Social Change and Political Participation in Turkey.* Princeton: Princeton University Press, 1976.

———. "Postauthoritarian Democracies: Turkey." In *Competitive Elections in Developing Countries,* ed. Myron Weiner and Ergun Özbudun, 328–68. Durham: Duke University Press (for the American Enterprise Institute), 1987.

Özbudun, Ergun, and Ali Kazancıgil, eds. *Atatürk: The Founder of a Modern State.* London: C. Hurst, 1981.

Parla, Taha. *The Social and Political Thought of Ziya Gökalp, 1876–1924.* Leiden: E. J. Brill, 1985.

———. *Türkiye'de Siyasal Kültürün Resmi Kaynakları, Cilt 1: Atatürk'ün Nutuk'u (The Official Sources of Turkish Political Culture, Vol. 1: Atatürk's Speech).* İstanbul: İletişim, 1991.

———. *Türkiye'de Siyasal Kültürün Resmi Kaynakları, Cilt 3: Kemalist Tek-Parti İdeolojisi ve CHP'nin Altı Ok'u (The Official Sources of Turkish Political Culture, Vol. 3: The Kemalist Single-Party Ideology and the RPP's Six Arrows).* İstanbul: İletişim, 1992.

Piscatori, James P., ed. *Islam in the Political Process.* Cambridge: Royal Institute of International Affairs, 1983.

———. *Islam in a World of Nation-States.* Cambridge: Cambridge University Press, 1986.

Pitkin, Hanna Fenichel. *Wittgenstein and Justice.* Berkeley: University of California Press, 1993 [1972].

Pocock, J. G. A. "The History of Political Thought: A Methodological Inquiry." In *Philosophy, Politics, and Society,* 2nd series, ed. Peter Laslett and W. G. Runciman. Oxford: Basil Blackwell, 1962.

———. *Politics, Language and Time.* London: Methuen, 1972.

———. "Modernity and Anti-Modernity in the Anglophone Tradition." In Eisenstadt, *Patterns of Modernity,* 44–59.

Popper, Karl. *The Open Society and Its Enemies.* Vols. 1 and 2. Princeton: Princeton University Press, 1962.

———. *The Poverty of Historicism.* London: ARK Paperbacks [1957], 1986.

Przeworski, Adam, and Henry Teune. *The Logic of Comparative Inquiry.* New York: Wiley & Sons, 1970.

Putnam, Hillary. "The French Revolution and the Holocaust: Can Ethics be Ahistorical?" In Deutsch, *Culture and Modernity.*

Pye, Lucian. "The Confrontation Between Discipline and Area Studies." In *Political Science and Area Studies: Rivals or Partners?* ed. Lucian Pye, 3–22. Bloomington: Indiana University Press, 1975.

Pye, Lucian, and Sidney Verba, eds. *Political Culture and Political Development*. Princeton: Princeton University Press, 1965.

Rabinow, Paul, and William M. Sullivan, eds. *Interpretive Social Science: A Second Look*. Berkeley: University of California Press, 1987.

Rahman, Fazlur. *Islam and Modernity: Transformation of an Intellectual Tradition*. Chicago: University of Chicago Press, 1982.

Randall, Vicky, and Robin Theobald. *Political Change and Underdevelopment: A Critical Introduction to Third World Politics*. Durham: Duke University Press, 1985.

Reed, Howard A. "Revival of Islam in Secular Turkey." *Middle East Journal* 8 (1954): 267–82.

———. "The Faculty of Divinity in Ankara." *Muslim World* 14, no. 47 (1956–57): 290–312, 22–35.

———. "The Religious Life of Modern Turkish Muslims." In *Islam and the West*, ed. Richard N. Frye, 108–148. The Hague: Mouton, 1957.

———. "Secularism and Islam in Turkish Politics." *Current History* 32 (June 1957): 333–38.

———. "Atatürk's Secularizing Legacy and the Continuing Vitality of Islam in Republican Turkey." In *Islam in the Contemporary World*, ed. C. K. Pullapilly, 316–39. Indianapolis: Cross Roads, 1970.

Ricci, David. *The Tragedy of Political Science: Politics, Scholarship, and Democracy*. New Haven: Yale University Press, 1984.

Richard, Nelly. "Postmodernism and Periphery." *Third Text* 2 (1987–88): 6–12.

Richards, Alan, and John Waterbury. *A Political Economy of the Middle East: State, Class and Economic Development*. Boulder: Westview, 1990.

Ricoeur, Paul. *From Text to Action: Essays in Hermeneutics, II*. Trans. Kathleen Blaney, John B. Thompson. Chicago: Northwestern University Press, 1991.

Riggs, Fred. "The Rise and Fall of 'Political Development.'" *Handbook of Political Behavior* 4, ed. S. C. Long. New York: Plenum, 1981.

Robins, Philip. *Turkey and the Middle East*. London: Royal Institute of International Affairs and Council on Foreign Relations, 1991.

Robinson, Richard D. "The Lesson of Turkey." *Middle East Journal* 5 (1951): 424–38.

Rodinson, Maxime. *Islam and Capitalism*. New York: Pantheon, 1973.

Root, Michael. *The Liberal Social Sciences*. Oxford: Basil Blackwell, 1993.

Rorty, Richard. "Philosophers, Novelists, and Intercultural Comparisons." In Deutsch, *Culture and Modernity*, 3–21.

Rorty, Richard, J. B. Schneewind, and Quentin Skinner, eds. *Philosophy in History: Essays on the Historiography of Philosophy*. Cambridge: Cambridge University Press, 1984.

Rose, Richard. "Comparing Forms of Comparative Analysis." *Political Studies* 34 (1991): 446–62.

Ross, Dorothy. *The Origins of American Social Science*. Cambridge: Cambridge University Press, 1991.

Rostow, Walt W. *The Stages of Economic Growth: A Non-Communist Manifesto*. Cambridge: Cambridge University Press, 1960.

Rouleau, Eric. "Turkey: Beyond Atatürk." *Foreign Policy* 103 (Summer 1996): 70–87.

Rudolph, Lloyd I., and Susanne Hoeber Rudolph. *The Modernity of Tradition: Political Development in India.* Chicago: University of Chicago Press, 1967.

Rustow, Dankwart A. "Politics and Islam in Turkey, 1920–1955." In *Islam and the West,* ed. Richard N. Frye, 67–107. The Hague: Mouton, 1957.

———. "The Near East." In *The Politics of the Developing Areas,* ed. Gabriel A. Almond and James S. Coleman, 369–530. Princeton: Princeton University Press, 1960.

———. "Turkey's Second Try at Democracy." *Yale Review* 51 (1962–63): 518–38.

———. "Politics and Westernization in the Near East." In *The Modern Middle East,* ed. Richard H. Nolte. New York: Atherton [Center of International Studies, Princeton University, 1956], 1963.

———. "Turkey: The Modernity of Tradition." In *Political Culture and Political Development,* ed. Lucian Pye and Sidney Verba, Princeton: Princeton University Press, 1965.

———. *A World of Nations: Problems of Political Modernization.* Washington, D.C.: Brookings Institution, 1967.

———. "Atatürk as Founder of a State." *Daedalus* 97 (Summer 1968): 793–828.

———. "The Middle East." In *Political Science and Area Studies: Rivals or Partners?* ed. Lucian Pye, 170–80. Bloomington: Indiana University Press, 1975.

———. "Turkey's Travails." *Foreign Affairs* 58 (1979): 82–102.

———. "Turkey's Liberal Revolution." *Middle East Review* 17 (Spring 1985): 5–11.

———. *Turkey: America's Forgotten Ally.* New York: Council on Foreign Relations, 1987.

———. "Political Parties in Turkey: An Overview." In Heper and Landau, *Political Parties and Democracy in Turkey,* 10–23.

———. "A Democratic Turkey Faces New Challenges." *Global Affairs* 8 (Spring 1993): 58–70.

———. "Turkish Democracy in Historical and Comparative Perspective." In *Politics in the Third Turkish Republic,* ed. Metin Heper and Ahmet Evin, 3–12. Boulder: Westview, 1994.

Sahliyeh, Emile, ed. *Religious Resurgence and Politics in the Contemporary World.* Albany: State University of New York Press, 1990.

Saylan, Gencay. *Religion and Politics: Emergence of Fundamentalism in Muslim Societies—The Turkish Case.* Vol. 3. University of Malta, Valletta: Mediterranean Institute Foundation for International Studies (Mediterranean Social Sciences Network, newsletter), 1989.

Schabert, Tilo. "Modernity and History I: What is Modernity?" In *The Promise of History,* ed. Athanasios Moulakis, 9–21. Berlin: Walter de Gruyter, 1985.

———. "Modernity and History II: On the Edge of Modernity?" In *The Promise of History,* ed. Athanasios Moulakis, 22–32. Berlin: Walter de Gruyter, 1985.

Schick, I., and E. Tonak, eds. *Turkey in Transition.* New York: Oxford University Press, 1987.

Schmitter, Philippe. "Still the Century of Corporatism?" *Review of Politics* 36 (January 1974): 85–121.

Searle, John. *Speech Acts: An Essay in the Philosophy of Language.* Cambridge: Cambridge University Press, 1969.

———. "Response: Meaning, Intentionality, and Speech Acts." In *John Searle and His Critics,* ed. E. Lepore and R. V. Gulick, 81–102. Oxford: Basil Blackwell, 1991.

Sen, Amartya. "The Threats to Secular India." *New York Review of Books* 40 (April 8, 1993): 26–33.

Serim, Ö., ed. *Milli Eğitim Mevzuatı (National Education Regulations).* Ankara: Alkim Kitapçılık & Yayıncılık, 1991.

Sewell, William H. "Three Temporalities" (pre-published copy). In *The Historic Turn in the Human Sciences,* ed. Terrence J. McDonald. Ann Arbor: University of Michigan Press, [1991], 1996.

Shapiro, Ian. "Realism in the Study of the History of Ideas." *History of Political Thought* 3, no. 3 (Winter 1982): 535–78.

Sharabi, Hisham, ed. *Theory, Politics and the Arab World: Critical Perspectives.* New York: Routledge, 1990.

Shaw, Stanford J. "Ottoman and Turkish Studies in the United States." In *The Ottoman State and Its Place in World History,* ed. Kemal H. Karpat, 118–26. Leiden: E. J. Brill, 1974.

Shaw, Stanford H., and Ezal Kural Shaw. *History of the Ottoman Empire and Modern Turkey.* London: Cambridge University Press, 1977.

Shklar, Judith. "Squaring the Hermeneutic Circle." *Social Research* 53 (1986): 449–73.

Sibley, Mulford Q. *Political Ideas and Ideologies: A History of Political Thought.* New York: Harper and Row, 1970.

Siraj ed-Din, Abu Bakr. "The Islamic and Christian Conceptions of the March of Time." *Islamic Quarterly* 1, no. 4 (1954): 229–35.

Sivan, Emmanuel. *Radical Islam: Medieval Theology and Modern Politics.* New Haven: Yale University Press, 1985.

Skinner, Quentin. *The Foundations of Modern Political Thought.* 2 vols. Cambridge: Cambridge University Press, 1978.

———. "The Idea of Negative Liberty: Philosophical and Historical Perspectives." In Rorty et al., *Philosophy in History,* 193–224.

———. *Meaning and Context: Quentin Skinner and His Critics,* ed. James Tully. Princeton: Princeton University Press, 1988.

———. "Language and Political Change." In Ball et al., *Political Innovation and Conceptual Change,* 6–23.

Skocpol, Theda. "Rentier State and Shi'a Islam in the Iranian Revolution, and Responses." *Theory and Society* 11 (1982): 265–83.

Smith, Wilfred Cantwell. "Turkey: Islamic Reformation?" In Smith, *Islam in Modern History,* 165–207. New York: New American Library, 1957.

———. *The Meaning and End of Religion.* New York: Macmillan, 1963.

———. "Retrospective Thoughts on *The Meaning and End of Religion.*" In *Religion in History: The Word, the Idea, the Reality,* ed. Gérard Vallée, 13–19. Waterloo, Ontario: Wilfrid Laurier University Press, 1992.

Springborg, Patricia. "Politics, Primordialism, and Orientalism: Marx, Aristotle, and the Myth of the Gemeinschaft." *American Political Science Review* 80, no. 1 (1986): 185–211.

Stirling, Paul. "Religious Change in Republican Turkey." *Middle East Journal* 12 (1958): 395–408.

Sunar, İlkay, and Sabri Sayari. "Democracy in Turkey: Problems and Prospects." In O'Donnell et al., *Transitions from Authoritarian Rule: Southern Europe,* 165–212.

Sunar, İlkay, and Binnaz Toprak. "Islam in Politics: The Case of Turkey." *Government and Opposition* 18, no. 4 (1983): 423–41.

Szyliowicz, Joseph S. "Elites and Modernization in Turkey." In *Political Elites and Political Development in the Middle East,* ed. Frank Tachau, 23–68. New York: Wiley & Sons, 1975.

Tachau, Frank. "The Face of Turkish Nationalism as Reflected in the Cyprus Dispute." *Middle East Journal* 20 (1959): 473–94.

———. *Turkey: The Politics of Authority, Democracy and Development.* New York: Praeger, 1984.

———, ed. *Political Elites and Political Development in the Middle East.* New York: Wiley & Sons, 1975.

Tachau, Frank, and Haluk Ülman. "The Attempt to Reconcile Rapid Modernization with Democracy." *Middle East Journal* 19 (1965): 153–68.

Tachau, Frank, and Mary-Jo D. Good. "The Anatomy of Political and Social Change: Turkish Parties, Parliaments, and Elections." *Comparative Politics* 5, no. 4 (1973): 551–73.

Tapper, Richard, ed. *Islam in Modern Turkey: Religion, Politics and Literature in a Secular State.* London: I. B. Tauris, 1991.

Taylor, Charles. "Foucault on Freedom and Truth." *Political Theory* 12 (May 1984): 152–83.

———. *Human Agency and Language: Philosophical Papers I.* Cambridge: Cambridge University Press, 1985.

———. *Philosophy and the Human Sciences: Philosophical Papers* 2. Cambridge: Cambridge University Press, 1985.

———. "Language and Human Nature." In Gibbons, *Interpreting Politics,* 101–32.

———. "The Hermeneutics of Conflict." In Skinner, *Meaning and Context,* 218–28.

———. "Comparison, History, and Truth." In *Myth and Philosophy,* ed. Frank E. Reynolds and David Tracy, 34–55. Albany: State University of New York Press, 1990.

———. "Inwardness and the Culture of Modernity." In *Philosophical Interventions in the Unfinished Project of Enlightenment,* ed. Alex Honneth, Thomas McCarthy, Claus Offe, and Albrecht Wellmer, 88–110. Cambridge: MIT Press, 1992.

———. "The Politics of Recognition." In *Multiculturalism and "The Politics of Recognition,"* ed. Amy Gutmann. Princeton: Princeton University Press, 1992.

Taylor, Steven, and Robert Bogdan. *Introduction to Qualitative Research Methods: The Search for Meanings.* 2nd ed. New York: Wiley [1974], 1984.

Tilly, Charles. *Big Structures, Large Processes, Huge Comparisons.* New York: Russell Sage Foundation, 1984.

Toprak, Binnaz. *Islam and Political Development in Turkey.* Leiden: E. J. Brill, 1981.

———. "Politicization of Islam in a Secular State: The National Salvation Party in Turkey." In *From Nationalism to Revolutionary Islam,* ed. S. A. Arjomand, 119–33. Albany: State University of New York Press, 1984.

———. "Islamist Intellectuals of the 1980s in Turkey." *Current Turkish Thought,* no. 62 (Spring 1987).

———. "Religion as a State Ideology in a Secular Setting." In *Aspects of Religion in Secular Turkey,* ed. Malcolm Wagstaff. Durham: Center for Middle Eastern Studies, University of Durham, 1990.

———. "Islam and Secularism in Turkey." In *Turkey: Political, Social and Economic Challenges in the 1990s*, ed. Ç. Balim et. al., 90–96. Leiden: E. J. Brill, 1994.

Toynbee, Arnold J. *Survey of International Affairs 1925: The Islamic World Since the Peace Settlement.* London: Humphrey Milford, 1929.

———. *Survey of International Affairs, 1928.* London: Humphrey Milford, 1929.

Trigg, Roger. *Understanding Social Science.* Oxford: Basil Blackwell, 1985.

Trimberger, Ellen K. *Revolution From Above.* New Brunswick, N.J.: Transaction, 1978.

Tully, James, ed. "The Pen Is the Mighty Sword: Quentin Skinner's Analysis of Politics." In Skinner, *Meaning and Context.*

———. "Wittgenstein and Political Philosophy." *Political Theory* 17, no. 2 (1989), 172–204.

Tunçay, Mete. *T.C.'nde Tek-Parti Yönetimi'nin Kurulması (1923–1931) (The Founding of the Single Party Regime in the Turkish Republic).* İstanbul: Cem Yayınevi [1981], 1992.

Turan, İlter. "Religion and Political Culture in Turkey: Islam in Modern Turkey." In *Islam in Modern Turkey*, ed. R. Tapper, 31–55. London: I. B. Tauris, 1991.

Valenzuela, J. Samuel, and Arturo Valenzuela. "Modernization and Dependency." *Comparative Politics* (July 1978): 535–57.

Van Der Veer, Peter. *Religious Nationalism: Hindus and Muslims in India.* Berkeley: University of California Press, 1994.

Voll, John O. *Islam: Continuity and Change in the Modern World.* Boulder: Westview, 1982.

———. "Islamic Revival and the Failure of the West." In *Religious Resurgence: Contemporary Cases in Islam, Christianity and Judaism*, ed. Richard Antoun and M. E. Hegland, 127–43. Syracuse: Syracuse University Press, 1987.

Wallis, Roy, and Steve Bruce. "Secularization: The Orthodox Model." In Bruce, *Religion and Modernization*, 8–30.

Weber, Max. "The Nature of Social Action." In *Weber: Selections in Translation*, ed. W. G. Runciman, 7–32. Cambridge: Cambridge University Press, [1914], 1978.

Webster, Donald E. "State Control of Social Change in Turkey." *American Sociological Review* 4 (1939): 247–58.

———. *The Turkey of Atatürk: Social Process in the Turkish Reformation.* Philadelphia: American Academy of Political and Social Science, 1939.

Weiker, Walter F. *The Turkish Revolution: Aspects of Military Politics.* Washington: Brookings Institution, 1963.

———. "Modern Turkish Studies." *Middle East Studies Association Bulletin* 3, no. 3 (1985): 1–16.

———. *The Modernization of Turkey.* New York: Holmes & Meier, 1981.

———. "Turkey, the Middle East, and Islam." *Middle East Review* 17, no. 3 (1985): 27–32.

Weiner, Myron, and Samuel P. Huntington, eds. *Understanding Political Development.* Boston: Little, Brown, 1987.

Weinsheimer, Joel C. *Gadamer's Hermeneutics: A Reading of Truth and Method.* New Haven: Yale University Press, 1985.

———. *Philosophical Hermeneutics and Literary Theory.* New Haven: Yale University Press, 1991.

White, Stephen. *Political Theory and Post-Modernity.* Cambridge: Cambridge University Press, 1990.

Wilson, Bryan R. "Reflections on a Many-Sided Controversy." In Bruce, *Religion and Modernization*, 195–210.

Winch, Peter. "Understanding a Primitive Society." In *Rationality*, ed. Brian Wilson, 78–112. Worcester: Basil Blackwell, 1970.

———. *The Idea of a Social Science*. 2nd ed. New York: Humanities Press, [1958], 1976.

———. *Trying to Make Sense*. Oxford: Basil Blackwell, 1987.

Winder, R. B. "Four Decades of Middle Eastern Study." *Middle East Journal* 41, no. 1 (1987): 40–59.

Wolin, Sheldon. *Politics and Vision*. Boston: Little, Brown, 1961.

Wollstonecraft, Mary. *A Vindication of the Rights of Men and A Vindication of the Rights of Women*. Cambridge: Cambridge University Press, 1995.

Wright, Robin. "Islam, Democracy, and the West." *Foreign Affairs* 71 (Summer 1992), 131–45.

Yalman, Ahmed Emin. "Islam in Turkey Today." *Moslem World* (from *Vatan*, Istanbul, Dec. 1941) 33 (1943): 70–71.

Yalman, Nur. "Some Observations on Secularism in Turkey: The Cultural Revolution in Turkey." *Daedalus* 102, no. 1 (1973): 139–68.

———. "On Secularism and Its Critics: Notes on Turkey, India, and Iran." *Contribution to Indian Sociology* 25 (1991): 233–66.

Yavuz, C., ed. *Medeni Kanunu (The Turkish Civil Code)*. Istanbul: Beta, 1993.

Yeşilada, Birol A. "Problems of Political Development in the Third Turkish Republic." *Polity* 21, no. 2 (1988): 350–72.

Young, Crawford. *The Politics of Cultural Pluralism*. Madison: University of Wisconsin Press, 1976.

Young, T. C., ed. *Near Eastern Culture and Society: A Symposium on the Meeting of East and West*. Princeton: Princeton University Press, 1951.

Zubaida, Sami. "Religion, the State, and Democracy: Contrasting Conceptions of Society in Egypt." In *Political Islam: Essays from Middle East Report*, ed. Joel Beinin and Joe Stork, 51–63. Berkeley: University of California, 1997.

Zürcher, Eric J. *Turkey: A Modern History*. London: I. B. Tauris, 1993.

Index

Yale Studies in Hermeneutics
Joel Weinsheimer, General Editor

Yale Studies in Hermeneutics provides a venue for inquiry into the theory of interpretation in all its varieties and domains. Titles in the series seek to expand and deepen our understanding of understanding while explicitly framing and situating themselves within the tradition of recognized hermeneutical thinkers from antiquity to the present.